St. John Capistran

ST. JOHN CAPISTRAN

A REFORMER IN BATTLE

BY
REV. JOHN HOFER

TRANSLATED BY
REV. PATRICK CUMMINS, O.S.B.

MEDIATRIX PRESS
MMXVIII

ISBN: 978-1-953746-42-9

Imprimi Potest
Ex abbatia Immac. Concept. die 29. Jun., 1943
✠ Stephanus Schappler, O.S.B.
Abbas Coadjutor

Nihil Obstat
Sti. Ludovici, die 30. Junii, 1943
Wm. Fischer, S.T.D. Censor Librorum

Imprimatur
Sti. Ludovici, die 30. Junii, 1943
✠ Joannes J. Glennon
Archiepiscopus

Cover art: *Maestro di San Giovanni da Capistrano*
Giovanni di Bartolomeo dell'Aquila, 1485.
Museo Nationale, Aquila, Italia.

Cover design: © Ryan Grant, 2019.

Mediatrix Press
607 E. 6th Ave.
Post Falls, ID 83854
www.mediatrixpress.com

TABLE OF CONTENTS

TRANSLATOR'S PREFACE

SCHOOLBOY memories led me to read this book. Reading led to translation. I wished to pass on to others this new and inspiring picture of the last crusader.

The picture is new. Its order is chronological. The Bollandists, who ordinarily follow the chronological order, made an exception in Capistran's case, because of lack of detail in the sources they had at hand. Hofer, having by long and careful search discovered a surprising number of significant details, is able to follow Capistran year by year on all his ways.

This new picture is also inspiring. The marvelous resurgence of the papacy, from lowest depth to topmost height, is familiar from Pastor's History. From Hofer's book, occasioned by a remark of Pastor, Capistran emerges as one of the chief instruments of papal restoration. Capistran is many-sided: missionary, educator, reformer, inquisitor, crusader. And he labored in many lands: Italy, France, Palestine; Bohemia, Poland, Germany, Hungary. But always and everywhere the soul of his incessant and multiplied activity was an unselfish and burning love for the vicar of Christ.

The German original, to which I refer professional historians, is fully documented. The translation retains only such notes as may interest the general reader. Substantial identity with the original has been my aim. Some unimportant details I have omitted. And I have simplified the author's stylistic diffusiveness. I have also omitted the citations for many quoted passages which were obtained from unpublished manuscript sources.

The emphasis rightly laid by biographers on the last five years of Capistran's life has led historians to underestimate the thirty-five years that preceded Capistran's journey across the Alps. Even to the hero of Belgrade, history has not been just. Much less just has history been to one who, during the forty years before Belgrade, raised papal supremacy from despair to triumph. Capistran was indeed the reformer, almost the second founder, of genuine Franciscanism. But Franciscanism, in Capistran's eyes, was but an instrument, a strong, patient, reliable instrument, in the hands of a rejuvenated papacy.

A glance at Capistran's first biographers will show why the saint's full stature is yet unknown.

Gabriel of Verona wrote in 1451, five years before the saint's death. Jerome of Udine wrote in 1457. Nicholas of Fara wrote in 1462, in the Abruzzi. Christopher of Varese wrote in that same year, in Vienna. John of Tagliacozzo, some years later, wrote two accounts, one dealing with the Turkish war, the other with the saint's death. Lastly, Peter of Odenburg wrote a panegyric, probably as introduction to his account of the miracles wrought at Capistran's grave in Illok.

Three of these biographers (Jerome, Nicholas, and John) were immediate witnesses, hence indispensable. But all of them were interested almost exclusively in the saint's last years. Bernardine of Aquila wrote in 1480. He, too, like the first six, was a Franciscan. But his interest, unlike theirs, sees in Capistran the great reformer. Hence for the brief period he covers (1445-51) his testimony is very valuable.

Enea Silvio Piccolomini, who became Pope Pius II (1458-64), wrote a frequently quoted sketch of his dead friend.

We thus see clearly that in our case documentary evidence is of particular importance. Two men deserve special mention in this field.

Luke Wadding (1657) was the first who carefully examined the letters, documents, and codices which Capistran willed to his native Capistrano. Death prevented Wadding from writing a biography.

Aniceto Chiappini, after studying Capistran's writings carefully, urged their publication, but did not attempt a life of the saint.

In the archives of Europe, Father Hofer found 600 Capistran letters, half of which have never been published. He found sketches of 150 sermons preached by Capistran in a dozen German cities.

Since Capistran, in preaching, freely utilized his own personal experiences, these sermons reveal biographical details hitherto quite unknown. The author has thus been encouraged to restore the chronological order, which even the Bollandists, contrary to their custom, abandoned in Capistran's case.

Capistran has always been a conundrum. He was the St. Paul of the fifteenth century. He was the saint with the heart of stone. The Reformation deepened these contradictory judgments. The Renaissance pitied the fanatic. Recent historiography (Voigt, for example) still sees with the eyes of Poggio. Catholic biographies (Hermann, Barberio), on the other hand, tend too much to the panegyrical.

To deny the mystical and the miraculous is to deny the existence of saints. But to affirm the saints means to be critical, as the Church is, in judging the genuineness of reported miracles.

Times change. A saint, while he transcends the moral defects of his age, does not transcend its intellectual limitations. To understand Capistran you must understand the age in which he lived. This duty, self-evident in statement, is seldom fulfilled. To defend the popes, paint them as they were. This word of Pastor applies also to the defender of the popes, St. John Capistran.

Thanks are due to Father Willibrord Beck, O.S.B., for generous and valuable assistance.

The title of the book here translated is: *Johannes von Capestrano, Ein Leben im Kampf um die Reform der Kirche*, von Johannes Hofer. Tyrolia-Verlag, Innsbruck-Wien-München.

PART I
FAMILY AND CAREER
(1386–1415)

CHAPTER I

Family and Home

"THE time into which I was born was a time of schism and turmoil. Two popes had been elected. Urban VI and Clement VII." Thus, in the year 1451, did St. John Capistran begin a sermon. Eight years before his birth, the schism he mentions had fallen disastrously upon Western Christendom. On September 20, 1378, the same Roman cardinals who, some three months before, had elected Pope Urban VI, now rejected him, and elected Robert of Geneva, a French cardinal, to the papal throne. Robert called himself Clement VII. Thenceforward, for many decades, two popes attempted to reign. When this disastrous schism ended, Capistran was thirty years old. His family history is so interwoven with the chaos in political conditions under the great schism that his story must begin with an account of those conditions.

Urban VI and Clement VII excommunicated each other, enlisted soldiers, and began to wage war. The kingdom of Naples, which from Norman times on had been a papal fief, was the first to suffer. Joanna I, Neapolitan queen since 1343, favored Clement VII, who reigned at Avignon in France. Urban VI deposed her and offered the Neapolitan throne to King Louis of Hungary, who belonged to the house of Anjou. Urban VI thus repeated the deed of Urban IV, who, more than a hundred years before, had called Charles of Anjou, ancestor of the Neapolitan and Hungarian Anjous, from France into Italy against the Hohenstaufens.

Louis of Hungary did not accept Urban's offer, but suggested that another Anjou, Charles, duke of Durazzo, be made king of Naples. Charles, at this time in Treviso, where he was general of a Hungarian army fighting against Venice, accepted Urban's gift, made peace with Venice, and started (August, 1380) from Verona to his kingdom in the south.

Queen Joanna was not idle. She quickly chose Louis of Anjou, brother of the French king, to be her adopted son, urging him to come with all possible speed. Louis accepted. The antipope in Avignon approved. But Charles of Durazzo already had the advantage. Otto of Brunswick, Joanna's fourth husband, fell into the hands of the Hungarians (June 24, 1381) at San Germano, and the Hungarians entered Naples. Joanna was taken prisoner, and ended her life by suicide (summer, 1382) in the castle of Muro. Louis of Anjou did indeed lead a splendidly equipped army over the Alps into Italy, and was everywhere celebrated in advance as victor. But Charles of Durazzo, equally valiant and cunning, kept out of the reach of the enemy and cut off their supplies. Sickness and desertion ruined Louis' grand army. His men died away "like dogs." He had to sell his jewelry. Many of his knights had to go on foot or ride on donkeys. His able field marshal, the Count of Savoy, died in 1383, and the next year he himself died of fever at Bari. Although his barons pledged loyalty to his son Louis II, the army dwindled to nothing. Some soldiers forced their way back to their native land, but others preferred to settle in Italy. Among the latter was one baron who, when hostilities ended, settled in the village of Capistrano in the Abruzzi mountains, and there became the father of St. John Capistran.

What was the nationality of this foreign nobleman? This is an unsettled question. Was he French? Was he German? Claims have been made for each. But we lack sufficient proof for either.[1] Nor is there adequate explanation of the political conditions that made it possible for a soldier in the defeated army of Louis of Anjou to build for himself a new position in life in the dominions of Charles of Durazzo, who ascended the throne of Naples as Charles III. In many parts of the country the party of Louis probably maintained itself for quite a long time. The Abruzzi certainly remained a stronghold of the Anjous. On the other hand we find a report that Charles III

---

[1] Capistran said his father was "ultramontano." But "ultramontane" applies to all northerners. Two centuries later his people were called "tedeschi" (Germans). But Capistran, in long years of preaching in Germany, never spoke of German descent.

entrusted the government of the village of Capistrano to his efficient general, Count Peter of Celano. Thus it seems that the knight who was to be Capistran's father adapted himself to the new situation by entering the service of the conqueror. He became a vassal of the duke of Celano, a rural nobleman residing in Capistrano. Here he won the affection of a daughter of the Amici family, a fairly well-to-do household. He must have married not later than 1385.

On June 24, 1386, about five o'clock in the afternoon, there was born to him a son who was baptized that very same day, and received the name John, in honor of the Baptist, whose feast day it was. John Capistran, as we shall call him from now on, was destined to give his birthplace, an insignificant hamlet in the Abruzzi, a world-wide renown. Capistrano itself is not an important place: a country town, with about eight thousand inhabitants, mostly merchants, peasants, and shepherds. Like most settlements in central and southern Italy, Capistrano is a mountain village. With its dense mass of rough stone buildings, it hangs like a gray mantle around the steep slope of the mountain which sinks toward the east down into the well-cultivated valley of the river Tirino. Fields strewn with blocks of limestone, numerous orchards of almond and olive, stretches of southern brushwood, characterize the landscape. Bare of forests near or far, it opens to the eye a beautiful panorama. The circling summits of the Apennines form a mighty framework. From the north you are greeted by the flattened horn of the Gran Sasso d' Italia; to the south your view is limited by the majestic group of the Majella mountains. To the northwest a paved road leads through gorges up to the high plateau of the Aterno, the center of the Abruzzi. A ride of two or three hours brings the traveler to Aquila, the capital of the Abruzzi, the highest province of Italy. Wheat and corn prosper here, and hemp and saffron, olives and almonds, even grapes in favored spots.

But the principal source of wealth is now, as it always was, herds of cattle and immense flocks of sheep. All summer long, on the extensive mountain pastures, the flocks graze, guarded by white dogs wearing spiked collars as a defense against the Abruzzi wolves.

In winter the shepherds drive their flocks into the warmer plains of Apulia. The shepherds, left to themselves the year round, became very wild and uncivilized, and thus gave to their country, the beautiful land of the Abruzzi, the bad name of home of brigands, a name which does not fit at all. On the contrary, the mountaineers are an imaginative and amiable race of men, not without artistic talent: a dreamy, reflective mountain clan, in striking contrast to the jovial and noisy Neapolitan breed down there in the smiling Campagna. Further, the Abruzzesi are brave, hardy, and venturesome. Like the Swiss, the Abruzzesi, especially toward the end of the Middle Ages, gladly served in foreign wars. All the Italian states hired them, and many a formidable leader of mercenaries came from this part of the country. This martial sense of the Abruzzesi came perhaps from a German strain in their blood. In the early Middle Ages the Lombards had dominated this territory, and perhaps nowhere else in foreign lands had German characteristics been so tenaciously preserved as in these rough valleys of the Apennines.

Here in this mountain town of Capistrano, John spent the days of his childhood. The nobility imitated courtly custom, and so the son of the baron of Capistrano was placed under the guidance of a palace-master, who was to train him, and teach him the elements of education. Learning was quite to the youngster's liking, and from this source arose no difficulty. The vivacious boy had an insatiable lifelong desire for learning. But his irascible temper did lead to domestic tragedies. Not yet six years old, he had a quarrel with his sisters, toward whom he used abusive words. His father reprimanded him, but refrained from punishing him personally. "Your teacher shall attend to that," was his sentence. Punishment over, the little penitent promised never to use bad words again. The immigrant knight, it seems, insisted on a strict life and courteous education for his children. Very soon the boy had his own horse. Even as Franciscan friar he never lost his fondness for horses, and references to horses are frequent in his sermons. In one sermon he enumerates twenty-two qualities of a good horse. It must have been a sacrifice for him to give up riding when he became a Franciscan.

Not before his great mission tours beyond the Alps did he again make use of a saddle horse.

Evidently John lost his father very early. But we cannot be sure whether the baron's early death is connected with the terrible catastrophe that befell his house. In two days' time twelve of Capistran's relations were slain; his father's house and the home of his mother's parents went up in flames. But neither the year nor the cause of these events is exactly known.[2] Probably the family became victims of the riotous disturbances which began with the death of Charles III and lasted many years. Charles had died in the year of John's birth. One party proclaimed the son of Louis of Anjou, Louis II, as king in place of the twelve-year-old Ladislaus, son of Charles. The other party declared in favor of Otto of Brunswick. A long struggle brought young Ladislaus at last to the throne. The massacre of Capistrano was perhaps an episode of this struggle. For many years John nourished bitter hatred against the murderers of his clan. Only his entrance into the Order gave him strength to forgive and forget. But terror of those days never left him. In 1452, when he was preaching peace sermons in Nuremberg, then at war with Margrave Albrecht of Brandenburg, he elucidated the horrors of civil war by depicting the gruesome fate of his own family.

To what extent family conditions were changed by this terrible stroke, we do not know. It does not seem to have entirely destroyed prosperity. At least his mother found means to let John go to the university when his time came to choose a vocation. Capistran's glowing enthusiasm for Ladislaus, and the manifest favors of the royal court, which opened for him the road to a splendid career, lead to the conclusion that his father had lost his life in the war from which Ladislaus emerged as victor.[3]

---

[2] The fact itself remained unknown till I found it attested by Capistran himself (in his sermons at Breslau and Nuremberg).

[3] Varese says that Capistran, while still a young boy, dissuaded his mother from a second marriage.

CHAPTER II

Education and Vocation

IN central Italy, Perugia was considered the best university. We meet famous names in the history of that university, Peter Damian, for instance, and Thomas Aquinas. Perugia was in the Papal States, beyond the borders of the Kingdom of Naples. Naples, under the iron rule of Ladislaus, enjoyed peace and order, but not so the other parts of Italy. For almost two centuries, since the downfall of the Hohenstaufens, Italy had never had one uncontested ruler. Many smaller potentates, filled with the imperial idea, tried to unify the whole peninsula, but their power was barely sufficient to keep the country continually disturbed. The cities, now wealthy and prosperous, were in perpetual civil war. Thus, toward the end of the Middle Ages, political Italy was a chaos of local wars. Street fighting and homicides were the order of the day. All Italian cities had a large contingent of exiles, called the outer class, in contrast to the citizens, called the inner class. Patriots contrasted the former splendor of Italy with the impotence of the present.

The cities of the Papal States offered the same hopeless aspect. The great statesman and general, Cardinal Alborno, a Spaniard, had succeeded in restoring the Papal States during the absence of the popes in Avignon (1307-78); but peace and order prevailed only a short time. Under the schism, papal dominion over central Italy again declined. None of the contesting popes had the money and men needed to assert himself as master, and party frenzy raged in the papal cities as it did anywhere else. In Perugia the struggle between nobility and common people ended victoriously for the latter. The leader of the defeated nobles, Braccio of Montone, a dauntless man, left his native town and went as exile to Florence. He and his fellow exiles succeeded in gaining the Roman pope, Boniface IX (1389-1404), successor of Urban VI, for an alliance against Perugia. Braccio had almost conquered the city, when the citizens offered full submission to the Pope, provided he would forbid the return of the exiles. On June 28, 1398, a treaty of peace was signed between Perugia and the Pope. The exiles were re-exiled. Braccio entered the service of King Ladislaus, who offered him assistance for a new attack on Perugia.

About 1400, when Capistran began his studies at Perugia, the city, now papal, may have enjoyed comparative peace. The university already had four faculties. The student's first years were given to the liberal arts. Then he had to choose one of the three professions: theology, medicine, or law. John chose the law. But along with civil law, a course of six to eight years, he followed also the course in canon law, requiring six years. Perugia's school could stand comparison with that of Bologna or Padua, and attracted the best jurists of Italy.

Yet even in those days the study of law was in its decline; the days of the classical jurists in Italy had passed. Among their last representatives were the three Perugian brothers, Ubaldi, especially the highly celebrated Baldo Ubaldi. Capistran was too late to hear him, or his brother Angelo, almost equally renowned. But he did have the third brother, Pietro, as his teacher, and recalled his memory in later years. The study of jurisprudence demanded the entire energy even of the most talented students. First came the various collections of divergent laws, then the views of the most famous jurists. "And into these depths was poured a labyrinthine mass of juristic material: citations, authorities, definitions, and definitions of definitions, divisions, distinctions, exceptions, replications, duplications. The few who with tireless zeal groped through the tangled mass, and left it in some sort of order, these are 'the great jurists of the age.' " At the end of this thorny path there waited not only a carefree life, but also a famous name. The great jurists of the Middle Ages were all but worshiped, both by nobles and by commons. The humanist, too, was honored. But a celebrated jurist stood above a celebrated humanist, as a prince stands above a schoolmaster.

The knightly son of Capistrano was ambitious to be a jurist.

His zeal was indefatigable. Whole nights he spent over his books. The proverb says, he remarks in a sermon at Vienna, that dissipation and smoke are the worst enemies of the eyes; but he could assure them from his own experience that studying at night is an enemy still worse. To keep awake he used to pluck his eyelashes, and thereby contracted lifelong eye-trouble. He had made up his mind to outstrip all companions. In the public debates, held not only in the lecture room but even in the market place, John missed no opportunity to let his light shine. For self-made men Capistran always had high esteem. One such instance impressed him during his years of study. In October, 1404, Cosmato de' Migliorati, who had studied law at Perugia, ascended St. Peter's chair as Pope Innocent VII. As a student this man had a hard struggle to provide his daily bread. In Perugia, Capistran admired the beautiful volumes that Migliorati had copied to earn needed money.

Capistran's purpose was hardly that of becoming a professor of law. Service in the government was his goal. His years of study over, he left the university, being satisfied with the licentiate. The title of doctor, to be granted after a solemn debate in the cathedral, was not a prerequisite for practicing law, but was rather a matter of honor. The expenses connected with that promotion, still more the wish to reserve this honor as ornament for a self-secured position in life, led him to postpone the great day. Similar reasons, probably, led him to delay his marriage. Soon after beginning his studies, still young in years, he had chosen a girl of noble descent to be his future wife. She was the daughter of the Count of San Valentino, an Abruzzi town much like Capistrano, and located about a day's journey to the southeast, on a slope of the Majella mountains. At the close of his studies (1409) he was old enough to marry; but he left university and bride behind, in favor of a public career, in the capital of the realm.

Capistran remained faithful to his law studies, pursuing them with passionate ardor all his life. This marked predilection for jurisprudence corresponded evidently with his talents, his amazing memory, and extraordinary sagacity. He found special pleasure in handling a hopelessly tangled case. Requests for opinion and advice in legal matters, coming from everywhere, were always willingly accepted.

On the other hand Capistran was hardly touched by the humanist movement of his time. The cause of this rests in the conditions prevailing at the period of his studies. The humanists were indeed already busy unearthing the treasures of classical literature, from which would spring the new educational ideal. But the universities in general, and the jurists in particular, held themselves at dignified distance from the innovators.

Capistran's first office was that of counselor in the royal court of Naples. That a young jurist, fresh from the university, was at once admitted to the highest court of the land was not indeed an event without parallel, but must nevertheless be looked upon as a token of royal esteem for the family of Capistran. These court sessions introduced the young lawyer into various political secrets, since here the highest political offenses were tried. The famous case against Count Ladislaus Arthur of St. Agatha and his son Ercole was just then pending. Since they were held to be partisans of the Anjous, Ladislaus had them arraigned for high treason. Investigation showed the father guilty, but the son innocent. A contemporary jurist, a personal acquaintance, reports that Capistran had candidly defended Ercole in the presence of the King, and had demanded his acquittal.

Did the King wish to be rid of the young Count, in order to be enabled to seize feudal tenure? Did he wish merely to frighten him? At any rate the court, by a pretended sentence, condemned Ercole to death. He was to be led with his father to the place of execution and there set free. On February 14, 1410, Count Arthur was executed in the presence of his son. As a result of the terror endured, the young man himself died soon after. Capistran may well have felt himself partly responsible in this judicial murder. The assertion of later historians, that under the pressure of these events he resigned his office, and embraced the religious life, is not true. But the remembrance of these first evil experiences does find an echo in his sermons, when he tells the advisers of princes and kings that "for vain profit they gamble away their eternal happiness." But as yet such thoughts were far away. Neither this shocking event nor the private life of the royal libertine could shake the loyalty which he had probably brought with him from home.

In many respects the character of the King was surely apt to awaken patriotic enthusiasm. Coming to manhood in the stormy days of civil war, Ladislaus had given proofs of courage and determination, and of more than common statesmanship. In his dreams of great deeds, Frederick II was his model. His aim was dominion over all Italy, leading to the imperial crown. "Emperor or nothing," was his motto. Cunningly he turned the schism to the best advantage for his own plans. He played protector to the Pope, occupied Rome and part of the Papal States under the pretext of anticipating a French attack, and already called himself king of Rome. Both sides were just then preparing a general council, in Pisa, to end the schism. But ecclesiastical peace did not suit the King's plans. To wreck the Council, he advanced into Florentine territory. Florence prepared for war, and Ladislaus retreated.

The Council ran its course. The assembled cardinals declared both popes deposed and (June 26, 1409) elected as pope the septuagenarian Minorite, Peter Philargi. He called himself Alexander V. But far from attaining unity, the Church had now three supreme pontiffs. The Pope at Rome was seriously threatened by the one at Pisa. Ladislaus sent ships to bring him to Gaeta. In the meantime Louis II of Anjou, son of Ladislaus' old opponent, strongly assisted by Florence, occupied Rome, and defeated Ladislaus (May 11, 1411) at Roccasecca. The Pisan pope, John XXIII, successor of Alexander V, made Rome his residence, deprived Ladislaus of his dominion over Naples, and excommunicated him. But history was repeated, and the young Anjou met the same fate as his father met twenty years earlier, against Charles of Durazzo. Provisions failed, his soldiers deserted and went to his enemy. Nothing remained but disgraceful retreat.

All these events, most of which happened during these first years in Naples, were suited to enkindle Capistran's enthusiasm for his King. Under this brave and crafty monarch, Naples became the leading city of Italy. The peninsula's fate lay in his hands. Notwithstanding the King's bad qualities, Capistran was fire and flame, ready to die for his cause. The royal house held him strongly fettered. As a nobleman, he was expected to be present at court festivities. When in later years he came to speak of the dangers of dancing, he utilized his own experience, telling the people that up to his thirtieth year he had often danced at the royal court.

Sooner than he expected, John had opportunity to suffer a serious injustice in the royal service.

King Ladislaus and Pope John XXIII, similar in political selfishness, soon became friends. On June 24, 1412, they signed a peace treaty at Naples. Ladislaus, discovering all at once that after all John XXIII was the right Pope, elected by divine inspiration, withdrew his protection from the Roman Pontiff. Amid great dangers Gregory XII fled to the city of Rimini, where Malatesta protected him. Although oppressed by need, Gregory refused to accept a pension of 50,000 florins. Ladislaus, on the other hand, received as a reward for his treason, besides other favors, also four cities in the Papal States, including Perugia, as security for 220,000 florins to which the Pisan Pope had pledged himself.

Ladislaus himself now came to Perugia, the most northern city of his kingdom, situated near the borders of his enemies, the Florentines. By a second act of treachery he sacrificed also his famous military leader, Braccio, once exiled from Perugia. Ladislaus promised the Perugians that he would treat all emigrants as his own enemies, and would hand Braccio over alive or dead. But Braccio heard of the royal betrayal in time and deserted to the Florentines. Ladislaus appointed a prominent citizen as captain in Perugia, and this man asked the favor of having Capistran as judge. In each city of the kingdom a captain had full powers of government as plenipotentiary of the king. He had a judge as assistant and representative in administrative and judicial matters. Besides captain and judge, also a notary was appointed. These three resided in the courthouse and were partly supported by fees. What was wanting had to be supplied by the city.

Capistran s transfer may have been a result of his own desire.

Thus, after a short separation, he was returning to the company of his former professors and friends and had opportunity to continue his favorite studies again. Perhaps he gave lectures in the university when his official duties permitted. One of the students there became his close friend. This was a young man, so poor that he lived on alms, and even collected the remnants of candles to study at night. This student later became the famous Cardinal Giuliano Cesarini, whom Capistran described as "his best friend and companion in the study of law for many years." Thus spoke Capistran, after Cesarini had lost his life in battle against the Turks at Varna in 1444.

Capistran's appointment was a new token of royal confidence. After the disturbances of the last years the city needed a strong hand. Robbery and thievery were in full swing. Party struggles had dulled the conscience of the citizens and weakened the sense of right and wrong. One of the most influential men of the city attempted to extort the condemnation of a personal antagonist. When bribery failed, he threatened death. Capistran could not be moved. He declared the accused man innocent and acquitted him. A strict sense of justice was part of his nature. "Not for a mountain of gold could he have been moved to give an unjust sentence," he declared later in the pulpit. Neither to himself nor to anybody else would he remit the least obligation.

A tradition reaching back into the days of Capistran brings the following anecdote, which shows his conscience in conflict with deeply rooted prejudices. He doubted the admissibility of torture, and showed its uselessness in the following manner. From his stable he secretly removed the saddle, then ordered his valet to saddle and bring his horse. The terrified youth reported that the saddle had disappeared. Capistran accused him of theft and had him tortured. Overcome by pain the poor fellow confessed himself guilty, mentioning even the place where he had hidden the booty. Nothing of course was found there. Tortured again, the unhappy man asserted he had sold the saddle. Capistran now knew enough. He compensated the servant generously for the pains he had endured, and resolved never again to resort to torture. Thus the story. It shows that Capistran lived in the memory of the people as a judge of rare qualities.

Capistran's coming brought hard times for the Fraticelli. This sect, founded by apostate Franciscans, rejected all popes since John XXII as heretics. Their sect, they claimed, was the true Church of Christ and the real Order of St. Francis of Assisi. Their secret machinations threatened not only the Church but also the state. The schism had made them more energetic. Their hiding places were especially numerous in the territory of Perugia. In those days the extirpation of heretics fell under the jurisdiction of the secular authorities, and the new judge fulfilled his duty with the greatest zeal.

The people of Perugia liked this new judge. He was strict, but impartial and courageous, and very kind to the poor. He gave much care to his personal appearance, especially to his curly hair, which waved over his shoulders like fine threads of gold. "Not for a thousand ducats would he have sold his hair," he confessed later. When the small wiry figure of "Messer Giovanni" appeared on the streets, everybody greeted him.

Capistran's administration satisfied also the expectations of the King, whose aim was to reconcile the Perugians with the new government of Naples and thereby to prepare the city for permanent incorporation. Capistran certainly knew the King's plans, not only regarding these few cities of the Papal States, but for dominion over all Italy. Capistran's wish, to be allowed to die for his royal master, is to be taken as an expression of his readiness to place himself entirely at the disposal of the King in executing these dangerous plans. Thus we understand, first, his self-accusation in later years, that he had as judge served the King better than he had served God in the religious order; secondly, similar remarks of his biographers, who say that, to please the King, he was not afraid to displease God. As a mature religious, with ideas purged of all worldliness, he deeply regretted that he had so persistently supported the brutal and unscrupulous politics of a militarist king.

Ladislaus was forging straight ahead. All Italy was to bow under his scepter. As shortly before he had betrayed his own general, Braccio, so now he betrayed his confederate, John XXIII.

When Ladislaus invaded the Papal States, Pope and cardinals fled to Florence, and the King's troops devastated Rome. Ladislaus was determined to drive the Pope entirely out of Italy. In March, 1414, he occupied Rome a second time. One good result came of these rascalities. Extremely afflicted, John XXIII appeared at the General Council of Constance. Shortly before the Council went into session, King Ladislaus died quite unexpectedly. He was not yet forty years old. Seized by a terrible sickness at Perugia, he was brought to Rome in a sedan chair, and from there by ship to Naples. In view of the beautiful city he expired, amid terrible pains, August 6, 1414. His last days had been horrible. Rumor said he had been poisoned, but the real evil was the dissolute life which had quickly consumed his strength. He was mourned over at Naples, and throughout the country. The demise of the enterprising monarch was everywhere felt as a national calamity. He left no one fit to be his successor. When the government was taken over by his sister, Joanna II, a childless widow and ugly woman, dull, vicious, and despised by the people, troubles began at once. Even loyal adherents of the crown favored the Angevin party. The troops were recalled from Etruria to protect the center of the kingdom. Perugia itself was no longer safe. When the captain left the city and did not return, the municipality reasserted its own power and appointed Judge Capistran to be captain of the city.

This advance in rank may have been the reason that induced Capistran now at length to marry. Too long his bride had been waiting for this event. The wedding indeed was celebrated, but the marriage was never consummated, and was soon dissolved.[1] This dissolution of his recent marriage is connected with those events which became the turning point, not only in his social position, but in his whole life, to which they gave an entirely new direction.

Before we enter into this new epoch in his life, we must answer the question: What was his religious and moral behavior up to St. Magdalen's Day, July 22, 1415, the day of his conversion?

Capistran's occasional remarks distinguish three stages in his

[1] A virginal marriage seems to have been, not an original intention, but a result, first of political turmoil, then of his conversion.

life. With joy and consolation he recalls the days of his childhood. A strong sense of modesty and a deeply founded respect for his parents were his safeguards. When he heard indecent words, he blushed and ran away. With his life in the Order he is likewise satisfied. He doubted, indeed, whether he had served God during the thirty-five years since his profession as faithfully as he had formerly served his king. Thus he spoke in a sermon at Vienna, 1451. Yet he goes on to declare that he would have died rather than commit a mortal sin. But he utterly condemns the fifteen years between leaving his parental home and entering the Order. Those years remain an object of bitter remorse. "I squandered those years," he complains in the pulpit at Breslau. "How I regret it! I still do penance for it. Oh, that wild beasts had torn me to pieces after baptism, before I offended Thy divine majesty!"

Saints are severe on themselves. We must weigh such expressions with caution and ask for the underlying facts. Capistran tells us that he had neglected to receive Holy Communion.[2] Only after his entrance into the Order of St. Francis at the age of thirty, did he receive his first Holy Communion. Yet this fact cannot be taken as a sign of irreligion, or even as a high degree of lukewarmness, since he frequently went to confession. During his years of study he confessed once a month. Not to forget sins, he wrote them down. Why did he so persistently neglect a duty strictly binding on all the faithful? Perhaps general custom had more to do with it than his own disposition. But his moral behavior stands forth in clear light when he asserts, equivalently, that this neglect was the only positive grievous sin of his life, as far as exterior acts are concerned.

When he says that during all those years he lived in the state of mortal sin, his proof is that he had never gone to Holy Communion. In favor of this somber view he adduces otherwise only his worldly- minded disposition, which prompted him to aim solely at wealth, honors, and pleasure. "With such inclinations," he

---

[2] Before Bernardine of Siena's time a wide-spread custom in Italy put off Communion till later years, even till the hour of death. As a result many died without the sacraments. See *Analecta Bollandiana*, XXV, 325.

asserts later on, "it can hardly be assumed that I did not seriously sin." It seems certain that he kept himself free from sensual aberrations, though many pitfalls were laid for him, and his nature was prone to sensual allurements. Even in the years of his religious life his southern blood put his steadfastness to hard tests. Purity governed his relations with his intended bride, and even beyond the wedding feast he practiced continence. This noble attitude was prompted not so much by ascetic considerations as by a highly developed sense of modesty, honor, and self-respect. Love for a blameless and esteemed name shielded him in countless temptations against justice. "When I had to give a sentence or make terms of peace, I always proceeded most justly, yet not for God's sake but for my own reputation." Yet, child of the world, he neglected his inner soul. He complains of his complete indifference in regard to thoughts: sins of this kind escaped his attention entirely. For years he nourished a spirit of hatred and revenge against the murderers of his relatives. The meaning of the great commandment, which finds its fulfillment in love for enemies, had not yet dawned on him. His energy against heretics can therefore hardly be ascribed to genuine religious promptings. The prosecution of heretics as guilty of high treason served rather secular aims than ecclesiastical purposes. In Naples this procedure had been introduced by Emperor Frederick II. In the struggles between Church and state John adhered unreservedly, without the least scruple, to the cause of his king.

In the little information we have of his early religious life, we of a later age find many anomalies. But in the Middle Ages the simultaneous practice of piety on the one hand, and worldly-minded activity on the other, had nothing exceptional about it. A nobleman who carefully curls his hair, or runs eagerly after pleasures and seeks revenge on his enemies, and still goes to confession often, and who recites the Office of the Blessed Virgin, may have been even in those days a rarity, but not a contradiction. Nor was Capistran's life a weak-kneed vacillation between piety and worldliness. His piety may have been rather external, not deeply internal; but strong principles of goodness must have been active in the young nobleman. His inflexible sense of justice indicates a strong, settled character guided by clear and firm norms of conduct. And amid all the dark shadows there is no trace of illicit sensual enjoyment. Neither exterior seduction nor his lively nature led him astray. An inherited solidity of temperament and careful boyhood training enabled him to lead the life of a cavalier, without fear and without reproach. The real danger in his nature lay in another direction: "By nature I am slicker than the devil, and prouder than Satan." King Ladislaus, the brutal despot, knew how to choose his men. The judge of Perugia was a useful tool.

PART II
CONVERSION, PROFESSION, ORDINATION
(1415-17)

CHAPTER III

Imprisonment and Conversion

DURING the summer of 1415 the judge of Perugia got ready to visit his native town, Capistrano, to procure the money for his solemn promotion to the doctorate. At that moment came the events which frustrated his promotion and thereby ended his career in the world.

Since King Ladislaus' death, Perugia, the most northern stronghold of the kingdom, lacked military defense. Neither of the two popes was able to regain the city for the Papal States. The Pisan pope, John XXIII, had gone to the General Council at Constance; and the Roman pope, Gregory XII, lived as a fugitive at Rimini. The nobles who had fled from Perugia as exiles some years before now began to stir. Their chief, Braccio of Montone, waited in the territory of Bologna, which John XXIII had confided to his care. When the Council of Constance (May 29, 1415) declared John devoid of the papal dignity, Braccio occupied all Bolognese strongholds, and demanded for their return 60,000 florins. With this sum he planned an attack on Perugia. But in this endeavor he was surprised by Carlo Malatesta, the lord of Rimini. Of all the Italian potentates, Malatesta was the only one who to the end had supported the Roman, Gregory XII. Now that Gregory, too, after the deposition of the Pisan pope, was preparing freely to resign the papal dignity, Malatesta thought the time ripe to lay hands on Perugia. In this war between Perugia and Carlo Malatesta, Capistran's future was to be decided.

Perugia sent Capistran to meet Malatesta and arrange for peace. On his way he fell into the hands of one of the exiled nobles, who had already occupied a number of fortified places in the neighborhood of Perugia. In Brufa, a little village in a fertile plain between Etruria and Perugia, John was kept prisoner. On the top of a hill stood the castle, a little round building with eight towers.

While Perugia seemingly submitted to Malatesta, poor Capistran, the mediator, pined away in one of the towers of Brufa, with water and bread to sustain life, and heavy iron chains on his feet.

Convinced his life was in danger, he planned a desperate escape. Calculating the height of the tower, with his teeth he tore the bed linen and then his cloak into strips. When he let down the improvised rope, the end was still far from the ground. However, he let himself down, but did not get far. The rope, not being strong enough, broke, and he dropped to the ground, where he remained lying, his thighbone fractured. A farmer working nearby ran up, recognized the fugitive, and made ready to call the guard. Capistran reached for a tool and uttered terrible threats. The frightened farmer ran away. But the jailers, missing their prisoner, soon found him totally exhausted, hiding in the shrubbery. Instead of medical treatment, he now found a more severe imprisonment. Down in the lowest and darkest dungeon, fastened with chains to the wall, up to his knees in water, with an iron chain round his waist, he could not even move. After three days of terrible pain, his strength left him and he fell in a swoon. This was the hour that God had prepared.

A deafening noise brought the sleeping man back to consciousness. The room was lighted, as if high noon had penetrated the walls. The drowsy man imagined himself to be free. Lifting his head and seeing before him a form in the habit of a Franciscan, he stretched out his arms to embrace the visitor, but the visitor vanished. When Capistran now leaned his head back, he noticed that his hair was cut, "just as you see me now," as he said years later.

His treatment soon became milder. He was being held for ransom. Hence medical treatment was allowed. The initial neglect left his leg in a condition that caused him much inconvenience all his life long. Jail life gave him time for contemplation. He had no difficulty in explaining the figure of the vision as St. Francis; the mysterious loss of his precious hair, his close-cropped skull, in full Franciscan fashion, was an unmistakable hint that he should become a Franciscan. Invisible hands were destroying his secular dress. The worldling shuddered with horror. In spite of the evident miracle, he was overcome by sadness, which soon turned into bitterness. He gave vent to fits of anger. Never, he gnashed, would he become a priest, still less a friar. Days of anguish followed. "He wrestled with God like Israel," wrote one of his intimate confreres. About a week later, at noon, when he was reciting the Office of the Blessed Virgin, the Franciscan again stood before him, chiding him this time for obstinacy. Thoroughly frightened, he began to stammer: he was ready to do anything that God demanded of him. Then and there he was told to leave everything and follow our Lord in the habit he had seen. "I saw finally that it was God's holy will that I should leave the world and serve Him alone." Thus he spoke to a friend, describing the end of his long struggle. It was July 22, the feast of the penitent Magdalen.

These events in the prison of Brufa were repeatedly mentioned by Capistran; even in the pulpit he seems to have touched on them. They are not a legend of later development. Capistran's own testimony leaves no doubt that his conversion and vocation were a wonderful act of God's direct intervention and that his captivity played only a secondary role. There is no reason to put him into the class of disappointed and crushed souls that seek the cloister to find rest and protection from a wicked world. He who came forth from the tower of Brufa was not a disappointed man that needed repose. The freshness and energy of his nature remained intact. In his impetuous zeal to begin the new life he could hardly wait on events. His jailer, well disposed, procured for him some gray Franciscan cloth and the necessary sewing requisites, Capistran promising to pay. He made the best Franciscan habit he could and began to wear it. The news spread quickly, but his enemies, not trusting him, strengthened the guard. Capistran answered that dissimulation was not his nature. Let them but send him a Franciscan whom they trusted.

This wish was granted. A highly esteemed padre from a neighboring Franciscan monastery came to visit the prisoner. The grave religious, when he saw the well-known Messer Giovanni in this fantastic costume, began to laugh, and asked him: "To what order does this habit belong?" But he was soon convinced that the prisoner had a higher call, and offered himself as hostage. This report hastened negotiations for ransom. Meantime Capistran received a genuine habit. But, according to canon law, a prisoner could not be invested. On the other hand, the captive persistently begged for that favor. So the brothers got around the difficulty by simply leaving a habit in his cell. As ransom, the reasonable sum of forty ducats was agreed upon. Accompanied by his spiritual adviser, Capistran returned in secular clothes to Perugia, where he was heartily welcomed by friends and companions.

From Perugia he hurried to Capistrano and informed his wife of his irrevocable resolution to become a Franciscan, and restored her dowry to her. Marriage contracted but not consummated can, according to Church law, be dissolved by one partner alone against the will of the other, on condition of entrance into a religious order. Capistran availed himself of this privilege. His young wife made no objection. Rather, she announced she would follow his example and remain a virgin.[1] His paternal inheritance he left to his mother. Then he made a few visits, difficult ones, to five "archenemies" of his house, was reconciled to them, asked their pardon, and promised to remain their friend henceforth. Returning to Perugia, he sold his books and other belongings. From the sum realized he paid his ransom. What was left he gave away.

Then came the closing scene, a public farewell to his dignity. He followed strictly the custom of his age. Mounted backward on a donkey, wearing an immense foolscap, covered with the names of crimes which he considered himself guilty of, he rode out into the market place, where great criminals, especially heretics, were led to execution. True to his axiom to spare neither himself nor others, his last sentence as judge was against himself. Living in new light, he saw clearly that he had been more faithful to the world than to God, and thus gave back what the world had given him: the reputation of an esteemed and sagacious nobleman. Incidents of this kind were not as strange in those days as they would be in ours. Nevertheless such scenes were not witnessed daily. Gossip filled Perugia. Street urchins threw stones at him. His friends were ashamed. Even some

---

[1] Nevertheless, urged by relatives, this woman did later on take a husband.

of the clergy called him a fool. A soldier on watch, reading the misdeeds on the foolscap, felt in duty bound to arrest him. The captain scolded the soldier's stupidity, and dismissed Capistran kindly.

At Monteripido, near Perugia, he asked for admittance to the Order. The guardian of the monastery, Marcus of Bergamo, was a wise and experienced man, himself a latecomer, who, like Capistran, had studied law in the Perugian university. Still Capistran's request met with difficulties. The brethren simply knew that he had been a married man; that he had until lately led a worldly life; that political changes in Perugia had struck him hard and led him to break with the world. Any religious superior would wonder whether the young man were not a victim of his fate and in a state of religious excitement. A sudden religious change, a sudden leap from worldly habits to the highest asceticism, so frequent in the later Middle Ages, often produced a tension of life which could not endure. Capistran's heroic deeds after his conversion did not yet have the stamp of durability. The brothers tried to discourage him. Vividly they described the hardships he would have to endure in the extremely poor institutes of the gray friars. He assured them he was determined to bear all this and more, even until death. At length they admitted him to the novitiate. On October 4, 1415, the feast of St. Francis of Assisi, he received the religious garb. Perugia, especially its university, heard the news and wondered.

CHAPTER IV

Fraticelli, Conventuals, Observants

WHEN Capistran entered Monteripido, the family of St. Francis of Assisi was two centuries old. The mustard seed planted by Francis had developed into a splendid tree. Pope Innocent III had given (1209) oral approval to the regulations laid down by Francis. When Francis died (1226) the number of the brethren was several thousand. Toward the end of that century the Order had from thirty to forty thousand members. After fluctuations, it had at least this number in the year 1400. This immense family was subdivided into thirty-four provinces and ten vicariates with houses numbering about fifteen hundred. And beyond the farthest provinces, in every land of the world then known, were found their missioners: from Lapland to the Congo, from the Azores to China. Every third year the provincial delegates met to elect a general, the director of the whole Order, who resided at Ara Coeli in Rome. Ara Coeli, high on the Capitoline Hill which overlooks the whole city, was a symbol of the Order, with which none of the other religious organizations could compete, either in number of members or in world wide activity.

But within this splendid outward development ran parallel a sad history of interior struggles. Beginning in the days of the holy founder, these contests, in a certain sense, still exist. They play a dominant part in the history of Capistran, and their consequences are far from being merely domestic. To the immense number of Franciscans proper we must add the second order, i.e., about fifteen thousand Poor Clares, and also the third order, which, according to Capistran's estimate, in 1450 numbered about six hundred thousand. By means of this third order, Franciscan life came in touch with all ranks of the people and with the entire Christian world. The seraphic spirit entrusted to its care was not an exclusively domestic affair, and the storms around the rule cast their waves far beyond the limits of the Order. Numerous people saw in St. Francis the guide to a deeper Christian standard of life. These imperishable values had to be preserved. That their preservation caused the Order such extraordinary difficulties is to be attributed to the Order's peculiar character.

Originally St. Francis had not intended to found a new order. He and his small group of companions wished to imitate as literally as possible the absolutely poor and apostolic mission life of Jesus and the apostles. But the surprisingly rapid increase of his followers impelled him to religious organization. This brought at once the serious question: How reconcile organization with the practical exercise of the vow of poverty? In the monastic orders individual members renounced the right to personal property, whereas no precise limits were set to possession by the community. Temporal prosperity was considered by Western monasticism, faced with cultural problems, as a normal condition. Wealth brought dangers, and many monasteries fell victims. If the Church was at times worldly-minded, monasteries that had grown too rich bore their full share of blame. The vow of poverty exemplified by pomp and luxury is a mockery of Christian ideals. This contrast was felt by the Christian conscience, sharpened in the days of the crusades. Thus arose with elemental force a religious movement which aimed at the restoration of genuine evangelical poverty. The noblest and most lasting fruit of that movement is St. Francis of Assisi and his Order.

With intrepid firmness Francis insisted on two things: first, that his brethren renounce personal property for themselves in the sense of the monastic vow; second, that all possession in common, especially of money and real estate, be excluded. The brothers cannot call anything their own, not even their poor domiciles. By alms and manual labor alone are they to meet their daily needs. Thus the Franciscan vow of poverty contained two obligations: the monastic one, which stresses the personal renunciation of property; and the primitive view of voluntary poverty, which demands practical restrictions in the use and enjoyment of earthly goods. But what about property rights over the few things needed for daily support? The question is oversubtle. Nobody disputes the extreme poverty of a beggar, though he possesses a beggar's sack. St. Francis would look on himself and his brethren as beggars, though they had property rights to their habits and to their tools. But this foundation of poverty, and the attempt to realize the ideal of evangelical poverty within the frame of monastic life, became the germ of protracted poverty disputes. Even in the days of St. Francis the continually increasing brotherhood needed permanent instruments, books for instance, which could not be called necessary for the support of bodily life.

From all sides the brethren were called on to preach. Francis and his first companions spoke without preparation, out of the depths of their hearts, and they performed wonders of conversions. But this grace is not granted to the average preacher. Nor would this method suffice for all kinds of sermons. The new heresies fought with the heavy armor of science. If the brethren were to meet them with equal weapons, they had to prepare by serious study. But may the brothers possess books? The Franciscan conscience awoke. Four years after Francis' death. Pope Gregory IX, the special friend and adviser of St. Francis, gave a famous explanation of the Rule. Therein the Franciscan vow of poverty is defined as follows: "The brothers have not, either individually or in common, any rights either of ownership or of use, over any goods whether movable or immovable." This decision was of immense importance, since it emphasizes renunciation of all rights of possession. Although this decision made clear that altissima *paupertas*, the distinctive mark of the Order, consists in community renunciation of all property rights to the things they used, still it stated implicitly that moderate use of these things would not touch the essence of the Franciscan vow of poverty, and that in this regard they enjoyed the same liberty as other orders of adapting themselves to prevailing conditions, provided they violated no positive restrictions of the Rule, for instance, the prohibition of money and real estate. This view became prevalent. By decrees of general chapters and by papal privileges, the original mode of living gradually softened. But the Order felt it was preserving the sacred inheritance of the holy founder, his altissima paupertas, as long as it did not claim any property rights in common.

But who would have to be considered proprietors of the houses, churches, books, and furniture of the brothers after benefactors and their heirs had died? The popes settled this question by themselves assuming proprietorship, in the name of the Apostolic See, over all Franciscan belongings; only the use remained with the brethren. The provincials, as administrators of the Apostolic See, were permitted to appoint secular procurators, who had to settle all questions involving ownership. Thus the Order enjoyed a juridically protected subsistence, without being proprietor, and consequently had the liberty of action necessary to display its full power. No other way lay open for the realization of the evangelical ideal of perfect poverty within the frame of a great religious community, if the Order was to acquit itself satisfactorily in all the tasks entrusted to it by the Church.

But with this regulation of the matter a certain minority in the Order was never satisfied. They saw in it an aberration, an apostasy from St. Francis. They clung tenaciously to the original manner of life, rejecting all "explanations" of the Rule and all papal privileges. They declared the main point was the *usus pauper*, the absolutely "poor way" of living, practiced in the beginning of the Order. In this they tolerated no change. Without the practice of poverty all renunciation of property was only an empty shell.

During the second half of the thirteenth century the two groups became more evident: the Community, as the members of the majority were called, and their opponents, for which the collective name "Spirituals" came into use. As leading minds came to champion the cause of the Spirituals, serious clashes with the Community could no longer be avoided. By 1311 (Council of Vienne) the leaders of the Spirituals were declaring they could no longer live with the Community. They must lead a separate life under their own superiors. With the accession of John XXII (1316) came a crisis for the Spirituals. The new Pope had long watched the dissensions in the Order. As Pope he intended to put an end to them. Spiritualism he suppressed at once, and mercilessly. Then he ordered the Community to conform themselves as regards poverty to the practice of other orders. That meant to abandon entirely the sacred principle of poverty in common. The Pope was inclined to regard this Franciscan peculiarity as the chief source of disturbance and dissension. His suggestion was promptly refused by the Community. Matters were complicated by the Pope's intervention in a theological dispute, which most intimately touched the struggles of the Order, the question, namely, of the poverty of Christ.

The mendicant friars had from the outset been exposed to violent attacks by some of the secular clergy. Jealousy had here its full share. Radical opponents of the friars went so far as to deny to all new orders the very right of existence. Absolute renunciation of secure revenues, they argued, was dangerous. Ecclesiastical authority was asked to suppress the new organizations. This called the great leaders of the mendicants to the fore, among them St. Bonaventure and St. Thomas Aquinas. It was the heyday of Scholasticism, and the immense apparatus of theological science was brought to bear on mendicant poverty. But some defenders of the mendicants were not satisfied with proving that mendicancy is permissible and possible, and is a suitable mode of attaining Christian perfection. Going still farther, they defended absolute poverty as the essential climax of Christian perfection. To the voluntary practice of poverty they attributed a value that does not belong to it. Moreover, they did not clearly distinguish between poverty as exterior renunciation, and poverty as interior virtue. Many of them found the ideal of Christian perfection in renunciation of the right to possess anything. Juridical renunciation, individual and common, the Franciscan formula of poverty, comes to represent simply the ideal of Christian perfection. Hence the attainment of the highest Christian perfection necessarily includes poverty. This exaggerated view of poverty, a reaction against medieval worldliness, a reaction which led even to heresy, was scientifically defended by these Spiritual theorists. Here, too, St. Thomas pursued the middle way of truth, and pointed out clearly the exaggerations of these theorists. Among the three religious vows, he said, poverty has the last place, and all the vows together are not perfection itself, but only means of perfection. The value of such means is judged by their appropriateness to the end. This sound doctrine of Aquinas seemed at first destined not to prevail. Franciscan theorists attacked him vehemently, and passionate controversies arose between Franciscans and Dominicans.

The crisis came when these controversies turned to the person of Jesus Christ. Opponents of the Minorites quoted Scripture to the effect that Christ and the apostles did indeed practice poverty, but held many things, for instance, alms, as common property. This assertion said nothing against the meritoriousness and value of conventual poverty. But, this assertion granted, the apex of Christian perfection did not include renunciation of property by the community. Thus the cornerstone of the Minorite theory, "No property rights either individually or communally," lost its Gospel support. The very foundation of the Order, the life work of St. Francis, seemed jeopardized. Thus the contest flamed still higher. Had not Christ and the apostles really renounced common property and even the right of use? On an affirmative answer the very existence of the Order seemed to depend. Scandalous conflicts occurred, not only in the universities, but even in the courts of the Inquisition.

In one case of this kind (1322) Pope John XXII himself intervened. From the beginning he agreed with the Dominicans, and prepared his decision in this sense. Franciscan champions were violently agitated. The general chapter, in session at Perugia (Pentecost, 1322), took the fatal step of anticipating the papal declaration by their own counterdeclaration to the Christian world. All they gained was that the irate Pope pursued still more energetically his reform of Franciscan poverty. In a public constitution he renounced his property rights to the possessions of the Order. A little later he published a dogmatic constitution on the poverty of Christ. The doctrine that "Christ and the apostles had no real right over the things which, according to the Gospel, they made use of," was condemned as contrary to Holy Scripture.

Just at this moment came the clash between John XXII and

Louis of Bavaria, the last great contest between pope and emperor in the Middle Ages. Political disturbances in Italy, mutual distrust and misunderstanding, led at last to open breach between the pope and the general of the Franciscans, Michael of Cesena. Michael fled (1328) with some prominent brothers of the Order to Louis of Bavaria, who gave them asylum in Munich. What scandal for the Christian world to see the head of the largest order of the Church at war with the pope! Michael's followers declared to the world that John XXII had, by his decrees against poverty, fallen into heresy, and must therefore be deposed by a council. But the majority of the Order remained loyal to the pope. The schismatics in Munich stood alone and soon died out. The Franciscans still adhered to the principle of conventual poverty, but the debate on Christ's poverty was over.

Thus ended the first century of Franciscan history. The rebellion left deep traces in the Order. Of the Spirituals, some identified themselves with the Community. But some groups retained their opposition to the papal decrees and attempted to realize their Franciscan ideal outside the Order. During the fourteenth century these groups received the name Fraticelli. Some of the Fraticelli remained orthodox, and lived under the jurisdiction of bishops. Later the most important of these groups, the adherents of Angelus Clarenus, came back to the Order. But there were also Fraticelli who followed the bad example of the apostate general, Michael of Cesena. Limited to some provinces in Italy, these schismatics were still strong enough to disturb the peace of the Church for more than a century. Public opinion continued to be very sensitive, inclined to side with the defenders of unadulterated poverty. Thus the Fraticelli gained ground rapidly, especially because in other things they taught nothing contrary to the doctrines of the Church. But their chief dogma was as follows: "Pope John XXII, by his denial of the absolute poverty of Christ, fell into heresy and thereby lost the papal dignity. His successors in the Apostolic See, as likewise all bishops and priests remaining loyal to him, are to be treated as heretics. Though they are lawfully ordained and administer the sacraments validly, yet, since they are excommunicated heretics, they commit mortal sin by exercising their office. Hence the faithful should receive the sacraments from their hands only in case of extreme necessity. The true Church exists at present only in the Fraticelli congregations. Only Fraticelli priests administer the sacraments worthily."

Acting in accordance with this view, Fraticelli priests made long trips to administer to distant adherents, to instruct them, and to encourage them to gain new members. Their main fields of activity were in the Marches, in Umbria and Tuscany. But they had colonies even in Rome. Wherever there was danger they remained in hiding. But some cities openly declared in favor of them, gave them houses and churches, and liberated imprisoned members by force of arms. Even some bishops were duped by their humble bearing and took them under protection. This sect, with its inner life carefully hidden from the public, was not only a threat to the unity of the Church, but also a focus of moral corruption. Age-old experience shows that the spirit of impurity follows, like an evil shadow, the hidden activities of secret sects. The disgusting heresy called "Freedom of Spirit," which justified lustful excesses with religious sophisms, had spread very far. Even ecclesiastically approved associations had to be watchful against this creeping poison. But in forbidden societies, which had to shun the light of day, the spirit of uncleanness found its best soil. In many places "Freedom of Spirit" found an asylum in Fraticelli communities.

The question of poverty has at different times threatened Church unity in the West. In the thirteenth century St. Francis conjured the danger. Fraticellism brought on a new wave of danger. To counteract this danger became a holy duty for the Minorites, particularly because the founders and leaders of the sect had gone forth from their own ranks. And the Fraticelli themselves directed their most violent attacks against the Order. Fraticellism was not easy to conquer. The Inquisition acted promptly whenever a member was seized. Literary opposition to the sect worked full time. But in truth the life of the conventual brothers themselves simply did not correspond with the original strictness of the Rule. The Fraticelli condemned them as traitors to St. Francis. The *fratres minores*, they said in derision, had become *fratres majores.*

Parallel, then, with Fraticellism ran loose tendencies in conventualism. During the fourteenth century monastic discipline sank deplorably. Since the principle of conventual poverty had been so sharply criticized by the highest authority, many lost enthusiasm for all ideals, and the lax elements prevailed. In many places the brothers began to accept without scruple real estate and regular revenues. Thus the Franciscan character faded more and more. The general discipline of the Order could and should have been preserved even under a milder interpretation of the practice of poverty. But the decline of monastic life as a whole had other causes. The fourteenth century was in general an evil time for monasteries. In Germany the struggle between Louis of Bavaria and the papal court brought endless disturbances into religious houses. After Louis died (1347), the Black Death overran Europe. The Franciscans are said to have lost two-thirds of their membership. But since the number of their houses rather increased than decreased, the gates were thrown wide open to fill the empty cells. Anybody and everybody was accepted, without much selection, the surest road to bring an order to ruin. Even boys under fourteen years were admitted to the novitiate. The rich legacies left by victims of the great plague were another danger. The great schism completed the ruin. In the Church, pope against pope, in the Order general against general, provincial against provincial. Religious superiors had to make all manner of concessions at the cost of discipline.

And yet, even in this century of deplorable decadence, the Seraphic Order gave proof of its indestructible vitality. Side by side with Fraticellism and Conventualism sprang up quite unobserved a new branch of the Order that brought it new life. Under the briars of abuse the seraphic spirit was nowhere extinct. In all provinces brothers were found who sincerely longed to follow the rule "literally," that is, in its original strictness. Since in the existing convents this pious desire could not be satisfied, some of these "pious brothers" began to retire to hermitages, where they could practice the first manner of living while remaining under obedience to their superiors. In Italy, in the year of John XXII's death (1334), John of Valle with four companions started a hermitage near Brugliano in Umbria. Other hermitages soon arose. But these brothers lacked prudence. They adapted a new manner of dress and admitted doubtful characters, probably Fraticelli, who pretended to be guided by holy zeal. In 1355 the young branch of reform had to be dissolved. But one of its first members, the lay brother Paul Vagnozzi, of the noble family of the Trinci, which ruled Foligno, again received permission to return to the solitude of Brugliano (1368). Venomous serpents infested the territory. The brothers had to wear rough wooden shoes. A froggy marsh nearby filled the air day and night with clamor. Only a few could endure the life. At times Paul had but one companion. But his heroic example conquered, and by and by Brugliano grew strong and vigorous, and this rough, barren place became the cradle of the reform. The brothers' occupation was prayer. For livelihood they begged, and received alms kneeling. Their faces were haggard, their feet bare, their garments the poorest.

Since the desert of Brugliano soon became too narrow, new hermitages were started. Former mistakes were avoided, and the superiors of the Order found no cause for intervention. Like their conventual brethren they obtained papal privileges and accepted donations of permanent settlements, without bothering about "rights of property" or "rights of use." They avoided all peculiarities, and remained in complete harmony with the convents. They did not even have a distinctive name, but were considered simply members of the Order who kept apart for the sake of a stricter observance of the Rule. Anyone who found life in the hermitage too hard was at liberty to return to the conventual life. They abstained from criticizing their brethren in the convents, and defended them against the attacks of the Fraticelli. True sons of the Church as well as of St. Francis, these "devout brothers" were the best antidote to Fraticellism. And this was their first great task. The convents themselves called these reformers from the wilderness as advance guards against the Fraticelli.

The Fraticelli were especially malignant in Perugia and the

surrounding territory. Rich citizens offered them their country houses. The Franciscan convent of Perugia suffered seriously under their attacks. One of them would hold up a Franciscan in the market place, tear his cowl or collar in the presence of a laughing crowd, with the scoffing remark: "Brother, St. Francis did not teach you to wear that." The brothers hardly dared to step out of their convent. Finally the convent decided to call Paul Trinci from Brugliano, offering him the chapel of St. Francis in Monteripido, situated beyond the city limits. The reform (1374) accepted the place, and the favor of the people soon turned to the new settlers. The secret activities of the Perugian Fraticelli began to come to light. A citizen overheard one of the Fraticelli claiming that he himself was the future Pope, while others contradicted him roughly. Now the citizens turned suddenly against them and expelled them. Some of the Fraticelli resisted, and their house was bombarded with stones for three days, until they fled.

But during the schism Fraticellism began to revive everywhere, also around Perugia. Capistran as judge of the city had to deal with them. But the reform movement, too, developed energetically. Paul Trinci was made commissary over twelve reformed settlements in Umbria, and even in the Roman province the reform found entrance. After Trinci's death (1390), John of Stroncone became the leader, and carried on the reform in the same tactful manner. Yet in 1400 the number of the brethren was, at least in Italy, in comparison with the whole Order, remarkably small. Capistran reckoned them at one hundred.

At the time of his entrance into the novitiate the number had doubled. The reform had, in all Italy, from thirty to forty colonies, mostly hermitages, i.e., small convents beyond the city limits. The name "Conventuals" was now reserved for those who lived in the spacious buildings. The brothers of the reform, *fratres de observantia,* were called "Observants," but the people called them simply "the pious brothers," *fratres devoti.* In German chronicles of the fifteenth century, the term preferably applied to Capistran is *Pater devotus,* i.e., the devout father. The Observants differed from the Conventuals principally by greater poverty. They strictly observed the rule of not accepting real estate or regular revenues. Their only resources were manual labor and alms, and they led a life almost exclusively contemplative. They had few priests; sometimes two or three settlements had only one priest, who said Mass for them alternately. Their pastoral work was still very limited. On begging tours they gave short exhortations, and occasionally assisted priests in parishes.

Capistran's entrance in Monteripido near Perugia marks the turning point in the history of the Observants, the beginning of a prodigious growth. Capistran became the organizer and leader of the reform movement. The further history of the Observance is interwoven with the history of Capistran's forty years in the habit of St. Francis.

CHAPTER V

Profession and Ordination

IN the novitiate at Monteripido, Capistran drew the spirit of the Observance from its purest sources. In the little monastery, on a hill a few hundred steps north of Perugia, beyond the gate of St. Angelo, had lived and died brother Aegidius, the well-known companion of St. Francis. His cell was ornamented with paintings from the thirteenth and fourteenth century. The guardian of the cloister, Marcus of Bergamo, and the novice master, the lay brother Onofrio, were full-fledged types of the Franciscan ideal. Onofrio took his new disciple into a hard school. Patience and self-denial are always put to severe monastic tests, in which real faults, but also harmless traits, furnish material. Such means of education, when used by a good spiritual director and accepted by the disciple in the right spirit, may lead to the desired result. Masters of high reputation, such as Philip Neri, made use of this method to eradicate pride.

Brother Onofrio easily found opportunities to humiliate the worldly nobleman. Capistran had care of the sacristy, an office that presents to a neophyte many chances for spoiling or breaking things, and for other blunders. But even without cause Capistran underwent harsh corrections. He was sometimes called to the parlor by parties who wished the advice of the famous jurist. The guardian gave his permission. After his return, Onofrio would sarcastically ask him why he had not stayed in the world if he liked such vanities. The novices, ordered to wash the church linen, stood round the wash tub, waiting for the boiling water to cool. The novice master sent all the novices abruptly away, with the exception of Capistran, the sacristan. Him he called a worthless sluggard, then threw a steaming piece of the boiling linen into his face. Capistran always remained grateful to his master, saying he would never have acquired the virtue of humility had he not gone through the school of Onofrio.

Far more difficult than these outward humiliations were his own interior battles. His extraordinary conversion and vocation had not made him all at once a different man. His vision in prison gave him a flood of new light, a real revolution of his judgments on the value of life. That vision, like St. Paul's, had lasting effects: an absolute break with everything he had loved and valued and a new kind of life from which formerly he had recoiled. In the beginning he had a horror of everything past, offices as well as studies. Jurisprudence itself seemed now so void and empty that he regretted having wasted so much time on it. But even remarkably gifted persons, like St. Paul, have to taste the bitterness of the struggle between the spirit and the flesh. In the circle of Capistran's confreres the question arose: What had been for each the most difficult obstacle at the beginning? Capistran's had been, he said simply, to resist the onslaught of sensual imaginations and emotions. He had experienced and observed so much evil, especially at the dissolute court of Naples! All this now returned to his mind and bothered his imagination. His escape from serious lapses is to be credited to his good education and to his innate disgust for everything unclean rather than to a determined practice of virtue. Only as a religious had he become aware that a person can sin also in thought.

His efforts were heroic. He scalded his body, in the most delicate parts, with marks that were still visible in old age. Once he threw himself into a pile of soiled laundry and remained there until dirt and vermin had extinguished every other sensation. Fleas, he said, should have his body, rather than lewdness and the devil. Still, temptations of that kind may have been more burdensome than dangerous for him. The world was far behind him. When his wife came to see him, the superior permitted the meeting. With tears she entreated him to return. But he admonished her so impressively to follow his example, that she renewed her promise not to take another husband.

The danger lay in another direction. "Prouder than Satan, sharper than the devil," he had styled himself. Now he strove to reach humility and simplicity. But his methods were excessive. "In order to break my pride," he says, "I scourged myself even seven times a day." Also in fasting and night-watching he overdid matters. Before his first Holy Communion (he had, before entrance, never gone to Communion), he fasted three full days. As sacristan he found pretexts to watch and pray all night. Excitement before entrance, the new mode of life, and his excessive self-chastisements, threw him on a sickbed before the novitiate was over. The doctor gave him up, and he received the last sacraments; but his strong nature surmounted the crisis. About his fitness for the Order, the superiors had no doubt. The general of the Order, Anthony of Pireto, after a visit to the novitiate, said: "If he perseveres, he will become a glory of the Order." He was admitted to the vows on October 4, 1416.

Where Capistran spent the first years after his profession, is quite unknown. By birth he belonged to the Abruzzi, where the Observance was not yet firmly established. The first house, St. Giuliano near Aquila, had been opened in 1415. Whether Capistran was sent there or remained for some time in Perugia or was sent elsewhere for theological studies, is all a matter of conjecture. The Observants had no higher schools of their own in Italy, and had so far put little emphasis on education. What was then demanded of candidates for the priesthood was far beneath the requirements of our time. This highly educated jurist might be left to his own counsel in the matter of studies. And, in fact, theology, the sacred science, remained his daily bread all his life. Always overburdened with external labors, he still acquired an imposing proficiency in theological knowledge. His familiarity with Holy Scripture amazed theologians who attended his sermons, some of which were mosaics of Scripture quotations. He would give, from memory, book, chapter, and verse for each quotation as it came. Correctness was often verified by listeners who made notes.

He was familiar also with theological literature. Among the Church Fathers, St. Jerome was his favorite. But for deeper study of the great Scholastics he hardly found sufficient leisure. Certainly he never pledged himself to any particular school, not even that of his own Order. He had entered the Order as a mature and accomplished man, and learned his theology by way of private study. Although he never became a complete Scholastic, the Dominican, Thomas Aquinas, was his guide and master. "He is my special patron; his works I study more deeply than those of any non-canonized author." Thus he spoke from the pulpit, during a sermon in Breslau. He placed Thomas even above the great Franciscan theologian, Duns Scotus, who was just then again coming to great fame in the Franciscan schools.

His old love for jurisprudence again revived. But civil law had no longer any attraction for him, and he hardly ever looked at a book of that kind. The study of canon law, however, became ever dearer to him. All those entrusted with the care of souls, he used to repeat, are bound to have a thorough knowledge of Church law. In canon law, he said, is hidden the juice of theology. In a sermon at Vienna, he declared: "When I first went to the cloister, the time I had spent in studying civil and canon law seemed to me to have been lost. But later on, when I got acquainted with theology, I would not have bartered the *Corpus juris* for a thousand worlds. Canon law is a great support of theology." His style was formed chiefly under the influence of the law and the Bible. Acuteness and clearness of expression, vivid, concrete language and lively rhythm, are the characteristic marks of that style.

The year 1417 was probably the year of Capistran's ordination. He began to preach that same year. The increasing activity of the Franciscans against the Fraticelli may have been the cause of Capistran's hurried promotion to holy orders, as the fight against Fraticellism called for capable preachers. Since the Fraticelli theologians employed their knowledge with dialectic adroitness, infected districts had to be visited by fervent missioners, able to refute these leaders. One result was that in certain districts the Fraticelli took to flight to escape secular authorities. Some of their settlements were turned over to the Observants. At the close of the year 1418 we find Capistran preparing a campaign against Fraticellism.

PART III
UNDER MARTIN V
(1417-31)

CHAPTER VI

Capistran and Bernardine

DURING Capistran's year of novitiate the forty-year-old schism approached its end. Gregory XII having voluntarily resigned (June 4, 1415), the apostolic chair remained unoccupied for two years and a half, during which the Church was governed by the Council of Constance. On November 11, 1417, about the time Capistran received holy orders, Otto Colonna, a Roman, was elected in Constance as pope, taking the name of Martin V. At the news of the end of the schism, people could hardly speak for joy, says one of the chronicles.

On May 16, 1418, Martin V left Constance, and traveled slowly over the Alps. On the plains along the Po, Capistran was awaiting him. On October 24, 1418, the papal train arrived at Mantua, and the Pope held court there until February 6, 1419. In those first days Capistran obtained an audience, and informed the Pope of the pernicious activities of the Fraticelli in central Italy. His petition to be made inquisitor was promptly granted. This decision is easily intelligible, though details are lacking. From his past career Capistran knew more about Fraticellism than did his confreres in their remote hermitages. Naturally he would prompt his superiors to sharper battle against these false brethren. Such work meant for him a direct continuation of his past activity as judge. These anarchic sects he regarded as dangerous foes, not only to state and society, but also to the Church. Mere preaching was not sufficient, since the Fraticelli enjoyed the protection of noblemen and bishops. As long as they found refuge at the courts of the mighty, their expulsion from a few villages availed little. Supreme authority was needed. And now was die time for action: the schism was over; the new Pope was on his way to Rome. A few days after Capistran's appointment as inquisitor, the Pope, in a circular letter to all bishops and inquisitors, gave stringent orders for sharp procedure against the Fraticelli and their protectors. Bishops and inquisitors are commanded to proceed against the protectors of these heretics, even if they are of episcopal or royal rank.

We do not know what were the exact powers that Capistran received at Mantua or how he exercised them. But his first meeting with the first Pope after the schism is of great importance. From now on he remained in close contact with all the popes of his time, Martin V, Eugene IV, Nicholas V, and Callistus III. With the last three of these he had been on friendly terms long before their election. He frequented the papal court as confidant, and remained in correspondence with Rome when absent. His intimate relations with the popes had not developed slowly during the years, but had been directly sought by himself. Just ordained, he negotiates with Pope Martin V as soon as the latter enters Italian territory. Appointment as inquisitor in 1418 is the first of a long line of papal letters to Capistran. The decree against the Fraticelli, dated November 14, 1418, was inspired and probably in great part written by him. Herein we see the special character of his activity: battle against all powers that threaten the Church. "Although I have not the ultimate responsibility," he writes to a cardinal, "I am nevertheless determined to spend my strength to the last breath in defending the flock of Christ." The three chief enemies of the Church—heretics, Jews, and Turks—could be restrained only by the combined powers of Church and state. Inquisitorial power was to him the most indispensable weapon against heretics. Against the Hussites his trump card was always a reference to his papal authorization; the documents containing such authorization he carried with him everywhere. At the end he had about sixty such documents. This union of statesmanship and military spirit was a family inheritance. His conversion had not changed his natural disposition. There was no need it should. "Every other occupation has to make room for the defense of the faith; this is my most cherished activity; this I appreciate higher than any other work." Thus he spoke to a cardinal. Under King Ladislaus he had dreamed of the death of a hero. As Franciscan friar he longed for martyrdom.

Yet Capistran was not exclusively an inquisitor, a soldier for the faith. First and foremost he was a shepherd of souls. Pastoral and missionary work, in its most comprehensive meaning, claimed his time, talent, and strength, from the day of his ordination.

The first fruit of the young reform movement was a new style of preaching. Pioneer in this field was Bernardine Albizzeschi of Massa near Siena. An incomparable power of speech, unction, powerful conviction, and a charming serenity, amiability, and piety, made Bernardine of Siena the favorite of the Italian people. Through him the Franciscan Observance became so widely known that the Observants justly venerated him as their patriarch, although he was in no way their founder.

Capistran was some years ordained before he made personal acquaintance with Bernardine. From then on a most intimate bond of friendship united these two souls, however differently gifted. Bernardine began to be famous when he had been twenty years a Franciscan. He joined the Order under the influence of the pestilence year, in 1400, at the age of twenty. But he had no need of conversion, since he had lived through the years of childhood and adolescence in angelic innocence. During the process of beatification, Capistran repeatedly assured the Pope he would let himself be burned for his belief that Bernardine had never committed a grievous sin. Bernardine lived for some time in a hermitage of the Observants near Siena. After his ordination to the priesthood (1404), he founded, again near Siena, a new settlement of the Observance. There he lived in seclusion till 1417, giving his time to prayer and study, interrupted only by an occasional sermon. But gradually he came to devote himself entirely to the office of preaching. As guardian of Fiesole, the oldest convent of Tuscany, he preached at Santa Croce in Florence (1417). Toward the end of that year he traveled via Genoa to Milan. The Milanese, the first to discover the great orator in him, relished his eloquence and engaged him for the Lenten sermons of 1418. Bernardine, who recognized ever more clearly his mission to preach to all Italy, that same year preached in Ligurian and Piedmontese territories. In 1419 he again preached Lenten sermons in Milan. The rich, proud city prepared a most enthusiastic reception. "Like ants the people streamed to his sermons." One year saw more Easter Communions than had been seen in ten previous years.

From Milan he went to Bergamo, a city torn by party strife. Then he gave missions in the villages on the shore of Lake Como. Along the Lira he went north into the Alps, where the inhabitants had been sorely neglected. Up the river Tessin he pushed his way into the valley of the Upper Rhine. The grateful mountaineers called the road on which he had come St. Bernardine's Pass. By the end of 1419 we find him again in Milanese territory. Two cities, Treviglio and Caravaggio, were in bitter feud. Bernardine raised his pulpit in the open field, halfway between the rival cities. The citizens of both had to come in peace if they wanted to hear Bernardine. Reconciliation followed, and that place was called Field of Peace. During Lent, 1420, Bernardine preached in Mantua. As further stations of that year are mentioned Cremona, Piacenza, and Lodi. He returned via Emilia to Siena. But Lombardy, which called again and became an especially fruitful field, saw him again in 1421, and he remained there for the next two or three years.

Bernardine's example inspired others. True missionary spirit is a Franciscan heritage. St. Francis and his first companions, genuine apostles, went from place to place, preaching wherever they found people: in the church, on the streets, in public squares. And preaching remained a chief occupation of the Order. But with the fall of discipline in the Order toward the end of the thirteenth century, the mission spirit also weakened. That century had been the century of sermons, but by 1400 preaching had reached a low level in all Italy. Sermons were infrequent and unsatisfactory. With Bernardine's complaint that "few preach, though many say Mass," various contemporaries agreed. Distinguished promoters of reform, for instance Gerson, declared that the reform of preaching was the greatest need of their time.

The Observant movement among Franciscans met this longing for reform. The fifteenth century saw a second spring in the Order, with an energetic revival of the itinerant mission spirit. Whole crowds of Franciscan preachers, Observants especially, crossed and recrossed the peninsula from the Alps to Sicily. For decades many of them preached almost daily. The standard-bearer in this movement was Bernardine of Siena, who, in favor of preaching, gave up even the confessional. That whole century bears the impress of his eloquence. Robert of Lecce, a Franciscan, himself one of the most outstanding pulpit orators of the century, asserts that all the great mendicant preachers, not Franciscans alone, looked on Bernardine as their model. Not himself over-modest, he still looked on Bernardine, whom he had never seen, as his father and teacher. He mentions some twenty great orators of his time who were disciples of Bernardine, and at the head of this list puts the name of Capistran. On this last point Robert is in error.

Until recently the assumption prevailed that Capistran studied theology under Bernardine, and was trained by him as preacher. This error must have crept into tradition very early. Capistran's boundless veneration for Bernardine was clearly the source of the error. In fact, the two men never met before 1420. When Capistran came to Mantua in 1418, Bernardine was indeed near, preaching in the cities along the Po. But the documents Capistran was seeking in Mantua show that he was at that time busy in central Italy, the home of the sect. His own view of his personal relations to Bernardine differ entirely from the traditional view. In a recently found letter he writes about Bernardine these surprising words: "He was my superior, but I his teacher." This teaching has no reference to eloquence, in which Capistran cheerfully acknowledged Bernardine's superiority. Lessons in canon law are probably meant. But not even as preacher can Capistran be considered a pupil of Bernardine, his style being so entirely different. Highly as he venerated his friend, he simply could not use Bernardine's sermons. He did indeed carry Bernardine's fame beyond the Alps; but among the many books he always took with him on his tours there were no sermons of Bernardine. Robert of Lecce, on the contrary, that conceited man, admits that he studied Bernardine's sermons and preached them word for word. Capistran, with amiable frankness, tells his audiences in Vienna or Leipzig that he had no sermons of Bernardine with him. He preferred his own manuscripts, with which he was more familiar. Capistran must have developed his own style of preaching before he ever knew Bernardine.

After his return from Mantua, Capistran lived in Aquila, not of course at St. Francesco, the Conventual house in the city, but with the Observants in San Giuliano, a few miles from the city, amid romantic scenery at the entrance into a rocky valley. San Giuliano today is an extensive building, which harbors a theological seminary of the Order. A part of the ancient dwelling has been preserved, a wretched cell, hardly wide enough to hold an ordinary bed. Capistran's home, as far as he could claim a fixed home, was San Giuliano in Aquila. He loved Aquila more than any other city and lived in intimate relations with its people, whereas he hardly ever mentions Capistrano, his native city. Aquila even seemed destined to become his episcopal city. But his aversion to the episcopal office was stronger than the wishes of the popes. Even in his last years and from afar off, he kept his eyes on his beloved Aquila. A letter from him is, in turn, an event for the city. Although he may scold the citizens, like a father chiding naughty children, they read his letters publicly and solemnly.

Capistran deserved this veneration, for the city owed him much. To the kings of Naples, Aquila had been a source of trouble from its very foundation. Its existence was owing to Frederick II, who wished to have a stronghold in the Abruzzi and invited the scattered colonists to form a town, that he might use the concentrated power of these mountaineers against the stubborn barons. To the new settlement he gave the proud name of Aquila ("eagle city"). It was and still is an eagle's nest, built on a plateau of the Gran Sasso, which dominates the plain of the Aterno. The city soon became conscious of its power and struggled for independence. King Manfred, Frederick's son, destroyed it. After the fall of the Hohenstaufens the city, under the Anjous, arose from its ruins and quickly attained its former prominence. All the surrounding peasant communities, ninety-nine in number, acknowledged Aquila as their mistress. Symbol of this union was the great fountain of Aquila, cut into the living rock, which spurted water from ninety-nine spouts into one common basin. In 1300 the peasant republic could muster

15,000 valiant warriors. When from the towers of the eagle city bells sounded alarm, the peasants hurried from their mountain glens and gathered to defend their citadel.

Immense flocks of sheep were the chief wealth of the country. In the hands of the town weavers the wool became cloth, and for the dyeing of these woolen goods extensive fields of saffron were planted. Half of Europe ordered this precious dye-stuff from Aquila. Of saffron markets alone nine were held every year. Thus the peasant republic in the Abruzzi enjoyed a comfortable existence, as long as wars, civil or general, did not put the destiny of the city in question. In a sermon at Vienna, Capistran said that the King of Naples had told him personally that the city brought him annually 110,000 ducats. Aquila, he added, was a great and populous city, but was too much inclined to mutiny and strife. The blood of men, the blood of beasts, it was all the same for the people of Aquila.

Capistran early attained a leading position in San Giuliano. In the year 1421 the general received orders from the Pope to appoint provincial vicars for the Italian provinces. Bernardine of Siena was made vicar for Tuscany and Umbria. Since Capistran exercised the office of a vicar in 1422, he was evidently one of those appointed the year before. The number of the settlements under his supervision must have been small. According to his own statement there were not thirty convents of the Observance in all Italy at the time of his entrance, but from now on their number increased rapidly. Already in 1418 Bernardine was building a larger monastery. About a mile from Milan arose the first great monastery of the Observance in Italy, called Santa Maria degli Angeli. Capistran's first known foundations date from 1422. His fame as a preacher was beginning. In Aquila he found the same response as Bernardine had found in Milan, and from now on Capistran was much in demand everywhere. Milan and Aquila were the two starting points of the great Franciscan mission movement of the fifteenth century; and Bernardine and Capistran were the leaders.

CHAPTER VII

Rome, Siena, Perugia

FOR the jubilee year 1422, superiors sent their best preachers to Rome. The Franciscans sent Capistran, not Bernardine. This decision may have been owing to Capistran's personal acquaintance with the Pope. Two sermons made special stir. That pilgrims were loud in their criticisms of things Roman is small wonder after Rome's long desolation. The Pope told Capistran to inspire the strangers with a higher appreciation of what Rome really meant. Capistran had always been a fervent patriot, proud of being an Italian. To meet an Italian abroad gave him particular joy. Italy, in spite of her political chaos, was the queen of all Christian countries. He gladly complied with the Pope's wish and exerted mighty efforts to produce a masterpiece, which he delivered in the open air, in Campo Fiori. His prodigious memory never showed to better advantage. The sermon, he says, contained 500 Catholic conclusions.

The other sermon, which attacked gambling, displeased the papal court, for Rome had its officially approved gambling establishment, which brought in large revenues. The bold preacher was ordered to come to the Pope, and was there told that the exchequer needed these revenues. The finances of the Papal States were indeed in a serious condition. But Capistran remained immovable. Such things, he told the Pope, would not be tolerated even among the Saracens. The casino was closed, the account books were burned, and games of chance forbidden in Rome by herald's public announcement.

Capistran seems to have influenced the Pope in another matter, even more delicate. Martin V has been considered the most pro-Jewish of all the popes. Jewish historians never tire praising the humane sentiments of the Colonna Pope. Not satisfied with the protection which all popes had extended to the Jews, he granted them privileges that were contrary to canon law. September 21, 1421, he allowed the Jews in Spain the practice of medicine; in fact, Christians might freely call in Jewish physicians. On February 20, 1422, appeared a papal edict against anti-Jewish preachers. Shortly after the jubilee year both decrees were laconically and peremptorily revoked. Capistran's influence at the papal court had been felt in the Jewish question also. Stern insistence on laws against the Jews was a principal element in his reformatory activity. This sudden change in the Jewish policies of Martin V, which has always puzzled historians, must be attributed to Capistran.

Capistran's stay in Rome was beneficial to the Observance. The Pope empowered him to take over five new settlements. On November 11, the fifth anniversary of the Pope's election, he himself received the privilege, in those days exceptional and much desired, of having at his deathbed a confessor of his own choice.

Capistran's next great task shows the high esteem he enjoyed at the papal court. The Council of Constance had decreed that after five years a new general council should be convoked. This council opened its sessions in Pavia in April, 1423, but because of the plague was transferred to Siena in June. Pope Martin's reluctance in calling the council was justified by the course of events. On the question of the pre-eminence of pope over council the assembly fell promptly into discord. In January, 1424, many members left the Synod, discouraged by growing dissensions. On March 7 the papal legates posted the decree of dissolution on the church door, and left the city. The following day, Ash Wednesday, the Council dissolved itself, and its members left Siena, where, on the same day, Capistran began his daily course of Lenten sermons. Very probably Martin V had sent him there to preach during the Council, just as, later on, Eugene IV sent several Observant preachers to the Council of Basle.

These Siena discourses are the first sermons of Capistran of which we have precise record. Immense was the material which the young orator intended to treat. Each daily instruction had two themes: one mystical, the other scholastic. The first he calls "the sweetness of the loving soul"; the other, "thoughts on the seven sacraments." As a daily conclusion he adds an explanation of the day's Gospel. Thus each sermon was practically three sermons. The time required went far beyond the measure to which we are accustomed. Thorough religious revival in all classes of society was the ideal, an ideal that remains, but methods have changed. Our retreats and missions rest on a compact system of religious truths and exercises, psychologically selected and arranged. Our aim is depth, that of Capistran's day was rather breadth. Convinced that moral weakness is caused chiefly by religious ignorance, Bernardine and his school aimed at thorough instruction in all spheres of Christian faith and morals. Where they had a longer stretch of time, in Advent say, or Lent, they often chose a scholastic tract as guide. Nor did they always escape the dangers of excessive scholasticizing in the pulpit.

Capistran himself is an example. The comprehensive exactness of a dogmatic textbook characterizes his cycle on the sacraments. Very subtle questions appear, for instance, whether there would be sacraments if sin had not been. The sacramental appointments of the Old Testament, and similar questions, of interest for theological students indeed, had surely little immediate importance for practical piety. Opposition soon arose. When the people of Siena asked him to leave learning alone and to preach against vice, he promptly changed his plan. Dropping both cycles, he simply explained the Gospel of the day. The opposition to the method of the itinerant preachers came chiefly from the secular clergy, who believed the traditional sermon on the Sunday Gospel was quite sufficient. Although Bernardine's frequent preaching often brought ridicule and mockery, he did not yield. If there were only three old women in the church, he said, he would preach just the same. And Capistran's concessions to the people of Siena were a transient accident. The itinerant preachers clung to the thematic sermon as their characteristic style, and Bernardine occasionally defended this form of sermon, also from the pulpit, with good-natured sarcasm. Preachers who would not leave the well-trodden paths are like druggists who would sell pills and powders, not according to the patient's need, but according to the stock they have in store. After a short homily on the Epistle or Gospel of the day, Bernardine turned to his systematic theme. And his eloquence established this method for good.

Capistran's peculiarity as preacher is not easy to grasp. Of his innumerable sermons during thirty-five years of activity in Italy, time has preserved only a few sketches, and some tracts based on these sketches. Only Capistran's Latin sermons, delivered during his last years in various cities beyond the Alps, were preserved in shorthand notes.

One of the causes which accelerated the end of the Council of Siena was the war which the Pope had to wage against Braccio, the despotic ruler of Perugia. Since his conquest of Perugia, in 1416, this audacious robber-chief had enlarged his territory by subjugating parts of Naples and of the Papal States. The Pope had tried kindness, making Braccio papal vicar in Perugia, Assisi, Todi, and Jesi. Braccio wanted more. In 1423 he besieged Aquila, intending to march against Rome; but Aquila withstood him an entire year. The Franciscans preached peace, one of them even in the camp of Braccio, who listened quietly and consented to receive a peace delegation. The parley (July 11, 1423) was without results, since Braccio wished to have the city delivered to one of his captains. The siege continued. Cautiously and methodically Martin V prepared a coalition against Braccio. But in this coalition the laurels go to Aquila, whose heroic resistance of thirteen months saved Rome and Naples from becoming the prey of Braccio. In a bloody battle (June 5, 1424), just outside the walls of Aquila, the despot was slain. He was buried on the spot like a beast, though later he was laid to rest in consecrated ground. Outstanding politician and soldier, Braccio was still a thoroughly wicked man, who despised priest and Mass, and believed neither in God nor in a future life.

After Perugia's restoration Martin V took care to renew the city, also morally and religiously. This task was entrusted to Bernardine, who in the fall of 1425 preached a great mission, in which Capistran probably shared. The one year which, according to contemporary evidence, he spent in Bernardine's company, has to be placed between 1424 and 1426. Now Bernardine, during the Lent of 1424, was in Florence; then, till June, he was in the adjacent Prato; in July he was in Rome; during Advent he preached in Volterra; during Lent, 1425, he was again in Florence, at Easter and Pentecost in Siena, then in Arezzo. From a contemporary document we know that three great preachers (Bernardine, Capistran, and Matthew of Girgenti) were together about this time. Guido Antonio, count of Urbino, asked the Pope to give extraordinary powers to these three preachers, and the Pope granted the petition (May 18, 1425). This Guido Antonio, whose second wife was a niece of the Pope, stood in high esteem in Rome as a virile defender of the rights of the Church. He must have been prominent in the war against Braccio. Very probably the Pope had entrusted him with the government of Umbria, in place of the overthrown Braccio. In any event, he was given the title of Duke of Spoleto. The request mentioned above presupposes that he himself had asked for the three famous missioners, whose fame, he says, is known to all Italy.

On his journey from Prato to Rome, Bernardine may have stopped at Siena, where Capistran was perhaps still preaching. From there they may have gone together to Rome. Thus it is plausible that Capistran was a fellow laborer with Bernardine from June, 1424, till the end of 1425.

No idle companionship was this. Each had his full share in the immense task which in those days fell to the lot of a missioner. Preaching and administering the sacraments were by no means their only obligations. No matter how low religious and political conditions were, Christian thinking and feeling were still strong enough to stamp the appearance of a great missioner as an event of the first rank. Stores were closed, trade and industry stopped, the whole city made retreat. To satisfy the enormous conflux of people, the pulpit was erected in a public square or in a meadow outside the city. The magistrates solemnly escorted the preacher from his residence to the pulpit, and the city authorities occupied a rostrum near the pulpit, in front of all the people. The city council often vested the preacher with unlimited authority to settle all feuds and dissensions, or even to give the city new statutes. In this country of endless party struggles, restoration of peace was the most difficult and most important task. Bernardine would preach peace, while Capistran arranged difficulties between the quarreling parties. "They loved each other beyond measure," says an account of the time. Bernardine excelled in eloquence, but Capistran had the advantage of juridical knowledge, theoretical and practical. Bernardine limited his activity to the pulpit. He announced publicly: "I give myself exclusively to preaching of the word of God, believing that is the best I can do. Confessions I will not hear, either of men or of women. I see that if I want to do many things, I will do nothing well." Bernardine was always sickly. In capacity for work Capistran excelled, and he was also more versatile. In July, 1425, he was empowered by Cardinal Giordano Orsini, papal penitentiary and protector of the Franciscan Order, under oral instruction from the Pope, to treat with full authority all cases, even those reserved to the bishops. The Pope's reason ran thus: "Penitents from all sides daily claim your attention."

The great mission in Perugia is one of the peaks in Bernardine's life. From Assisi, where he spent the feast of Portiuncula, he came north to Perugia, and there he preached incessantly from September 19 till the end of October. Bishop Peter Donati governed the city as papal legate. A codex written by Capistran, containing summaries of Bernardine's sermons preached in Perugia, shows that Capistran went with Bernardine to Perugia, presumably by the express wish of the Pope. He knew the city and its conditions from childhood. Bernardine lived with the Observants of Monteripido, and from there he went every morning to the city to preach in the square. Nowhere else did he meet such success. Umbria's capital remained ever after his favorite city. Religiously and morally the city had sunk very low, partly in consequence of the endless feuds and contests in and about the town during the last decades. Eight years under Braccio had certainly not civilized the population. Bernardine, sent by God to renew the face of the city, attacked sin unsparingly. He promised in one sermon to let them look into the face of the devil. To that next sermon they came in crowds, wondering what would happen. He began. Suddenly pausing, he reminded them of his promise. Then he cried out in a terrifying tone: "You wish to see the devil? Just look into each other's faces. Devils is what you are. You love, and seek, and do, the works of the devil." Then followed a horrid picture of their moral condition.

Not only did the Perugians tolerate such language, but they repented, thoroughly and efficaciously. The city promptly passed laws against the worst vices of the community, such as gambling, blasphemy, sodomy, sacrilegious immorality, usury, and certain public entertainments. In their first fervor the city authorities went to work so energetically that the papal legate had to modify their penal statutes. Even thus these "statutes of Bernardine," as they were called, were harsh enough: heavy fines, loss of citizenship, penitentiary, loss of hand or foot, death by fire. Rivaling Bernardine's "devil-sermon," the preface to the statutes calls the houses of Perugia "temples of Satan." The "battle of stones," a favorite but barbaric contest during Easterweek, was entirely abrogated. The public dances on the feast of St. Herculano, the patron of Perugia, were canceled, since they had been sources of drunkenness and debauchery. Money thus saved was devoted to candles for the church. Such laws certainly testify a sincere will for thorough and lasting renewal. Regulations appear to prevent relapse. Cards and dice are not to be made or imported. Dove-catching, a favored opportunity for seducing boys, was to be stopped. Men are forbidden to enter boys' schools. Enclosure in convents was strictly regulated. Execution of these statutes was entrusted to a committee of five.

Reconciliations were so frequent during these weeks that Bernardine wondered how so many enmities could exist in one city. Perugia remained grateful to her apostle and savior, and Bernardine's heart continued to love the corrupt, but penitent and responsive city. Looking out over crowded masses, he addressed them with the words of the apostle: "My children, of whom I am in labor again, until Christ be formed in you" (Gal. 4:19). At the end of the six weeks' mission, he condemned in public trial all objects which till then had been tools of vice. On Sunday, October 28, the people brought immense numbers of jewels, ornaments, cards, dice, and so on, and burned them on a pile of wood in the middle of the market place. An eyewitness remarks: "The fire was so gigantic it cannot be described. In that fire burned things of immeasurable value." On All Saints Day the citizens renewed the spectacle on their own initiative. This "bonfire of vanities" had been practiced already in other great cities, Rome for instance, and Bologna. It now became a fixture of the mission program. In face of frequent opposition, Bemardine's school held fast to the practice.

Were the effects of these missions lasting? When the missioner departed, did everything return to the old fashion? This is frequently asserted. But the statement needs qualification, at least for Perugia. Two years later, in his native city of Siena, Bernardine praises the Perugians, declaring that nowhere had he experienced such a thorough change as in that corrupt city. Its thirty churches were now well filled, the confessionals were thronged. The difference between Siena and Perugia, he says, is like that between earth and heaven. He ascribes the lasting effects of Perugia's conversion to the strict measures of the government.

CHAPTER VIII

The Name of Jesus

AS visible reminder of the blessed mission preached by Bernardine, the Perugians adorned the walls of their churches with the name of Jesus, in the age-old form of the letters IHS. The gold for each one of these gigantic emblems was valued at more than 100 florins. Bernardine never gave a mission without preaching a sermon on the name of Jesus, and through him the devotion to the holy name became a characteristic of Franciscan missions. In itself this devotion was nothing new; we need but remember St. Paul and St. Bernard. The Franciscans merely gave to the devotion a definite form and figure. Like the manger and the stations of the cross, the holy name of Jesus became in time an acknowledged sign of Catholic devotion.

According to Capistran, Bernardine's sermon on the name of Jesus was based on a tract of the famous leader of the Spiritualists, Ubertino of Casale, whose little book contained a symbolic representation of the name of Jesus, namely, the letters IHS in the middle of a sun disk, from the rim of which streamed outward twelve rays, in sign of Him who said: "I am the light of the world." In a sermon at Alessandria, Bernardine described this image. A clever boy went to an artist, who drew on paper what the boy described. Holding this picture on high, the boy ran about in the market place, crying out continually: Jesus, Jesus! Other boys followed his example. Bernardine, gifted with a fine insight into popular needs, ordered quantities of these pictures, and distributed them on his missions. In preaching he used the same picture, enlarged and painted in beautiful colors, the disk in gold, its halo upon sky-blue background, and in the midst the three letters. In his preaching he trained the people to kneel down when he showed them the painting, according to the word of the Apostle: "In the name of Jesus all knees shall bow of those in heaven, on earth, and under the earth." He admonished them to place the most holy name everywhere: on medals worn round the neck; in their homes, on buildings, private and public, on churches and courthouses. The name of Jesus should gleam forth everywhere as a symbol of all-embracing dominion. In processions, besides church banners and reliquaries, also a holy name standard was carried, which stood near the pulpit when he preached.

Criticism raised its voice against the new devotion. The humanists ridiculed what they called "Jesusness." "Christiani," they said, not "Jesuani," was the traditional name of the faithful. Poggio Bracciolini, otherwise indifferent in religion, condemned separation between the names of Jesus and Christ. But also strictly ecclesiastical circles found fault with the new cult. The Augustinian, Andrew Bigli, scion of a prominent Milanese family, professor of rhetoric and philosophy in Bologna, wrote a special tract condemning this form of devotion as an unsound innovation. Christians, he said, had at all times given highest honor to the sign of the Cross; now they venerated the "sign of Bernardine"; as if the letters of a name could better impress the heart than the lifelike representation of the Crucified. Such had always been, he argued, the method of heretics and schismatics: to introduce innovations; to invent new devotions which served curiosity rather than edification. Still he would not condemn the authors of this devotion since they probably had the best of intentions.

New types of devotion always have to meet such attacks, for instance, in our own days, that to the Sacred Heart of Jesus. Within limits Catholic self-criticism is sound and wholesome, and prevents abuses. Yet it is difficult to distinguish genuine developments from malformations. Many opponents of Bernardine, intelligent and zealous men, thought that too many religious exercises and devotions existed already, that exterior piety was to some degree overburdened. Justified reform was directed also against this frailty. But in Bernardine's case personal opposition played quite a part. Andrew Bigli was himself a blameless religious, but belonged to the opponents of the Observance; like many others, he disliked the enthusiasm aroused by the itinerants, disliked the throngs of people who ran to their sermons. The saints, he said, had always kept within the bounds of discretion. Further, the leaders of the movement were regarded as uneducated men. This circumstance helped to send into the opposite camp this learned man, Bigli by name, who went far beyond the mark in attacking the holy name devotion. But it was Bernardine's misfortune to have as opponent a man who was looked upon as a second *doctor angelicus.* A further misfortune arose when Bernardine spoke publicly against Manfredi of Vercelli, one of the most celebrated Dominican orators.

Manfredi and Bernardine preached at the same time in northern Italy. Manfredi's principal theme was the nearness of the world's end, in those days a favorite subject. The disconsolate times of the schism had kindled morbid expectations. Many saw no remedy. St. Vincent Ferrer, one of the most powerful missioners of the day, had repeated incessantly that the end was near, that the antichrist was already born. As proof he pointed to the schism. The papacy, he said, is the sun: the sun is divided, it can no longer shine. Whole crowds of men and women, young and old, left their homes and families, and followed the preacher through France, preparing themselves by prayer and penance for the approaching end. A similar movement followed the sermons of Manfredi. The great Franciscan preachers also spoke of the signs of the approaching end, but they did not pretend to know precise dates. Manfredi, on the contrary, attempted to show from the Apocalypse that the catastrophe was near at hand and drew consequences leading to confusion. Married people, he said, were no longer obliged to conjugal duties; even against the will of the partner they could renounce family life, and give themselves entirely to care for their souls. About a hundred men and more than three hundred women applied his advice, entered the Third Order of St. Dominic, and followed him everywhere.

These absurdities disconcerted Bernardine, who thought that his own activity might be discredited. The mendicant orders had lost much of their former reputation. For a while he kept silence, but the commotion around Manfredi grew daily greater. In Bologna, where he spent four months, some eccentric women of his party claimed to have had visions of angels. Rumor said Manfredi would become pope. Now Bernardine broke silence. Martin V was concerned. In Florence, where Manfredi's company presented itself, the Pope told them to return to their house. The Pontiff feared a revival of the Flagellant movement. But the company, instead of obeying, followed Manfredi when by papal order he went to Rome. There they lived during the following years in quiet seclusion. Otherwise nothing blameworthy was said about Manfredi or his followers. In fact, Martin V appreciated the zealous missioner's untiring though ineffective efforts to bring the Fraticelli back to the Church. The Romans showed great interest in Manfredi and his community, who of course, regarded Bernardine as their opponent; and the Dominicans were not pleased that he had come forward so energetically against one of their Order. Even St. Antonine of Florence shows Dominican prejudice in his praises of Manfredi, and in his unfavorable remarks on Bernardine's cult of the holy name of Jesus.

But Bernardine was not the only critic of the eccentric and unwholesome Manfredian movement. Equally opposed was the above- mentioned Augustinian, Andrew Bigli. The latter now published a tract (1424), which attacked not only the cult of the name of Jesus, but also in general "the customs, the disciples, and the doctrine of brother Bernardine." He places Bemardine's activity, as missioner and as pioneer of the Observance, in a most unfavorable light. Though Bernardine's talent as a pulpit orator and his blameless life are recognized, he is accused of self-conceit since "he says Mass like a prelate, eager to assemble great crowds about him." Bigli sees a new schism emerging. What irritated him in particular was Bernardine's doctrine that the members of the Observance alone practiced the true and genuine Rule of St. Francis. Thus Bigli made himself spokesman for Conventuals of the different orders, who watched with growing annoyance the rapid increase of the Observance movement, which was popularly favored everywhere. As the best point for an attack on Bernardine lay in the new-fashioned devotion to the name of Jesus, complaints were sent to Rome, designating that custom as at least offensive.

Over Bernardine's head a storm gathered, that broke in Lent, 1426, when he was preaching in Viterbo. Though only forty-six years old. Bernardine had the appearance of an old man. Haggard, emaciated, bald-headed and toothless, yet with flaming cheeks, he had the appearance of an ancient prophet. The burning of vanities was a frightful spectacle. Authorities and people went in solemn procession to the pyre. From all church towers the bells tolled mournfully while the flames flared up to heaven. The people went so far as to burn up even the houses noted for gambling and bad living. When Bernardine suddenly raised on high the standard with the gleaming sign of the holy name, invoking that name with his mighty voice, the people were overcome by awe, and cried out: "Mercy! Mercy!" The Lenten season was almost over when Bernardine received orders from Rome to stop preaching, and to vindicate himself before the Pope. Like a lightning stroke from a clear sky this message fell on the general enthusiasm. Bernardine could not prevent a large company from accompanying him when, on Easter Tuesday, obedient to the Pope's command, he started for Rome. Hundreds of people, says a chronicler who was with them, went with him, to see the end of the procedure on the spot.

Martin V gave audience, and made it clear to the defendant that he did not approve these new customs, and that for the time being he must not preach or leave Rome without papal permission. Bernardine was insulted on the streets as if he were a condemned heretic. But the papal commission, after searching his writings and sermons, found nothing blameworthy. The investigation was, according to custom, to have the form of a debate. The Manfredians acted as if they were already victors. They destroyed all signs of the name of Jesus. Their priests refused absolution to penitents who would not submit in that respect. This blind fanaticism pained Bernardine more than his own misfortunes.

Capistran, preaching a Lenten course at Rieti, heard the news from friends, and Bernardine himself sent to ask his help in the imminent debate. Capistran dropped everything, hurried to Aquila to get the necessary scientific material, and thence to Rome. He, too, was followed by a train of people, moved by veneration for Bernardine or by curiosity. Confident of final victory, Capistran risked a public demonstration. Outside the walls of Rome he turned his company into a procession. Carrying high the standard of the name of Jesus, he led his company through the streets to St. Peter's. As they marched, they sang hymns to the name, the procession continually swelling. Martin V gladly admitted Capistran to the debate. Few details are extant. Besides the Franciscans, among them Matthew of Gigenti, fifty-two Dominicans and ten Augustinian hermits are mentioned as participants. The Pope decided that the new devotion was to be tolerated. But a cross was to appear with the name of Jesus to avoid the accusation that the people were adoring the three letters. Since then a cross has been attached to the middle letter (H).

Pope Martin fully restored the honor of the accused. With his court he took part in a grandiose procession in honor of the holy name, Capistran carrying the standard, and Bernardine was ordered by the Pope to preach in Rome. In St. Peter's and other churches he delivered 114 sermons. "O how fickle is the world," he exclaimed later, referring to those agitated days. "When I was called to Rome, some would gladly have baked me, others would have roasted me. But when I was again allowed to preach, woe to the man who had dared to say an unkind word against me!" Finally the Pope gave him a chapel in Rome,[1] as headquarters for the Society of the Holy Name of Jesus.

Other Italian cities followed the example of Rome and celebrated with feasts the happy end of the trial. Florence placed the name of Jesus in mighty letters of gold upon the façade of Santa Croce. Viterbo displayed it upon the two principal gates of the city and on numerous private houses. In Siena the sign was painted in the famous hall of Mappamondo. On the façade of the courthouse it was sculptured in stone. Bologna, Venice, and other cities, did in like manner. According to Capistran, there was soon scarcely a

[1] This oratory was later given to St. Ignatius of Loyola, who had a special veneration for St. Bernardine. In 1575 Cardinal Alexander Farnese replaced the oratory by the magnificent church called Il Gesù. Thus the Name of Jesus became the emblem of the Jesuits.

church in Italy without this sign.

But all this turn of events did not silence the critics. They took special offense when masses of people followed the standard of the holy name. Whether or not Martin V's toleration of this custom at the close of the proceedings against Bernardine, was merely in view of the public sentiment and against his personal wishes, we do not know. At any rate, later on (the year is not known) he forbade the symbol to be carried in public or to be exposed for veneration in the pulpit. This law still remains. But no restriction was laid on the sermon itself, or on the representation of the name in the flaming sun disk, whether on pictures or medals or the fronts of buildings. In spite of multiplied opposition, the sign of the holy name held triumphant march through Italy and then through all other Christian countries. Even today it can be seen sculptured on many churches and other buildings, private and public, not only in Italy, but also in cities beyond the Alps. Gradually it became a common Christian symbol. So familiar is it in the liturgy of today that few have the least idea what opposed emotions this pious symbol once aroused.[2]

After the proceedings against Bernardine, Capistran returned to Aquila. Surrounded by an immense concourse of people, he celebrated the victory of the holy name of Jesus. During the sermon, which was delivered in the open, the listeners held lighted candles in their hands. Blessed Bernardine of Fossa, then a little boy in his father's arms, carried with him a lifelong memory of the moment when the preacher lifted the name of Jesus high above the vast throng.

[2] To this devotion is due the insertion of the name "Jesus" in the Hail Mary.—In 1911 a Name-of-Jesus Congress was held in Baltimore.

CHAPTER IX

The Jews and the Missioner

ABOUT this time the Fraticelli seem to have again claimed Capistran's attention. He had received authorization from Rome (May 27, 1426) to proceed, not only against individuals, but also against whole communities. And the Dominican Manfredi published a tract against the Fraticelli. Nearly all the great preachers united to combat this sect. Bernardine's sermons against them still exist. Capistran considered it his special mission to eradicate Fraticellism. So too did James of the Marches, who went immediately into the Marches, the chief seat of the sect. Capistran was delayed by delicate and pressing problems at home.

In extreme perplexity, several cities in the Abruzzi called him to be mediator. Exiles from Aquila, Sulmona, and Teramo were scattered through the country and were a source of disturbance. Since the subjugation of Naples by Charles I of Anjou, Sulmona in particular had never found rest. With Queen Joanna's approval, Capistran tried to bring peace to the unhappy city. Maria Contelmo, the countess of Popoli and Massana, supported his efforts energetically. On November 6, 1426, an agreement was signed, granting return to those who had been exiled, though excluding them from any share in the government.

Next came the extremely complicated affair between Lanciano and Ortona. Lanciano, south of Pescara, about a mile inland from the Adriatic, had long been a thriving center of commerce. But Ortona, two miles to the north, was the only seaport in the Abruzzi. From Lanciano's attempts to get a port of its own arose a long-standing quarrel. Nearly two centuries back, in 1252, when the Hohenstaufens still ruled Naples, we find mention of a treaty between the two cities. As often as Lanciano obtained the privilege of a harbor, the Ortonese had the privilege revoked. Thus the grant of a harbor at San Vito, south of Ortona, was revoked within the year (1395). The merchants then boycotted Ortona, which appealed to Queen Joanna II, urging loss of revenue. Lanciano countered with bribery.

Capistran was now demanded as arbitrator. With both cities he stood in intimate relations. One of the five new Observant settlements of 1422 was in Frisa, near Lanciano. The Ortonese he calls his benefactors, the people of Lanciano his spiritual children. December 8, 1426, Capistran preached in the church of San Francesco in Lanciano. In the church itself the citizens made him plenipotentiary to Ortona. Cries filled the air: "Just as you think best. San Vito, Lanciano, the tower, the harbor: we put everything into your hands." January 2, 1427, he invited the Ortonese to a meeting, leaving the choice of the place to them, but asking them to bear in mind that he must make the trip on foot. February 7, 1427, peace was signed in St. Thomas' Church in Ortona. Capistran read the ten paragraphs of the document. The chief features were: mutual cooperation in both political and economic matters, mutual citizenship between the two cities, one heart and one mind in all their dealings. In gratitude Lanciano built for the Observants a large monastery, called "Angel of Peace," to preserve the memory of the peace treaty. This treaty, however, was not lasting. Capistran, in later years, saw the old quarrel flare up again, in horrible outbursts of passion. Poor missioners; to be peacemakers in this passionate and fickle people. Besides, the feeble government under Joanna II, and succession disputes after her death, left the missioners without proper support.

After peace was concluded at Ortona, Capistran visited Naples, the capital. The visit was a sensation. The frivolous court saw the dancing cavalier of former days now clothed in the Franciscan habit. Queen and court appeared occasionally at his sermons. Did the aging woman profit by this invitation to penance?

Two purposes probably drew Capistran to Naples. First, the peace treaty between Lanciano and Ortona, which required royal sanction. Secondly, the Jewish question. From the Queen he obtained (May 3, 1427) decrees that became famous. He seems to have discovered Jewish influence in the feuds between the two cities; at any rate, he certainly treated the Jews there with severity, restricting them to one street, limiting their trade liberties, and breaking their economic predominance by the banishment of some of them. But he knew that similar conditions prevailed also in other cities. All through the Abruzzi the Jews enjoyed a privileged position which defied all ecclesiastical and state regulations. Sulmona, Capistran's native diocese, had been from ancient times the center of Jewish life and Jewish culture in Italy. Powerful in trade, the Jews enjoyed the special favor of princes. Jewish fugitives from Spain and Portugal swelled their number. The regulations of the Roman law, purposing to restrict communication between Christians and Jews, were still on the statute books, but these laws, ecclesiastical and civil, were doubly protective. The Jews had to be protected against persecution and plunder, the Christians against harmful influences and economic chicanery. That the royal people of Christ should be subservient to a nation of deicides was to him unbearable. With all the itinerants, he insisted that rulers must revoke the many privileges granted to the Jews.

Capistran's particular insistence on this point should be attributed, not merely to natural inclination and a special view of his missionary duties, but especially to the Jewish position in his native country. Under Robert of Naples (1309-43) the laws had been strictly enforced, particularly that of wearing the odious badge: a red cross on the breast for men, a blue veil for women. But under Ladislaus the Jews were given great privileges. Why not? These privileges brought money into the royal purse. In Sulmona, Aquila, Lanciano, and other cities, the Jews had their own schools and cemeteries, did not have to wear the badge, had separate jurisdiction, were on a par with other citizens in regard to taxes. Queen Joanna approved these privileges and increased them. Capistran, having protested at the papal court, now did the same in Naples. Well armed with facts, he demanded that the government re-establish the laws and revoke all contrary privileges.

For the moment his success was complete. Queen Joanna gave full consent. Her decree (May 3, 1427) states that the Jews of the kingdom were again loaning money at interest, that they no longer wore the badge, and did not observe other regulations. Hence she empowers Capistran to re-enforce all these ecclesiastical and civil laws and to punish at his own discretion those who should refuse obedience. All privileges granted by former rulers of Naples, especially those granted by her brother Ladislaus, are revoked. Under threat of full confiscation, the Jews are bound to hand to Capistran for destruction the originals of their privileges. Capistran's authorization and consequent decisions shall never be revoked. Contrary regulations, made through oversight or otherwise, shall be null and void. All magistrates of the realm are ordered to submit without further notification to these directions. Duke Louis, Joanna's viceroy, extended the decree to the province of Calabria. Capistran, to insure success, asked the Pope's approval, and also authorization to execute similar decrees in other countries. He also asked the Pope to extend his powers against the Fraticelli, to include all other kinds of heresy. Both wishes were granted (June 7, 1427).

Capistran's plan is clear. He intended to use his fame as pulpit orator, with consequent influence on princes and cities, in fully restoring anti-Jewish legislation. But he was destined, as often in later years, to bitter disappointment. His well-planned program met successful opposition. The Jews in the Abruzzi, through their procurator Vitale d' Abramo of Aquila, applied to the Pope, whose Jewish physician and confidant. Maestro Salamone di Ventura of Anagni, did the rest. The Pope admonished Queen Joanna to be less rigorous. She in turn sent to the Jews in the Abruzzi (August 20, 1427) a charter reinstating them in all their previous privileges. The phrase in the former edict, that "she had issued the same by her own impulse without prompting from anyone," she here openly admits as false, since it was issued at the urging of John Capistran. Thus the anti-Jewish campaign collapsed. But from now on the Jews of Italy feared and hated Capistran, comparing him to Aman in the Old Testament.

These activities are but significant episodes in his missionary career. To a preacher of great fame little time was granted for rest and study and prayer. Daily preaching in Advent and Lent was but part of his yearly program. Another part included the great pilgrimages, such as the one to St. Michael on Monte Gargano. May 8, the feast of the angel's appearance, saw an immense crowd of pilgrims making their way over the steep, winding paths to that revered shrine. August 2, the feast of Portiuncula, regularly called Capistran to Assisi. August 29 called him to Aquila, to preach the indulgences granted by Celestine V, who lies buried in the Celestine monastery of that city. The extensive esplanade in front of that Pope's memorial church is well suited for mass meetings. To pilgrimages were added frequent calls to act as peacemaker. Sermons far exceeded in length anything that is customary in our days. Filling the office of a preacher alone might suffice for one man's energy. We can understand why Bernardine at last gave himself entirely to preaching. The daily sermon belonged to the itinerant's program, just as distinctly as daily Mass and breviary. Capistran had in addition the duties of superior. From 1421 on he seems to have acted as provincial vicar in the Abruzzi. To this office belonged, among other duties, that of deciding on new settlements, and directing their foundations. In such cases he was compelled at times to set aside his mission work.

Unusually talented though he was, the program assigned to him taxed his time to the utmost. But we need not think that this life of ceaseless change was against his taste. On the contrary, it seems to have corresponded with his inclinations. He refused bishoprics as being too narrow. Martin V offered him the see of Chieti (1428), a diocese where he was well known and where he had made five foundations. Yet he declined the honor decisively, telling the Pope that he did not wish to be locked up in one diocese.[1]

This public activity was not usual among the Observants. Even Bernardine for twenty years led the silent and retired life of the "devout brothers" before he began the wanderer's life. Capistran had spent in retirement not much more than the one year of novitiate. Only a short span of time separated his missionary

---

[1] Bernardine, who had been offered in succession three bishoprics, said in similar fashion that he would rather be bishop of all Italian cities than of just one.

activity from his former public life. Such a development is an exception, which finds its explanation, not only in the peculiar circumstances of the time, but above all in the extraordinary disposition of this man. The fact that his confreres and superiors trusted him thoroughly from the very beginning, betrays farsightedness on their part.

The Observants had indeed no reason to restrain the able and educated members of the order in their energetic activity, which was not at all contrary to the original Franciscan ideal. Francis of Assisi did not plan the foundation of an order directly contemplative. Rather, his particular mission is the sanctification of active life. His unique union with Christ prompted him to work incessantly for Christ's kingdom. In the first decades his disciples preferred solitude, and the brothers preached only occasionally. They obeyed the law of gradual maturing. All great reform movements started in solitude. But the time must come when the Observants enter as co-laborers in the immense field which the Church had to cultivate in those days. That time came when, from leading circles in the world, educated, experienced men asked for the poor habit of the Observance. Capistran's vocation was not an exception. Almost at the same time came Dominico de Ganghali, born in 1394 at Monteprandone in the Marches, for which reason he is called James of the Marches (Giacomo della Marca). He had been a student of jurisprudence at Perugia, and had practiced law for some time in Florence. After being refused admission to the Carthusians, he joined the Observants (1416) at Portiuncula near Assisi, the cradle of the Franciscan Order. A fourth renowned member of the Order appears about the time of the holy name dispute, in Bernardine's own company. This was Albert of Sarteano in Tuscany. First a Conventual, fascinated by humanist studies, he turned under Bernardine's influence to more serious views and joined the Observants.

Bernardine, Capistran, James of the Marches, and Albert of Sarteano, the Order considers the "four pillars" of the Observance. The first three have been canonized by the Church. Albert and others, like Matthew of Girgenti, are honored as Blessed. These leaders reached the high aim proposed by St. Francis: sanctification of activity by Gospel ideals. The sacrifices laid on the itinerant preacher were not ordinary sacrifices. They could not profit by the well-regulated life of the community. To give them freedom of action, superiors or even the Pope gave them privileges that allowed far-reaching independence. In many cases these privileges turned into tragedy.

Capistran recognized these dangers from the beginning and took precautions. As superior he followed the golden middle way. But in his own person he exemplified the original form of the Franciscan life, without the least diminution or alleviation. The first seven years he went barefoot. After that he wore sandals. Only in his last years, beyond the Alps, did he wear shoes. He kept strictly to the old rule of traveling on foot, although the difficulties of long journeys forced him in his last years to ride. When he had to stay overnight in private houses, he would strip the bed completely. He shared the begging tours of the brethren, going from door to door. What went beyond the needs of the day was promptly divided among other poor people. When invited to a meal, he would leave the dishes untouched, and eat the bread in his wallet, asserting that what he had himself collected tasted better. The three Lents customary in the Order he observed strictly, even on journeys and in sickness. He abstained from meat altogether. His usual meal consisted of beans, eggs, or fish. Wine he would take, but mixed with so much water that it hardly could be called wine. As a rule he took only one meal a day; only after strenuous marches would he take lunch in the evening.

Such austerities presuppose a strong physique. We must not forget that he had enjoyed all the freedom and convenience of a secular life until he was full-grown. Well nourished in childhood, steeled by sports and hunting, not weakened by debauchery, he was physically well prepared for the great exertions demanded from his body during the forty years of his apostolate. His sinewy little body, with surprisingly long arms that reached to his knees, must have been from the very beginning in an excellent state of health. Hence his dislike of medicine. Even when suffering from fever he would not omit preaching. However, it is true that he was exhausted at a comparatively early age. In his fifties he felt the approach of old age. Yet even in his last years he was able to perform tasks surprising in a man of his age. His leadership can be attributed, not primarily to his astonishing intellectual and bodily exertions, but to his persistent determination to realize in his own person the ideal of the Order, namely, sanctified activity. By example more than by teaching he pointed out the path which the Observance would henceforth follow.

CHAPTER X

Trastevere and Assisi

THE Observants were to the fifteenth century what Francis had been to the thirteenth. More than accident links the great reform Council of Constance (1414-18) with Bernardine of Siena and Capistran, the most popular heralds of interior reform. One lasting and valuable fruit of their efforts for a spiritual renewal is the astonishing growth of the Observance itself.

As the mission movement grew and flourished, great numbers asked for admission. The preachers urged them on, painting in vivid colors the dangers of life in the world and the advantages of the religious state. Capistran, while still a novice, said he would gain at least a hundred others for the Observance. His novice master rebuked him for bragging, but the reality went far beyond the expectations of the novice. According to his own estimate, his sermons brought four thousand to the Order. The first century of the Order was thus repeated, though on a smaller scale in consequence of general conditions. Bernardine of Siena alone is credited with ten thousand vocations to the religious life. Perfect restoration of Franciscan poverty together with renunciation of every source of secured income made the growth of the Observants easy. Capistran explains: "Cloisters depending on secure revenues have to ask themselves how many they can keep; if the monastery is for forty; forty can come. We, on the contrary, can accept as many as may come. We do not ask how many we can feed, but how many God has called."

Men of mature age asked for admission. Great excitement arose over the entrance of James Sannuzio of Amatrice in the Abruzzi. In 1428, when Capistran was preaching on Monte Gargano, Sannuzio came asking to be accepted, asserting that he had not yet consummated his marriage. Hence Church law was not against his entrance; it was a repetition of Capistran's case. But Capistran repeatedly refused. When Sannuzio renewed his petition at Viesti, Capistran was convinced of his sincerity and accepted him. Then gossip got busy. Although the Bishop of Aquila, the Franciscan provincial, and several noblemen insisted on dismissal to avoid grave scandal, Capistran remained firm. In a rather sharp circular letter he defended himself and his novice emphatically, saying he could see no reason to distrust the repeated protestations of a man who was ready to leave everything, that he might serve God alone in such a strict order. He has no regrets for having accepted him, and under no condition will he ask him to leave: "I would rather die ten thousand times. With what right do they insist on his dismissal? I hold him not by iron chains, but by the bonds of love; not in the prison of this world, but in the earthly paradise of my Lord. I have not deprived him of his spouse, but I gave him the virginal mother of our Lord, with the choirs of virgins, angels, and saints. There could be no question of scandal. Our Lord did not say: Woe to the orders! But He did say: Woe to the world on account of scandals! For scandals of this sort Christ came into the world. I do not regret in the least that I myself gave the same scandal."

This rapid growth of the Observance displeased the parent order. The mutual harmony yielded to suspicion and strain. This rapid increase had disadvantages for the Conventuals. Excellent men, such as the talented and highly educated Albert of Sarteano, went over to the Observance. Bernardine of Siena had been originally a Conventual. Repeatedly prompted by magistrates or people, the Conventuals had occasion to relinquish a convent to the brothers of the reform, and these losses they sometimes felt as humiliations. In 1415 they lost the Portiuncula; five years later they lost the venerable sanctuary of Monte Alverno, where St. Francis received the stigmata. But these changes inflicted no real damage on the Order. The Observants were by no means outsiders, but confreres, whose life and activity added credit to the whole Order, and rejoicing to the better elements among the Conventuals. The progress of the reform brought a better spirit into the whole Order.

The program of the Observance contained nothing impossible.

No new organization was needed; only the removal of abuses. The Observants, demanding nothing that could obstruct the activity of the Order, by their apostolic work showed that sincere fidelity to the Rule brought success. Why were the Conventuals, who in number far exceeded the Observants, so lacking in great preachers? Adoption of the Observance would, it is true, mean sacrifice for those who had grown old in an easier mode of life since absolute and thoroughgoing renunciation of permanent maintenance was not easy. Bernardine and his followers went in destitution from one place to another, depending entirely on charity. Abrupt change to the original strictness of the Rule presupposed an idealism that was not found in the majority of the Conventuals.

Although we must beware of too general a sentence of condemnation, evidence from many countries leaves no doubt that the Conventuals of the fifteenth century were in state of decadence. Not only had certain harsh demands of the Rule been mitigated, but the inmates of some cloisters did not even lead a Christian life. Laxity in discipline, a vanishing spirit of prayer, had led, if not exactly to scandals, at least to neglect of divine service and to deterioration of churches. Lacking good will to reform, the Conventuals began to see in the Observants personal opponents, disobedient subjects, mischief-makers. That individual Observants were guilty of acts of imprudence and encroachment, need not be denied. Numerical preponderance alone would have enabled the Conventuals, not merely to regulate the reform movement, but even to suppress it. Things might have come to this extreme, had not the Church taken the reform under her protection. The contest was carried on, not so much in the body of the Order itself, as in the papal court. In order to exist, the Observants had to obtain a certain degree of independence, which could be gained only by the intervention of papal authority.

The reform was thus made secure. But the danger arose of division in the Order. Any persistent reform will lead to one of two results: general reform of the whole Order, or division into branches, one reformed and the other non-reformed. The Observance is the second great reform in Franciscan history. The first was the Spiritualist movement in the second half of the thirteenth century, an attempt that ended in tragedy. The valuable elements of renewal which Spiritualism contained were not made use of. The second reform movement, the Observance, remained indeed victorious, but it came too late to embrace the whole Order. It persisted by the sacrifice of unity. In 1517, exactly a hundred years after Capistran's ordination, the struggle issued in the separation which still endures.

Capistran himself, however decisively his influence was felt, did not favor a separation. On the contrary, he fought for unity more tenaciously than others. Without his interference the events of 1517 might have come much earlier. At the time of his entrance complete separation of a considerable group of Observants was expected. In three French provinces (Burgundy, France, and Thuringia), the Observants had obtained from the Pope (1407) the privilege of freedom from the jurisdiction of their provincials. In the following year the Franciscan general, by papal order, appointed a special vicar-general for these three provinces. The Order petitioned annulment, but schism prevented definite regulation. The Council of Constance favored the French Observants and allowed them (September 23, 1415) to elect a provincial vicar for each province. This vicar had to be approved by the provincial, but could thereafter act independently. This regulation made the first breach in the unity of the Order.

The Conventuals tried to have the decree of Constance revoked, or at least to prevent its extension to other provinces. The general chapters of the order regularly passed resolutions against exemption, but just as regularly such decrees were annulled by the Pope. Thus the chapter of Mantua (1418) enjoined upon all the brethren obedience to their provincials and attendance at the provincial chapter, which alone would appoint guardians over them. The French Observants had the decree of Constance renewed by Martin V (1420). The general chapter of Forlì (1421) excommunicated all brethren who obeyed the vicars in place of the provincials; but the same year, by order of the Pope, the newly elected general, Angelus Salvetti, had to provide vicars for the

Observants in Italy. At this time, as mentioned before, Bernardine and Capistran became vicars. Salvetti tried sincerely to remove at least the greatest abuses in regard to poverty. However, the reform decrees of the chapter of Forlì were vitiated by a clause allowing the general to dispense those provinces in which the execution would meet with too great difficulties.

That lax elements predominated is shown by the chapter of Ferrara, which elected as general Antonio of Massa, a man disinclined to any kind of reform. This same chapter excommunicated the Observants under vicars, and commanded this decree to be published in churches. The general chapter of Casale (1427) unearthed paragraphs from a penal code, directed by John XXII a hundred years before against the separatist efforts of the Spirituals. But a few weeks later (August 8, 1427) the Pope gave permission to the Observants in the realm of Duke Louis of Bavaria to have their own vicar.

Each party began to accuse the other at the papal court. In 1429 the general superiors of several orders united in complaining that the Observants, under the pretext of a better discipline, were penetrating everywhere. Martin V then renewed a still existing law, forbidding the Observants to start new foundations in places where mendicant cloisters already existed. The Observants, in turn, complained that they were molested by the Conventuals in many ways. The Pope assigned the affair to two cardinals, one the protector of the Franciscan Order, Cardinal Giordano Orsini. These two dignitaries, in a circular letter of April 15, 1429, commanded the Observants to report in Rome on June 8. Probably the same invitation was sent also to the Conventuals. As the Observants never came to chapters, here was welcome opportunity to give the Observants a piece of the Conventual mind. The Conventual speaker, a bishop, collected material for weeks. Three points were raised: Sequestration in very small hermitages with only a few inmates, multiplication of houses unfavorable to the Conventuals, and abuses in the office of preaching.

This third point was a boomerang. There were abuses on both sides, chiefly the authorization of unqualified persons as preachers.

Among the Observants the example of Bernardine and other great pulpit orators invited imitation. For this work, however, their men were inadequately prepared. Studies were extremely deficient. But neither with the Conventuals could Rome, very exact on this point, be satisfied. We know this from Capistran's correspondence with a provincial of Apulia, who had ordered a lay brother to preach. This happened in 1428, only a year before the Roman meeting. Capistran gave full vent to his disgust. He apostrophizes the seven liberal arts, commiserating their dethronement by Brother Lawrence. To the provincial who stubbornly defended the preaching brother, he gives the following advice: Since the brothers take care of preaching, do you now go to the kitchen, take care of the cooking, and wash the dirty feet of duncecap Lawrence, If the Pope should hear of the affair, what disgrace on the provincial and the whole Order. Capistran says he has already been rebuked by Pope and cardinal protector for not reporting unqualified preachers. He must now report the provincial, unless this nuisance is abolished.

In the Roman conference, held at San Francesco in Trastevere, each party is said to have been represented by eighty men. The Observants were not hopeful. Capistran told them to choose a speaker to represent their case, and they asked him to do so. The Conventual orator was called first. A three-hour philippic followed. All heresies, it said, began with innovations, like those now in vogue among the Observants, who go about barefoot, wear a shabby habit, and refuse to touch money. Let them return to common sense or end outside the Church.

When the speaker concluded, Capistran came forward, genuflected with his brethren before the cardinals, and begged permission to speak. But the cardinals said: "It is time for dinner; let us go." Capistran broke out impetuously: "Three long hours for a ranting bishop! Now suddenly time for dinner." The chairman yielded. If the Conventuals thought their mighty eloquence had overawed their simple opponents, they were now undeceived. In extemporaneous speech, with resourcefulness and wonderful memory, Capistran refuted, point by point, his opponent's carefully prepared oration. The Observants had found a leader of superior caliber. Thundering philippics had lost their force. The meeting ended with the usual exhortation to keep silence on the controversy now ended, and to live again in harmony and peace. The cardinal gave good example by inviting both speakers, the bishop and Capistran, to his house for dinner. That this peaceful closing meant final settlement was an illusion. Capistran turned from defensive to offensive and persuaded the Pope that the time had now come to reform the whole Order.

A decade brings many changes. The Observance, at first glad to be let alone, was now ready to attack, to abolish abuses. It was high time. The laxness of the general, Antonio of Massa, called peremptorily for redress. Provisionally the Pope gave him as coadjutor the procurator of the Order, William of Casale, without whose approval the general was not allowed to give orders. But complete reform would have been highly welcome to the Pope. The conciliar theory was taking shape, and the conviction was growing that final reform of the Church in head and members could be attained only by a general council, just as the schism had been ended by a council. The Council of Constance had decreed that the pope must call a general council for the year 1431. A thorough reform of the largest order in the Church, a reform generally known to be needed, would greatly strengthen the pope's position in view of the approaching council.

The details of the plan may well be owing to Capistran. The first step was the revival (November 7, 1428) of the *syndici apostolici* (i.e., Minorite judges officiating in the name of the pope), an office abrogated by John XXII. This decree of John XXII had occasioned the unhappy poverty quarrels of the previous century. Conventuals, in defending abuses, were accustomed to refer to that document as proof that the highest authority in the Church wished the abandonment of community poverty. The reasons that had moved the popes of the thirteenth century to meet all juridical objections against the introduction of collective poverty by vesting all property rights in the Apostolic See, were now felt anew, since the Observants earnestly insisted on re-establishing absolute conventual poverty. Plain lay brothers could be indifferent to the question about who had property claims, but not juridically trained brothers. Capistran, as juridical adviser and leader of the Observants, wished to place the Observance upon a clear and safe juridical basis. This first measure paved the way for the contemplated general reform.

One month after the Roman meeting, a *capitulum generalissimum* was called with a twofold object: first, to remove all abuses, especially those against poverty; secondly, to bring the Observants to give up their own vicars and return entirely to obedience under the provincials and the general. As meeting place, Liége was first proposed, but the Pope preferred Assisi, at the tomb of the holy founder. The Spanish cardinal, John Cervantes, was appointed to preside over the chapter.

The chapter opened on Corpus Christi (June 15). Its first decree removed from office the ruling general on the charge of negligent administration. The deposed general was appointed to the episcopal see of his native city, Massa. The chapter then chose as general, William of Casale, whom the history of the Order praises as a man of erudition, eloquent and pious, dignified in his manners, prudent as superior, diligent and efficient as administrator. Though himself a Conventual, he was favorably disposed toward the reform, and thus the Observants declared themselves willing to give up their own vicars. This difficult point met with opposition. The French Observants insisted on their independence, guaranteed by the decree of Constance, until such time as reform in head and members should be an accomplished fact. Even Bernardine of Siena approved this idea. Not so Capistran. He called the French Observants "enemies of the work of peace." His demand prevailed. The French vicar-general and provincial vicars were deposed, and the decree of Constance (1415) was explicitly revoked.

The Conventuals, on the other hand, had to pledge themselves to the revival of discipline according to the holy Rule. Those convents which, contrary to the Rule, had accepted real estate, were ordered to sell it and to use the proceeds for the settling of their liabilities and for the needs of the brethren. Secular procurators were reinstalled in all provinces. The use of cash money is strictly prohibited, and, if the general superior attempts to dispense from this regulation, he shall, without further sentence, be considered deposed. These acts of Assisi, or, as they were called in honor of the ruling Pope, these Martinian constitutions, contained no new obligations and even mitigated some older obligations. The constitutions were solemnly published on June 21. When Capistran mounted the rostrum and read the decrees to an immense audience, enthusiasm ran high. Shouts were heard: "We will stand by you. We will all be one order again, in life and in death." The next day everybody took an oath to carry out the decrees of the reform. William of Casale swore a special oath, never to ask dispensation from the first oath. The work of the reform seemed assured. The general was expected to visit the provinces and convents at once. Capistran was appointed to accompany him.

And yet. Is it possible to re-establish discipline once lost? In a few weeks the Observants were thoroughly disillusioned. The Conventuals assembled in Assisi were undoubtedly earnest and sincere. But when the first enthusiasm died down, when cold facts were faced, many recoiled from their solemn oaths. Under difficulties in the provinces, the solemn oath could become a source of endless scruples. Hence already in Assisi some members begged the cardinal to release them secretly from the oath. Even William of Casale shared these fears. On July 27, 1430, Martin V approved the constitutions of Assisi, but at the same time released the general from his oath.

The reform did not indeed depend on the oath. But in an essential point Casale had abandoned the reform from the very start, even before he went on his visitation tour. Absolute renunciation of every kind of secured revenues, either in money or real estate, was certainly the chief cause why many convents refused to accept the reform. Cloisters which from the time immemorial had existed on secure income based on pious legacies had now to be placed on an entirely new economic basis. Such a situation presupposed great readiness for sacrifices in the majority. The leaders of the Order were faced with the question whether it would not be the lesser evil to have the irregular but widespread condition sanctioned by the pope once and for all. At bottom the question was between two forms of poverty, not of intolerable abuse and misconduct. Considerations of this sort may have caused the general, William of Casale, to obtain from the Pope the bull *Ad statum* (August 23, 1430), which robs the Assisi chapter of its cornerstone, since it permits all minor brethren to possess, and to acquire also in future, all kinds of real estate, or other secure income. What until then had been exceptionally allowed or tolerated became now the regular and normal condition. The characteristic of Franciscan poverty, the sixth chapter of the Rule, so especially dear to the holy founder, was now surrendered. Conventualism becomes legally justified, and the great reform is frustrated. Division of the Order became inevitable.

Equipped with this ominous bull, the general began his visitation. By abandoning those points of the Assisi program which he thought impossible to execute, he evidently hoped to save at least a part of the reform. But for Capistran the tour had lost all attractiveness. The very text of the papal letters of passport showed how little the constitutions of Assisi were observed. Those regulations limited the suite of the general expressly to one secretary and one servant. The passport provides for a train of ten persons, partly on foot, partly on horseback. A servant was there to carry money. All this may have been the recent fashion. But if William of Casale wished to restore appreciation of poverty, he should himself have given a good example. Capistran, much to his chagrin, had to go horseback, against the expressly renewed prohibition of Assisi. This initial feebleness affected all of Casale's efforts. He did indeed abolish many abuses, but his energy collapsed before resistance, and he was satisfied with merely saving appearances. His words were ever warm in defending the reform, but he never found courage for effective measures. After four months, Capistran abandoned the hopeless task. The time spent in it remained a painful memory.

At this period Capistran seems to have been thinking of going abroad. His authorization as inquisitor had been renewed, and was extended to other countries. He may have had in view especially the Hussite danger, which for a decade had been hovering over

Bohemia. The crusade approved by Pope Martin collapsed with the defeat of King Sigismund. The Hussites now took the offensive. Victorious at home, they invaded surrounding countries, Lausitz, Meissen, Saxony. Two armies, which were gathered in northern Germany dared not attack them. In the year 1430 those incendiaries devastated Saxony and Franconia. About a hundred fortified cities and nearly ten times as many open villages were laid in ashes. The elector of Brandenburg finally bought them off. Three thousand wagons, each requiring from six to fourteen horses, brought their booty back to Bohemia. The delegates to Assisi reported these Hussite horrors.

In the constitutions of Assisi, Capistran directs the attention of the whole Order to this danger. The brethren are exhorted to strengthen the people in their faith against heretics and schismatics, and especially to attack the devilish and damned heresy of the Hussites. This call to a relentless war against the Bohemian heretics was needed. Tired of the hopeless battle, many advised a treaty of peace with the Hussites at the next council. Posters with such demands were fastened even on the Vatican gates. Pope Martin decisively rejected such insinuations and forbade all conferences with Hussites on matters of faith. Capistran's plans against the Hussites waited long for realization while other important ecclesiastical matters now came into the foreground.

A new storm against the papacy was preparing. The conciliar illusion, which was gaining ground especially among jurists, had for its war cry the reconstruction of the whole ecclesiastical constitution. In subordination of the Pope to the council lay salvation for the Church. No wonder Martin V postponed the council as long as he could. When at last he moved (February, 1431), he began by appointing an early friend of Capistran, the excellent Giuliano Cesarini, to preside over the deliberations. But the Pope did not live to see the opening of that council. A stroke of apoplexy ended his life on February 20. Capistran was present at his bedside a few hours before he died.

Pope Martin V has justly been called "the new founder of the papal kingdom, the restorer of Rome." The lamentations at his funeral showed that the Church of God and the city of Rome had lost the best of fathers. The Observants had lost a great protector. We do not know in full the personal relations of Capistran with the Colonna pope, but evidently he stood very high in Martin V's esteem. Even if this Pope was personally not so deeply interested in the Observance as was his successor, it still remains true that the astounding growth of the Observants in Italy was chiefly owing to the benevolence of Martin V.

Cardinal Gabriel Condulmerio, a Venetian, was elected (March 3, 1431) to succeed Martin V and took the name of Eugene IV. Capistran greeted the election with great joy. The new Pope had long been his familiar friend. Condulmerio, an Augustinian, had been a fervent pioneer of reform. On an island near Venice, together with Cardinal Antonio Correr, he had founded the Augustinian monastery of San Giorgio, which became the motherhouse of a reform congregation. Three days after the election, when Capistran paid his first visit, the Pope told him he hoped now to make their old friendship fruitful. Two weeks later came two papal decrees. The Conventuals, while forbidding the Observants to have their own vicars, were lax in reform regulations. Hence the Observants were again demanding their own vicars. Eugene consented. He called (March 10) a general chapter of the Italian Observants to meet on Pentecost at Bologna, where they should install new vicars. But he went a good deal farther. He published anew the Martinian reform in the bull *Vinea Domini Sabaoth*, revoking all dispensations and mitigations granted since then to the Conventuals and holding the general, Casale, to his Assisi oath. Conditions were thus reversed. The constitutions of Assisi became binding on the Conventuals, while the Observants were allowed to have their vicars.

We can hardly say that this was owing to Capistran. Eugene IV was inclined to excessively harsh measures against abuses and irregularities. Especially in matters of religious discipline he knew no mercy. He himself, even as Pope, led the life of a strict religious. With four monks, two Benedictines and two Augustinians, he kept each hour of the breviary. His diet was most simple. But his impetuous zeal often proved unsuccessful. Within the year he had to revoke the bull *Vinea Domini*, thus granting to the Conventuals the mitigations conceded by his predecessor. These concessions have remained since then the fundamental basis of Conventualism. The attempted unification of 1430 had ended, not in reform, but in relaxation.

The Italian Observants met (Pentecost, 1431) at Bologna, and installed provincial vicars. They did not elect a vicar-general, but the Pope let the brothers know his wish that Capistran should have supervision over the Italian Observants. Also in non-Italian countries the office of provincial vicars was revived or continued. But the Italian Observants remained for the time being in greater dependence on higher superiors than elsewhere. Capistran even now did not wish definite separation. Had he so wished, he would have had easy sailing under Eugene IV. To the honor of the leading Observants be it said that their zeal was never partisanship. For the welfare of the whole Order, of the Church, they refused to separate from the antagonistic majority as long as they still hoped to gain them. Positive separation would lead to the ruin of the Order. The last impulse to reform would disappear, and laxity would assume scandalous proportions. But not all Observants were far-sighted and patient. Capistran's effort to save the union met with frequent criticism and censure, and in later years he was often reminded of his failure in the reform of 1430.

PART IV
UNDER EUGENE IV
(1431–47)

CHAPTER XI

For Bernardine and Against Döring

A GROUP of Observants now declared against the Martinian constitution, and separated from the Order under the leadership of Philip of Berbegall, a Spiritualist of the most radical kind. The Rule of St. Francis, he argued, is simply inviolable. Even the form of the habit and the cowl which Francis wore cannot be changed without mortal sin. The Martinian constitution has no obligatory force, since it does not harmonize with the "pure Rule." Capistran tried to bring the Spaniard back to his senses. "You seem to assert that the Rule does not need to obey the Church, but that the Church has to serve the Rule. Do you know that our seraphic Father St. Francis, in the holy Rule itself, repeatedly asserts the very contrary? The Church is not derived from our Rule, but our Rule from the Church." These self-evident principles had been overlooked by zealots of poverty, by the Spiritualists of the thirteenth and fourteenth centuries, and most of all by the Fraticelli, who, Capistran says, have deceived Berbegall.

Similar tendencies were not lacking among the Italian Observants, as we shall see later. Their suppression is owing to the spirit of their leaders. Paul Trinci and John Stroncone were simple lay brothers, genuinely humble and submissive. But timid brothers were now asking themselves how faithful adherence to the Rule was compatible with papal explanations of the Rule. What a blessing that such men as Bernardine and Capistran held supreme leadership! In constitutional questions Capistran was the real director of the reform. Unflinchingly faithful to the Franciscan ideal, he also saw soberly and clearly the foundation on which reform must be based. Scruples against papal regulations had no right to exist. In the old quarrel over the form of habit and cowl, revived by Berbegall, Capistran said simply: "Let us suppose our holy Father

Francis wore the cowl as you do. But do not suppose he was thereby laying down a law which even the pope would not be allowed to revise. Above poverty stands obedience. The devil has ensnared many zealots for poverty by the net of stubborn disobedience."

As example Capistran adduces Michael of Cesena, who had apostatized under John XXII. We must note that historians are inclined to find excuses for Cesena, but Capistran stigmatizes him unreservedly as a heretic. To the presumption of Michael of Cesena, who would not submit humbly to the decisions of the Church in regard to the poverty of Christ, Capistran traces the heresy of Fraticellism. What distinguishes Capistran from the great leaders of Spiritualism in his reverence for papal authority, his absolute confidence in the visible representative of Christ on earth. "Reform," he writes against Berbegall, "is pleasing to God, in harmony with the Rule, it is just and holy when it is approved by God and His true representative, our Holy Father, who is, as it were, God on earth, more than a man, less than God, the only vicar of Christ."

Capistran lived on good terms with the new general, William of Casale, whose letters to him are very friendly and who treated him as a well-trusted confidant. But while Capistran realized the immense difficulties faced by his well-intentioned general, frequent events were further widening the chasm between the Conventuals and the Observants. Pope Martin V had scarcely breathed his last, when the Conventuals took possession of Monte Alverno and carried away the documents and holy vessels. The citizens of Florence complained to the new Pope. Then Casale received orders (November 28, 1431) from Eugene IV to restore Alverno promptly to the Observants and to bring back there anything that had been carried away. To secure the Observants in the quiet possession of Alverno, the Pope, a few years later, entrusted the guild of the Florentine wool-weavers with the protection of the monastery.

A similar event is reported from Ragusa. In this flourishing little republic on the Adriatic a Franciscan convent existed from early times. When discipline gave way to a scandalous laxity, the citizens sent a deputation to the general of the Order, and obtained reform.

Now, in the year 1431, Angelus of Rieti, who had guided the convent to general satisfaction, was transferred to Venice. Ragusa, fearing a return to former conditions, wrote to the Pope, to the cardinal protector, to the general, to Capistran. Ragusa wished to have Capistran as vicar in case Angelus could not return. Ragusa's wishes were listened to, though Capistran could not go there himself, principally because Eugene IV needed him. The Pope's first wish was to give Capistran the bishopric of Aquila. But, though Aquila was his second home, Capistran again declined, as he had done two years before when Chieti was offered to him. Then, said the Pope, do you find a bishop for Aquila. Capistran suggested Amicus de Roccha, canon of Aquila, an efficient jurist. Amicus governed the Church of Aquila for over thirty years, and was made a cardinal in 1467. Presumably the impending council prompted the Pope to keep the most prominent Observant preachers near him. Among the six chosen ones were Albert of Sarteano, James of the Marches, and Capistran. Bernardine, the greatest preacher of them all, is not on the list. He was again under fire.

After his Roman trial, Bernardine had again toured Italy, chiefly Romagna and the Marches. In Reggio he induced the people to replace the party signs on their houses by the monogram of Jesus. Even the inhabitants of Forlì, "hard as stone," were vanquished. But Bernardine's acquittal by the Pope had not silenced his opponents. The Augustinian hermit, Andrew de Cassia, attacked him violently in two pamphlets, both of them being directed not only against the cult of the holy name of Jesus, but also against Bernardine's mission work in general. Cassia's view of conditions is quite new and stands alone. All other sources complain bitterly of the miserable state of the Church. But Cassia tells us that during the pontificate of Martin, Rome and the Roman Curia lived in peace and security. The Church lay before the Pope like a pleasure garden, until Bernardine began to preach. Bernardine is the villain that broke in like a wolf upon the harmless and unsuspecting Christian people, whom he misled in such numbers that Martin V could not deal strictly with him without risking the peace and the security of the Church. Had the Pope been strict, Bernardine would have gone the way of Hus and

Jerome of Prague.

This document illuminates the meaning which, even in clerical circles, was sometimes attached to the slogan "reform in head and members." Certainly, the itinerant preachers may not have been always free from excrescences. But the Franciscan Observance was in general a genuine and profound movement of reform, gladdening all genuinely religious men. Only jealousy and irritability could so slander and insult a man like Bernardine. In expressive abusiveness Cassia reminds us of Martin Luther. He regards Bernardine's symbol of the holy name as a picture and badge of antichrist. Bernardine and the Observants he calls "the goats." In their activity he sees signs of the antichrist.

After Pope Martin's death, denunciations of Bernardine increased. In 1431 he was attacked from the pulpit of his native city, Siena. Called home from Romagna, he soon silenced his antagonists. In Bologna, where he preached a series of sermons in the cathedral of San Petronio, the canons affixed a beautifully executed "name of Jesus" to the high altar as a memorial. Bernardine had scarcely left Bologna when a Franciscan thundered against him from the same pulpit. A Dominican, in his capacity of inquisitor, removed the holy name and replaced it by a crucifix. Bernardine returned to Bologna and preached for another two weeks in St. Petronio. The Bishop forced his opponent publicly to retract his accusations. By orders of the Pope the holy name was replaced in St. Petronio. Still his enemies succeeded. Inquisitorial proceedings against Bernardine were taken up in Rome, and on November 29, 1431, he was summoned before the Roman Inquisition to defend himself against the accusation of heresy.

The proceedings were kept secret from the Holy Father on account of his predilection for the Observants. But the people of Siena heard of this affair in time and informed the Pope through their ambassador. The Pope himself promptly took over the affair, canceled the summons of Bernardine, and closed the mouth of the opponents by an explicit document (January 7, 1432) in which he publicly censured the procedure of the Inquisition and restored the honor of the accused by a noble testimonial before the whole world.

The bull reads almost like an announcement of Bernardine's canonization, which did in fact follow eighteen years later. The Pope scornfully refutes all suspicions against the orthodoxy of Bernardine, whom he calls "the most relentless foe of all heresy, the great apostle, and the teacher of the Catholic faith." Capistran again had been behind the scenes.

As we know from his sermon on the newly canonized Bernardine, he it was who obtained from the Pope that bull of justification.

Clerical animosity against Bernardine stands in sharp contrast with humanist views, especially those expressed by Poggio, whose sarcasm otherwise spared nothing holy. Poggio has no word of blame for Bernardine, though he slanders and blackens all the other Observants. The construction of a monastery in Tuscany involved some relatives of Poggio, who appealed to the Pope and had the erection of the building forbidden. Then he wrote a tract (December 15, 1429) in which he asserts: "Not the desire for a stricter order of life prompted the Observants to separation from the Conventuals, but only their quarrelsomeness and vagabondage. The excellent and irreproachable sermons of Bernardine are above criticism. But his unworthy followers, beneath the dirty garments of vagrant beggars, hide proud and vicious souls, whose aim is not an ascetic life, not the following of Christ, but a life of luxury in lovely Tuscany under Jupiter Nectar of Gangheretto." Their unedifying manner of life was the reason, he elsewhere insinuates, why they were summoned to account in Rome.

Such accusations from the pen of an offended humanist were little trusted by the public. But the social standing of the accusers left the attacked party in disfavor. Albert Sarteano, the humanist among the Observants, though a friend of Poggio, refuted Poggio's accusation. Dislike of the Observants, Albert argues, came from Poggio's love of paganism. With eloquent words Albert describes the solitary, unworldly life of the Observants, in whose company he himself had now spent fourteen years. "Many lead a life of excelling purity; others lead a good life; none at all a bad life." Sarteano's description shows that the reform, all in all, stood as high as can be expected of a numerous order.

The conciliar movement was now approaching its climax. Eugene IV, while partly responsible for the severe storms of the following years, was still one of the worthiest of popes. His tall, haggard frame, his earnest demeanor, inspired men with awe. But prudent moderation was not his forte. He dissolved the Council of Basle (December, 1431) before it had really started work. The members protested in a circular letter, and continued their deliberations with greater fervor. The cardinals censured the Pope's hasty procedure. A new schism was feared. Rupture threatened the relations between Eugene and Sigismund, who came to Italy (1432) to receive the imperial crown. His friendly relations with the Duke of Milan, an energetic opponent of the Pope, filled the latter with grave misgivings. Bernardine of Siena entered as mediator, in July, 1432, when Sigismund came to Siena on his way to Rome. Sigismund was prejudiced against Bernardine in consequence of malicious accusations which declared that Bernardine had influenced the Pope to refuse the imperial crown to the King. In a private audience, Bernardine unraveled the web of lies, and the King listened to his sermons, attended his Mass, visited him repeatedly, and attached him to his suite. Thus Pope and King were drawn together. On May 31, 1433, Eugene IV placed the imperial crown on this last representative of the Luxemburg line.

Emperor Sigismund won lasting merit in promoting mutual understanding between the Pope and the Council and thus preventing a schism. The Pope, influenced by the revolutionary movement in Milan, yielded, revoked (December, 1433) the decree of dissolution, and declared legal the sessions so far held, but without binding himself to the approval of all resolutions so far passed, particularly the agreements with the Hussites. The assembly at Basle had quickly made peace with the Bohemians, hoping thus to please the Christian world and to increase the importance of the Council. A Hussite embassy appeared in Basle (January, 1433). At its head were Procopius the Great, bishop of the radical Taborites, and Master John of Rokytzana, the leader of the Utraquists, the more moderate wing of the Hussites. Three months of discussion led to no satisfactory results, and the conferences were continued at Prague. The peace concluded at the national assembly (November 30, 1433) between the Utraquists and the Council, was based on the concessions contained in the Compactata of Prague.

The most important among these concessions was the permission, under certain restrictions, to give Holy Communion to lay people under both species. The radical faction of the Hussites refused to accept the Compactata. They wanted no peace with the Roman Church. But Catholics and Utraquists, now united, won the bloody battle near Lipan (May 30, 1434), where thirteen thousand bodies lay on the battlefield, among them the body of Procopius the Great. But although the Hussite war was ended, the Hussite schism continued. The Compact did not lead the Utraquists back to the Church, at least not the Utraquists of Rokytzana. However, the concessions made to them by the Council of Basle hid this fact from the Catholics of other countries. Perhaps the Compact inflicted more harm on the Catholic Church in Bohemia than did even the disastrous Hussite wars. When, two decades later, Capistran undertook the conversion of the Utraquists, he found at the beginning of his mission his greatest obstacle in the *Compactata* of Prague.

During the last years of Martin V and the first years of Eugene IV, Capistran was occupied against the Fraticelli. Two letters from Martin V permitted him to pardon relapsed Fraticelli when it was a case of seduction or of ignorance. Capistran, therefore, was not the merciless zealot he is so often pictured. Even as inquisitor he studied each character individually.

For the Observants the most important event of the time was their acceptance of guardianship over the Holy Land (1433), whereas previously Conventuals and Observants had shared this privilege together. On July 9, 1433, Capistran, with a great number of confreres, appeared before the Pope to ask his blessing for these friars before their journey to the East. The joyful event was made known to all Observants by a circular letter.

But the continued favors of the new Pope to the Observants did not deter the Conventuals from warfare against the reform. At the general chapter of Bologna (Pentecost, 1433), which was the first under the new general, William of Casale, the Conventuals succeeded in obtaining new relaxations for themselves, and in limiting still more the rights of the Observants. Spokesman for the Conventuals at that chapter was the notorious provincial of Saxony, Matthias Döring.

Matthias Döring, born at Kyritz in Brandenburg, is the Conventualist counterpart of Capistran. He received his scientific education after his entrance into the Order, at the university of Erfurt. His unusual talent quickly made him a leader. He received the title of Doctor (1424), and accepted a professorial chair in the university, but only for a short time. The provincial chapter soon elected him (1427) provincial, a position he held for thirty-four years, a rare occurrence in the history of the Order. Talent for leadership and strict adherence to the Conventual manner of life gained him the perfect confidence of his confreres. But the Observance soon found entrance into Saxony, Brandenburg being their first convent. To keep this movement from spreading was one of Döring's chief aims during his long term in office. But as calm objectivity was not an easy task for his strong and passionate temper, in his very first effort, a controversy with the Spanish Dominican, Paul of Burgos, he did not shrink from personal abuse. In the Council of Basle he took the liveliest interest and was admitted as representative of the Saxon province in July, 1432, at a time when the Pope's bull of dissolution was still in force. Educated in Erfurt, one of the chief German centers of the conciliar movement, Döring sided with the radicals and spoke repeatedly for their ideas. As deputy of the Council he went (1433) to Denmark with invitations to attend the Council. He stayed on in Basle even after the Council itself became schismatic. In opposition to the Saxon branch, the Franciscans generally, both Conventuals and Observants, preserved fidelity to Eugene IV. The general of the order, William of Casale, was an especially reliable supporter of the new Pope.

Soon after Easter, 1434, a revolution drove the Pope from Rome. The Roman people took the Capitol by storm, and once more declared a republic. Eugene IV, pursued by a hail of stones, got away by boat down the Tiber to Ostia. Thus began an exile of nearly two years, spent mostly at Florence. Hence Capistran, too, during this period labored chiefly in northern Italy. During Lent of 1434 he had been at Agnone in the territory of Naples. But in October of the same year we find him, for the first time as far as we know, in one of the large cities of Lombardy, the city of Ferrara. The bishop of that city, St. John Tossignani, himself a fervent reformer, had declared war against unbecoming fashions. Styles that defied both good taste and good morals were an almost ineradicable plague, against which not only missioners but also secular magistrates strove energetically. In these rich cities of northern Italy women began to wear dresses with long trains, a style which opponents of the fashion asserted had come from the brothels of Milan.

The Bishop of Ferrara, after deliberating in many conferences about a way to stop the evil, at last (October 12, 1434), in a great assembly of preachers and jurists, forbade these trailing gowns under pain of excommunication. Harlots were allowed to retain this style of dress. Capistran published and justified this resolution from the pulpit. Similar commands were published in Padua by Albert Sarteano, and in Forlì by James of the Marches. To his studies on this question we owe Capistran's tract, of cultural and historical importance, on the proper limits of ornament and pomp. The work excels in careful weighing of all conditions and circumstances affecting moral judgment in questions of luxurious clothing. The chief circumstances are social position, custom and usage, danger of scandal, and intention. During the Renaissance, Italy's devotion to art often threatened to degenerate into senseless luxury. Capistran, having been himself a victim of vanity and finery, now excelled as preacher against this new aberration. His unrelenting earnestness passes from time to time into biting sarcasm.

CHAPTER XII

In Italy

FROM 1435 on, Capistran was engaged directly in papal missions. Queen Joanna II died that year (February 2). To prevent repetition of struggles for the throne, which fifty years before had followed the death of Joanna I, Pope Martin V had acknowledged the claims of Louis III of Anjou, and of his brothers René and Charles, that is, if Joanna should die without children. But Joanna had her own ideas, and in 1421 adopted the valiant Alfonso V, king of Aragon, as her son and successor. Alfonso occupied Naples, but soon offended the Queen by arrogant behavior. She dropped him, and transferred the throne of Naples to the Pope's candidate, Louis III of Anjou. When he died, she chose his brother, Duke René of Lorraine. A year later the Queen herself died, and war for the throne began between Alfonso and René.

Pope Eugene IV, reserving final decision, appointed the militant bishop Giovanni Vitelleschi viceroy of the vacant kingdom. Vitelleschi, more soldier than priest, was for the moment fully occupied in the Papal States, having with an iron hand re-established papal supremacy in Rome (October, 1434). In a proclamation (June 6. 1435), the Pope commanded both parties, Angevins and Aragonians, to cease fighting. Capistran, expert in Neapolitan affairs, was sent there by the Pope to bring the warring parties to peace. As René was still a prisoner in Burgundy, his mother Isabella was to take over the government for the time. But Alfonso had Naples completely under control. To move Alfonso to renounce his claim seems to have been the particular mission of Capistran. Several hard months went into this ecclesiastico-political mission. It was a time of extreme exertion, and often marked by dangerous journeys and difficult conferences.

Capistran brought a message to the prince of Faventino, in

Capua, just captured by Alfonso. The war, it said, was unjust, since Alfonso could not prove his claims to Naples. A commission of twelve jurists tried to defend the rights of the King. No particular acuteness was needed to uncover the shallowness of the Aragonese demonstration. Neither the feudal rights of the Pope nor the adoption of René by Joanna could be contested. But Capistran's memory and quickness at repartee won the admiration of the royal lawyers. Without any notes he repeated in detail all their arguments. But the discussion had merely academical value, since Alfonso was determined to keep Naples. At Gaeta, a fortified seaport, Capistran met the King himself, who was preparing to battle a fleet from Genoa coming to the rescue of the starving city. Capistran conjured him to refrain. The Aragonese took the risk and suffered a crushing defeat (August 25, 1435). Alfonso himself, with two of his brothers and about a hundred Spanish and Sicilian noblemen, fell into the hands of the victors, who brought him captive to Milan.

Capistran returned to the papal court in Florence. Two documents (October 13) show clearly that his political missions did not make him lose sight either of pastoral work or of the affairs of the Observance. The first document gives extraordinary faculties for absolving his penitents, of which latter a great throng is indicated. The second document authorizes the acceptance of five new foundations.

Toward the end of 1435, as papal commissioner, he had to mediate a second time in the matter of the Neapolitan succession. Isabella, René's mother, had arrived at Gaeta (October 8). The city honored her as Queen. In René's name she took possession of the kingdom; entering the capital city on October 18, the amiable Queen quickly gained the favor of the people. But Pope Eugene IV still delayed formal transfer of the kingdom to René. This delay may have been on account of his strained relation with the Council of Basle, which had its strongest support in France. The Pope seemingly expected, as a kind of balance for giving Naples to René, that France should cease to protect the Council.

Meantime Vitelleschi was to go to Naples as papal viceroy.

Capistran was to meet the heads of both parties, to prepare the way for the cardinal. He traveled over the Abruzzi to visit the duke of Bari, James Caldola, the most powerful pillar of the Angevin party. At Airola, near Benevento, Capistran met James and his brother Raymond. They accepted the Pope's proposal and declared they would support him with all their power. Marriage between the daughter of Raymond and a nephew of the Pope, helped to pave the way to success.

Capistran now hurried on to Naples, where he presented his message to the privy council in the presence of Queen Isabella, and again found, with certain reservations, full-hearted acceptance. On December 19, he reported to the Pope the good results of his mission. On the same day he wrote Vitelleschi, urging him to come at the earliest opportunity, since the noblemen and the common people awaited him as an angel of peace. Not mere obedience to the Pope gave Capistran such fervor in these political problems. His old patriotism had been rekindled. How deeply Naples had sunk since the glorious days of King Ladislaus! Now a new era of peace and prosperity beckoned. The union of the Pope with France, the newly founded dominion of the Angevins over Naples, could become a blessing for the whole peninsula. Such was Capistran's expectation. This marriage, he writes to Vitelleschi, could give peace to all Italy, this bride is a second Esther. "A new light arises, the joy of men and the jubilation of the people." The cardinal should urge the Pope to act quickly, as no one could foresee what might happen; postponement is always dangerous. His warnings were only too well justified. Alfonso V, a smooth diplomat, had been very active in his prison and had gained Philip Maria Visconti, the duke of Milan, for his plans. The Duke not only set him free (Christmas, 1435), but also promised assistance in a new war to recover Naples.

After a short stay in Naples, Capistran visited other parts of the realm (Nola, Baroli, and Andria), where he spoke with the Prince of Taranto, the strongest partisan of the Aragonian. In January, 1436, he is active in the territory of Manfredonia. On January 20 he writes from Monte Gargano to the Pope, urging haste: "Why do you delay and let the time pass uselessly? What fame you could gain by restoring peace to all Italy!"

But the favorable moment was allowed to pass. Vitelleschi was busy in the Papal States; the government in Naples remained inactive; Eugene IV would not abandon his policy of delay. February 2, 1436, Alfonso landed at Gaeta, and the war for the throne was reopened. On July 11, Capistran writes from Gaeta, now again in the power of Alfonso. Such mediation back and forth between enemy camps would have been impossible except to one who was not suspected of ambition. Even so his life was repeatedly in danger. But here his mission, as far as the struggle for the throne was concerned, came to its end.

Northern Italy now offered the preacher a splendid field of labor. In 1436 he was in Bologna, where Eugene IV now resided. In a circular letter Capistran sent to the members of the Third Order the good news that the Pope had removed certain regulations made more than a hundred years before by John XXII when the quarrel was at its height. From the very beginning the Tertiaries had encountered much contradiction in secular and religious circles. "Many barked, saying the Tertiaries were the devil's own race." Thus spoke Capistran in a sermon at Vienna. Afterward, when the Inquisition was dealing with the Fraticelli and Beguins, the Tertiaries, especially communities of Tertiaries, were under the suspicion of favoring heretical associations. To keep the Fraticelli from hiding under the cover of the Third Order, John XXII added to the bull of condemnation (*Sancta Romana atque universalis Ecclesia*) an explanation that the Rule of the Third Order did not permit living together in communities. This explanation was generally interpreted as strictly prohibiting community life for Tertiaries. And beyond doubt that Rule has chiefly in view people who live in the world. But for those Tertiaries who were not bound by any family ties, community life in some monastic form would certainly facilitate Christian perfection. Hence, during the course of the fourteenth century, Tertiaries often settled together in cloister-like communities. The painful legal incertitude, repeatedly used by the enemies of the Third Order as a weapon, was now removed by Capistran's efforts. Eugene IV, on Capistran's repeated request, revoked every prohibition against Tertiaries living in communities. Further, the Pope allowed them to choose for themselves a father confessor, who could absolve them from all censures which they might have incurred under the bull of John XXII. Capistran's love for the Third Order may be measured by his remark that, since the Council of Constance, he had obtained for the Third Order about a hundred bulls. In the year 1450 Capistran computed the membership in Italy alone at more than half a million.

Now (1436) came a new proof of confidence. Conditions in the convents of the Oriental vicarage, especially in a convent at Kaffa on the Crimean peninsula, required immediate visitation. William appointed Capistran as his commissioner, visitator, and reformer of those convents, particularly the one at Kaffa, and Capistran promptly prepared to go to the Orient via Greece. The Oriental vicarage included Macedonia, Constantinople, the southern coast of the Black Sea, and from there on into Turkestan and India. His particular destination was Kaffa, and clearly he was not to visit the Holy Land, called Provincia Syria, or Terra Sancta, which was separate from the Oriental vicarage. To guarantee full freedom, the general provided him (January 20, 1437) with the powers of a *vicarius a latere*. But at the last moment someone else had to be appointed in Capistran's place. The reason seems to have been the Pope's wish to have Capistran near him, since the transfer of the Council from Basle to Ferrara had been determined.

In Capistran's place the Observant, James Primadizzi of Bologna, went to the Orient. On July 11, 1437, Capistran presented in papal audience the brothers chosen for the journey to Kaffa. Primadizzi was entrusted with additional work in the Orient. The reunion of the schismatic Churches of the East with Rome seemed to be near realization. Preliminary discussions were already in full swing. In this regard the Franciscans, who had their settlements all over the Orient, had done splendid work for the Church. Albert of Sarteano and Bartholomew of Giano had gone to Greece in 1435, to urge attendance at the general council. Primadizzi was to get in touch with the Armenian schismatics and prompt them to come. As the Greeks had really agreed to come, Eugene IV determined to transfer the Council from Basle to Ferrara as a place more accessible to Orientals.

The summer of 1437 found Capistran engaged in reforming a famous but decadent convent of Poor Clares in Ferrara. Command had come directly from the Pope. A convent of that kind in the Council city itself would certainly have made a bad impression. A standing accusation raised by the friends of the Council was that the Pope was not eager to reform the Church. Capistran made the necessary changes in St. William's convent. But he told the Pope that as long as the present abbess continued in office the reform would not last. Hence Capistran had to return to Ferrara and install a new abbess. Further, the convent was withdrawn from the spiritual guidance of the Conventuals and placed under the care of the Observants. But even so Capistran did not succeed. Toward the end of August the Bishop of Ferrara informed him that almost all the nuns in St. William had again accepted property.

Another disagreeable task was waiting, this time in the monastery of the Jesuates in Venice, a community founded about eighty years before by Blessed John Colombini. The Jesuates, Brothers of Mercy, led an extremely strict life. They wore a white habit, a leather belt, a brown cloak, and sandals. Soon after their foundation these "Poor Men of Christ" were suspected of contact with the Fraticelli. They were even accused of leading loose lives and of fostering heretical ideas. To substantiate these accusations their antagonists used as a tool a little book, Mirror for Simple Souls, composed by one of the Jesuates. The saintly bishop of Venice, Lorenzo Giustiniani, after investigation, had found them guiltless. As the accusations were not silenced, the Pope commanded the Bishop to proceed to a more thorough investigation, in which he would be assisted by Capistran, a man "famous for holy life, spotless reputation, and distinguished wisdom." Capistran went to Venice in September. The Bishop of Ferrara, who had been a member of the Jesuate Order himself for twenty-five years, defended their innocence in several letters to Capistran, who did in fact find that the charges were calumnies. He openly declared their complete innocence, and the Bishop held a public demonstration in their favor.

But Capistran did discover abuses in Venice. In a detailed report to the Pope he speaks of heretical and superstitious pamphlets. A woman named Mina, now deceased, had been even the object of a superstitious cult. She pretended she had been pregnant for forty-five years and asserted she would give birth to a boy and a girl. The boy would become pope, and the girl would defend women in the faith. She herself, she said, had received the keys of the kingdom of heaven. Hence she had demanded from her devotees the honors corresponding to such dignity, genuflections, for instance, and kissing of her hands. Even a priest was involved in this extravagant nonsense. Capistran had a mind to have the corpse of Mina unearthed and burned. The priest was arrested. Capistran asked permission to proceed rigorously, saying: "Most Holy Father, where the faith is at stake, justice must prevail. Your enemies seek every occasion to trump up charges against you. What will they do if they can accuse your Holiness of carelessness in matters of faith?"

Giustiniani appointed Capistran as inquisitor of his diocese. This led to proceedings against a second priest, the brother of a Dominican. This priest had protectors at the papal court, and Capistran, upon returning to Rome, found to his great surprise that the Pope was indignant, believing that Capistran was guilty of partisanship and of dislike toward the former inquisitor at Venice, a Dominican. The simple truth was that the priest, according to the testimony of his own friends, had received a very mild sentence. Also, in direct contradiction to the facts, reports came that Capistran had preached against the Jesuates. For the first twelve days he was not admitted to see the Pope at all. He had to call the Bishop of Ferrara to his aid. This Bishop had in the meantime received from his former confreres in Venice reports showing that the Jesuates venerated Capistran as their protector and benefactor.

William of Casale had brought to the Council in Bologna twelve Franciscan professors of theology. The Greek Emperor had been expected on All Saints Day, 1437, but was delayed. Meanwhile the theologians discussed the primacy of the pope, the divine attributes, and the dogma of the Holy Trinity. The Council in Basle opposed to the utmost the Pope's plan of transferring the Council to northern Italy and insisted on Basle or Avignon, or then some city in Savoy. In October, Cardinal Cesarini left the rebellious council and went back to Italy. Only one cardinal remained in Basle, Louis Allemand of Arles, the leader of the opposition.

During Advent, 1437, Capistran preached in Verona, called thither by Cardinal Antonio Correr. Correr, like Cesarini, Capranica, and Albergati, was one of the worthiest members of the Sacred College. Like Eugene IV he had been canon of San Giorgio in Venice. He had accepted the purple from his uncle, Gregory XII, on condition that his confrere, Condulmerio, the future Pope Eugene IV, would also become cardinal. Strictly religious, the cardinal had chosen Capistran years before as private chaplain, companion, and familiar friend. This position was now of practical value, as at the end of the year Capistran fell seriously ill. Cardinal Cesarini, returning from Basle to Ferrara, passed through Verona and found his dear friend sick abed. This meeting was destined to be momentous. From Cesarini, Capistran learned all details of the discussions in Basle, especially those concerning the Hussite question. When, years after, he met the Utraquists in Bohemia, he referred explicitly to these meetings with Cesarini in Verona.

For Lent, 1438, he was expected in Ferrara. For the opening of the Council the Prince of Ferrara wished a Lenten preacher of great fame. But Tossignani, the bishop of Ferrara, consoled his sick friend in a letter (January 11, 1438). He would find a substitute. Let Capistran take needed rest; it would be wrong to endanger his life. The Bishop also informs him that on January 8 the Council had been solemnly opened at Ferrara, and that the first session had been held on January 10. The Pope and the Greek Emperor were awaited daily. In fact, Eugene IV came to Ferrara on January 27; the Emperor, accompanied by Albert of Sarteano, on March 4. Capistran recuperated in time to undertake the Lenten course at Verona.

His topic was usury, a favorite subject with Franciscan preachers, one on which their views were very strict. They taught that any and all interest on a mere loan was usury, and was consequently condemned. This held good also for Saracens and

Jews, who must be forced to restore all they had gained by taking interest. Capistran had a special liking for this theme. With juridical profundity he treats different forms of loans. He investigates all circumstances and conditions that could make compensation for a loan permissible. Considering usury a capital sin of his age, he proceeds with unmitigated harshness. Evidently he made a deep impression in Verona. Here, as later in Germany, he was requested by lawyers, noblemen, and prominent citizens to publish these sermons. Thus arose his famous treatise *De cupiditate*, which by its very title shows his idea of money. Of all his published writings this seems to have had the greatest circulation.

Albert of Sarteano had advised Capistran to get in touch with the humanist circle in Verona. Guarini, Albert's teacher, was chiefly intended. Even Bernardine profited by his few free moments. We may doubt that Capistran followed Bernardine's example. But Albert's proposal seems to indicate that Capistran, the inveterate jurist, did not in principle condemn humanist studies, though apparently he never had leisure for them. Thus in Verona Cardinal Correr imposed on him a second tract, dealing with the plenitude of papal power. Reluctantly Capistran entered on this new task: "A burden I am not able to carry," he says in the introduction. "When I left you and considered the matter on my bed of straw in the silence of the night, I said to myself: 'Poor ignoramus, why did you undertake such a task?' " This long work was hardly finished before 1440.

While Capistran in Verona, suffering from stomach ailment and attacks of fever, was defending papal authority, the assembly of Basle openly declared against the Pope. His daring to transfer the Council to Ferrara and to begin the conferences with the Greeks independently, made them reckless. They declared (March 14) as a truth of faith that the pope could not transfer a general council. Ten days later they put the Pope under sentence of suspension and threatened all partakers in the "conventicle of Ferrara" with gravest penalties. Council stood against council. It was only a question of time when Basle would proceed to depose Eugene IV and set up an antipope. But Eugene did not let himself be intimidated.

Conferences with the Greeks were solemnly inaugurated in the cathedral of Ferrara (April 9) and continued after Easter in the church of the Franciscans. Capistran did not participate in these conferences, since he was still in Verona, at least till Pentecost of that year. Where he spent the summer is not known. Presumably the affairs of the Observance claimed much of his time, as these had come up for discussion in Basle.

Since 1430 the relation between Conventuals and Observants had remained in the same confusion as before. The Conventuals stubbornly insisted that, on the basis of the Martinian reform, provincial vicars no longer existed. But Pope Eugene IV had repeatedly granted these vicars to single provinces. In Italy, Capistran, not in name but in fact, was vicar-general of the Observants. However, since such regulations were local, sometimes merely oral, the Conventuals maintained the original prohibition. Against the decrees of the general chapter of Bologna (1433) the French Observants appealed to the Council of Basle, at that time still legitimate. The general of the Order, William of Casale, came personally to Basle and attempted to mediate. As far as we can see he had nothing against provincial vicars. But the office of vicar-general, heading the provincial vicars with the powers of a general, was a thorn in his side since it meant cleavage in the Order itself. He labored to have the decree of Constance revoked, but the fathers of the Council, anxious to appear before the world as strict and severe reformers, sided with the French Observants, and approved anew the decree of Constance. But they added a clause: until new orders would regulate the affair. The disputed decree was, in fact, soon annulled.

The general chapter of Toulouse (Pentecost, 1437), united the provinces of Francia and Turonia under one vicar, subject to the general. This new arrangement, supposedly agreed to by the Observants, represented a sort of middle way. It gave the Observance a certain degree of independence and leadership. On the other hand it abolished the vicar-general and thus drew the reform convents more closely into the general order. The Observants in Bosnia and Hungary had already been put under one vicar. But the general chapter of Toulouse (1437) made other regulations that put the Observants at a disadvantage.

In Capistran's audience (July 11, 1437), at which Primadizzi with the brothers who were to accompany him to the Orient presented themselves to the Pope, the latter admonished the numerous Observants surrounding him to remain faithful to the reform, and not to worry about the censures of the chapter of Toulouse. This occurrence shows clearly how impossible the situation had become. William of Casale was occasionally forced to resort to a kind of double-dealing, by declaring null and void decrees which he himself as president of the general chapter had approved. To illustrate. At Osimo in the Marches the Observant vicar accepted (1437), at the wish of the Bishop and people, a new foundation, which the provincial of that district promptly canceled, although the vicar had all the required documents of authorization. The general, as often happened, could not be reached for many months. Hence complaints among the Observants continued to increase.

William of Casale intended to come personally to the Portiuncula feast in Assisi (1438). But, as sickness kept him in Siena, he met the wishes of the brothers by appointing for Italy two fully authorized commissaries to guide the reform convents. The commissary for the Kingdom of Naples was the highly respected Nicholas of Osimo. Commissary for the rest of Italy was Bernardine, whom William called to his sickbed in Siena. Bernardine accepted reluctantly. Since the Pope had entrusted Capistran with a sort of supreme direction of the Observance in all Italy, the appointment of Bernardine finds its explanation: first, in Capistran's state of health; secondly, in the urgent apostolic labors which kept him in northern Italy.

CHAPTER XIII

From Trent to Palestine

THE city of Trent had invited Capistran (Pentecost, 1438) to be their preacher. "Let him not despise their little city, so sorely tried and disturbed. As he often went to cities that had not called him, he should be the more willing to come to those that invite him. Their hearts are hard as stone, but the sweet sound of his voice can stop rivers and soften rocks." The Prince Bishop also asked him to come. In the first half of October, Capistran began his mission in Trent.

Clearly, then, Capistran had little to do in the question of union with the Greeks. During the sessions of the Council on this question (October 8, 1438, until the beginning of January, 1439), Capistran was preaching in Trent. The tradition ascribing to Capistran a special share in this matter of reunion with the Greeks, is wrong. On the contrary, we find in his correspondence expressions which minimize the value of these reunion conferences. Referring to the fate of the union agreed upon at the Second Council of Lyons (1274) and so promptly dissolved again, he concludes that little can be expected from members separated from their head, from twigs cut off from the vine. He was not at all friendly to the thought that the best forces of the Church should be spent in these doubtful efforts at reunion with the schismatic Churches of the East at a time when the Western Church itself was passing through a most dangerous crisis. His words sound like a warning of the coming sixteenth century, when he writes to a prelate: "To save a toe, we may at last lose an eye. Let the framework of the Western Church at least remain strong and unimpaired."

To conferences like these Capistran preferred the direct care of souls. He found fertile soil in Trent, a city that was in a deplorable condition as a result of dissension with its overlord, the Prince Bishop Alexander, born prince of Masovia. A letter to the

Bishop (October 17) shows that Capistran held the Bishop himself partly responsible. Capistran begins the letter with expressions of humility, accusing himself of ingratitude for not having yet answered the Bishop's letters. He is an old ox who moves slowly and always needs the goad. Then he generalizes on the ingratitude of men, and the duty of benefactors to increase their favors. All enmities may be overcome by kindness. With surprising frankness he admonishes the dignitary: "Illustrious Prince, look not at what others do, but see what fits your own greatness. Be to your people not a harsh tyrant, a raging boar, but a kind bishop." The long letter develops in detail the way to restore Christian thinking and feeling, mutual charity and harmony, among the people of Trent.

An interesting episode dates from this time. In the case of a youth of good family who was awaiting execution, Capistran begs the sovereign to have pity. Graphically he describes to the Bishop the unspeakable grief of the young man's relatives. When he came down from the pulpit, the weeping women of Trent, he says, pressed round him. The mother's tears streamed down her cheeks. The father begged to die in place of his son. We do not know what the crime was. Justice in those days was very liberal with the death sentence. Capistran adjures the episcopal ruler to pity the poor fellow for the love of Christ, who took upon Himself the disgrace of the Cross. Where youth, ignorance, or seduction intervene, mildness should predominate. A week later Capistran renews his petition. He does not wish to interfere with justice, but a bishop is bound to practice also mercy. The young man is ready, in case of pardon, to join the Franciscan Observance; and a penitent life in such a strict order would satisfy justice to perfection. The outcome is unknown.

Capistran was in Trent for Christmas, 1438, probably also for Lent the following year, and preached at the diocesan synod (April 22). These conferences for priests he published in tract form under the title *Speculum clericorum*, one of his best known books.

This Mirror of the Clergy is characteristic of Capistran's views and methods. Reform of head and members must begin with the clergy. To preach to the clergy was a duty of the preacher of penance. But it cannot be said that preachers always showed tact.

Many indulged in a flood of harsh criticism against prevailing abuses. People relished these severe lectures against the clergy. Bernardine of Siena once remarked that the best way to wake up a sleepy audience is to inveigh against prelates and monks. In harmony with St. Francis, who had such deep veneration for prelates, Franciscan preachers avoided this abuse of the pulpit. Instead of telling the people the shortcomings of the clergy, they gave special instructions to the clergy in closed meetings. Bernardine claims he obtained better results with one conference for priests than he would have obtained by thundering publicly against their faults in twenty Lenten series of sermons.

Capistran followed the same method. His apostolic frankness did not halt before high dignitaries. He warned one hot-headed prelate not to throw ecclesiastical censures carelessly around as little children do flowers. Another prelate gets detailed instructions on his duties to the poor. The general of the Vallombrosians is reminded in detail of all his obligations. An anecdote reveals Capistran at his best. A cardinal wished to go to confession. Capistran demurred, but the prince of the Church insisted. Capistran changed his tone: "Very well, then. Kneel down there. I'm judge now."

The dignity of the priesthood of the New Testament, his frequent theme to the people, is also the soul of his instructions in the Mirror of the Clergy. His text is: "The priests also that come to the Lord, let them be sanctified, lest He strike them" (Exod. 19:22). The book has three parts: first, the reverence due to the clerical state; second, the consequent sanctity binding on the priest; third, the punishments that await an unworthy priest. Canon law is often called the "marrow of theology." It certainly was that to Capistran. In his sermons, books, and letters, law has its full rights.

The third part of his Mirror of the Clergy is by far the longest, the other parts forming rather an introduction. Guided by the story of the Exodus, he details to the clergy the plagues inflicted by canon law. One third of the whole treatise deals with excommunications, thirty-eight of them being reserved to the pope, and sixty to the bishops. The clergy's neglected education caused widespread ignorance of the ecclesiastical regulations. Capistran had much truth on his side when he said that canon law was the "wine of theology." The penitential code reveals what ideals the Church has of the office of the priest. The number and the rigor of ecclesiastical penances must surely have made a wholesome impression on undutiful priests.

What Capistran says of the dignity of the clerical state and of priestly sanctity is even today worthy of meditation. Always guided by Holy Scripture and the Fathers of the Church, the preacher paints the grandeur of the priesthood from seven points of view. The priesthood is the highest majesty on earth, excelling that of the Roman emperor. "Well then, venerable brother, make haste to follow, not Judas, but Peter and the other holy apostles and disciples of Christ. Preserve this excelling dignity in all honor that you may deserve the respect of kings and princes through stainless sanctity." Like Christ, the priest is mediator and intercessor, who reconciles the human race with God. "Therefore, excellent fathers, live so that your prayers may find gracious hearing with God. Christ is mediator by nature, the priest by grace. As shepherd and guide, he has to go ahead of his flock. The priest must be first in knowledge and holiness, just as he is first in dignity and honor. What the head is in the body, the priesthood is in the Church. As long as the head is united to the members, so long can the whole body be healthy. Separate the head from the body, and all hope of life is destroyed. Even if the clerical state deteriorates, as long as it retains union with the members, that is, the obedience of the faithful, so long there is still hope for reform and improvement. But if members are separated from the head, that is, if the faithful refuse obedience, then the whole body is in danger.

"Look at Bohemia. More than 300,000 men have fallen by the sword as a result of the Hussite heresy. Refusing to obey the prelates of the Church, they perished, like the thousands who defied Moses and Aaron. Far above earthly treasures are the values which the priesthood bestows on mankind through the seven sacraments. Through the power of consecration the priest stands higher than the Mother of God. Mind, therefore, and consider, O priest, with what tender care you have to guard and preserve your state, your dignity, your consecration, and how you have to be an example for those living now and later. The eyes of all the people are watching you, or better, us, for I am myself one of you. We are placed before the eyes of men like a target for the arrow. With pain and effort, tears and sweat, priests must daily implore the gift of piety."

The duties of the priestly state, clerical dress for instance, lead Capistran into details. Banquets require six rules of behavior. Some passages sound exceedingly rigorous. The obligation of keeping the tonsure shaven binds under mortal sin. Drinking wine without the addition of water is not free from venial sin. What shame for a cleric to breathe the odor of wine into the faces of other people! The instructions on priestly chastity reveal modest restraint. How these brief sketches were developed orally, we do not know.

The Council had been transferred to Florence (1439). On July 6, 1439, the union of the schismatic Greeks with the Latin Church was celebrated. Bernardine, Capistran, James of the Marches, and Albert of Sarteano, the four pillars of the Observance, attended the solemnity. Cardinal Cesarini read the Bull of Union in Latin, Archbishop Bessarion in Greek. The union was also a victory of the papacy over the conciliar movement. The Greeks confessed expressly that the pope is the head of the universal Church, and that he receives his power, not from the community of the faithful, but directly from Christ. Even if the union had no lasting effect, it enhanced esteem for the papacy at a most critical time.

A few days earlier the council at Basle had deposed "Gabriel, formerly called Eugene IV." But this decree now aroused only disgust, even in such countries as France and Germany. In many places the decree was simply torn from the church doors. The Synod of Basle on November 5 elected the rich Duke Amadeus of Savoy to be pope. He called himself Felix V. But from now on the schismatic Council declined quickly to an inglorious end.

Eugene IV simply went on to reunite also the other schismatical Churches of the East. To the Franciscans belongs the credit for preparing the union with the Armenians. Primadizzi's mission had been a complete success. He gained the good will of the

Armenians, and personally led the delegation to Italy. In a public session of the Council (November 22, 1439) the Armenians returned to the Roman Church. Albert Sarteano, after bringing the Greeks back to the fold, prepared for a still more difficult journey. Eugene IV sent him to Ethiopia, to reunite this ancient Christian country with the Roman Church.

About this time Capistran himself went to the Orient, his destination being Palestine. His journey had nothing to do with reunion, but rather with the disturbed conditions among the Franciscans in the Holy Land. The first Observant custos, the Venetian Jacob Delfino, was evidently not qualified for his office. The chief cause of abuses seems to have been the secular procurator whom the brothers had appointed. A layman of lowly circumstances, altogether uncultured, he had still such influence that all affairs had to go through his hands. The brothers were simply afraid of him.

The Italian Observants wished Delfino to be replaced by Nicholas of Osimo. Osimo was in every respect an exemplary religious. His weak health made him less qualified as itinerant missioner, but he was perfectly qualified to be custos of the Holy Land. At a hint from the Pope the general promptly made him guardian of Jerusalem. But, without explanation, his appointment was just as promptly revoked. Suspicion pointed to intrigues of the procurator. Also in Italy some brothers opposed Osimo's appointment. Albert of Sarteano did his utmost to have Osimo transferred to the Orient, sending petitions to the Pope and to the general, but without success. Osimo himself did not wish the office intended for him. Cardinal Cesarini, protector of the holy places, now took a hand in the matter, and Eugene IV appointed the Sicilian Gandolfi as custos. But when various difficulties arose also against Gandolfi, Cesarini simply ordered his friend Capistran to go over and put things in order.

This journey was Capistran's greatest, but also one about which we know least. Even the time is disputed. The period from the middle of 1439 till the spring of 1440 is the only possible period. According to later accounts he traveled by way of Cyprus, where he became acquainted with the merchant, John Martini of Venice, a good friend of the Observants, in whose house all brothers going to the Holy Land used to stay. This very man Capistran appointed as the new procurator. The former procurator was deposed, and Capistran forbade all brothers any intercourse with him. Anyone disobeying this regulation was sent back to Europe. Under Gandolfi's guidance the reputation of the brothers, tarnished by the past years, was quickly restored.

Capistran's memories of this trip to Palestine seem not to have been pleasant. Surprisingly, his first biographers, Fara, Udine, and Varese, do not even mention it, and he himself seldom spoke of it. He had an almost morbid aversion for the sea. Thus he wrote soon after his return: "The very sight of it is worse than death itself."[1]

[1] Fear of the sea was very common in those days.

CHAPTER XIV

Defender of the Papacy

AFTER his return from Palestine, Capistran was detained in Milan for more than two years. He came there to succeed Bernardine of Siena, who after two decades had returned to preach in the metropolis of Lombardy. What changes those years had brought! Bernardine's perpetual lack of sturdy health had made him an old man. Plagued with gout, he rode a little donkey from place to place. Milan, too, was changed. Political confusion had led to moral disorder. Bernardine's task had been twofold: first, to urge the people to save their souls; secondly, to reconcile Duke Philip Maria to the Pope. The Duke's leaning toward Felix V, and his enmity against Florence, which held faithfully to the Pope, might result in Milan's openly placing itself under obedience to the antipope. But here Bernardine showed lack of human wisdom. He criticized and opposed the slavish attitude of the Milanese toward their tyrant. The laws of the Duke were not the word of God; and his decrees were not relics. If the duke uttered threats, Bernardine smiled and went on preaching as usual. The viscount, fearing public opinion, would not risk the use of force. Instead, he invited Capistran, and the order of the Pope followed.

The old Duke lived in his castle in the midst of the city, separated by courtyards and walls from the outside world. Morbid fear of assassination and his own repulsive ugliness made him shrink from the public eye. A mixture of tyrant and hypocrite, Philip Maria made it a point to call the most renowned pulpit orators to his city. Bernardine at his departure sent Capistran a message, to "go fishing" in Milan where a "great catch" awaited him. Capistran came (1440), but seemed at first destined for a short stay. Late in the evening of Good Friday a messenger handed him a letter from the Pope. Eugene IV was entrusting him with a new and extremely difficult mission, namely, to accompany the Armenian embassy back to their country and there provide for ecclesiastical regulation. Immediately after Easter he was to present himself to the Pope in Florence.

On Holy Saturday, Capistran wrote to Bernardine, his nearest superior, whom he supposed to be in Florence. His long letter shows how immensely difficult he found this papal commission. His health was not good, and he was depressed in mind. Functional disturbances tortured him. "Stomach, spleen, liver, intestines, all are in uproar, and torment me alternately. Only fifty-four years old, I feel like an old worn-out man. I am already a prey of death. I cannot do any more. Father; I simply cannot. I would rather die than live longer. Let the youngsters work and fight. Let the veterans die in peace. The Holy Father knows I never shirked work or danger; dangers on rivers and seas, on roads infested by robbers. As often as he called, I went without delay to face the mighty ones of the world, to the barons of Naples, to tyrants, to the enemies of the Pope. In rain and snow, in summer's heat, I traversed the Campagna, the Papal States, the Marches, Tuscany, and Romagna. I often wonder how I passed through so many perils." Bitter memories well up in him. "Is it not true? The papal court thinks of the Minor brothers when they are needed for a strenuous or dangerous mission; then promptly forgets them and their work and their success. Well, they are simply Minor brothers; sheep meant for the slaughter house."

Obstacles rise before him. Turbulent times, the confusion of wars, make it impossible to take his books along. And then that horrible sea! And apart from personal difficulties, he simply cannot reconcile himself to the idea of sacrificing Italy's best abilities to these uncertain efforts at reunion. The Observants had already given a considerable number of brothers, among them famous preachers, to the East. "It is not proper, for the sake of Armenians and Hindus, to rob Italy, the noble queen of countries." How can he leave Milan, where his work promises the best results? Let Bernardine intercede for him. "If possible, let this chalice be removed. If not, God's holy will be done." This was his last word on that dark Good Friday night.

Resignation appears still clearer in a letter addressed a few days later to a cardinal at the papal court, since he had begun to doubt that Bernardine was in Florence. After explaining his difficulties to the Cardinal, presumably Cesarini, he says: "If the Pope decides otherwise, I will not refuse, even if I have to drag myself there half-dead, or if I have to go through thorns, fire, or water." The chalice did pass by. Duke Philip Maria wrote immediately to the Pope and obtained the revocation of the order, against which the general, William of Casale, had also protested.

Thus Capistran went on laboring in his beloved Milan. Some interruptions occurred. According to tradition, he preached in Rome the praises of Francesca de' Ponziani (St. Frances of Rome), who had died there on March 9th of that year (1440) in the odor of sanctity. He was likewise present with St. Bernardine at the feast of the Portiuncula in Assisi. And here affairs of great importance to the Observants were treated.

The causes which in the thirteenth century had produced the Spirituals were again at work. The Observance, too, had to bring reality into harmony with the ideals of St. Francis. As the Community had been threatened by the Spirituals, so now the Observants were endangered by the extravagant group gathered around the Spaniard, Philip Berbegall. In Italy, too, some were afraid that the program of life and work customary in the Observance was dangerous to perfect Franciscan poverty. Scrupulously they restricted poverty to the mere use of the most necessary means of subsistence. They took offense at the use of silver in church vessels, at the eating of meat, at the style of conventual buildings, which they said were too large and too expensive. The brethren were still bound, they said, to observe literally the evangelical rules of poverty, for instance, to take nothing with them on a journey. Against papal explanation these zealots reacted like the old Spiritualists: only in what the Rule allows may superiors be obeyed. But Spiritual leaders had been great men, like the famous philosophers and theologians John Olivi and Ubertino of Casale. These new zealots were a circle of simple, uneducated lay persons.

All those who stood high in knowledge and education were determined opponents of all exaggerations. They followed the golden middle way, outlined by usage and tradition as well as by papal explanations. And they led holy lives. Leadership was in the best hands.

Nicholas of Osimo, much revered by the Observants, laid down a few guiding principles, which were commented on by Bernardine, Capistran, and others, as also by William of Casale. Capistran's views manifest restrained anger at certain brothers who would not listen to reason. Only what the Rule allows, they say. But who is to decide what is allowed by the Rule: a simple imbecile, or the Apostolic See? Let the brethren abide by the decisions of the Holy See, especially by the explanations of Pope Gregory IX, the friend of St. Francis. Neither these nor later explanations contain anything indicating an obligation to follow literally the evangelical counsel, for instance, not to take anything on a journey. Those who assert this obligation are nothing but disturbers of the peace, and will be punished if they do not cease. What should be considered superfluous was sufficiently pointed out by Pope Clement V, and lately again by the constitutions of Assisi. Why then, he asks, these everlasting scruples and doubts, wherewith we have become an object of aversion and disgust, not only to the Roman Curia, but almost to the whole world?

He goes on to lay open the deeper source of these scruples. "We vow poverty. Well and good. But do we not just as solemnly promise obedience and chastity? I should like to ask you which stands higher, poverty or humility? Verily, one that judges reasonably, will give the higher rank to humility. Many proud paupers have gone with Lucifer down to hell. But those who are humble of heart are triumphant in heaven, like our Queen, the heavenly harpist, who sings: 'The humble hath He exalted.' The culmination of perfection is not poverty, but love built on humility. Poverty, the renunciation of property, is not itself the essence of perfection. It is a support on the way to perfection."

A hundred years earlier these views of Capistran would have sounded half-heretical, not only to the Spirituals, but also to his own confreres. Capistran's views are identical with those defended by St. Thomas Aquinas, which had been attacked by the Franciscan poverty theorists. Capistran merely repeats the earlier arguments when he urges, first, that Christ Himself had allowed the apostles to carry money for the time of need; secondly, that the state of a bishop, though a higher state than that of a religious, does not bind to renunciation of property. What a change had taken place! In the course of a century those difficulties had become meaningless. In practical poverty the Conventuals hardly differed from other religious orders. The Franciscan peculiarity having been given up along the whole line, why dispute about its superiority? The situation was now utterly different. Decisive for the Observants was the ruling of John XXII, the Pope who canonized St. Thomas and brought to victory in the Church the principles which Thomas represented. Like John XXII, Capistran was a jurist and a follower of Aquinas.

Capistran's predilection for Thomas is revealed in his views on poverty. Thus was he able, theoretically at least, to settle the long controversy. As inquisitor he gave the death blow to Fraticellism. As leader of the Observants, he simply followed the way laid down by Thomas Aquinas, the way which the Church has ever since acknowledged as the only secure one. Capistran thus rendered fertile for the whole Church the truly religious values of the spiritual movements of the Order. The Observance takes over and preserves the values of both schools. Bernardine and Capistran are genuine successors of Bonaventure, the noblest and best representative of the Community during the age of struggle. But they are also successors of the great Spiritual leader, Ubertino of Casale. By making devotion to the name of Jesus the very center of their mission activity, they made the mystical currents of spiritualism forever fruitful in the devotional life of the Church. The principles enunciated by Nicholas of Osimo, approved by Bernardine and Capistran, were made known to the Observants of Italy by a circular letter from San Damiano in Assisi on July 31. 1440. The brethren are earnestly admonished, in doubts concerning the discipline of the Order, to abide by the decisions of their superiors. Opponents are threatened with punishments.

Another major problem was that of education. Bernardine, who had long recognized the absolute need of thorough studies, went from Assisi to Perugia, in order to teach moral theology in the convent of Monteripido. This he did by order of the Pope. Cases of crass ignorance had probably been reported to the Roman Curia. These lectures of Bernardine had their amusing side. The guardian at Perugia, a saintly man, thought he had incurred innumerable excommunications and overwhelmed Bernardine with doubts and questions. Many other brothers, too, felt scruples of conscience, probably not altogether without reason. Very few of them possessed the necessary knowledge for hearing confessions. Bernardine suspended one after another of those who fell short of the required knowledge for that office. Probably Capistran, too, lectured to his confreres in the convent near Milan where he had his domicile. But a few occasional lessons could not remedy the evil. A well-ordered plan of studies remained the most urgent problem of the Observants.

Capistran returned to Milan at the latest in September. One of his most important tasks was to keep Duke Philip Maria from publicly acknowledging the antipope. Felix V had been crowned (July 24, 1440), and the Council threatened with excommunication all who would refuse obedience. But a general schism did not seem imminent. England, France, and Castile rejected the antipope. Germany remained neutral. But some German princes and the universities of Cologne, Erfurt, and Vienna declared in favor of Felix V, as did also the German Franciscan Conventuals, under the leadership of Matthias Döring. Affairs in Italy were even less favorable. The two leading powers, Milan and Naples, were doubtful. Alfonso, fighting for the possession of Naples, welcomed the antipope as a means of intimidating the Pope. The Duke of Milan had sent Francesco Sforza, the greatest military leader in Italy, to threaten the boundaries of the Papal States.

Capistran had started his treatise on the plenitude of papal power two years before. This work he now finished and published. Among numerous contemporary treatises, Capistran's is the most vigorous and positive, defending the Catholic traditional doctrine against all conciliar writers. He begins with a prayer to St. Jerome and St. Francis. May Jerome, the conqueror of heresies, take over anew the defense of the truth. May Francis, with his tears and stigmata, eradicate all discord and grant the Church once more unity and peace. He considers, first, the institution of the papacy and the election of the pope; secondly, the limits of the papal power; thirdly, what is to be done when the papal incumbent proves to be incompetent for his office.

That Capistran's theological and canonical exposition had much influence on his contemporaries, may be doubted. Defense of the monarchical constitution of the Church of Christ was necessary. But the opponents of conciliar omnipotence often fell into the opposite extreme. Capistran defends to the full the ancient theories of the authority of the pope also in secular matters. With unmitigated strictness he holds to the doctrine of the two lights and the two swords. As Moses was set by the Lord as master over Pharaoh, so is the pope set over emperors and kings of the whole world, even of the infidel world. The pope can annul the decrees of a council without mentioning the council at all. He can change any positive right. Only the divine law and the natural law are beyond the reach of papal authority. Remarkable is Capistran's formulation of the perfect poverty of Christ, the chief foundation of the adversaries of papal dominion. Capistran invokes the constitution *Quia vir reprobus*, wherein, a hundred years before, Pope John XXII expounded the doctrine of Christ's all-comprehensive dominion. Guided by that constitution, Capistran here rejects the very cornerstone of the old Franciscan theory of poverty.

It is one thing, he argues, to say that Christ had no property rights in anything, and another thing to say that Christ did not avail himself of His property rights. The first is wrong, the second is true, as Scripture testifies.

The tract is not complete. The third part breaks off abruptly, probably, like so many others of his literary works, for want of time. But it did get the attention of opponents. Even Silvio Piccolomini, who at that time still defended jealously the pre-eminence of the council over the pope, wrote a private letter in which he remarks angrily that certain people, in order to ingratiate themselves, would like to subject everything to the pope. Of the antipope, the father-in-law of the Duke of Milan, Capistran speaks in terms of the greatest abhorrence: "We see already the abomination of desolation: this Amadeus of Savoy." That he also preached in this tone in Milan is indicated in his correspondence. On the 5th of October he informs his general, William, of his intention to stay in Milan until the following Easter, unless a higher command calls him elsewhere or schism should capture Milan. What he would do in the second case, he says, he had already publicly announced. "Of four things I abhor one, the other three I choose. I abhor schism. After twenty hard years in the Order, I do not wish the shame and eternal ruin of a schismatic. Three things I choose with a cheerful heart: exile, prison, execution, even under cruel torments." He was spared the choice. He continued his work in Milan, not only till Easter 1441, but until midsummer of the following year.

CHAPTER XV

Capistran as a Writer

ONE series of Lenten sermons was devoted chiefly to the duties of judges, lawyers, and other servants of the public welfare. These detailed instructions he published under the title of Mirror of Conscience. The impulse to publish came from two Milan jurists and statesmen. The dedication reveals the very high esteem which court jurists enjoyed. In almost humanist style, Capistran praises the condescension of his friends. Why do these "men of the sun" come to play with the little "flake of ashes," John Capistrano? Why do they demand honey from the rock and oil from the rough stone? He complains of the continually increasing difficulties of the study of law. One school of law supplants another. Accursius, the light of the century past, had given way to Bartolus and Baldus. In canon law similar conditions prevail. In the turmoil of opinions and views, the poor judge, rather *juris perditus* than *juris peritus*,[1] seems to move in the swarm of lawyers as in a swarm of vipers and dragons; and what is worse, many queer-headed fellows, "to speak of people like myself," make it their business to invent new solutions in order to appear smarter than others. The judge should not follow the opinion of others. He should ascend to the springs of truth instead of drinking from rills.

He descends to minutest detail regarding the judges, the lawyers, the assessors, the consultors, the procurators, the witnesses, and other persons who are concerned with the practice of law. Perfect justice keeps the judge independent of evidence presented, if he is in possession of the truth through other channels. Neither hatred nor favor, neither dread nor greed, but fear of God alone shall dictate the sentence. May we excuse a judge who passes

---

[1] Editor's note: A ruination of law rather than an expert of law.

an unjust sentence out of fear of losing his possessions or even his life? "I have known those who say 'Yes,' jurists and advocates of flesh and dust." A judge must submit to all evils rather than condemn an innocent person. Capistran lashes also the sins of lawyers, their garrulous, lambasting, noisy behavior before court, and especially their ugly greed. In the famous words of Alanus: "Money conquers, money triumphs, money rules." Experience shows that wicked lawyers on their deathbed often lose the gift of speech. During lifetime they used their tongue to twist the truth, now they must leave the world with their tongue tied. Just lawyers, on the other hand, are like soldiers who, suffering from a thousand wounds, still fight for their country. Such lawyers win the crown of eternal life.

Counselors of princes he warns against rash advice. Princes he admonishes to take only counselors of mature age, who excel in upright life and profound knowledge. Good counselors should advise peace rather than war. Legal assistants he warns against directing their clients to conceal truth in order to escape punishment. They tell their clients: "If you tell the truth, you lose your suit"; instead of saying: "If you hide the truth you will lose your soul." If they are not judged by men, they will most surely be judged by God.

He makes excursions to the battlefield. In particular he cites a case that happened when the Saracens stormed Acre (May 10, 1291). A Christian soldier went forward all alone to attack the enemy. His act led to the capture and destruction of this last Christian stronghold in Palestine. Hence his deed was condemned by contemporaries as foolish and rash. Capistran is inclined to judge differently. Granted the probable situation, he comes to the conclusion that this warrior was rather to be praised than censured. He had judged it better to die for his faith and his city than to live in ignominy. Had the others but followed his example, they would doubtlessly have gained the victory, and Acre would still be in Christian hands. Numbers do not mean as much as valor and skill. Knowledge spurs courage. No one is easily afraid in what he knows thoroughly. A small well-trained troop accomplishes more in a battle than a large but unskilled army. He who wills victory must fight skillfully and train his soldiers well.

This leads to a further question. Is flight allowed? Not during the battle, is the answer. Look at Acre. Its inhabitants had the duty of persevering to the end instead of fleeing to the harbor. See how many of them lost their lives just the same. Against a stronghold the aggressor fights with greater danger than the besieged. Still, after the battle is decided, if the enemies have been victors, and the citizens have surrendered, then flight is allowed. Only the clergy are bound to remain. The army with its leaders may retreat, although it would be more perfect to resist and fall in battle.

When Capistran wrote these expositions he had not the least presentiment that this case of conscience would one day become for himself extremely practical. Fifteen years later, as leader of the crusaders in besieged Belgrade, he exemplified literally what he had here written down. But even here, in the midst of a didactic treatise, his longing for the death of a hero breaks through. He admits that there is also an unbloody martyrdom, "To bear insults patiently, to love one's enemies, to preserve peace of heart, to subdue the desires of the flesh with the sword of the spirit, to hunger at a well-set table, to freeze when luxurious clothing is at hand, to live in depressing poverty amid the riches of the world: this is a bloodless martyrdom. Still, death is more bitter than all this. Martyrdom of blood deserves the highest honor."

A related question is that of flight during the time of a plague. This question was frequent. Capistran, basing his view on the Bible and history, sees in plague a scourge of God for the sins of men. The usual counsels for behavior during plagues he interprets chiefly in a spiritual sense. These rules, good in themselves, would be abused if they led anyone to prefer the perishable life of the body, "which we have in common with flies and fleas," to the salvation of the soul.

This topic leads him to give advice also to physicians and patients. Doctors' fees are not forgotten. With his usual sharpness he inveighs against the custom of calling in unbelieving doctors, particularly Jewish doctors. This custom is a serious offense against canon law. But, he is told, even the judges employ Jewish physicians. This he cannot approve. He will not approve even when St. Thomas says that those who are free from the danger of seduction may converse with infidels. Even if popes act thus, it is not laudable. But it is nobody's business to judge them. In general, he speaks very highly of the medical vocation. He addresses the physicians as "illustrious gentlemen and fathers," to whom, after God, our life is entrusted. Although averse to medical assistance, he taught people to honor the physicians who use healing forces created by God. But physicians in their turn must not undervalue the power of prayer. And since they themselves have not much time for prayer, they should look on priests as co-operators. Even an uneducated cleric may, by prayer, obtain more from God than all the healing powers of plants and stones.

This *Mirror of Conscience* contains, he said, sufficient material for four Lenten series, i.e., for two hundred sermons. How could such lectures serve the general public? First, they were prefaced by a homily on the Gospel of the day. Secondly, his reflections were suited to listeners in all states of life. The one great truth he inculcates again and again: "What will it profit a man to gain the whole world, and suffer the loss of his soul?"

These Milanese treatises mark, practically, the end of Capistran's literary activity. Since he was a missioner, the greatest part of his literary works grew out of his pastoral practice. His tracts are simply collections of material for his series of sermons. Careful elaboration was impossible for missioners, who were almost daily in the pulpit. Capistran's general preparation consisted in collecting as much material as possible on all points of faith and morals. Special preparation, generally by night, consisted in a sketch, filled out from his rich collections. When the series of sermons found favor, the preacher was often asked to write them down for wider circles.

This happened more frequently in North Italy, where populations were more dense, wealthy, and cultivated. Thus arose the treatise called *The Last Judgment*. The materials also of this tract, he says, would suffice for four Lenten series. In this work he embodies his own commentary on the Apocalypse, two writings of Giovampaolo di Fondi on the end of the world, and excerpts from famous prophecies on the same theme. Capistran's interest in this subject grew with the years. Later on, in German territory, he loved to explain the fifteen signs of the coming end of the world, which St. Jerome had compiled from Jewish sources. Personally convinced that the end was near, he still carefully avoided all alarming prophecies. He emphasized rather, when occasion offered, the absolute uncertainty of the end.

Four other treatises should be noted. The first discusses eternal punishment, the second blasphemy and perjury, the third fasting, and the fourth the sacrament of penance. These, too, are easily recognized as Lenten series.

For confessors he composed the *Interrogatorium*, a list of questions to aid them in training the faithful to make a good examination of conscience. These questions deal with the Decalogue, the seven capital sins, the corporal and spiritual works of mercy, the three theological and the four cardinal virtues, the seven gifts of the Holy Ghost, the seven sacraments, and the vocational duties of one's state of life. They end with a review of thought, word, and deed. Superstitious views and practices are prominent, as for instance: Do you believe that women can become witches? That they can ride through the air at night? Do you believe that when a man perishes by fire or water, this was decreed for him, and consequently he could not escape? Capistran here opposed belief in witchcraft, whereas Bernardine of Siena was still subject to this popular superstition, and even preached against witches.

Canon law remained his favorite field of literary activity. For systematic work he had no time. His lectures on the Decretals either antedate his entrance into the Order, or are the fruit of his brief activity as teacher. Otherwise his canonical treatises are recapitulations, dealing with penal power and discipline, or they are applications to particular cases. One such case, a marriage question, became famous. Philip Maria had given his natural daughter, Bianca, in marriage to Francesco Sforza. But the marquis of Ferrara, Niccolò d' Este, wanting Bianca for his son Lionello, contested the validity of her marriage to Sforza. More than a hundred jurists were asked for their views, and Capistran is said to have been the only one who defended the validity of the marriage. At any rate the marriage of Bianca with Sforza remained intact. Difficult cases of conscience came to Capistran from all directions. Such work pleased him. "I am glad to have your questions; they give me much pleasure," he writes to one correspondent. But too much is too much. He writes thus: "I received your letter during Lent, at a time when I must admit that I could hardly breathe, so much was demanded of me on all sides." Collections of these cases of conscience were compiled and published.

Finally, the affairs of his Order kept his pen busy. The disputes on Franciscan ideals led to three works: his tract, already mentioned, against the Spanish separatist Philip Berbegall; a commentary on the famous explanation of the Rule given by Clement V; an explanation of the Rule of St. Francis, written in the vernacular. Of his explanation of the Rule of the Poor Clares we shall hear later on. The Third Order also continued to claim his attention. In spite of the energetic measures of Eugene IV, opposition would not come to rest. Capistran's *Defensorium tertii ordinis*, written in 1440, was reprinted twice in recent years.

None of his works is exclusively theoretical. Even his tract, called *The Precious Blood of Christ*, served a most practical purpose. The question was this: Could the supposed relics of the precious blood, preserved and revered in many places of pilgrimage, be adored? Capistran himself, when he was legate to the Netherlands (in January, 1443), investigated one of the most renowned "blood miracles," the one at Brussels. In later years he became involved in the violent controversies on the "blood miracle" of Wilsnack in Germany.

Judging by manuscript remains, we regard as his three most famous works, apart from his later controversies with the Hussites, *The Mirror of Clerics, the Mirror of Conscience*, and his tract on usury. Capistran himself seems to have considered the tract on the authority of the pope the best of his writings. When he rededicated this work to the successor of Eugene IV, the great lover of books,

Nicholas V, the latter in turn gave him 200 gold florins to buy books. In the second half of the fifteenth century the printing press becomes the criterion of literary fame. According to this rule Capistran was little in demand. Only his tract on usury is found among the incunabula. Antonio Amici of Aquila, a century later, had Capistran's juridical works printed. Most of his writings, however, are still in manuscript. But the many works falsely attributed to him prove that he had a wide reputation.

The incompleteness of his works probably discouraged publication. Capistran, it is true, always took a number of books with him on his journeys, mostly in a sack on his back, but he certainly could not take all his literary sources everywhere. Affairs of the Order absorbed him more and more. Bernardine, commissioner general for the reform in Italy, had been long weary of his office. He was made for preaching, so he told the Pope, not for the office of superior. The Pope simply confirmed him in his position (November 10, 1440), but allowed him to accept a coadjutor with all powers of a plenipotentiary for any length of time. But, though acknowledged also by William of Casale, Bernardine had reason to complain of official molestation. New aggressions of Conventuals against Observants seem to have set in toward the end of the year 1440. Capistran, called to assist Bernardine, counteracted these efforts from Milan and obtained a mandate from Eugene IV. Bernardine, from his cherished hermitage in Capriola near Siena, wrote (February 14, 1441) a grateful letter to Capistran.

From another letter of Bernardine we learn that Eugene IV, while he protected the Observance, still insisted on avoiding everything that might justify Conventuals in resisting the reform. In particular Bernardine warns against improper criticism of the Conventuals and against wandering back and forth from one province to another. On the feast of St. Mary Magdalen (July 22) all the vicars, each with one brother, are to meet at the Portiuncula for consultation. Capistran is ordered to visit Bernardine soon after Easter, in Florence. On Whitsunday he is to preside as *visitator* over the provincial chapter in Milan, and then come with some efficient brothers. Furthermore, he will have to act as commander-in-chief.

Capistran had pledged himself to go, after Easter, to Bergamo, but in the end he could not go either to Florence or to Bergamo as some important affair, perhaps the above-mentioned marriage case, kept him in Milan. Bernardine, who was also invited to come to Milan but had to decline, writes to Capistran (May 18), to give his time to the province of Genoa, especially to the newly founded Observant settlement.

Until the beginning of June, Capistran remained in Milan, and he may have been present at the chapter in Assisi toward the end of July. At the latest in November (1441) he is again active in Milan. On November 10, William of Casale confirms him as commissary and *visitator* of the Milan province. The general died soon after (February 22, 1442). In his last hours he was troubled with the thought of not having carefully fulfilled the duties of his office. At the approach of his agony he had himself laid on the floor and begged the surrounding brothers, Conventuals as well as Observants, forgiveness for the faults he had committed.

It is difficult to judge William of Casale correctly. Three successive re-elections as general, an exception in Franciscan history, show that the Conventuals recognized in him one who was averse to revolutionary reforms. On the other hand he was benevolent to the reform and its leaders, to Capistran, for instance, and to St. Colette. To his provincials should probably be attributed those measures that were felt by the Observants to be so antagonistic that even the peaceful Bernardine finally came to complain about Casale. Again we are astonished to find that Pope Eugene IV, the ardent friend of the reform, had such a high opinion of him. Casale enjoyed the great privilege of going unannounced to the Pope. During his sickness the Pope requested regular reports from a cardinal, provided the patient with medical care, and took care of his funeral expenses. The deeper reasons for this papal benevolence may be looked for, not so much in Casale's activity for his Order, as in the unswervingly loyal services he had rendered to the Church in the critical times of the Council of Basle.

CHAPTER XVI

In France and the Netherlands

THE coming election of a general was the first in the reign of Eugene IV. The Pope, thoroughly in favor of the Observance, intended to use the vacancy for his own plans of reform. Instead of appointing a vicar-general for the vacancy, he himself took charge of important affairs personally, appointing a board of brothers to manage current business. The chapter at Padua was to be like the one in Assisi twelve years before, a *capitulum generalissimum*, formed by representatives of both branches, Conventuals and Observants. Albert of Sarteano was the Pope's choice. A happy incident seemed to prepare the way. At the Padua chapter Albert had been unanimously elected provincial. As provincial of Padua he would preside over the meeting. To call the attention of the whole Order still more to his personality, the Pope now appointed him vicar-general of the whole Order.

The end of divisions seemed near. In a letter to Sarteano, but meant for the whole Order, the Pope leaves no room for misunderstanding. He first praises the rapid growth of the Order: "You have marched on into every corner of the earth." Then he turns to question the scholars of the Order. "What are men supposed to think of the Order of St. Francis when they see its different factions, its quarrels, its threatening division? When they see the former home of peace, love, and holy life now breeding dissensions; such discord, beloved sons, is a stain on your Order."

Bernardine's wish to be released from his office, that of vicar-general of the Italian Observants, was now gratified, and the Pope did not appoint a successor. In favor of unification, the Pope further withdrew drew from the Observants the privilege of accepting new foundations, and refused them every exemption from the general. The Observants in general seem not to have shared these rosy hopes of the Pope. Bernardine was against the election of Albert, whether because he considered his election hopeless, or because he feared even worse entanglements if an Observant became general. James of the Marches apparently shared the same view. On the other hand Albert's personality gave grounds for hope. The Conventuals still considered him one of their own party. Capistran seems to have shared the hope of those who believed that the revival of the unification effort at Assisi twelve years before might, with Albert at the head, be successful.

The most difficult preparatory task was laid on the shoulders of Capistran. The Ultramontane provinces, especially those in northern France, the mainstay of the separatists, must be persuaded to give up their position. Hence Sarteano appointed Capistran as his commissary and *visitator* to the north. Eugene IV confirmed this appointment, adding the following commissions: first, to publish everywhere Sarteano's appointment as vicar-general of the whole Order, so that no one could claim ignorance of this fact; secondly, to re-establish everywhere harmony among the brethren; thirdly, to bring back to the obedience of the Pope those who adhered to the schism of Basle; fourthly, to visit all convents and remove prevailing abuses. Capistran's remonstrances met with a prompt veto.

Apparently Capistran started his journey in September. Though cautioned by Pope Eugene to stay out of the antipope's territory, he felt he needed no such cautions, and traveled straight through Savoy to Burgundy. During November and December he visited the Burgundian convents, and celebrated Christmas in Verdun. The journey was unusually fatiguing, particularly for a southerner, now for the first time in mid-European winter. His report dwells on snow, frost, ice, swollen rivers, and dangers from brigands.

The Burgundian provincial resisted, but unsuccessfully. He came with an armed guard, but was deposed. A different kind of difficulty awaited Capistran in St. Colette's convents. This woman, born at Corbie in Flanders, was a staunch character, animated by the most tender piety. In the midst of the great schism she had started twenty convents according to the Rule of St. Clare. William of Casale approved their Rule in 1434. Colette had changed the Rule of St. Clare in some points. But in contrast to the French Observants, these Poor Clares held strictly to the common superior, and refused all offers of independence, in which they saw the stain of disobedience. They acknowledged the energetic activity of the Observants, but said they would not like to live and die with them. Colette's convents were now subject to Capistran's visitation. He met St. Colette, probably in Besançon, where (November 8, 1442) he confirmed the arrangements of the former general concerning Franciscan guidance of these convents. A legend has added details of this meeting. When Capistran demands that Colette eliminate certain rigors from her rule, she prays, and he relents. There may really have been differences of opinion, but hardly in point of strictness. However, if, as seems probable, Capistran demanded from Colette perfect assimilation to the Italian Poor Clares, he was not successful. The Sisters of St. Colette have preserved their own status down to our own days.

Capistran observed with satisfaction that Felix V had scarcely any adherents worthy of note. The rich and mighty Philip of Burgundy and the Netherlands had remained loyal to Eugene IV. Still Capistran encountered many passionate opponents. In Dijon probably occurred the following scene. One of the courtiers, a magister, applied to Felix V the words of Gamaliel, saying that, if the schism of Basle is of human origin, it will fail; but if it is of God, it cannot be destroyed. This skeptical position was held by many so-called neutrals. Capistran answered that the schism had failed already. Not even the flies now bother about Felix V, much less do princes consider him. Those who do hold to him are either such as elected him or are dependent on him or are ashamed to admit their mistake. Like a mad elephant, the magister jumped from his seat, ran toward Capistran, and shouted: "Now you will have to answer. Christ was hung on the Cross. He did not work any miracle there, and nobody was converted. Answer now. Answer." Capistran in turn: "What has that to do with our case?" The other: "You insist that Felix is not pope, because the princes do not acknowledge him." Capistran: "Excuse me, honorable magister. This comparison came from you, not from me. I say that Felix is not pope, because he is not canonically elected." "I have heard many legates on this question," cried the magister, "but never one like you." "Had I thought," said Capistran, "that I would enrage you, I would have kept silent." From Verdun he sent the magister a brief statement of the principles governing the relations of the pope to the council.

One fruit of his contacts with defenders of the antipope was a circular letter to several prelates, in which he introduces the Church as complaining of her own children: "Unhappy mother that I am! Children I have brought up and exalted, but they have despised me. As long as they lived in harmony, they honored the Father, they loved the mother, and all together sought the good pleasure of God. Now all seek their own advantage, not that of my Bridegroom. From lowest to highest, from the prophet to the priest, they serve avarice, practice deceit, and grieve the daughter of my people. Alas, from head to heel there is not a sound spot in my body. Who would not weep and lament? Oh, illustrious mother, where are the children of thy womb? Like a brood of vipers they consume thy bowels; like vampires they suck thy blood; they gnaw at thy vitals, corrode thy joints and nerves. Who will now dare to blame thee for lamenting and weeping? Thou hast become the laughing stock of barbarians, of Tartars, Jews, Saracens, and Turks, of heathens and public sinners, of the wise and of the simple." This jeremiad seems to have been intended primarily for Archbishop Tudeschi of Palermo, a renowned canonist who had been made cardinal by Felix V. He was now at the head of an embassy, intended to move the German Empire to the support of the antipope. Capistran had become personally acquainted with Tudeschi at the court of Naples.

Capistran arrived in the Netherlands at the beginning of 1443. Duke Philip had sent him an urgent invitation. The Duchess desired for her son, the future duke, Charles the Bold, the blessing of the venerable father. He found to his surprise that the Observants in province of Francia were quite ready to meet his wishes. In St. Omer he met an assembly of forty-two brothers, headed by John de Maubert, the vicar-general of the French Observants, who declared their readiness to obey the Pope and Albert Sarteano. They made reservations in regard to the future general, but gave up their special privileges, including those granted at Constance. In the convent of the Poor Clares at St. Omer, strict reform was introduced. With many tears the nuns brought articles, big and small, from their cells into a common room, and again resumed strict community life.

In Bruges, Capistran went to meet the provincial vicar of the Observants, Symon Philomene, whose reputation in Italy was bad. Capistran had strict orders from the Pope to depose him. But Symon, who at first seems to have opposed Capistran's legation, did not after all prove to be, in Capistran's words, "a venomous dragon." On the contrary he proved himself as meek as a lamb, docile and tractable. In the presence of fifty brethren he laid his office into the hands of Capistran, handed him the seal of the province, revoked his appellations, and declared himself satisfied with any provisions the Pope might make. The provincial chapter then re-elected Symon as provincial vicar in canonical form. But Capistran soon discovered that this easy compliance was owing to his own plenitude of powers, and perhaps also to his energetic manner. Scarcely had he left St. Omer when the citizens sent him a letter with the urgent petition to leave everything about the brothers as it was before. Provoked by this improper divulging of the affairs of the Order, he answered the magistrate in the words of Samson: "Had you not plowed with my heifer, you had not found out my riddle" (Judg. 14:18). The general chapter at Padua, he added, would certainly find a solution that would bring general satisfaction. Let them trust to the prudence of the Pope.

To save time, since he had to be in Padua by the beginning of June he appointed some commissaries. To Paris he sent John Maubert. For the German provinces he had already appointed Henry Werl, the able provincial of the province of Cologne.

A last adventure awaited him on the banks of the Po. The ferryman refused to transport him, his three companions, and his beast of burden, to the other shore. Capistran walked up and down, helpless, until all at once he noticed an abandoned boat, with only its nose above the water. With the donkey's halter the brothers pulled the boat to the shore, emptied out sand and mud, and put it in condition as best they could. Capistran encouraged them. Trusting in God's protection, he blessed the stream, and entered the boat, together with the brothers and the donkey. The hazardous enterprise ended successfully.

About two thousand brothers are said to have assembled in Padua (June 9, 1443). But the German Franciscans were poorly represented. Under the leadership of the Saxon provincial, Matthias Döring, most of them adhered to the antipope, and Matthias called an opposition chapter in Berne. Further, keeping the authorship strictly secret, he wrote a book called *Refutation of Papal Primacy*, one of the most radical conciliar treatises of the fifteenth century. The book attempted to give new life to the *Defensor pacis*, written by Marsilius of Padua more than a hundred years before. Like Marsilius, Döring denies to the Church all right in secular affairs. He subjects the Church to the emperor, and reserves the highest power in matters ecclesiastical to the council.

Twelve years had passed since the last *capitulum generalissimum* in Assisi. How strained the relations between Conventuals and Observants had become was revealed at once in ugly fashion.

William of Casale's election at Assisi, twelve years before, was marked with the greatest harmony. But at Padua, from the very beginning, regrettable scenes were witnessed. The Conventuals came to the chapter firmly determined to prevent by all means the election of any Observant, even that of Albert. When Sarteano in the opening session read the papal message, in which Eugene IV probably made known his wish regarding the person he would like to see elected, the storm broke loose. Clamoring, "Liberty, liberty," a crowd of Conventuals stormed the platform, tore the papal letter from Albert's hands, and dragged Albert himself out of the room. His cry that they were all excommunicated was drowned by the roaring noise. Some of the Observants are said to have received a thrashing. A contemporary chronicler says he could tell still worse things, but prefers silence.

The whole procedure proved that Bernardine of Siena had

judged the situation correctly. He now calmed the storm with the declaration that, as far as he was concerned, neither Albert nor any other Observant should be chosen. In the ensuing election he gave his vote to Antonio Rusconi, a moderate Conventual. Rusconi actually became general. When the chapter ended, both parties hurried to see the Pope, who had transferred his residence from Florence to Siena. Capistran, the leader of the Observant delegation, was by now completely disillusioned. At the audience he said bluntly: "Holy Father, with a crowd like that we can no longer live together." The Pope confirmed the general, elected against his wishes, out of consideration for the Duke of Milan, from whose territory Rusconi came. Further, the new general was an outstanding pulpit orator and a great scholar. Indignant at the events that marked the election, the Pope was now willing to grant full separation by giving the reform its own independent general. But the Italian Observants were still afraid of this last decisive step. They wished to preserve union in the family of St. Francis by having at least a common head. On the other hand they wished such a measure of liberty as would free them from being restrained by provincials or general. Eugene IV consented, and appointed a commission of four cardinals to decide all questions that might emerge.

Capistran took care of the preliminary work. The general vicariate for the Observants was made permanent, and was changed into two general vicariates, independent of each other: cismontane and ultramontane. The jurisdictional limitation of vicars, as well as the regulation of their relation to general and ministers, proved difficult. The monastery of Siena saw many days of animated discussions. The Observants, favored by the Pope, succeeded in having the faculties of the general assigned in full measure to the two vicars-general of the reform. Still the general remained a point of unity since he appointed or at least confirmed the vicars-general, since he alone could summon a general chapter, also of the Observants, and since he had the right to inspect the houses of the Observants and the activities of the vicars-general. On the other hand infliction of penances on one vicar depended on the consent of all other vicars. And provincial vicars and guardians were elected by the Observants themselves. Moreover, Conventuals were permitted to join the Observants, but Observants could not withdraw from their own superiors. The prohibition laid on the reform of taking over houses from the Conventuals remained in force. Whether the appointment of the two Observant vicars was granted to the general for good, or only for this first instance, is doubtful. In any case it was scarcely more than a formality, since the Pope himself commanded the new general to install Capistran as vicar-general for the cismontanes, and John Maubert for the ultramontanes.

Thus the chapter of Padua marks another epoch in the development of the Franciscan Order. Separation of the two orders was now a reality. Only personal union remained. Besides, the reform itself was divided into two independent families. Lastly, a section of the German Conventuals did not acknowledge the new general at all, but put up an antigeneral in the person of Matthias Döring.

Thus the reputation of the Order suffered seriously. The scandalous events of the chapter in Padua could not be hidden from the public. They were still fresh in memory when, fourteen years later. Conventuals and Observants prepared to meet again at a general chapter in Milan. Francis Sforza, by that time duke of Milan, declared he would prevent the repetition of such excesses in his capital.

Albert of Sarteano was a special target of gossip. Conventuals said he was the cause of the whole scandal by his ambition for the generalate. The well-deserving man grieved over the affair more than was necessary. Even in the pulpit he expatiated on the recent chapter. A contemporary Franciscan, Bernardine of Aquila, was present in the square of Perugia and heard Albert justify himself. With a vehemence no one had ever seen in him before, he turned against the Conventuals with a philippic so furious that a Conventual, a master in theology, turned away bathed in perspiration.

Other Observants, too, were affected. Many brothers could not forgive Bernardine and James of the Marches the position they had taken. Thus Bernardine's chalice of bitterness was filled up in his last years. His own confreres drew away from him, saying he had given up the fight for the reform. Happily for the Observance, its fate now rested in the hands of a man who possessed sufficient energy to overcome resistance in its own ranks, and to lead it on into the future with a firm hand.

CHAPTER XVII

Vicar-general of the Observants

CAPISTRAN, now leader of the cismontane Observants, went first to Monte Alverno, to make a retreat. On September 24, the octave of the Stigmata of St. Francis, he sent a detailed circular to his new subordinates. From the height of the memorable mount he looks down with grateful heart at the growth of the Observance. It has found its way to the ends of the earth. To that family of his he gives the testimony of great sanctity. For his exalted office he feels himself altogether unfit, and that not only by reason of his advanced age. He considers that his appointment is rather a punishment for the numerous faults of his wretched life. But, being now prince over the house of Israel, he must exhort them to strict observance of the Rule.

His twelve chapters enter into the smallest details. Nothing is overlooked, not even the hint to be careful with the light in their cells, to avoid the danger of fire. Nearest to his heart is the rising generation, Full seventeen years is the age for acceptance of novices. Let the vicars not be in a hurry with reception. Candidates must be virile, not look like boys; they must be able to bear the burden of the religious life. Never deceive young people. On the contrary reveal to applicants the full strictness of the life. Tell them they can no longer wear shoes or shirts, and they are to expect no bed-linen: they are never to put off their habit, even for sleep or in sickness. Novices either give their clothes away or send them home.

Thorough training of youth was Pope Eugene IV's repeated injunction. Every Observant province must establish a special house of studies. Brothers qualified for study are exempted from other wearisome work, even from copying books. With ardent words he praises the office of preacher. Then he emphasizes the importance of poverty. This delicate point of monastic discipline needs constant watchfulness. All that the brothers have should be brought to superiors for inspection. Prohibition of money is to be carried through in all strictness. Even gifts of money deposited on the altar are not to be kept, and everything in the nature of real estate must be banished. In begging they are to give the Conventuals precedence. The visitators should treat failing brothers with moderation, and guard their reputation when there is question of secret faults. The purpose of penance is the improvement of the failing brother. The superiors shall not punish when excited. Scourging must be done by the culprits themselves.

During hard work the brothers are allowed to eat meat more than once a day. But when they are guests, they shall not demand meat, but be satisfied with what is offered by their host. Certain exaggerated gestures of esteem he abolishes, for instance, that of going on one's knees as often as one is addressed by a superior. Subordinates shall not be excessively burdened with work, lest religious life suffer. At least twice a week they shall go to confession. Those who are not priests go to Communion every two weeks. He warns earnestly against useless gossip and correspondence, and still more against aimless running back and forth from one settlement to another. They must not visit Rome without express permission of their superiors. This point, he says, was emphasized by Pope Eugene IV himself. He aims at removing even the more remote dangers to chastity. They shall permit nuns to confess only once a month. In the presence of seculars the brothers shall not take off their habit when bathing, but may use a lighter tunic. Dramatic presentations that involve change of costume are forbidden (i.e., in mystery plays).

Finally Capistran inculcates absolute fidelity and loyalty to the Apostolic See. Provincial vicars must take the oath of fidelity to Holy Church, since the schism, like a cancer, threatens to turn into heresy. Capistran's closing words are dedicated to the mission among the heathens or, as he calls it, "the ideal of martyrdom." No brother shall be obliged to go. He warns against imprudent fervor. Those chosen must be free from human and worldly ambitions, low in their own estimation, patient in difficulties, kind in their conduct, entirely on fire with love of God and neighbor. Let them long for martyrdom in order to glorify God's power, truthfulness, and kindness, and to save souls. With stirring eloquence the lonely writer on Monte Alverno depicts what the martyrs have suffered for Christ, and paints with glowing colors the joys that await the missioner when he has courageously shared the ignominy of the Cross.

This beautiful letter, which deserves to be taken to heart even today, is a splendid monument to the prince of the Franciscan Observance. The ardent appeal must have made the deepest impression on the brothers. They knew Capistran. What he asked of others he did himself. With the exactness of a novice the vicar-general observed even the smallest prescriptions of the Rule.

His office imposed much travel. His first journey seems to have brought him to Naples, where great political changes had just occurred. Alfonso had vanquished René. The Pope now abandoned resistance and made an agreement with the victorious King (June 14, 1443), acknowledging Alfonso as feudal lord of Naples. The King in turn acknowledged Eugene IV as legitimate Pope, thus assuring the Pope's victory over his antagonists at Basle and over his other political opponents in Italy. King Alfonso recalled his subjects, among them Archbishop Tudeschi of Palermo, from Basle. While Capistran was composing his circular on Monte Alverno, the Pope entered Rome.

In the tedious negotiations that followed, Capistran was papal envoy. He was invoked as mediator by Aquila, which had always sided with the Angevins and had resisted the Aragonese to the utmost. The victor decided to reduce this stubborn opponent to impotence. Destruction, as in the days of the Hohenstaufens, threatened the city anew, but Capistran succeeded, at the last moment, in reconciling King and city, thus saving his beloved Aquila from ruin. In our own times Aquila has erected a marble memorial, containing the names of those to whom the community feels itself most indebted. The long list is justly headed by the name of John Capistran. King Alfonso had no cause to regret his act of mercy. He later told Capistran personally that this flourishing center of the Abruzzi brought him annually a revenue of 110,000 ducats.

At the beginning of 1444, Capistran was occupied with important affairs in Rome. His circular from Alverno had met with opposition, the chapter on studies being the bone of contention. This measure, today almost self-understood, met obstacles. The dispensations granted to professors and pupils, especially to those studying in universities, had indirectly caused the relaxation of discipline and thereby contributed a great deal to the decay of religious life in the Order. Some excessively zealous brothers went so far as to put the whole blame for weakened discipline on higher studies. This idea now awoke to new life. Should the reform, too, be now led astray? The prescription about houses of study required that some of the brothers devote themselves entirely to study, and this Capistran expressly demanded. That meant residence at universities to prepare themselves for their teaching office. And we must remember that in those days the demands for systematic theological knowledge in candidates for the priesthood were very low. Bishops were, as a rule, satisfied if candidates obtained an indispensable minimum of knowledge by private lessons, given by other priests or in a monastery. Why should the Observants, dedicated principally to the contemplative life, not be satisfied with this average knowledge?

The leaders of the reform thought otherwise. They saw clearly that this low level in average clerical education represented a serious defect in the Church, and that consequently one of the first obligations of an Order which aimed at general reform of the whole Church was to make order in its own house. Bernardine's dogma said that the deeper reason for the serious defects in Italian moral and religious life lay in the great ignorance of clergy and people. Thoroughgoing and profound revival of Christian doctrine was the very aim of the Franciscan itinerants. But for this great mission only such brothers were qualified as far excelled the average. Preachers, untrained and shallow, had often degenerated into absurdity. Unlettered brothers, trying to cover their want of knowledge and ability by imitating certain exterior manners of great pulpit orators, had evoked the ridicule of the humanists, who thereby justified their own dislike of religious orders, and led some Observants to demand the adoption of humanist studies to meet the humanists with their own weapons.

What Capistran demanded was thorough, comprehensive education of clerics and priests, to make them good preachers and pastors of souls. On this point he would not yield, however much hurt by criticism. "Brother John," it was freely predicted, "will fail in this plan, just as he failed to unify the Order." Capistran did not let himself be discouraged. The circular from the Observant monastery in Trastevere (Rome) to all vicars in Italy, is sharp in tone, indicating determination to break down resistance in a vital question. As long as he was not superior, he writes, they had willingly followed him. Now they have become his opponents. This seems to him surprising, especially since the matter concerns the glorification of God, the welfare of souls, and the growth of the Observance, things for which he certainly might have expected the most willing obedience.

His displeasure strikes primarily those brothers who were guided, not by objective reasons, but by their own ease and comfort, and their inborn dislike of books, a vice which Capistran, the great lover of literature, loathed above all things. He finds no term strong enough to stigmatize this spiritual stupidity. "The priest cannot dispense holiness if he does not possess it himself. The Church needs the power of the keys. Is no science necessary for the proper use of those keys? Is knowledge not counted among the seven gifts of the Holy Ghost? O ignorance, thou foolish and blind mother of all errors, who has now beguiled thee? How can a person know if he does not learn? How can he learn without teachers? O stupid and idle gossip of the ignorant! An enemy of nature is he who despises knowledge: the longing for knowledge lies in the nature of man. Therefore he that despises knowledge sins against human nature. To neglect the gifts of the Holy Ghost is to despise the Spirit who gives those gifts. Beware, dearest ones, lest you fall under the curse which says: 'Wisdom will not enter into a malicious soul, nor dwell in a body subject to sins.' Do you consider it more useful to spend your time in complaints and criticism, in idle conversations, in faultfinding, than to spend it in the attainment of knowledge?

"You prophesy a repetition of the same failure that met my plan of reform. Was it wrong that I labored with all my power for the reform of the whole Order? If only I could see that reform reached before I depart from this world! I wish for nothing but your progress, your prosperity and honor. Forgive me, please, that I am planning to lift you higher. Or are you, without study, able to have a clear idea of faith, hope, and charity, prudence, fortitude, temperance, and the other virtues? Of the gifts, of the corporal and spiritual works of mercy; of the difference of sins, their degrees and species? Must you not deal with these things? How do you expect to justify your ignorance? How shall your light shine before men if you yourselves are obscurantists, hiding in the general darkness? Together with your followers you will fall into the ditch.

"Further, do you not need guardians? Has not the guardian to take care of souls? Is he able to do that without having studied? As to the preacher: if he learns only stories, or recites his script like a grind organ, will he not become the laughing stock of the streets? How disgraceful is the reproach of heresy! What a shame when preachers have to recant in the one sermon what they said in the former, like the dog returning to his vomit. And you, my father confessors, how quickly you lift your hands for absolution! Do you realize that the judge is responsible for false sentences? Do you not believe that the Lord will demand an account of your ignorance? The lips of the priest shall keep knowledge, and they shall seek the law at his mouth: because he is the angel of the Lord of hosts (Mal. 2:7). But angel, messenger, he will not be if he does not announce the truth; and the truth is not made known by one who does not know it; and one cannot know it unless he learns it; and he cannot learn it without a teacher. And you flee from teachers and still feel satisfied. The crafty devil will test your ignorance as he once did Eve's.

"Let no one claim the example of St. Francis. Only to a very few, and by miracle, was knowledge granted without studies. Did not Anthony of Padua, with St. Francis' permission, spend five uninterrupted years in study? The danger lies not in knowledge, but in the abuse of knowledge."

As to himself, he concludes, there is no return. "It is the will of our Holy Father Eugene IV, and also my wish, that brethren who are capable give themselves to study. If you do not obey, let the fault be on your conscience, not on mine. I hereby command, under obedience, all vicars to read this circular to the brothers and to explain it clearly."

Capistran did not merely decree, he put his hand to the work himself. At times he exercised the teacher's office. But, above all, he prepared the upsurge of study among the Italian Observants. The first necessity was a manual for confessors. The *Summa Pisana* of the Dominican Bartholomew a Sancto Concordio, who had died a hundred years before, served as a basis. To this work Nicholas Osimo had, about 1440, independently of Capistran, composed a supplement. But Osimo's work, called *Quadriga*, did not meet with Capistran's approval. Probably by order of Bernardine of Siena, who was then vicar-general, he had subjected the *Pisanella* as well as the *Quadriga* to a thorough revision. On the basis of this preliminary work Osimo now prepared an improved edition of the *Quadriga*, which appeared toward the end of 1444 in the convent of the Holy Angels at Milan.

The stimulus given by Capistran led to rich fruit. Since the publication of the *Pisana* this kind of literature had ceased almost entirely for a century. It now took a new swing upward, and its promoters were the Observants of northern Italy. In the second half of the fifteenth century appeared the popular manual, *The Confessional*, by the Milanese, Bartholomew de Caimis; then the *Summa* of Baptist Salis, of the Genoese province; and finally the famous *Summa angelica* by Angelus Chiovasso. Capistran's influence can easily be recognized in the predominantly juridical tone of these works. Together with the *Corpus Juris Canonici* these summas were now the chief pillars of ecclesiastical law. Capistran's success went far beyond the bounds of his family. In the field of practical theology the Franciscan Observant held, by the end of the Middle Ages, the undoubted leadership. The *Summa angelica* supplanted all other compendiums. Violently attacked by Luther, it was honored as one of the books which he threw into the fire at Wittenberg in 1520.

Another important affair probably kept Capistran busy in Rome at the beginning of 1444. In the first decades of the fifteenth century the Turks had been suddenly and providentially halted in their advance against Hungary. They had indeed won a splendid victory over King Sigismund of Hungary at Nicopolis (1396). But a few years later the Mongolians from the east broke into the Turkish Empire. The battle of Angora (1402) saw the Turkish power collapse. But, sad to say, Europe neglected this fine opportunity. While the Christian West wasted its power in political and ecclesiastical wrangles, the Turks had time to recuperate. Under Murad II (1421-51) the struggle began again. With the fall of Semendria (1439) all Serbia came under Turkish control. A year later Murad stood before Belgrade, which blocked his way to Hungary.

Hungary was divided by two contenders for the throne. Albrecht II of Hapsburg, son-in-law of Emperor Sigismund and king of Bohemia and Hungary, was a ruler of rare qualities, who would have been able to master the Turks. But he died in the second year of his reign. His posthumous son, Ladislaus, was rejected, both by Bohemia and by Hungary. Bohemia entered into a period of anarchy. The leader of the Utraquist nobility, the ambitious George Podebrad, who was only twenty years old, seized the reins of government. In Hungary too, though the Polish king, Wladislaus, had the larger following, Ladislaus of Hapsburg gained a smaller part of the nobility. Protection of the southern Hungarian borders was entrusted by Wladislaus to a nobleman from Wallachia, John Hunyadi, who in the service of Emperor Sigismund had received knighthood and the castle of Hunyad. To honor Hunyadi's military prowess against the Hussites, Sigismund had made him voivode of Transylvania and count of Temesvar.

Hunyadi now opened war against the Crescent and for many years he was the soul of that war. In the spring of 1441, while flying columns of the Turks were seriously damaging southern Hungary, Hunyadi surprised and defeated their main army near Belgrade. The next year he drove two other Turkish armies out of Transylvania. The West now began to notice this southeastern storm center. In Capistran's correspondence we find in these years for the first time notices regarding the Turks. His circular to the adherents of the Council of Basle had deplored the madness of ecclesiastical dissension in view of the danger threatening Hungary from the Turks. On his journey to Burgundy he had heard of the Hungarian victory, for which Pope Eugene IV had ordered solemn thanksgiving services in Florence. The same was done by the Duke of Burgundy in Dijon, and by many prelates in their sees. From Brussels, Capistran wrote to the provincial of Cologne, encouraging him to promote similar celebrations.

Now, at the beginning of 1444, Eugene IV addressed an encyclical letter to Christendom, admonishing all nations to prosecute the war so happily commenced. Among his messengers were many Observants. Albert of Sarteano and James of the Marches were sent to the Patriarch of Aquileia. To Hungary the Pope sent his best diplomat, Cardinal Cesarini, who arranged an armistice in the struggle for the throne. Venice fitted out a powerful fleet. But the rulers of the West in general paid little attention to the Pope's appeal. Only from the lower classes were troops recruited to go to Hungary. In July, 1443, the crusaders had marched into Serbia under the leadership of Wladislaus and Hunyadi. On November 3 the Turks were defeated in the bloody battle of Nisch. The crusaders pushed southeast, beyond Sofia, but approaching winter suspended further activities. The Turks, following the returning victors, suffered one more defeat on Christmas Eve.

In that same year (1443) the celebrated Skanderbeg, the Albanian George Kastriota, was repeatedly successful in his operations against the Turks. Hence Murad II was inclined to make peace. Thus things in Hungary looked fairly well. But then, quite suddenly, the Sultan of Egypt started a furious attack on Rhodes, which was defended by the Knights of St. John. To save Rhodes, this most important Christian bulwark in the East, a great fleet was necessary, but the finances of the Pope, just returned to the devastated Papal States, were exhausted. He appealed to the sacrificial spirit of the Christian world. The fiery pontiff had far-reaching plans. The fleet, so he intended, was to drive on far beyond Rhodes and prepare the reconquest of the Holy Land. He again chose Observants to preach the crusade and collect gifts for the good cause.

This crusade probably led Capistran, at the beginning of 1444, to Rome. Soon afterward he went to Naples. King Alfonso was the first to be approached, since he had promised, in the treaty of Terracina, to build warships for use against the Turks. During the spring Capistran reached Sicily, where the royal governor prepared a splendid reception for him in Palermo. A solemn procession met him a mile from the city. Refusing the invitation to take quarters in the royal palace, he went to live with his confreres. His sermons drew enormous crowds, so dense that at times he could hardly move. People cut pieces from his habit. These signs of veneration and enthusiasm were not uncommon when great preachers appeared in the midst of a warmhearted and effervescent Christian people.

At the height of his Sicilian activity he received a message from the continent which affected him deeply. He interrupted his work and returned straight to Italy. On May 20 his most beloved confrere, Bernardine of Siena, had died in Aquila.

CHAPTER XVIII

Bernardine's Death and Canonization

IN spite of growing illness Bernardine had spent his last year in preaching, especially in Vicenza, Verona, and Venice. At Siena he finished his treatise on the eight beatitudes. The death of Brother Vincent, his inseparable companion for the last twenty-two years, gave his health a serious shock. "My life is now worse than death," he said, while preaching over the departed brother. His confreres continued to stand aloof. In April, 1444, he preached in his native city of Massa, then torn by party strife. More effective than his sermons was the miraculous healing of a Spaniard, a leper, who led a miserable life outside the city. When this man, meeting Bernardine, begged him for footwear, Bernardine promptly took off his sandals and gave them to him. As he walked away the leper felt violent pains in the soles of his feet. Thinking of sharp pebbles, he took off the sandals. The crusts were falling from his wounds and paining the healthy flesh beneath. As he moved on, the incident was repeated. Soon he became aware that the terrible sickness had left him entirely.

At the end of April, Bernardine took leave of his confreres in Capriola. Thinking to find Capistran in the Abruzzi, he went there. Approaching death may have prompted him to visit his most faithful friend and confrere, who was now also his superior, with the hope of dying in his arms. He passed through Perugia, Assisi, Foligno, and Spoleto, preaching as he went. In Rieti, where he arrived on May 12, the mayor received him with high honors, and the citizens met him with a torchlight procession. Bernardine was hardly able to stand. But at the banquet which the mayor gave in his honor he was so cheerful that the guests remarked they had never had such a happy meal.

However, when he came near Aquila all strength left him and he was carried by the brothers on a stretcher into the city. The

Conventuals of San Francesco put him to rest in the cell which stood always ready for Capistran. Even in death the apostle of Italy was still the peacemaker. Aquila was torn by bloody perils. During the preceding Holy Week seven prominent citizens had been slain. The revenge was planned for the feast of Christ's Ascension. On the eve of this day, Wednesday, May 20, 10 o'clock at night. Bernardine died.

When his corpse was laid out on Ascension Day, news spread that a poor little boy had been suddenly cured. Pasquale de Ciculo, twelve years old, a cripple from birth, used to sit at the church door selling candles. As soon as he saw Bernardine's body on the bier, he dragged himself there, praying: "Bernardine, I know that you are a saint. On my knees I recommend myself to you. Pray to our Lord Jesus for me." The report that Pasquale was jumping around in perfect health brought the whole city into great commotion, with bells pealing from all church towers.

The next morning Bernardine's body was carried in triumph through the streets; tears flowed freely, and the hostile parties made peace. When Capistran arrived, probably in the first half of June, Bernardine had not yet been buried. His hands and forehead showed spots, but the body as a whole remained intact. On June 13, Capistran was eyewitness of a wonder, which is referred to repeatedly in his sermons and letters. The solemn mood evoked by Bernardine's death quickly evaporated, and feuds pursued their usual way. Sunday, June 14, was the day appointed for battle. A second time Bernardine saved the city from blood. On the Saturday before, blood came forth from his closed coffin and fell on the church floor. At once the coffin was opened. The blood came from the nose, and had saturated his habit and pillow. Twenty-four days had elapsed since his death, yet the blood looked like that of a living person. The people eagerly gathered it up with cloths. Later, when Bernardine's relics were everywhere in demand, Capistran often lamented that he had secured only a portion of this precious relic. He now transferred Bernardine's body from the coffin of wood to one of iron, bound with iron chains. This coffin he deposited in a chapel of the Franciscan church, since he had no doubt that

Bernardine would shortly be canonized.

All Italy mourned the death of the great missioner. Numerous cities, especially the cities of northern Italy such as Treviso, Vicenza, and Padua, prepared grandiose celebrations. In central Italy, Siena and Perugia vied with each other. The Perugian city council decreed an imposing funeral celebration for Bernardine, "the mirror and model of preachers, the restorer of Christian faith, the lover and advocate of the Perugian people." The celebration took place on Sunday, June 14. In the market place, in front of the cathedral, stood the catafalque, covered with precious hangings, illuminated by an ocean of lights. The Bishop held the services, and all the religious orders of the city were present with lighted candles. A young Augustinian delivered the memorial sermon, in which he declared that Bernardine was already among the saints, in view of the miracles which he was daily working. Siena held its funeral services on June 15. The day was an official holiday; all business houses remained closed. The report from Aquila covering Bernardine's last hours and the miracles that followed was publicly read. An Observant preached. For three days processions crossed the city, with the officials, the Bishop, and the abbots participating. These scenes were repeated in the other cities and villages of the republic. The expenses were born by the state.

The Sienese naturally burned with longing to bring the corpse of their esteemed fellow citizen back home. On June 19 they sent out two delegations: one to Rome, one to Aquila. The latter, on July 19, sent back certified reports of thirty miracles wrought at Bernardine's grave. But the corpse they could not obtain. At Rome, Eugene IV expressed the best hopes for speedy canonization. But return of the body, he said, would lead to most serious disturbances of the peace. Aquila was determined to frustrate every attempt of this kind even by force of arms. Even today the highest honor for an Italian city is that of harboring the body of a saint. Religious reasons were supported by material advantages. The grave of Bernardine would draw a new stream of pilgrims to Aquila. The Sienese had to be contented with Bernardine's poor garments and personal books. His donkey carried these belongings of his dead master back to

Siena. There the people fell on him with scissors and knives, till the poor animal was completely cropped. Everyone wanted a tuft of hair as souvenir.

Siena remained fervent in its efforts for early canonization. Pope Eugene IV himself counted on rapid procedure. To advance the great reformer of Italy to the dignity of the altar would give more lasting effect to the efforts of the reforming Pope. Canonical procedure, not having the strict forms and rules of our time, varied from one case to another. Eugene IV appointed a commission of three cardinals, who in turn selected two bishops as a subcommission. But the chief burden rested on Capistran's shoulders. His intimate relations with the departed, and still more his ability in legal matters, placed the affair almost entirely into his hands. For nearly six years this new obligation taxed his time and attention to the utmost. The two chief tasks were: proof of heroic virtues in the life of the deceased, and examination of the miracles through his intercession. In contrast to our modern attitude, emphasis at that time lay upon the miracles. Only two miracles are required today for beatification, and two more for canonization, whereas heroism in virtue is the chief problem. But at that time the number of miracles was the most decisive factor. Hence the necessity of investigating miracles on the spot. Reliable testimonies on Bernardine's conduct had also of course to be officially recorded. Sermons in later years show how circumspectly Capistran proceeded. Results were submitted to the commission in Rome or to the Pope. February 2, 1445, Capistran reports three readings in public consistory of reports of the miracles wrought through the intercession of his blessed confrere.

Of Capistran's ceaseless journeys during these six years, Aquila and Rome are the two poles. Only toward the end of the long process did he again extend his visits to northern Italy. Even preaching had occasionally to be sacrificed. Toward the end of 1444 he came to Rome, where two important affairs besides the process kept him for several weeks.

From the East had come news of the catastrophe near Varna. The Hungarians, against Cesarini's advice, had accepted the peace which Murad II offered. But when Murad went to Asia, the Hungarians, urged by Christian admirals, violated the treaty and went south under Wladislaus and Hunyadi. Murad returned with lightning speed from Asia and met the crusaders at Varna (November 10, 1444). Wladislaus and Hunyadi retreated. A Janizary slew Cesarini, the cardinal legate. Hunyadi's series of successful campaigns had come to nought.

The defeat at Varna plunged the West into deep mourning. Capistran lamented the loss of his old friend Cesarini. Eugene IV, who did not lose courage, called on Christendom to renew the war against the Crescent. On January 13, 1445, Capistran, with other Observants, was appointed to preach the crusade.

A few days before this, the Pope empowered the two vicars-general of the Observants, Capistran and Maubert, to start each fourteen new colonies. And the Pope's mind found still clearer expression when he transferred the Roman cloister, Ara Coeli, to the Observants. Roman pilgrims are well acquainted with this beautiful church, situated on the northern summit of the Capitoline, and approached by a stairway of 148 marble steps. This stairway, 50 feet wide, is a votive gift of Rome to the Queen of Heaven at the time of the plague. Ara Coeli stands on the site of one of the greatest sanctuaries of pagan Rome, the temple of Juno. In earlier ages Benedictines had lived there. Since the time of its transfer to the Franciscans by Pope Innocent IV, it had been the residence of the general of the whole Order. As in many other Conventual monasteries, discipline had relaxed; buildings and services were neglected. The inhabitants of this cloister, said Eugene IV, bear the name of St. Francis but do not keep his Rule. He insisted that in this cloister, distinguished by its site, such brethren were required as would by their very life edify visitors. Hence he removed the Conventuals, and three Roman citizens took over the administration. All real estate was sold, and the money used for church and cloister. Capistran now made of Ara Coeli a center for all Observants by giving also the ultramontane representative a home there. From all nations he invited brothers to come to Ara Coeli to assist their countrymen who might visit Rome as pilgrims.

Also among the Poor Clares the Observance made gratifying progress. During this Roman sojourn Capistran wrote for them an explanation of the Rule, urged to do so by Abbess Elizabeth of the Corpus Christi convent in Milan.

In general, relations between Observants and Conventuals were now better, since the Observants, guided by their own superiors, could develop unmolested. Numerous foundations reveal an immense influx of novices. Now that complaints and quarrels had ceased, said the Pope, the Observants enjoyed the tranquillity indispensable for study and meditation. The new order of things was to be made permanent. Rusconi's confirmation of the two Observant vicars-general had been intended to last only till the next general chapter, to take place at Pentecost, 1446, in Montpellier. That this chapter would try to overturn this regulation, was almost certain. The Conventuals were urging ultramontane Observants to come to Montpellier. The Observant superior, John Maubert, promptly consented; but his vicars were divided in opinion. The separatist efforts of the ultramontane family favored the plan of the Conventuals. The Observants of Burgundy had just withdrawn from Maubert, who, an infirm and peaceable man, ordered his followers to win their opponents rather by good example than by controversy. He trusted that Capistran, the organizer of the Observance, with whom he maintained contact, would see that things came out right. And in fact the Pope, advised by Capistran, prepared suitable measures. The general chapter of Montpellier was to be confronted by the accomplished facts.

At the meeting of the Italian Observants, held as usual at Assisi on the feast of the Portiuncula (1445), only four brothers were allowed from each province. The regulations given by Capistran from Monte Alverno underwent explanation and partial mitigation.

Toward the close of 1445 Capistran seems to have been in Rome, occupied with preparing the papal bull. This bull, *Ut sacra ordinis minorum religio*, dated January 11, 1446, declares that the twofold general vicariate of the Observants is permanent. Both vicars-general are to be elected by the Observants themselves. The general retains only the right of approval, a right which he must exercise within three days. Similarly the provincial vicars chosen by the Observants must be approved by the provincial ministers within the same period. Observant chapters are called and presided over by Observant vicars. The right of visitation, also retained by the general, was almost illusory, since corrections and punishments depended on majority consent of the Observant brothers.

The vicars-general, so the Pope wished, were to be elected before the general chapter of Montpellier. The cismontanes held a preparatory chapter in Ara Coeli, which was presided over personally by the Pope, who also paid the expenses. Into his hands Capistran laid down his office of vicar-general, since it had been determined that no one should be in office longer than three years. James Primadizzi of Bologna was elected the new vicar-general. In the absence of the general, Rusconi, then in France, the Pope himself approved the election lest ratification be postponed too long. At the same time he somewhat severely warned the general not to do anything against the Observants in the forthcoming chapter. Since the Observants had gained continually in merit and number, thus honoring the whole Order, he should instruct his provincials not to meddle with them. In fact, the general refused to approve Primadizzi, saying that the chapter had been called without his consent. But a chapter called and presided over by the Pope himself, so Eugene IV reminded him, needs no further approval. He must at once acknowledge Primadizzi. Only now did Rusconi yield.

Capistran's term of office had been decisive in the struggle between Observance and Conventualism. The bull of January 11, 1446, is rightly called the bull of separation. Conventuals and Observants henceforth walked separate paths. The general still remained the official head of the Observants. The Observants even now shrank from cutting this last thin thread of union. Individual groups of Observants even refused to obey the Observant vicars and remained under obedience to the general. In vain Eugene IV tried to prevent these Observant dissensions, which threatened especially the ultramontane family. The fact that Capistran was the originator of the separation bull clears up the question of responsibility. Capistran had changed his views. Since the events at Padua he had given up all hope of maintaining the unity of the Order. Later on he admitted, with something like contrition, that he had wronged the French Observants, whose efforts for independent superiors he had so energetically frustrated. He regretted also that he had in this matter contradicted Bernardine of Siena, saying: "He was a man of the spirit, and I am a man of the flesh."

The bull of separation, while it guaranteed to the Observance untrammeled development, ended definitely the good relations which had existed, especially in Italy, between Conventuals and Observants. The general protested vigorously against the bull. What hurt most was the regulation that any Conventual could join the Reform, whereas the Observants were forbidden under pain of excommunication to join the Conventuals. This measure is the chief source of the mounting antagonism of Conventuals against the Reform. Their position is quite intelligible. In losing their better elements they lost the best supports of discipline. On the other hand the Reform, too, would have been seriously endangered if dissatisfied characters could pass to convents with easier discipline. Further, the transfer of a Conventual to the Observance was not an easy procedure. Such brothers had to undergo a two-year term of probation, during which they were not allowed to preach or to accept any kind of office. Besides, superiors were instructed to be most cautious in accepting Conventuals.

Released from his office of vicar-general, Capistran had now more leisure for the canonization process. The greater part of the next two years he spent in the Abruzzi, especially in Aquila. But two new foundations claimed much of his time. The Poor Clare convent (dell' Eucharistia), which he had established in 1447, grew quickly from fourteen to sixty sisters. He may also be considered the founder of the great hospital of Aquila, which the citizens built as atonement for the bloody excesses in Bernardine's last year. By papal ordinance all smaller homes for the sick in Aquila were amalgamated into one large modern hospital. Capistran made the plan, and the citizens worked without pay. Capistran was often seen at work there, carrying a bucket of lime or sand on his head. Even so, expenses mounted to 80,000 ducats. Capistran wanted this house of physical suffering to be cheerful and agreeable. In the courtyard, surrounded by colonnades, were a fountain and flower beds. The rooms were ornamented and brightened with paintings. Capistran probably never saw the building after its completion.

The process of canonization did not lack reports of miracles. But these reports were not examined with the rigor now demanded. Capistran himself was direct witness only in rare cases. Those cured were brought before him by their relatives or other witnesses. He examined their reliability with such care as he considered sufficient. But nothing in the records indicates that physicians were called in to testify. Even sworn testimony seems as a rule not to have been required. Modern procedure, certainly, is not the only effective procedure. But the procedure in Bernardine's case proves the wisdom of the Church in insisting on most careful investigation.

Capistran, even by standards then known, was not rigorous enough. To illustrate. Miracles of dead persons being raised to life, upon which he laid the greatest emphasis, rest, in large measure, on testimony that leaves us doubtful. Fifty-five such are catalogued in the Liber miraculorum. Of these Capistran himself investigated fourteen, and defended them as genuine in the presence of Pope and cardinals. Today these cases would scarcely be admitted as proved. With few exceptions these fifty-five cases are those of children, some stillborn, some still in infancy. When the cause of death is mentioned, cases of drowning are a majority. How long the victims had been "lifeless" is generally not reported. One man is said to have been dead half an hour; a stillborn child, three to four hours. Bernardine is impetuously invoked by the distressed relatives, and life returns. In such cases the fact of death was insufficiently certified. The record sometimes says the person was thought to be dead. But even these cases were quietly admitted into the list.

Boundless veneration for Bernardine made Capistran predisposed to accept as genuine all reports that were submitted. Clearly genuine miracles, as, for instance, the healing of Pasquale, the boy of Aquila, may have led him, in view of the increasing popular enthusiasm, to be less cautious rather than more so. He, too, shared the credulity of his age. But, even in his time, men felt the need of careful investigation before admitting the reality of such wonderful events as the raising of the dead to life. Capistran tells the story of a man who doubted the supposed resuscitation of the dead in Bernardine's process. The man argued that seventy hours were required to establish that a man was really dead. Capistran declares that this argumentation is a blasphemy, since Christ had not remained that long in the grave. And he sees punishment in the fact that this man, not long afterward, lost his life by a fall from his horse. But if that critic went too far in one direction, Capistran was inclined to go too far in the other.

Views went to extremes also on the question of Bernardine's personality. The popular voice was inclined to anticipate the judgment of the Church. A certain bishop, on the contrary, sent a herald with a bell through the city, ordering all pictures of Bernardine to be at once either burned or surrendered. Capistran wrote to the Bishop. Even the Pope, he says, kept Bernardine's picture in his private apartment. Capistran goes on to lament that the humanists are zealously reviving the memory of pagan heroes without much opposition on the part of the Church. Ironically he suggests to the Bishop, who perhaps was a friend and patron of the humanists, to replace Bernardine's picture with that of some famous pirate or gangster. Another bishop sarcastically remarked: "I know that at my table blessed Bernardine often consumed chicken and fish with as much relish as I did."

Further, Bernardine's old opponents started again to discredit the purity of his doctrine. Eugene IV defended Bernardine's honor in a public letter (November 7, 1446). The Pope wished to have the canonization as soon as possible. He said to Capistran: "This year I shall canonize Nicholas of Tolentino, and next year, Bernardine." Capistran is said to have answered: "Holy Father, someone else will canonize Bernardine." In fact, Eugene did not live to see the end of the process. He fell sick in January, 1447. During his illness he had the consolation of seeing the Germans abandon their almost schismatic position. On February 7 the German delegates gathered round the bed of the dying Pontiff and swore the oath of obedience. He died on February 23, 1447.

PART V
UNDER NICHOLAS V
(1447-55)

CHAPTER XIX

The Jews and the Humanists

ON the day of Pope Eugene's death Capistran was in Aquila, praying the breviary with a confrere, whose name was Nicholas. When they came to their usual daily prayer for the Pope, Capistran told his companion to insert the name Nicholas. Brother Nicholas smiled at what he thought was a jest. The prayer ended, Brother Nicholas said: "If I become pope I will make you a cardinal." But Capistran was not joking. He answered with deep seriousness: "No, not you. But the next pope will be called Nicholas. Pope Eugene lives no more." In the sermon that day he spoke in similar fashion.

On March 6, 1447, after a short conclave, Cardinal Thomas Parentucelli was elected Pope, taking the name of Nicholas V. Capistran, who had long been an adviser of Cardinal Parentucelli, came to Rome after Easter to see the new Pope.[1] While he was commending to Nicholas V his heart's desire, the canonization of Bernardine, he made the jesting remark that since the Pope's name was no longer Thomas, he might now believe in Bernardine's miracles without touching them with his hands. To such free and easy manners Nicholas V was not averse. In contrast to his predecessor, who personified the dignity of papal sovereignty, Nicholas preferred familiar manners. He would invite visitors to sit down beside him, and took those who hesitated by the arm and made them sit down.

Scarcely six weeks after his election (April 14) Nicholas V issued a bull defending Bernardine against the attacks of opponents

[1] One tradition reports a spicy bit of repartee. When Thomas Parentucelli became bishop of Bologna, Capistran told him he was destined to be pope. The bishop answered: "You have the right name. You are a *capo strano* (queer-head)." Capistran retorted: "And your name is like your faith. You are now an unbelieving Thomas. But you will soon lose both your name and your unbelief."

who had reappeared after Eugene's death. All accusations against the deceased had to be withdrawn. Wherever the Observants demanded it, this bull was to be read in the churches. The Pope also appointed a new commission of cardinals to continue the process.

Capistran did not lose sight of other problems. His faculties against the Fraticelli were renewed. He began a new campaign against the Jews. The laws which he had obtained twenty years before from Joanna II and which had been extended to the Papal States by Martin V, had become obsolete. What, if anything, he did in this direction under Eugene IV, is not known. The war for the throne in Naples, and the entanglements under Eugene, may have distracted public attention from the Jews. In Spain, at the demand of princes and priests, Eugene IV had renewed former restrictions. Toward the end of his reign he published similar edicts for the Papal States. The new edicts of Nicholas V (June 23, 1447) are doubtless attributable to Capistran. By arbitrary interpretation of their privileges, thus the document says, the Jews have become guilty of many encroachments against Christians. Hence former regulations are renewed. Interest on loans of money is strictly forbidden, and interest already paid must be restored. The wearing of distinctive badges is again commanded. To prevent subterfuges the protective measures of Martin V and Eugene IV are expressly revoked. This bull of 1447 is harsher than that of 1427. Capistran is said to have expressed to the Pope his willingness to load all Jews of Italy on ships and carry them to foreign lands; however, this may have been said in jest. But the bull, if literally executed, would have become a catastrophe for Italian Jewry. The Jewish communities took measures against the "machinations" of this "wicked Aman," as they called Capistran, and obtained interpretations and exceptions. For instance, Nicholas V allowed the Marquis d'Este to continue his toleration of Jews since otherwise his country would suffer great loss. In the Papal States the Pope granted postponement of the regulations. To make strict laws was easy; to execute them was very difficult. Officials, prelates included, were inclined to mitigate these laws and even to frustrate them, often enough for selfish reasons. For instance, the papal government continued to maintain good relations with the Jews of Ancona, an important seaport; and this it did simply for economic reasons. The governor of Ancona, Cardinal Recanati, was known as a protector of Jews. Even a hundred years later, when the Jews were exiled from the Papal States under Pius V, the Jewish community of Ancona was exempted. In spite of all failures, Capistran with undaunted perseverance never gave up the struggle.

But we do find it surprising that, according to all indications, he did not attack the humanists, who, though few in number, brought greater dangers to practical Christianity than did the Fraticelli, Jews, Hussites, and Turks together. The latter threatened the Church from without, whereas the humanists introduced an interior process of decay, a decay more dangerous because it did not involve open denial of Christian teaching. Thus Lorenzo Valla, in his dialogue of lust, does allow the representative of Christian morality to triumph. But this triumph is merely apparent. The reader feels that sensuality is inculcated as the ideal of life, while the Christian moral law is presented as bigotry, as decadence from the old pagan wisdom of life. Valla clothed his paganism in philosophical garb. But his friend, Antonio Beccadelli, the tumble-bug of world literature, tried to lend poetic beauty to the vice of lust, even to that most disgusting form of lust against which Bernardine fought so energetically as a national vice which disgraced and poisoned Italy. From humanist circles came the first systematic attacks against the existence of the Catholic orders. Voluntary virginity they characterized as unnatural torture. They held religious life in general up to ridicule. It was modern man's open declaration of war against the religion of the Cross.

But humanist influences were at the time greatly underestimated. Take Capistran himself as illustration. No other man worked harder than he to save the Church from her enemies. He tried to separate Christianity from Judaism. He dislodged the Fraticelli from their last hiding-places. He showed superhuman strength against the Utraquists in Bohemia. And he sacrificed his life in a heroic effort to stem the Turkish invasion. But the antichristian humanist spirit, originating in his own country, seems to have escaped his attention. His literary remains are indeed not complete enough to form an absolutely correct judgment on this particular point. Yet the writings of Valla and Beccadelli and others of their kind could hardly have remained unknown to him. The court of Naples was a favorite focus for humanists. Valla and Beccadelli met congenial welcome there.

Capistran may indeed have raised his voice against them, as did other Observant preachers. Antonio da Rho denounced Beccadelli, ordering his sordid pamphlets to be publicly burned. Capistran's friend, Antonio da Bitonto, attacked Lorenzo Valla. But of any energetic action on the part of Capistran we have no record. He simply did not realize this particular danger. Jurist and inquisitor, he was too little acquainted with the humanist movement; for him the enemies of Christianity are the unbaptized and the heretics. He is still dedicated to the medieval system of defense, i.e., the use of force, spiritual and secular, against non-Christians and apostates.

We do not mean to say that the Observants, and in particular Capistran, failed in their efforts to counteract the new paganism. They did not fail. First of all, they had a share in Christian humanism, which met pagan humanism on its own ground and combined the new educational ideas with the spirit of piety. Such Christian humanists were, for example, Cardinal Cesarini; the Camaldolese, Ambrogio Traversari; the noble Guarino in Verona; the Observant, Albert of Sarteano; and especially the great educator, Vittorino da Feltre in Mantua. All these were proof that classical education and Christian asceticism did not represent contradictory principles. Then with the pious Nicholas V, Christian humanism ascended the papal throne. The Rome of Peter became the center of the modern movement, exerting influence even on Valla and Beccadelli. Many disasters were thus prevented in spite of the deep shadows that mark the age of the papal renaissance, initiated by Nicholas V.

The Franciscan Order should have led the forces of Christian humanism. But in Capistran's time the Order was not yet able for the task. Leadership in culture presupposes a religious organization that is strong and well developed. The Franciscan Conventuals, however, were not progressing, but in great measure regressing. The Observance was busy in overcoming the difficulties which beset every new organization, especially when that organization is devoted to reform. Where even studies absolutely necessary for the priesthood met stubborn opposition, what room could be found for humanist studies? Voices in that direction were indeed heard. At a provincial council in Aquila, in the days of Nicholas V, requests were heard to take up literary studies, at least for the purpose of self-defense. The proposal was rejected by the majority. Let brethren, thus ran the decision, give themselves to prayer, to devotion, to the service of God. The Lord Himself will take care of His family. As God did in the past, so in the future He will send us well-educated men, able to defend the Order. These arguments, though not convincing, are intelligible, in view of the Order's immaturity in the field of study, and likewise in view of the general obscurantism that led even many universities to declare against introducing humanist plans of study.

But we cannot say that the Observants of Italy were opposed in principle to humanist studies. Preachers, it is true, were sometimes guilty of exaggerations and mistakes. But the best Observant preachers, sometimes when advanced in age and when overwhelmed with work, often took instruction from the humanists. Sarteano studied Greek under Guarino, and did so with such fervor that he mastered the language in ten months. Albert and Bernardine studied rhetoric under that same master. Frequent missions to the Orient brought the Observants into the homelands of humanism. After twelve years in Constantinople, Bartholomew of Giano returned laden with Greek literature, and busied himself with its translation. Capistran himself did not look on these efforts with indifference or contempt. His correspondence with Francesco Barbaro, the foremost representative of humanism in the Republic of Venice, shows his appreciation of the spiritual advantages he gained from contact with humanist circles. He, too, had busied himself with Greek and with the works of ancient philosophers and orators. Quintilian was his teacher in oratory. But systematic study of the ancient masters was impossible in his excessively burdened life.

Another point deserves reflection. The Observance, by its very existence, served as a strong bulwark against the new pagan flood, as the humanists knew. Hence their intense hatred of the Observants. But with all their cleverness and wit they were no match for the great Observant preachers. Capistran, about the year 1450, estimates at four thousand the number of candidates won by himself for the Order. Many of these vocations were votaries of the new learning. Some of the leading Christian humanists owed their conversion to a preacher of penance. Sarteano was gained for the Observance by Bernardine. Maffeo Veggi, devoted to pagan muses, was converted and entered the Augustinian Order. As a boy of twelve, he had heard Bernardine preaching in Milan, and the impressions then received were never effaced. Enea Silvio went the same road. The memory of Bernardine became for him, after years of worldliness, the decisive call for return to duty. Bernardine and his kind were the providential apostles of the humanist era. Bernardine's canonization did not occasion any interruption of Capistran's apostolic activity. It was the answer to the Church's most pressing problem, the renewal and the intensification of religious life.

The canonization process continued to test Capistran's patience. Progress at times seemed to stand still. Opponents were never at a loss for new objections and difficulties. And miraculous cures seemed to cease. Bernardine had a rival. From Rieti came rumors of miracles taking place at the grave of a lay brother, Thomas, who had been a companion, first of Capistran on the visit to Palestine, and then of Albert Sarteano on the visit to Egypt. The Observants were now working miracles by turn, said the wits at the papal court. It was reported that Capistran hurried to the grave in Rieti and commanded the brother not to hold up Bernardine's process any longer. Often in those days he would groan: "O blessed Bernardine, pray for yourself." But he always preserved confidence. We are told that Bernardine appeared to him in Siena, consoling him with encouraging words. Urged probably by Capistran, Alfonso of Naples approached the Pope anew (August 28, 1448) with a petition for the promotion of the canonization. Siena, Lucca, and other cities did likewise. But the doubts raised against the canonization seem to have made a great impression on the Pope. Thus we understand the strong language used by Capistran in presenting the cause before the Pope and the cardinals. This is one sample: Let them throw Capistran's body and Bernardine's corpse into the fire together. If both burn, ascribe it to my sins; if we remain intact, acknowledge the holy will of God." He never tired exalting Bernardine's perpetual virginity. Bernardine went to his grave as pure as he came from his mother's womb. For this truth he would die at the stake. His devoted zeal touched the Pope, who asked him jestingly: "Who is going to take care of your canonization?" "I am a sinner," parried Capistran, "and such things are not for sinners." The Pope is reported to have said he would canonize Capistran if the latter died first. When Cardinal Bessarion became a member of the commission, things went better. The Pope ordered the bishop of Rieti, Angelus Capranica, to examine all the acts. Capranica took Capistran with him to visit Rome, Siena, Perugia, Aquila, and other cities.

Capistran was not neglecting his duties as provincial vicar. In 1448 he made four new foundations. The year 1449 brought further labor. Primadizzi's vicariate was ended. The general chapter, at the request of Cosimo de' Medici, was held at Mugello, near Florence, while the Conventuals met at Santa Croce in Florence. Cosimo was both magnanimous patron of humanists and liberal promoter of cloisters. He had the church of San Marco in Florence painted by Fiesole, and reserved a room for himself in the cloister there. People in general felt no contradiction between Renaissance culture and ecclesiastical spirit.

Capistran wrote a sketch of Bernardine's life for the general chapter at Mugello. When Bernardine joined the Order the Observance numbered about 130 brothers. When he died it numbered 4,000. The number of foundations had increased during that span of time from 20 to 230. At the Mugello chapter 270 houses, with more than 5,000 brethren, were represented. Among these representatives were Capistran, James of the Marches, and Albert of Sarteano, all three already old men. Still in vigorous manhood were Marcus of Bologna and Antonio da Bitonto. The younger generation was represented by Michael Carcano of Milan, and particularly by Robert of Lecce, only twenty-three years old but already celebrated among preachers. His eloquence captured Perugia, where the plague had prepared the ground for him. In the following decades he was destined to eclipse all other preachers.

What esteem the Observance enjoyed, in spite of the humanists, is shown by the fact that Cosimo, modern, serious, and cultured, counted it a special honor to appear with his sons at the general chapter. But precisely this growing esteem and influence made the Conventuals reluctant to lose this distinguished branch of the Order. After the death of Eugene IV they tried to have the bull of separation suppressed. At the papal court the position of the Observants became less favorable, not because the new Pope was ill disposed toward them; but in these questions Nicholas was not as independent as his predecessor, whose care for the Observance was not merely official but also personal. Under Nicholas V the provincial of Tours in France obtained permission for Observants to return to the Conventuals. Italian Observants expressed similar wishes. These demands came generally from brothers who were not on good terms with their superiors or who found life in the reform too burdensome. The spokesman of these malcontents was soon Robert of Lecce, who was not proof against the dangers that threaten an itinerant preacher of unusual fame. He became the source of many sad hours for superiors and confreres. Under these clouds the Conventuals might manage to regain control.

Rusconi ordered the general chapter at Mugello to remove to Santa Croce. The Pope compelled the general to retract his order, and thus, a month before Pentecost, the Observant chapter was opened at Mugello. Unanimously the chapter elected Capistran as vicar-general of the cismontane family. According to Eugene's IV's regulation, the general was obliged to confirm him within three days. But the general waited on papal prompting. On May 23 Nicholas commanded the general to confirm the election of

Capistran. The Pope's tone is threatening. If the general will not aid the new vicar in every way, the vicar will find in the Pope a more permanent protector. At the Conventual chapter in Santa Croce the Observants did not appear. But they did participate in the great procession which, after the close of the chapter, moved from Santa Croce to the Palazzo Vecchio, the proud citadel of the Florentine Republic. There the immense procession was received by the city council. During the solemn service Capistran delivered the festive sermon from the steps of the Palazzo. Since Bernardine's death he was the most popular representative of the Order in Italy. Crowds of people thronged to meet him when he came to the chapter.

Rusconi, who had been re-elected general, died soon after, at the age of forty-one. The language used by Eugene IV and by Nicholas V shows that he was no friend of the reform. Even among the Conventuals he does not seem to have left the best memory. After the general chapter he had disputed so vehemently with the guardian of Santa Croce, Francis della Rovere (later Pope Sixtus IV), that the latter fled from the general's anger to the house of his relatives. The Pope entrusted the guidance of the Order, until the election of a new general, to Angelus Christophori, a native of Perugia.

Bernardine's fame had passed beyond the Alps to the north. At the chapter of Mugello, Capistran met the German Franciscan, Caspar of Augsburg, who was on his way to thank Bernardine for restored health. Paralyzed in hands and feet, he had vowed, in case of cure, to make a pilgrimage on foot to Aquila.

Capistran, after a month in Tuscany, went to Rome, to confer with Bishop Capranica. The second half of the year 1449 he seems to have spent in the eastern parts of central Italy. In July he was to start a long-planned foundation in his native city, Capistrano. The last months of 1449 he spent near Fabriano, where Nicholas V had again retired to escape the plague. In the Observant cloister, Valle Eremitica, near Fabriano, Capistran found an excellent library, established by James of the Marches. The interest of his Order and the progress of Bernardine's canonization forced Capistran to remain near the Pope. Here he asked authorization to erect twenty new foundations. Space for the rapidly developing communities was everywhere too small. The papal document (October 14) ascribes this flowering of vocations to the good example of the brothers and the sermons of Capistran.

Similar progress is noted among the Poor Clares. The Perugian convent was now placed under obedience to the Observance. Sisters who could not make up their mind to join the Observance were sent to other convents. From Foligno came twenty-four Observant nuns to organize the reform in Perugia. From Foligno and Perugia a whole line of St. Clare convents accepted the reform.

CHAPTER XX

Brescia and Venice

AT Fabriano the Pope finally assured Capistran that during the coming year of jubilee (1450) Bernardine would be canonized. Hence also the general chapter was convoked for that year, to lend greater splendor to the canonization.

This prolonged stay in Fabriano was prompted by the fact that the headquarters of the Fraticelli were in that district. Capistran and James had received from the Pope extensive powers against these heretics. Since Fabriano was under papal dominion, the inquisitors called in the secular power to deal with them; and thus the Fraticelli were rooted out in Majorati, Massa, Podii, and Meroli. From Massa, Capistran wrote (November 18) to the Pope's brother, Cardinal Philip, apostolic legate of Bologna, to inflame his fervor against these heretics. Every other work must give way to the defense of the faith. Much has been accomplished in Massa during the last six years. Many Fraticelli were converted. If obdurate, they were burned at the stake, for instance, in Fabriano itself, the "pope" of the sect. And in Florence, a second center of the movement, some of its chiefs met the same fate. But only a decade after Capistran's death did the sect die out, after harassing Italy for more than a century. The memory of the "wicked brothers" survives in local tradition to our day.

The jubilee year began on Christmas Eve, 1449. Pilgrims came to Rome like migrating starlings. Hospices and monasteries were ready. As the Conventuals had only a small convent in Rome, Capistran put Ara Coeli at their disposal. Three thousand Franciscans were expected. In the larger cities disciples of Bernardine preached in preparation for the jubilee: Antonio da Bitonto, in Florence; Andrea da S. Gemino, in Bologna; Marco da Bologna, in Aquila. For St. Peter's in Rome, Robert of Lecce was called. Capistran scored one success during that Lent. After several disputations, a prominent rabbi was converted. On Palm Sunday he was baptized, receiving the name of William. His example was followed during the course of that year by more than fifty other Roman Jews.

The canonization was decreed, finally and formally, on May 9, 1450. The latest delays came from Bernardine's criticism of evils among the clergy, and from his cult of the holy name of Jesus. The Pope met these scruples by decreeing that pictures of the new saint should not bear the sign of the holy name. Capistran agreed, provided Bernardine were canonized in the name of Jesus.

About eight hundred brothers took care of the pilgrims. Infirmarian at Ara Coeli was the Spanish lay brother, Diego of Alcala, now St. Didacus. Diego's foresight kept Ara Coeli well provided, though Rome itself suffered shortage. Of course Ara Coeli received more in alms than any other hospice. Bernardine's name was a charm.

Late on the vigil of Pentecost, Capistran had a last audience with Nicholas V. Obstacles still existed. The Pope acted as if he were still undecided what to do. Capistran was on the rack. The Pope, after teasing him, put an end to his torture with the decisive declaration: "Tomorrow I will canonize Bernardine." Capistran broke into tears. "You were in fear, it seems, Brother?" "True enough, Holy Father, never before did I tremble so much."

The canonization on Pentecost Sunday (May 26, 1450) has seldom been equaled in splendor. "In a thousand years there has not been a feast like this," asserts Capistran. Pope Nicholas preached the first sermon on the new saint. He was surrounded by 14 cardinals, 44 bishops, and more than 2,000 Franciscans. From Ara Coeli the mendicant procession had gone singing to St. Peter's. Those first in the procession reached St. Peter's before the last had left Ara Coeli. The ceremonies lasted from early morning till late evening. One of those present describes the scene as follows: "I never passed such a day. We entered the church, but we could not get out. We were wedged in, no one could make a step, movement was merely up and down. We thought we would die, so tired were we. The square in front was so crowded that a grain of millet thrown over those heads would scarcely have reached the ground."

The day was a day of glory and joy. Bernardine, the first Franciscan canonized since 1300, was followed within fifty years by four Observants and two Poor Clares. Three future saints were present at his canonization: Capistran, James, and Diego.

Italian cities honored their glorified apostle. Siena, his native city, and Aquila, where he died, bore the costs of the Roman canonization. Siena's own celebration surpassed even that for St. Catherine of Siena. After Perugia's festivities the city council reported: "This city once belonged to the devil; Bernardine tore it from his claws, and brought it back to a well-ordered life." Both Siena and Perugia made May 20, the day of Bernardine's death, an official holiday.

At the general chapter, Angelus Christophori had been chosen general. He promptly confirmed Capistran and Maubert as vicars-general. Maubert, prevented by sickness from coming to Rome, died in August, 1450. Albert of Sarteano died shortly before him. The new general was a man both learned and practical. But Capistran wrote to him that, whereas in former years he was a friend of the Observants, he had not been so since the Padua chapter.

The celebrations concluded, Capistran set out on visitations. August 15 he preached at Borgo San Sepolchro, in northern Umbria, at the foot of the Apennine mountains.[1] On the same day he crossed the mountain to Forlì in Emilia, and was there welcomed by the nobility, especially the Ordelaffi. From Forlì he went to Bologna and Ferrara, where he visited the Poor Clares. The abbess at Bologna was Catherine of Bologna, later canonized. To her and to the nuns in Ferrara he brought, as a gift from the Pope, a plenary indulgence at the hour of death. As a condition for gaining this indulgence, the only requirement was the faithful practice of the holy Rule. In Ferrara he confirmed the newly elected Abbess.

In 1451 Capistran went to Venice. He would have preferred Padua or Milan. From Venice he intended, after Easter, to go to

---

[1] Here we meet for the first time the name of Nicholas of Fara, whose biography of the saint is based on six years of closest association.

Dalmatia, Bosnia, and Hungary, since the Observants of those countries belonged to the cismontane family. During Bernardine's canonization he had chanced to meet, in the portico of St. Peter's, the apostolic legate of Bosnia, Thomas of Fara, who gave him consoling news about conditions beyond the Adriatic. King Stephen III of Bosnia had returned to Roman obedience. Observants there under Michael of Zara were extirpating the ancient Bosnian heresy of the Patarines, whose traitorous relations with the Turks had endangered the very existence of the kingdom. King Stephen was building cloisters for the Observance, and Michael of Zara was calling for Capistran. Michael of Bechen, the vicar of Hungaria, wrote that the Queen Mother and the barons of the realm urgently wished Capistran to come. In Transylvania especially the plague had carried off many brothers.

Even this extensive itinerary was destined to become still much wider. The Pope informed him that the King of the Romans, Frederick, wished to see him in Austria.

Frederick III, of the Styrian line of the Hapsburgs, had been the head of the German Empire since 1440. As guardian of Ladislaus, who was still a minor, he represented the interests of his ward in Bohemia and Hungary. The suggestion to invite Capistran came from Enea Silvio, the King's secretary. This adroit diplomat, abandoning the Council of Basle, had earnestly endeavored to reconcile the German Empire with the Pope, and had succeeded (1448) in obtaining a concordat. This step brought the schismatic Council to dissolution. On April 4, 1449, the antipope resigned. Three weeks later the Council, in its last session, acknowledged Nicholas V as legitimate Pope. The conclusion of peace would be sealed by the crowning of Frederick as emperor in Rome. In September, 1450, under the leadership of Enea and Archduke Albrecht, a brother of the King, an embassy went to Italy on a double mission: first, to prepare the coronation of Frederick; secondly, to arrange for Frederick's marriage to Eleanor, the daughter of the King of Portugal and niece of King Alfonso. Here in his native country Silvio saw the high esteem to which Capistran had risen, and recognized the value he would have for Austria. He obtained a papal command and promptly forwarded it to Capistran.

In his history of Frederick III, Enea Silvio says that Capistran received a threefold commission; to reform the degenerated Conventuals, to preach peace to the people, and in general to teach them the way of truth. Besides these general commissions, he mentions two that were special: first, the introduction of the Observance, which was still unknown in Austria and Styria, though Hungary had long since had Observant cloisters; secondly, Capistran, as promoter of peace, was to suppress the political contentions, which kept the Hapsburg dominion in ceaseless turmoil. Upper and Lower Austria were demanding more and more urgently that Frederick release their young sovereign, Ladislaus, from guardianship. Frederick was not to be moved, and kept a strict watch over his ward. Excitement ran so high that the royal councilors advised against the journey to Rome. No wonder Silvio wanted Capistran as peacemaker. Further, Capistran was not unknown beyond the Alps. Pilgrims told how sick persons had been cured when he applied a relic of Bernardine to them. When Capistran informed a German lay brother that he would soon go north, the brother replied that even nobles were saying: "If we only had a man like him, conditions would soon become better."

Until Easter, Capistran continued to preach, at Padua first, then at Vicenza and Verona. Envoys arrived at Verona from Brescia, the richest and most densely populated province of the Venetian Republic. Bernardine of Siena had preached at Brescia in 1422, and had abolished many abuses, for instance, indecent races. But after the preacher's departure the evil conditions returned, chiefly among the clergy and religious, conditions so deplorable that magistrates were obliged to intervene. The senators went in a body to the Bishop and demanded that the churches, especially the cathedral, be kept in suitable condition, and that the priests should lead respectable lives. In 1428 the council complained that the Abbot of St. Euphemia was wasting the endowments of monastery and hospital on loose women; and in 1433, that the Dominicans of St. Barnabas no longer kept their Rule. Two years later the city council banished the nuns of St. Cosmas on account of their disgraceful lives. In 1440 the nuns of St. Clara were found leading a life of shame. In this last case the council, lest the city be struck by God's wrath, passed a decree, after adequately punishing the two worst offenders, to drive these filthy women from the city, and to transfer the convent to the Franciscan Observants of St. Apollonia.

Brescia had 20 monasteries, 10 of them mendicant, housing in all about 1,600 religious. There were besides a great number of quasi-religious unions. Conditions were certainly not everywhere as bad as those mentioned. But we can see that Observant foundations were by no means superfluous. The magistrates of the city had endeavored to engage the best preachers of the time. In 1442 seven itinerant preachers had worked in Brescia at the same time. In 1444 Albert of Sarteano was active there. Two of his efforts bore lasting fruit: the foundation of a great modern hospital, like that of Capistran in Aquila and Sulmona; the foundation of a Poor Clare convent, peopled by fifty virgins and widows.

Conditions in Brescia were improving when Capistran entered the city in February, 1451. He was welcomed with immense enthusiasm, heightened by reports, from Vicenza and Verona, of the numerous miraculous cures which the charismatic preacher was now performing. The city council made extraordinary preparations. A committee of seven senators had special funds from the treasury to supply the needs of Capistran's suite, composed of nearly a hundred brothers and candidates. In the prison square, carpenters erected a pulpit and tribunes. Capistran was escorted by three hundred citizens on horseback, by the senators and their wives on foot. An eyewitness has left us a vivid account of the six days during which Capistran preached in Brescia.

Three hours before daybreak (February 10), ten thousand people were assembled. After a retinue of fifty mace-bearers escorted the preacher to the piazza, it was with great difficulty that he reached the pulpit, because everybody wanted to touch him. Some cut large pieces from his cloak, as if he were St. Peter. The number of sick people brought into the city was estimated at more than two thousand. On Sunday the province of Brescia streamed- into the city, together with crowds from Bergamo, Crema, Cremona and Milan. Rooms, balconies, even the city walls, were all occupied. People climbed into trees, and many branches broke under their burden. Looking out over the tossing waves of that human sea, even Capistran was startled. He calculated the number of his audience at 80,000; others mention a still higher number. St. Bernardine's relic, his headdress, evoked mighty emotion among the masses. Their exclamations are compared by a contemporary to the roar of the stormy ocean. After the sermon fifty young men were invested with the habit of the Order. On Tuesday, February 16, the missioner left the city.

Halfway between Brescia and Cremona he stopped in Prato Albino. Crowds of people immediately gathered, and many sick were brought to him. To satisfy them he had to preach, although he must hurry to be in Venice for Lent. After passing through Mantua, he returned to Padua, where he invested sixty-six novices, the costs being borne by the city. All in all, in these last months of his activity in Italy, he received three hundred novices, an extraordinary number even in those days.

Near Venice, as he related the events of the past weeks in an address to his confreres, he broke into sobs and could hardly continue speaking. These last weeks in Italy have certainly a superhuman stamp.

The Italian cities were used to scenes of emotional excitement as one famous speaker followed another. But the events in Brescia (February, 1451) went quite beyond the usual measure of religious manifestations. The reason lay not so much in Capistran's excellent qualities as a preacher, not even in his fame as a saintly man, but chiefly in his miraculous power as a healer.

Amid this universal acclaim, Venice at first stood aloof. Capistran's reception was cool. "We came now to a more quiet haven," remarks Fara. Certain circles, it is true, awaited his coming with great eagerness. The Venetian humanist and diplomat, Francesco Barbaro, mentioned above, wrote to him thus: "I hear you have received from above gifts worthy of praise, yea, of admiration. I rejoice that in our days God has given you these gifts." Capistran's answer warns him not to believe too easily in rumors, but to give the honor to God, from whom all good gifts come.

In the cool-headed business world of Venice the famous missioner found at first little attention. His companions complained that he was squandering precious time on these indifferent Venetians, while elsewhere his presence was longed for. In answer he pointed to the many lagoons, saying: "Many waters cannot extinguish love." By Midlent, he added, things would change. Until then the Lord had decreed an armistice. On Thursday, April 1, a mute boy received the gift of speech under the imposition of Capistran's hands. A few days later, April 5, he healed a man paralyzed in hands and feet. Onlookers broke into tears. The cure of a possessed woman completed the change.

This unhappy creature was brought into the Franciscan church while Capistran was celebrating Mass. At the consecration she began to scream fearfully. After Mass, Capistran approached her and blessed her. The first effect was terrifying. Her face changed color, her mouth foamed, she leaped into the air. Repeatedly she screamed: "How much I suffer today on your account!" Capistran quietly continued to pray the exorcism. Finally she sank to the ground and remained there motionless. Then she awoke as from a deep sleep, and went quietly home. The following day she came again, now a humble, modest woman. The terrible creature of yesterday could no longer be recognized.

During the rest of Lent, Venice presented an entirely different picture. No church was now big enough to hold the audiences. Therefore the pulpit was erected in the spacious piazza in front of the beautiful church of the Dominicans, SS. John and Paul. A guard opened the way to the pulpit for the preacher.

Capistran was now making his last preparations for the journey to Austria and Hungary. He would have a suite of twelve brethren: seven priests and five lay brothers. The seven priests, except Peter of Odenburg, were all Italians. Among them were the first three biographers of Capistran—Nicholas of Fara, Christopher of Varese, and Jerome of Udine. In the course of time Gabriel of Verona became the most prominent of his companions. Of the five lay brothers two had come from Germany, Michael and John, the first a Prussian, the other an Austrian. Capistran left Mark of Bologna in Italy as vicar-general of the cismontane Observants.

At Pentecost the general chapter of Barcelona was to provide a successor to the deceased John Maubert. Capistran wrote a letter to the chapter, expressing deep grief over the death of Maubert, this excellent leader of the army of Christ, and admonishing the assembled brethren to elect a holy and experienced man: "May the Holy Spirit give you a man of peace, who knows how to keep you in harmony; a man of kindness, to pardon faults committed through frailty and to have compassion on imperfect brethren; a man of prudence, to govern with consideration; a man of justice, to bring the obstinate to terms. Let him be a fervent promoter of our religious family. Let him remain united with the brethren in Italy to make you of one heart and mind with us, in word and in deed." The one chosen should promptly inform the brethren in Italy of all affairs that may prove detrimental to the whole family, since those nearer to the papal curia can more promptly obtain remedy. He himself would defend both branches of the Observant family. "And then, my dear fathers, both families will prosper, will be the edification of the world, the joy of the Church, the song of the angels, and the consolation of Christ. Let love, beautiful love, preside in your assemblies. And may joy dwell with her."

Capistran had to refuse an urgent invitation to Milan, which now had a new master, the famous free-lance leader, Francis Sforza, son-in-law of Philip Maria Visconti. The new ruler promptly adopted the role of a friend to humanists, though he had no understanding at all of higher learning. Personal piety, then, may not have been the reason why he wished to bring the most renowned preachers of Italy to Milan. Court fashion demanded both humanists and preachers. Capistran offered Robert of Lecce as substitute. But Sforza insisted on having Capistran and wrote to the Pope. Rome, it seems, had forgotten that Capistran was long since promised to Vienna. So Nicholas V sent Capistran orders to go to Milan. But Capistran did not receive this command till he was in Vienna. From there he wrote to the Duke, explaining the Pope's oversight, and promising to visit Milan after his return. Sforza was satisfied.

This forgetfulness at Rome is not surprising. So far nothing more had been planned than one of the usual visits to the King in his residence at Wiener-Neustadt. Such requests from princes and cities asking for famous preachers evidently reached Rome in great numbers.

What importance this journey to Austria would assume was not at that time suspected. Capistran himself was still reckoning upon a comparatively short absence from Italy, as he intended to preside personally at the general chapter in Aquila, to be held at Pentecost, 1452. The entire journey, through Styria, Austria, Hungary, Bosnia, and Dalmatia, was not to claim more than a year. Yet sometimes he had forebodings that he would not die in Italy.

On Easter Wednesday, April 28, he left Venice, and on the same day reached Caorle. Two days later he passed through Portogruaro. On May 7 he reached San Vito; thence to Udine, the capital of Friuli, where he held a provincial chapter. Sick people waited in long lines for him in front of the Franciscan church. Urgent requests made him pay a one-day visit to the neighboring town of Cividale. His last and longest pause on Italian ground was in Gemona, where he was received by the city with great pomp.

Emotion seized the small traveling party when (May 17) they reached the borders of Italy, near Pontafel. Capistran's joy in preaching to a non-Italian people was not fully shared by his companions. Nicholas Fara confesses that crossing the border cost him bitter tears. Italy, he complained, should never have allowed a John Capistran to leave his country.

With this feeling we can sympathize. Capistran stood at the zenith of public esteem when he left his dearly beloved Italy forever. The general feeling of the masses of the people finds expression in the metrical epistle of the humanist, Donato de Cittadella, who praises Capistran as the lamp of faith and Italy's greatest ornament.

CHAPTER XXI

From Italy to Vienna

THREE weeks had elapsed since Capistran left Venice. He now hurried on. On May 18 he arrived in Villach. Nicholas Fara says that the reception there cannot be described. "You would think the pope was entering the city." The next day, the vigil of St. Bernardine's feast, Capistran preached, speaking in Latin to an audience of Germans and Slovenians. An interpreter repeated the principal parts of the address. After the sermon the church became a hospital. Villach was just then suffering from a strange epidemic. People were suddenly attacked by extreme pains in the heart. General lameness followed, soon succeeded by death. Many had already succumbed. According to Varese's report, fourteen such patients were cured by Capistran's blessing. At his request most of those cured left their stretchers as votive gifts in the church. On the feast itself, the first anniversary of Bernardine's canonization, the priest John, former vicar at the principal church in Villach, was suddenly cured. Paralyzed in both hands, he had not for years been able to say Mass. Everybody now wanted to see the healed man, and such a turmoil followed that Capistran could hardly make his way out of the crowd. The excitement on both days and the unknown language explain why only thirty cures were recorded.

From Villach, a key point in the Alps, the news of these incidents spread rapidly through Carinthia and Styria. From huts on the mountains and from remote valleys people hastened to see the man of God. They came in solemn processions, led by their clergy, singing hymns, arrayed with all the ornaments of their churches, carrying banners, torches, and relics of saints, just as if they were receiving a papal legate. Bells rang solemnly through all the valleys, and flowers were spread on the roads.

From Villach the way went northward, along the lake of

Ossiach into the valley of Gurk. Bishop John Schallermann of Gurk had prepared a splendid reception. Fara remarks: "I really do not know what more he could have done if Christ Himself had come." Under the sound of the cathedral bells, accompanied by organ and song, the solemn procession entered the majestic and beautiful temple, where Capistran mounted the pulpit and preached on the Mother of God, to whom the cathedral is dedicated. After the Te Deum, the Bishop approached the high altar and sang some beautiful prayers, including, as Fara remarks, "a specially beautiful one in which Capistran's name was mentioned." From the cathedral the procession moved on to Strassburg, the episcopal castle, enthroned on a hill above the little city. The ruins of that castle remain today, eloquent testimony to the size and splendor of that ancient episcopal residence. Here Capistran and his suite were most cordially entertained. During the day he went down into the city, to visit the sick. John Schallermann became Capistran's sincere friend and protector. The noble and zealous prelate recognized in his guest a providential instrument for reforming the Church. Though they never met again, they continued correspondence. "Since the day you left me," wrote the Bishop, "I have never ceased praying for the success of your mission"; and in a circular to his people he requests them to do likewise.[1]

The ancient town of Friesach also received the Franciscans with all signs of veneration. A children's choir sang the Benedictus qui venit in nomine Domini. And they sang so sweetly that the brethren seemed to hear the voices of angels.

Over the ridge of Neumarkt and Unzmarkt, they came into the beautiful and well cultivated valley of the Mur. In Judenburg they paused again. Learning that King Frederick was intending to leave Wiener-Neustadt and go to Vienna, Capistran hastened on and arrived in Neustadt on May 30, a day sooner than he was expected. The King expressed regret, since he had planned a grandiose reception for his guest.

Wiener-Neustadt was then at the zenith of its history. It was

[1] Fara says of Bishop Schallermann: "I know not if Mary has on earth a more devout client."

repeatedly the residence of the sovereigns. Frederick III cherished a predilection for this city. In its parish church he had, eleven years before, accepted election as king of the Romans. It was one of the best fortified places in Germany. Though the splendor of the crown had faded, the city was still an imperial city. The court attracted the nobility. Imperial embassies were frequent.

When Capistran arrived, Enea Silvio, the King's secretary and counselor, who had prompted Capistran's journey, was not at home. Business kept him in Vienna where he awaited Capistran. As the King himself was soon to go to Vienna, discussions were postponed until they would all meet in the capital. "When we meet," wrote Enea from Vienna on June 5, "we will talk matters over in detail." Of the topics discussed at Neustadt, Capistran's companions knew only that he tried to dissuade the King from financial dealings with the Jews. In Austrian countries, which Frederick controlled as guardian of Ladislaus Posthumous, the Jewish question was once again acute. Thirty years before, the father of Ladislaus, Emperor Albrecht II, had, under the form of law, inflicted terrible penalties on the Jews. As atonement for sacrilegious treatment of the Blessed Sacrament in Enns, some were executed, and all others were forever exiled from Austria. Though this last regulation was still in force in 1450, Jews still lived in Vienna, and Frederick III was about to grant the Jews the legal right to settle in Austria again. Pope Nicholas V's bull of 1451 supported the King. But the people were opposed to letting the Jews return, and called the King Rex Judaeorum in place of Rex Romanorum. The nobility also protested decidedly against a return of the Jews.

Evidently Capistran tried to influence the King in this direction. The question was a delicate affair. In Wiener-Neustadt itself he could see the Jews enjoying the greatest liberties. Jewish quarters had spread far beyond their original limits. They had their own synagogue and school, their own hospital and bathhouse, and were, in general, treated as Christians were. Waruch, an able surgeon, stood high at court. Rabbi Israel Isserlein, the head of a prominent talmudic school and a man distinguished by great knowledge and noble character, in his old age was consumed by a longing for the Messias. "If I could see him only for a quarter of an hour, I would gladly die," was his frequent remark. A Jewish tradition says that he agreed to become a Christian if Capistran would go through fire for the truth of his doctrine, though nothing came of this proposal.

Capistran's admonitions can hardly have had any effect on the King, whose friendship for the Jews was based, not on principles of humaneness, but on his continued financial embarrassment, for which he could find no help except from the Jewish money-lenders. Religiously the King was beyond reproach. Still unmarried, he led an exemplary life. To the Church he rendered valuable services. His sovereign prerogatives in ecclesiastical affairs he exercised in favor of Church reform, giving particular attention to the restoration of monastic discipline. Thus, on January 3, 1450, he obtained from the Pope authorization to appoint a commission for reforming the Minorites in Wiener-Neustadt. But the introduction of a reform in Hapsburg countries offered special difficulties. In contrast to Hungary, Austria had no Observants; even the name was unknown there. To put Italians into German convents was useless, and in the countries near Germany the Observance itself had just started. Hence Capistran could do no more than give the King hopes of the future.

Five days after Capistran's arrival, Frederick left Neustadt and went to Vienna, but Capistran stayed a few days longer. The number of the sick brought to him in Neustadt was reckoned by his companions at 1,500; and 64 cures are recorded.

Crowded as these days were, Capistran was preoccupied with the question of the next step of his journey. He was still urged to go on to Hungary. But conditions in Bohemia drew his attention ever more strongly. He had seen how the court at Neustadt watched closely the developments there, since young Ladislaus was heir apparent of the Bohemian throne. The throne question was complicated by unsettled religious conditions. Almost two decades had elapsed since the Council of Basle made peace with the Hussites, but a peace ominous and unreal. Even in Italy Capistran had kept an eye on the Bohemian heresy. In Wiener-Neustadt he recognized the grave danger existing here in the middle of Europe. An ancient Christian kingdom, a rich and beautiful country, might be forever estranged from the Church. Capistran's love for the whole Western Church flamed up as never before. During his last night in Wiener-Neustadt, June 6, while he was at prayer, he recognized God's will. He was to go to Bohemia and put an end to Utraquist separatism. Exceedingly great joy came over him in view of the great work awaiting him.

Early on June 7 he started for Vienna, but was delayed by troops of pilgrims coming to Neustadt. Scarcely had he dismissed one group when another came in sight. And here it was, amid the green fields, the waving banners, the prayers, songs, and joyful exclamations of the pilgrims, that Capistran revealed to his companions the events of the night just past. They learned with consternation that now, instead of returning to their dear homeland, they were to go still farther to the north, into the land of the heretical Bohemians.

Vienna had begun to doubt whether Capistran would come at all. On June 4 the magistrates sent five messengers, among them two canons of St. Stephen. The next day the mayor of Vienna and several councilors requested Enea Silvio to write to Capistran, that he should not put them to shame by neglecting to visit their city. Enea wrote to Capistran that same day, insisting on the universal desire to see him in Vienna. After this long and troublesome journey from Italy to Austria, he must not now slight the metropolis of the provinces, the capital of the country, the imposing city, the royal residence. He promised the preacher the best results, suggesting that he might gain here perhaps more souls for Christ in one day than anywhere else in a whole year. The people were pious and easily stirred to good. In many regards Vienna might, of course, be called a Babylon, but it could also be called Sion. If it is Babylon, it needs your presence. If it is Sion, it is worthy of your visit.

Capistran did not need these urgings. Since he had decided to go to Bohemia, a visit to Vienna was self-understood, not only because the journey led that way, but because Vienna, whose university was a strong bulwark against the Hussite heresy, was the natural starting point for his new work.

He reached Vienna in the early afternoon, though he was not expected before evening. Preparations for his reception were in full swing. "With the full splendor of solemn procession," was the standard phrase in the reception of royal visitors or dignitaries of the Church. The "full splendor" consisted in holy relics and similar ecclesiastical treasures, which were carried by the students of the university. When Capistran approached, a multitude rushed out, some on horseback, some on foot. Enea Silvio relates as eyewitness how the masses pushed forward to see "the devout father." Many wept tears of joy; others stretched their hands to heaven or snatched at his garment to kiss it.

Capistran preached at once in the church of the Minorites, a beautiful Gothic temple, which stands today, quite isolated, on the Minorite piazza. Next to the church stood the convent, where rooms were held ready for guests. The magistrates assumed the expenses for food. The next day, by request of the cathedral chapter, Capistran preached in St. Stephen's. A secular priest, named John, acted as interpreter.

King Frederick and Enea Silvio promptly assented to the Bohemian visit. Important negotiations were already under way to settle the question of the Bohemian succession and to regulate other political and ecclesiastical affairs. Enea was preparing to go to Bohemia as representative of the King at the diet to meet in Prague. Capistran was satisfied to wait in Vienna for the results of that session. Return to Italy was now not so urgent, and he was earnestly planning to establish some Observant settlements in Austria. The city pleased the Italian brethren exceedingly. The magnificent buildings and the royal squares elicited their admiration; and Capistran himself found Vienna much more beautiful than Florence. The population was estimated, probably too high, at something between 80,000 and 100,000 souls. In his sermons Capistran repeatedly expressed his admiration for this great city. He told the Viennese that their boys sang more beautifully than those in Italy.

The university especially bound him to Vienna. It is not a mere accident that he stayed unusually long in the four university cities,

Vienna, Erfurt, Leipzig, and Cracow. His studies and also his former profession made him a member of the international league of the universities of the Middle Ages, and he felt especially at home in university cities. Here, under the most favorable conditions, he could preach in Latin. Students, professors, and others attached to the university, furnished alone a considerable audience.[2] The Viennese university showed him the highest esteem. In the theological faculties preaching played a very important role. Literary activity was almost exclusively limited to the publishing of Latin feastday sermons, though this academic eloquence seems not to have enjoyed a high reputation. Henry, an Augustinian hermit, once said mockingly: "In the whole university you will not find three masters who can really preach."

In Vienna, as everywhere else, Capistran had enormous audiences. The reports of 80,000 and more, given by him and his companions, are certainly exaggerated. Perhaps even Enea Silvio exaggerated when he spoke of 20,000 or 30,000. What is certain is that St. Stephen's church proved too small. The sermons were, therefore, as in Italy, held mostly in the open air, generally in the cemetery of St. Stephen, or in the piazza before the Carmelite church, where the magistrates had built a pulpit and a spacious stand. Sometimes he preached in a field outside the town. The clergy, the professors, and other prominent people had their places. King Frederick and Prince Ladislaus were often in the audience.

---

[2] Schrauf's history of the university says that the average number of students at this time was 1,038.

CHAPTER XXII

Preacher in Vienna

FROM June 7 to July 27 Capistran preached daily. We possess ample extracts of all these sermons except the first five. We know of no such memorials of his sermons in Italy, where the appearance of itinerant preachers had become a commonplace. Not so in Germany. Now and then indeed, an itinerant preacher could be heard also beyond the Alps, especially in the year of jubilee, 1451, when the indulgences were preached from city to city. But Capistran came preceded by his reputation. No wonder that pens caught up the words of this highly favored man of God. Archives and libraries, widely separated, still contain copies of more than 150 sermons which he preached in Germany from 1451 to 1453. Copies exist in Vienna, Ratisbon, Freiberg in Saxony, in Chemnitz, Meissen, Nuremberg, Bamberg, Erfurt, Halle, Leipzig, and Breslau. Literally exact copies they are not, but more or less faithful excerpts. The art of shorthand was not then practiced in Germany. The recorders took down catchwords and short sentences. Where the manuscripts offer a continuous text, we are dealing probably with reproductions from memory. Still they enable us to get some understanding of Capistran's art of preaching.

In general he follows the traditional rules. After some words on the Gospel or the Epistle of the day, he turns to the main theme. The first few days in Vienna his theme was grace. On the vigil of Pentecost (June 12) he began a treatise on faith, interrupted by dogmatic questions relating to the Holy Ghost. On Pentecost Tuesday the sequence, *Veni, Creator Spiritus*, furnishes him with twenty-two titles of the Holy Ghost.

During this Pentecost week multitudes of people poured into the city. "Vienna looks like Rome during a jubilee; all restaurants, inns, and taverns are filled," writes Fara. Pilgrims came from Styria,

Hungary, Moravia, and Bavaria. Sick pilgrims had reserved places, where in two long rows they waited until, after the sermon, Capistran came to touch them with the relics of St. Bernardine. "If Vienna did not have such a healthy climate and if the wind had not blown continually, the plague would certainly have broken out," writes Fara. Cures on Pentecost Monday brought emotion to a climax. That same evening hundreds of other patients were brought to the Minorite church. The patients themselves, their relatives and friends, all implored the holy name. When Capistran again appeared, the prayers became a deafening roar. Capistran was almost fainting. He again gave the blessing, and retired. But the crowds followed him into the convent, even to the door of his cell. The cloister resembled a fairground.

On Pentecost Wednesday he resumed the tract on faith. Eight names enclose the seven ages of the human race: Adam, Noe, Abraham, Moses, David, Babylonian Exile, Christ, End of the World. The seventh age has seven headings: Justice, Patience, Prudence, Grace, Penance, Poverty, Probation. For two centuries and a half, since 1200, humanity has been living in the sixth cycle, in the period of poverty, i.e., of the mendicant orders. This bird's-eye view of mankind's history recurs often in his sermons. He proves the Christian faith by ancient revelation. Of the twelve articles of the Creed to be proved in this fashion, only the second article, the divinity of Christ, is developed, and this chiefly under the sixth age, the age of the great prophets, the fulfillment of the Messianic prophecies by Christ.

The whole cycle is planned to convince chiefly the Jews, who were obliged to attend his sermons. Thus we understand why he dwelt at length on the Old Testament prophecies. These he applies, under thirty different headings, to the earthly life of the Messias.

One sermon covers the ten events in the youth of Jesus. A second sermon is devoted to the eleventh point, Christ's teaching career. A third sermon (Trinity Sunday, June 20) develops points 12 to 18, which lead over into the history of the Passion. The fourth sermon on June 21, the postponed feast of St. Anthony of Padua, dwells on the Passion prophecies, points 19 to 24. The fifth sermon (points 25 to 29), treats the events between the death of Jesus and the descent of the Holy Ghost. The sixth sermon, last in this cycle, deals with the Last Judgment. Eight words of Jesus offer him eight divisions.

Thursday, June 24, was Corpus Christi. The unusually large crowds of pilgrims made the magistrates fear a shortage of provisions. During the procession Capistran walked in the midst of the gaily dressed aldermen, as if he were the emperor of the whole world and they his servants. He preached in the afternoon, speaking of the Blessed Sacrament as prefigured in the miracles of the Old Testament. He reminds the Jews that in reality they believed in miracles and mysteries greater than those that are contained in the Eucharist. Friday he preached on John the Baptist, "the saint on whose feast I was born." Summing up the tract on the Last Judgment, he gave one sermon, June 28, on the pains of hell-fire. His sermons on the next two days, the feasts of St. Peter and St. Paul, were Christological sermons, one on the monarchical constitution of the Church, the other on Christ's prerogatives as King and High Priest.

His words on papal supremacy did not meet with full approval. In the struggle between the Council of Basle and the Pope the University of Vienna had been throughout on the side of the Council and of the antipope. Frederick III almost had to use force before the University submitted to Nicholas V. Capistran's friendship with the University nearly broke down. Some professors planned to come out publicly against him. But, after some consideration, they abandoned their plan.

On Tuesday, July 1, with a transition from Corpus Christi to the Visitation of the Blessed Virgin, he began a cycle of Marian sermons, in those days a favorite theme. Capistran especially felt urged to preach on Mary. To her he ascribed his recovery from extreme illness during his novitiate. She had appeared to him, and had given him a drink from a silver pitcher. Since then he greeted her whenever he drank or even rinsed his mouth. He recited the Hail Mary aloud before preaching. He taught the Germans to add the second part of the prayer, which so far had not been in vogue there. In regard to the Immaculate Conception, he was an opponent of Scotus, following St. Thomas Aquinas, who had not been able to find sufficient theological reasons for the support of that doctrine. When reminded that the Council of Basle had defined the doctrine of Scotus, he replied that the definition was made after the rupture of the Council with the Pope. But in his sermons on the Blessed Virgin his chief model was Bernardine. He gets a threefold division from the words of the Apocalypse: "Clothed with the sun, with the moon beneath her feet, her head crowned with twelve stars." Each of these three principal parts is divided into twelve, and these twelve are subdivided. The cycle ends with a sermon on Mary's Assumption. This period was closed, according to his custom, with a cycle of sermons on St. Bernardine.

His departure from Vienna, proposed for July 11, was postponed because a number of young men, most of them from university circles, asked to enter the Observance. The time had come for a foundation in Vienna, so much desired by King and people. "I cannot describe the veneration and good will they have here for our Order," he wrote to James of the Marches. "We have accepted many students, and other men from respected circles." He chose St. Theobald, formerly a convent of nuns, situated outside Vienna. On Sunday, July 11, the day set for the transfer, he spoke as follows: "I wished to leave tomorrow, but man proposes and God disposes. Our Holy Father, Nicholas V, sent me here to the King's court, and thus I am the King's prisoner, though of course the captivity is very pleasant. Hence I will stay with you another week. My sermon today will be brief, and after the sermon we will go out together to take possession of St. Theobald."

Judged by the topics covered, the sermon does not seem to have been brief. In jovial fashion he relates the incidents of St. Bernardine's life, speaks of the city of Aquila, and announces voluminous matter for the coming days, when he will preach on St. Bernardine and the advantages of the religious life. From the sermon on the following day we learn that St. Theobald is already opened: "When we marched out, it was very hot; but when we entered the church it began to rain." On Monday, July 12, he accepted ten novices. The storm that came on during the sermon he regards as attacks of the evil spirit. With satisfaction he dwells on the great number of vocations he had already awakened. It sounds self-conscious, yet naïve, when he asks: "Will perhaps one of those received today become a great preacher, and bring 4,000 brethren into the monastery?" His sermons on Bernardine are based on the twelve qualities which he finds in light.

On Saturday, July 17, he announces the "bonfire of vanities." His audience seems prepared for the sacrifice. "Forty-three times, enough for a Lenten season, I have now preached in this city. Many are now contrite." Let them bring their gambling tables, cards, false hair, and other vanities. In return he promises them partnership in all the works of his Order. The Queen, probably Ladislaus' mother, was the first to put gambling tables and headdress into the fire. Evidently the spectacle was repeated on St. Magdalen Day. These great "bonfires of vanities" in St. Stephen's piazza were a topic of conversation in Vienna for a long time after. In Italy, Capistran told them, he had burned such things to the value of about 20,000 ducats. Preaching on the penitent Magdalen, July 22, he said: "Today marks the thirty-sixth year that I have worn the habit." The sevenfold flame of love in the heart of the penitent was his theme. On July 27 he preached his last sermon in Vienna.

During these two months he had preached five series of sermons: on grace, on the promised Messias, on the Last Judgment, on Mary, on the advantages of the religious state. His pulpit oratory in other cities of Germany follows the same plan. He does not dwell too long on one theme. Wishes of his audience, or feasts that occur, furnish sufficient reasons for a new series. Hence his sermon cycles often remain unfinished. His lively temperament also leads him to interweave topics that stand in no relation whatever to the theme of his sermon. To illustrate. In comparing society to an organism, he had, after much detail, arrived at the teeth. Here he remembers a youth who had lost all his teeth through cancer of the jaw-bone and was suddenly cured at the grave of St. Bernardine in Aquila. He stops to give the story in detail, for the glorification of his holy confrere.

In sermons that sometimes lasted for hours and developed difficult trains of ideas, such parentheses were psychologically justified. Listeners had a moment of rest, and renewed their powers of attention. Some similar defense is needed for his complicated method of dividing his material. In the chief parts Capistran prefers the number three, but his subdivisions run from seven to twelve. The third part, for instance, of his sermon of the Last Judgment is divided into two great sections, and one of these has seven divisions; of these seven, one has seven subdivisions. The disadvantages of this method are evident. The natural flow of thought is hemmed, and unified impression is weakened. But, artificial though it is, the method, accompanied by frequent repetition, is an effective aid to understanding.

Capistran's use of Latin robbed him of direct influence on the multitude. But to those who knew Latin he offered, besides rich instruction, also aesthetic enjoyment. He was a master in the Latin of his age. The records show that he knew and wielded the full beauties of that medieval idiom now unjustly ridiculed. The Franciscan school paid notable attention to beautiful language. Its great preachers cultivated the ars prosandi. Headings were given in rhyme; speech had flow and rhythm. In these rules Capistran shows the greatest skill. Sometimes as many as twenty divisions have the same rhyme. Some devices, we must admit, are entirely contrary to our taste, as, for instance, the division of a speech according to the first letters of a word, or especially an almost incredible arbitrariness in word-derivations.

Regarding the contents of his sermons, we get from newly discovered sources an idea essentially different from that hitherto in vogue. The scanty reports of contemporary chroniclers, with their insistence on the "bonfires of vanities," led to the idea, still widely prevalent, that his sermons were fanatical outbursts against luxury, gambling, dancing, and similar follies. But, in truth, invective and moralizing occupy a comparatively small place in his sermons. We search them in vain for such gruesome pictures of corruption as occur in Enea Silvio and other humanists. He does, of course, condemn vice. Cursing was a national vice. He had been told, he said, that an Austrian could not speak without cursing. And cursing was connected with drinking. The Viennese made their living chiefly by making and selling wine. But even on this topic he was sparing. Those who are of sanguine temperament should not drink red wine, since that would produce more blood than white wine. As regards dissoluteness, the protocols of the university itself offer sufficient evidence of the accusations raised by Enea Silvio. But even against these shady sides of student life Capistran inveighs only incidentally.

With noblemen, too proud to study seriously, he is more severe. A nobleman himself, he could more easily tell them serious truths. Nobility of sentiment and character, the charter of noble deeds, is the definition of nobility to which he frequently returns. He quotes St. Jerome: "Why be called a nobleman, if in truth you are a rowdy or a beast?" Knowledge is the crown of kings, and God knows only one nobility: freedom from vice. He never dwells in detail on the vice of immorality, from which, according to Enea Silvio, scarcely a house in Vienna was free. Nobody, he says, doubts the wickedness of that vice. Adultery and impurity are notoriously wicked and lead to hell. Remember the word of the Apostle: Neither fornicators nor adulterers shall possess the kingdom of God.

Capistran's battle is directed rather against those vices which the public conscience seemed no longer to realize as wrong. The two chief vices he chastises are usury and gambling. Senseless luxury in clothing is found equally prevalent on both sides of the Alps. The trailing trains worn by women and some ecclesiastics call forth his sarcasm: "You surely sweep the streets clean," he tells the Viennese women. "My poor habit is worth as much as your goods of silk and purple and damask. If you wished to change with me, I would not consent. But I might take them for chasubles." Their immense ruffs remind him of the spiked collars worn by shepherd dogs in the Abruzzi. "Are you women here in Vienna afraid of the wolves? Take my advice: I will pray to God that the wolves spare you, and you give me your ruffs for the churches and the poor."

He is unusually severe on the sin of his own youth, costly and elaborate care of the hair. "This ugly custom the men in Italy have now left to the women. Here you have the reverse. Long hair does not benefit your health, but rather harms it. Sweat and dust gather, and you need an extra servant. Better spend that money for alms than turn your head into a lice-nest. I go entirely shorn. Is that not better? When the wind blows, your hair gets into your eyes, you may easily fall. To have your hair cut benefits soul, head, and ears. Poor wretches, who love their hair more than their soul." To the wives of such men he gives counsel: "When you are out of material for clothes, just cut off your husband's long hair while he is asleep, and make yourselves a new garment thereof." Occasionally he counts what they squander on their hair: eggs, wine, quicksilver, and different spices. "You are proud of your hair. To what purpose? You rob your wives daily of a dozen eggs to bathe your hair. How many chickens are thus lost! Enough in the end to buy a horse."

Nevertheless sallies of this kind are incidental. Dogma is his predilection, especially the more difficult topics of faith and morals. If at times he seems to be in the lecture hall rather than in the pulpit, we must recall that he preached in Latin, and that his addresses were meant primarily for the academically trained part of his audience. His German interpreter may have omitted portions that were too learned, though the rule seems to have been to translate completely. His interpreter on one occasion confessed his inability to make Capistran's technical terms intelligible to the people. Capistran changed his theme. Even his favored Marian sermons were dogmatic and exegetical, and required the strained attention of his audience. Sermons on the saints and their legends, so common in that age, were rarely preached either by Capistran or by Bernardine. Capistran never outgrew his doctrinal and scholastic method. Learned and explicit definitions come first.

Still the common assumption that his success was due exclusively to his personality is wrong. A closer study reveals his excellent oratorical qualities. His sermons are saturated with Scripture as his wonderful memory provided him with apt quotations promptly and in great number. He has perfect acquaintance with the holy books. Instead of pulpit commonplaces he draws new pictures, new comparisons, new proofs, from the inexhaustible treasure of Scripture, preferring the prophets, whom he allows, in long quotations, to speak directly to the audience. But where he feels the need, he carefully explains the meaning of the sacred words, and he is circumstantial and vivid when he narrates biblical events. He introduces Adam with this monologue: "What shall I do now? If I give in, I offend God. If I do not, Eve will give me no rest." He is a skillful painter of picturesque scenes, like that of the infant Moses in the bulrushes.

He shares the fondness of his age for the accommodated sense of Scripture.[1] The parable of the prodigal son he interprets, in one and the same sermon, in three different ways. First, the elder son represents the Jews, the younger son, the Gentiles. The heathens did not preserve the true faith, but adored idols, symbolized by the swine. The Romans built the Pantheon to adore demons. But God, through Constantine, led them to the true faith. Thus the heathen returned to himself and said: Father, I have sinned. But the Jews, the elder son, would not enter, even when the Father begged them to do so. Consequently they became sons of the devil.

Second. The younger son is any sinner. He takes his share, that is, his freedom, his five senses, and uses them for his own pleasure. Satisfying these desires is "feeding the swine." Seeing, then, so many servants of God, he comes to himself, returns to his Father, and says: Father, I have sinned; and the Father, full of compassion, receives him gladly. The elder son is those who are proud and just. Better the humble penitent than the man proud of being just.

Third. The elder son stands for the devils. They were created before us. Our Father looks upon our lowliness, while the devil, seeing how God has taken the younger son, i.e., human nature, to Himself, is jealous of men, because his pride keeps him from being saved. The festal garment which the Father orders to be brought is faith and sanctifying grace; the ring is hope; the shoes are the examples of the saints.

In a sermon on St. James he quotes the words of Christ: "Can

[1] Before the accommodated sense of Scripture comes the literal sense, which Capistran's sermons often distinguish from the spiritual sense.

you drink My chalice?" and appends a list of twelve different meanings which the word chalice has in Holy Scripture. Every detail of Scripture is grist for his mill. In the scene of the adulteress, since the old Pharisees went out first, he concludes that sins in old age are greater than the sins of young people. His explanations are sometimes bold. Susanna squandered oil when bathing; hence God allowed affliction. The mother of the Zebedees did not know that to stand at the left of Jesus means to be condemned. Jesus at the miraculous pond, by healing one man, taught the unity of the Church. The five loaves and the two fishes refer to penance. Ears of corn point to contrition, the five loaves of bread to five qualities of penance. Of the two small fishes, one comes out of bitter water, that is, the fear of punishment; the other comes from sweet water, that is, the hope of heaven. The one boy again symbolizes the unity of the Church. Such explanations, exaggerating the accommodated sense, still show his love of minute circumstances, and often shed surprising light on important truths.

The figurative language of Scripture kept him from becoming monotonous or unintelligible. A listener in Leipzig writes to a friend: "The grace of the word shines wonderfully in this man. He is a master in applying the sacred text to time, place, and circumstances."

Besides the inspired authors, he quotes, though far less frequently, other authors, ecclesiastical and secular. Of the great Fathers of the Church he cites most frequently Gregory the Great, Jerome, and Augustine. Of medieval authors and theologians he quotes Bernard of Clairvaux, Hugh and Richard of St. Victor, Thomas Aquinas. From the sequences of St. Thomas he recites entire stanzas. Of the ancients he quotes Aristotle, especially in defining and outlining; also Boethius and Seneca; more rarely Ovid, Horace, and Sallust. His own geography of the world beyond he prefers to that of the poets.

Like Bernardine he clothes the scholastic skeleton with flesh and blood. Nature and human life are an endless source of comparisons. His favorite illustration for an impenitent sinner is the mole whose eyes are covered with a tender membrane which breaks at the time of its death. He sees and dies. So, too, the sinner. Punishment opens his eyes, which were closed by sin. He sees and dies. In new-born snakes, devouring their mother's entrails, he sees apostate children devouring the Church. Snakes slough their skin, to put on a new man. In Italy he had watched a snake, which jammed itself down into a pile of pebbles and stripped off its skin. The donkey keeps close eye on the spot where it fell and never goes there again. Animals illustrate concord, sociability, even modesty.

Contrition is derived from conterere, which means "to grind." Grinding needs two stones, the upper one of hope, and the lower one of fear. Humility is a vessel, filled to the brim, and air-tight. Such a vessel retains the water, even if you make a hole in the bottom. But if you make a fissure at the top the water promptly runs out below. Let the least breath of haughtiness enter the human heart, and the water of divine grace leaves it. He is blunt in humbling pride. No animal equals man in evil-smelling excrement. The sense organs betray what man hides within. Take the eyes. What do they produce? Certainly no balm. Our ears? Surely no wax. Our nose? Certainly no honey. Our mouth? No syrup. And our flesh! Even during lifetime it breeds worms, lice, and vermin. Such is man's misery!

The daily routine of human life is symbolic. He recalls his Italian homeland, its silkworms, its industry, its farming, its sugar and cotton. He portrays the wine-fakers who put in honey and brandy, to give their drink strength and sweetness. Fearing the Viennese wine dealers may learn similar tricks, he says: "If I were sure of this, I would never say Mass here again." He describes the busy women preparing delicacies from bitter fruits.

Drastically he paints the crosses of married life. The husband comes home and would like to rest. His wife begins to complain: "Unhappy hour, when I came to you. My neighbor is so beautifully dressed, she wears grand ruffles and gold rings and precious stones. And I, poor wretch, am despised, because I got into your hands." And the poor man broods over his poverty. Again he dwells on the hour of his death. His children, friends, property, wife. What will she do? Whom will she marry? But she plays the role of the hapless, unconsolable one, saying: "Leave me something. I promise you I shall never marry again." The poor fellow believes, bequeaths to her a fortune, more than a dowry. But she thinks: "Now he may go, I have what I wanted." When he is near death she says: "Bring a candle, hold it near his mouth. Curse it. The candle is out. He doesn't want to die." But when he does die, her only thought is whom to marry next.

Sometimes whole sermons, ever a series of sermons, are built up on one sense-image: the noble horse, the parts of a ship, the weapons of war, the qualities of purple. He utilizes especially his own experiences. The lofty pines on Monte Alverno, the stony road from Jerusalem to Mount Olivet, liturgical usage in Rome, pilgrims in Assisi for the Portiuncula. That all undertakings must be well planned, he illustrates by a description of the great hospital in Aquila.

As a royal officer he had once imprisoned mutinous soldiers. Although they had everything they needed, they tried to throw themselves out of the window. How hard it is to lose freedom! With an astonishing candor he speaks of the most intimate things in his own life, his errors, his marriage, his conversion, if they but serve to clarify his subject. His sermons thus become an important source for his biography. But with equal unconcern he speaks of his great deeds as a religious. He has a special liking for numbers: his dates of birth, of conversion, of entrance into the Order; twenty-five attacks were made on his life; between Villach and Nuremberg he employed successively twenty-four interpreters. He has led four thousand youths into the Order. He has written fourteen hundred letters of affiliation. With exact statistics he gives his listeners a picture of the Observance.

In contents, then, his sermons are webs of many and multicolored strands: Scripture and the Fathers, pictures and comparisons, legends and personal experiences. Equally rich in variety is his language. He is master of the scale, from joviality to pathos. He imitates the cry of the crow. He mimics mothers silencing their children, to show how God calls sinners. He knows, in Italy, the contemporary representative of the family of Aquinas.

The stories he tells of the immense girth of that holy man would hardly suit the pulpit taste of our own days. He is also master of sublime rhetoric. Apostrophe is his strong point. He summons the spirits of people long since dead. "Where is your glory now, where your triumphs, O Caesar, where your wealth? In the devil's cavern. Nero, where is your cruelty now? Humbled, in eternal damnation. Maximian, where are your treasures, your pleasures, your power, your titles? In the habitation of the devil." He paints the transient nature of earthly power and greatness, leading his listeners to a long line of deathbeds. "When the pope dies, he is no longer pope. When the cardinal dies, he is no longer cardinal. When a patriarch dies, he can no longer be patriarch." And thus in dreadful monotone through the long line of ecclesiastical and secular dignitaries: a real dance of death in the pulpit.

CHAPTER XXIII

Holiness and Miracles

CAPISTRAN'S southern vivacity, his continual changes of tone, his ceaseless gesticulation, did not always appeal to sedate Germans. He had to defend himself. Preaching on the Last Judgment, he pronounced with thundering voice the words: "Depart from me, you cursed." Here he suddenly paused, and inserted a defense of rhetoric. "If you have read Cicero or Augustine, then you know how much tone and gesture mean to the people, who are more impressed by what they see than by what they hear. When you wish to lead them to devotion, you must raise your voice. But when you say, 'Depart from me, ye cursed,' then you must shout like thunder. That is demanded by the meaning of the words. But the words, 'Come, ye blessed of my Father,' are to be spoken gently." Then he continued his sermon.

He had to face still more serious contradiction. In Italy people had the custom, during certain sermons, of crying aloud for mercy: "Misericordia! Misericordia!" Capistran led his German listeners to the same practice on seeing the relics of St. Bernardine. Such expressions, natural in a southern people, were certainly hazardous among northerners, and aroused opposition. To adapt a well-tried method to foreign conditions needs time. But Capistran, hurrying from one city to another, had often to sacrifice his night's rest for the immediate preparation of a two-hour sermon for the following morning.

The aging missioner's days were truly exhausting. Holy Mass, the sermon, repetition by the interpreter, claimed the whole forenoon. Then came his breviary. Then he visited the sick. After dinner many came for audience. After Vespers he again visited the sick, sometimes until nightfall. Much of the night went to study and correspondence. Time for sleep he had long since limited to four hours, or even three. Now he curtailed it still more. "I sleep two hours, sometimes only one hour," he said in a Viennese pulpit. He gloried in his gift of awaking when he wished to. He called this a particular grace. But he felt this battle against sleep. "I would rather just now rest than preach. But I belong not to myself, but to you." And he did profit by an occasional free hour for rest. But his general ascetic manner of living stayed with him into old age. He had abstained so long from meat that his stomach refused to take it. When, during a serious illness, he obeyed a papal order, the meat gave him such nausea that the order had to be withdrawn. "I get along on eggs or fish just as well as these fine gentlemen with their endless line of dishes." Human nature needs little nourishment, as Boethius remarks. Even in his old age he continued to use instruments of penance. Simply and frankly he describes a hairshirt, and concludes: "When you have slept one night in that fashion you feel as if you had slept on needles."

His very appearance betrayed heroic abnegation. "I saw him in Vienna: a little old man, haggard, lean, withered, mere bones and skin." That is the famous description by Enea Silvio. But these severities were not a burden that he dragged along. Unchangeable cheerfulness is the characteristic repeated with surprising regularity in descriptions of him. "I never met a more joyful man," says Jerome of Udine. Enea Silvio, gifted with a fine sense of observation, cannot suppress his astonishment at the constant good humor of this man, who seemed to live on work and self-denial. "No one ever saw him gloomy. You saw always the same expression of happiness and tireless energy."

His natural disposition was his ally. He was amused when a literary opponent, who did not know him personally, represented him as a melancholy man. "Radically mistaken diagnosis," he said, since his temperament was rather a mixture of the choleric and the sanguine. He had indeed his hours of gloom and dejection, but he soon reasserted himself. In general he was the dauntless adventurer, whom resistance and failure do not break but inflame. Like St. Bernardine he believed in success rather than in failure. From their seraphic father both had inherited the holy cheerfulness of the children of God. Bernardine was habitually joking and laughing. The German Franciscan, Frederick of Thorn, whom Capistran called from Italy to Vienna as interpreter, preached on the exuberant gaiety of Bernardine, who had told him how he learned to shriek while preaching. "Brother Frederick, I learned that from the donkeys in Siena. A fair was held there while I was preaching, and the donkeys brayed during the whole sermon. So I had to bray, too." Even in the pulpit these serious preachers, on certain occasions, did not disdain to use a most jovial tone. Joviality was not the least of the motives which drew the crowds to these men. Radiant face and vivacious mind, says Varese, made Capistran's sermons so attractive.

The goal of all asceticism is joyful self-dominion, which releases man's higher powers. Capistran had this complete self-control. All admired his careful use of time, and his quiet and well-planned method of work. All problems, great and small, were ranged in proper order with calm equanimity. His leisure was labor, his labor leisure. He worked incessantly, but without becoming a slave of work. At a time when he was overloaded with work he received from a friend a donation of cookies and wine and fish. He answers, not with a scribbled word of thanks, but with an attractive and ingenious little essay on the symbolic meaning of those gifts. He never succumbed to the common temptation of gaining time at the cost of devotion. He held steadily to the ideal of Franciscan piety, profound contemplation followed by energetic activity. Deeply concentrated in saying his office, he kept the canonical hours also while traveling. He preferred to recite the breviary with a confrere, pronouncing each word, each syllable, slowly and clearly. Voluntary devotions, like the penitential psalms, the office for the poor souls, the Little Office of the Blessed Virgin, he would in cases of necessity postpone at the moment, to be said during his next journey.

Saintliness rather than extraordinary ability drew attention to him. Listen to the words of his companion, Nicholas Fara: "A holy soul, filled with spiritual joy, streamed forth visibly over the whole appearance of this man. You could easily find him in a crowd of

Franciscans, though you had never seen him before."

Ignorance of northern languages deprived Capistran of the confessional. But instead he was continually besieged by multitudes of sick people. On his mission tours, this care for the sick, traditional among Observants, assumed peculiar forms. "The people have a faith I have never seen before," he writes to Aquila. "They come long distances, even three, four, and five hundred miles. They call to God, and cry for mercy. They beg St. Bernardine for help. Their tears would soften hearts of marble." Deeply touched, almost ill himself with compassion, he traverses the long lines of patients, who, supported on crutches or lying on cots, wait for his blessing. Sudden and perfect cures are reported, few of course in comparison with those who were not cured. Capistran insisted that cases of cure should be carefully recorded, not only to glorify the new saint, to whose intercession he ascribed all the graces, but also to put to shame the old opponents of Bernardine and of the Observance. These reports, however brief, contain all essentials: name and residence of the person cured, sometimes also his state of life and age; the nature and duration of the sickness; day and place of cure. Nicholas Fara, the first recorder, reports two hundred cures at Vienna.

Fara was succeeded by a Bavarian Franciscan, Conrad of Freyenstadt, who prepared a full list of what were called Bernardine's miracles. This liber miraculorum contains 2,507 reports of miracles, under seven headings: raised from the dead, saved from death, blind restored to sight, lamed and crippled cured, lepers cured, deaf and mute restored, and those cured of various diseases. Of the fifteen hundred cures assigned to Capistran's tour beyond the Alps, about one half falls into the first four months, from the end of May to the beginning of October, 1451; the other half is distributed over the following four years. This decrease in the number of recorded miracles may well be partly due to lack of recorders, and to their increasing negligence, which gives rise to repeated complaints. But we must also note that Capistran's appearance did not call forth everywhere the same enthusiasm. National characteristics, general religious conditions, apathy following the first excitement, reduced the concourse of sick people seeking help. In Capistran's second period in Vienna, in 1455, though like the first one it lasted several weeks, the liber miraculorum registers only two cures. Of course this fact is no argument against the genuineness of the cures recorded.

A strong presumption in favor of genuineness is found in the fact that persons who participated in the events are the witnesses. In some places the secular authorities investigated these cures, and furnished official documents. But as a rule Capistran's companions did the recording. Considering the limits of time, the pressure of the multitudes, and the great number of reported cures, only summary procedure was possible. Further, the brothers depended on interpreters, and thus often give us distorted names. Again, the declarations about the nature of the illness are often so general and vague that the nature of the cure remains obscure. In the group of the deaf, for instance, we read that a person had formerly heard poorly or little, and that after Capistran's blessing he again heard well.

Thorough examination of the course of the disease was hardly ever made. Medical judgment is nowhere noted. The pilgrims, who sometimes came from great distances, soon dispersed again in all directions. Thus the lasting effect of the cures could hardly be established. Rumors are heard asserting that these cures were not lasting, that after Capistran's departure the patients came back to the church to get their crutches. We must reckon with the possibility that many of those cures were the natural effect of extreme emotion. All these conditions made official attestation extremely difficult. Looking back today, we would prefer well documented reports of a small number of cures. But the point of view at that time was different. Capistran and his companions felt obliged, for the glory of God in his servant Bernardine, not to lose anything reported to them as a special grace. That they were guided by the fullest sincerity is proved on every page of the liber miraculorum, which enabled contemporaries to investigate the veracity of the reports. Conrad of Freyenstadt omitted numerous reports because they did not contain the names of those who were healed.

This defect may be partly responsible for contemporary criticism. But this criticism went beyond all reasonable bounds. Some mocked Capistran's miracles by inventing ridiculous reports. Thus a man was said to have sent his wife to Vienna, secretly hoping she would die, so he might marry again. But the woman came back in perfect health, and found her husband in bed with the disease she had lost. If his blind dog were cured, said another, he would believe Capistran's miracles. The dog did get its eyesight back, but the man became blind on the spot. And so on. Thus people at a distance might easily be skeptical or neutral. They did not hear the reports of the liber miraculorum with its exact details, but only exaggerated rumors.

Further, Capistran's personal opponents were not likely to believe in his charismatic gifts. To these opponents belonged men like Matthias Döring, head of the German Franciscan Conventuals, who was completely upset by the advance of the great Observant leader. More weight attaches to the views of men who stood closer to Capistran during these years. Thus Enea Silvio is very reserved when he speaks of the miraculous cures by Capistran, and seems to be neutral on the question of their genuineness. Canon Tocke of Magdeburg roundly denies any true miracles, as does likewise an unknown chronicler who had heard Capistran preach in Judenburg and Vienna. But these reports do not in any way indicate that their authors had sufficient interest to observe at first hand Capistran's visits to the sick.

The *liber miraculorum* must remain our chief guide in discussing the authenticity of Capistran's miracles. Take as illustration the following passage. "Conrad of Nuremberg, of the Order of St. Augustine, suffering from gout, lay in the corridor of the cloister. He was blessed, promptly threw away his stick, and walked about in perfect health. In his joy he kissed the ground in the presence of all of us." The phrase, "under the eyes of the brethren," recurs regularly in the *liber miraculorum*. Capistran used to test the cures on the spot. He made the deaf and dumb repeat the words he told them. He took away crutches from the lame and told them to walk. Writing to Italy about these wonders, Capistran says: "We have seen them with our own eyes and touched them with our own hands." In some cases persistence of the cure is particularly stressed. To illustrate. "John Honer, a Viennese and sixty-eight years old, an educated man, formerly beadle[1] in the faculty of arts, lame for thirty years, so that he could hardly walk with crutches, was blessed by the father, and went away quite easily, without any support, and is today still as healthy as a man of twenty." Other well-known personalities in Vienna are registered as thoroughly cured. The author of these reports is a member of the new convent of St. Theobald in Vienna. It is difficult to imagine how this man, a few years after the events, when the people he mentions as cured still lived at the same place, could have written such things if they were not true.

Capistran is often blamed for making so much ado about these healings. But we must remember that he himself ascribed all these favors to the intercession of St. Bernardine. Witnesses of these events, however, especially his own confreres, were convinced that he himself was the wonder-worker. Healing often came simply from his blessing. His biographers report similar events from the very beginning of his Franciscan life. The cures reported from that period are few. Prophecy and power over demons are prominent. His general reputation as a wonder-worker came during Bernardine's canonization. Bishop Capranica, who first directed the process, ascribed at least some of the cures to Capistran. The jurist Sulperti compares him to St. Francis of Assisi and St. Anthony of Padua. But the full tide of extraordinary events began in Lombardy in the year 1451, and reached its climax that same year in Vienna.

Capistran, surrounded by this supernatural abundance, lived months of intensity and enthusiasm, as his own and Fara's letters plainly testify. Nothing similar has been seen since the days of the apostles, says Fara. But empty enthusiasm could not satisfy Capistran. These wonderful acts of God were only the preparation for far greater things which were to come, and for which God had chosen him as the instrument. In Bohemia, he told his brethren,

[1] Editor's note: A ceremonial official.

they would experience things even far more wonderful. Others, too, shared these keen expectations. What crusades and council, parliaments and papal legates, had not done, this man sent from God would accomplish. Thus spoke even very sober contemporaries. The enthusiasm which his mere name released everywhere would sweep away all heresy from Bohemia and bring the whole kingdom back to the Church. Capistran thought, and told his brethren, that he was to die in Bohemia and find there his last resting place.

In this anticipation he was mistaken, for his Hussite mission did not have the decisive success he had hoped for. Nor did he die in Bohemia. But these expectations, a fruit of his lively imagination, show how concentrated he was on achieving great things for the kingdom of God. The chief of the great ecclesiastical problems, so he rightly thought, was the subjugation of the Utraquist separatists. His apostolic spirit had outgrown the narrowness of his earlier years. His predilection for Italy, his disinclination to withdraw any spiritual forces from the queen of the provinces, was a weakness, now changed into apostolic strength. The task which he undertakes will probably keep him permanently beyond the Alps. "He has decided never to return to Italy," writes Fara. His fear is that he may be forced to return. Only a papal command, so he informs his brethren in Italy, can bring him back. But he warns them earnestly against seeking such a command. Hindering such an important work would lie on their consciences. Even physically he seemed rejuvenated. Ten years earlier he felt he was at the end of his career, and desired rest. Now he is really an old man, after the superhuman labors of these past years. But we hear no more complaints, no more calls to be released. He runs from work to work like a man in the bloom of youth.

CHAPTER XXIV

History of Utraquism

"IN body I am still with you, but in spirit I am already in Bohemia." Thus he spoke in the Viennese pulpit. He must go to Prague to dispute with Rokytzana and his adherents. He must convert them, at least refute them, even if it costs his life. On every occasion he combats Utraquist doctrine. His sermons in Vienna were attended by Bohemian ambassadors and pilgrims.

On July 27 he delivered his parting sermon. "Fifty days we have been here. We came on June 7, and today is July 27." First he must give thanks, thanks to the Most Holy Trinity, the Blessed Virgin, the apostles and evangelists, the martyrs and confessors, virgins and widows, the patriarchs, prophets, and all the saints. He thanks Pope Nicholas V who sent him. He thanks the august King of the Romans who called him, "who even deigned to visit me in my cell." He thanks Ladislaus and Albrecht. He thanks the venerable University of Vienna, all its masters of theology, law, medicine, and the arts. He thanks all who had honored his sermons: mayor, magistrates, and citizens. Lastly he thanks the Queen, who came repeatedly to his sermons, giving a good example to all other noble ladies.

Secondly he commends all present and absent to the divine Majesty, to the Blessed Virgin, and to all the saints. He commends to his audience the souls of their ancestors, who perhaps still suffer in purgatory. "I commend to you also the clergy and the religious, the poor, the students, all churches, orders, cloisters, and hospitals. In the name of the newly established convent of St. Theobald, I thank the King for its foundation, and Duke Albrecht for the altar in honor of St. Bernardine. I hope that St. Theobald will be the first of many foundations. I leave here twenty brothers, among them my two eyes, my right eye, Brother Michael, an able member of your university; my left eye, an old companion from Milan, Brother Jerome. Brother Michael I leave as guardian and representative. Brother Jerome as vicar of the convent."

Thirdly, he must give them something. But what? "We have received generous alms. What shall I give you in return? I have nothing, I am nothing. Yet I am something. Only if I had no charity would I be nothing. In charity, then, I give you myself. I give myself to the august King of the Romans, to the King of Hungary, to the Austrian nobility. I give myself as servant to the venerable University. I dare not say as a son. For I am not worthy of that. To all in general I grant a share in the good works of the Order. And thus I put my life into your hands, and press you all to my heart."

What was the situation in Bohemia when Capistran approached? Fifteen years before, on July 5, 1436, the Hussite representatives had promised obedience to the delegates of the Council of Basle. The conciliar delegates had then released them from the ban and declared them true sons of the Church. That peace was based on the "four articles of Prague." These four articles were: first, free preaching of the Gospel by capable priests; second, the reception of Holy Communion under both species; third, renunciation of worldly possessions by the clergy; fourth, punishment of grievous sins.

But this peace was delusive from the start. The Hussites had indeed been victorious on the battlefield. Their adversaries, the crusaders, were dispersed. But the victors needed peace even more than the conquered. In the fifteenth century, in Catholic Europe, how could an openly declared un-Catholic state assert itself for any length of time? This reformed Hussite state Church, to survive at all, must either return to the Mother Church, or appeal to the schismatic Church of the East. The Hussites rejected the name of heretics as the greatest insult. They wanted to be and remain Catholic Christians. But in the great Catholic house they wanted a room to their own taste. This was their reason for sending representatives to Basle. On the other hand the Council needed agreement with the unconquered Hussites as support. After many negotiations, repeatedly interrupted and always renewed, the agreement had been reached. The four articles of Prague, limited by a few additions, were declared Catholic. Grievous sins were to be punished by the secular power, but only by those legitimately authorized. The word of God should be freely preached, but only by approved preachers and under reservation of the papal supremacy. Secular power and earthly goods have to be given up, but only by those members of the clergy who have pledged themselves to do so by vow. But the chalice for the laity met far greater difficulties.

The chalice movement antedated the Hussite upheaval. It was prepared by a popular Eucharistic movement. Bohemian preachers and authors, during the entire fourteenth century, had been urging frequent and even daily reception of Holy Communion. But this genuinely religious movement fell into the hands of misguided leaders. As the Fraticelli accused the Church of apostatizing from apostolic poverty, so these zealots accused her of neglecting the administration of the Holy Eucharist. Back to the entire Christ, they cried, back to Communion under both species. These zealots did not know that the Church had withdrawn the chalice from the laity in order to reduce the danger of profanation and to refute erroneous opinions about the manner of Christ's Eucharistic presence.

The year 1380 is generally assigned as the beginning of the movement, though a pastor in Prague had before that time preached the necessity of the chalice for laymen. But the real originator of the doctrine was Master Peter of Dresden. Exiled from Dresden, he settled in Prague and found there sympathy and adherents. Under Jacobell of Mies three parish churches introduced the practice in Prague. People were aroused. Sharing in the chalice was to be a panacea for all evils. For Hus, who was in Constance, the chalice for the laity was only one of many ecclesiastical reforms. But the masses of the Bohemian people found in the chalice a visible symbol of resistance, a party banner, a catchword to inflame passion. These followers of Hus were now called Utraquists, that is, those who receive Communion under both species. The Hussite wars became crusades for the holy chalice. This national situation strongly influenced the Council of Basle. Peace with Bohemia meant granting the chalice. The Council, while demanding full acceptance of Catholic doctrine on the Eucharist, granted Utraquists the chalice for the laity. This compact, signed November 26, 1433, ran as follows: In Bohemia and Moravia, Holy Communion shall be given under both species to all adults who demand it; but the priests must impress on the people that the whole Christ is present under each of the two species.

Some churches became Utraquist, others remained Unionist. The Taborites, who opposed every effort for peace with the Church, were subdued the next year (1434). In 1435 the Diet of Prague accepted the Compact in principle. And the Diet of Iglau, in the following year (1436) brought solemn reconciliation with the Church.

Which of the Utraquist factions would gain dominion in Bohemia? On this question depended the fate of the reconciliation based on the Compact. Some parties, like the one headed by Master Pribram, satisfied with the concession of the chalice, were determined to stand firmly on Catholic ground in everything else. But the overwhelming majority had long since been under the energetic control of the Hussite leader, Master John Rokytzana, who was organizing a Utraquist separate Church. Capistran's mission meant a contest with this man, an energetic leader like himself, and equally talented.

John came from a poor family of cloth-makers in Rokytzana, near Pilsen. Prompted by need rather than real vocation, he tried to join the Augustinian canons in his native city. The superiors did not trust the arrogant youth and dismissed him. He returned to Prague and there finished his studies. Hussite ideas found in him a passionate and gifted champion. He was an excellent orator and clever negotiator, born for ruling and organizing. After John Hus had died and after Archbishop Conrad of Prague had joined the Hussites and been excommunicated by the Pope, Rokytzana assumed full management of the whole Utraquist Church. Whether he was ever validly ordained remained a disputed question. On his moral conduct we have contradictory reports.

Officially Rokytzana was preacher at the Teyn church. But in this cathedral pulpit he was a demagogue rather than a theologian.

Nature had given him iron lungs. From Jacobell of Mies, the creator of the Hussite Church, he had inherited unshakable zeal for the chalice, but also a certain respect for the tradition of the Roman Church as the guardian of the ancient faith. The Roman Church, however, had fallen into some errors; to correct these errors was the mission of Hussitism. The chief correction lay in the absolute necessity for all Christians to receive Holy Communion under both species. The practical consequences of this fundamental principle had been drawn by Jacobell of Mies, who, after baptizing infants, gave them Communion under both species. Contemporaries accused Rokytzana of errors in his teaching on the Eucharist. On this point the Hussite sects were divided, but Rokytzana was very tolerant toward them all. To be archbishop of Prague was his great ambition. The death of Archbishop Conrad (1431) opened the door. He went, therefore, to the Council, just opening in Basle, as Bohemian agent. Tenacious in wresting from the Council all possible Hussite concessions, he finally agreed to the Compact, on the promise of Sigismund to labor for his installation in Prague.

The Utraquists of the Rokytzana type accepted the Compact, not at all as a concession granted by the Church for reasons of pastoral prudence, but as a victory of their national reform over the reluctant Church. According to their view, the universal Church, assembled in council, after long and persistent refusal, had finally, by removing the ban, acknowledged and approved the Hussite teachings.

The granting of Communion in the form instituted by Christ they welcomed as the beginning of a general reform of the Church. Nor did they feel bound to accept the conditions and declarations of the Council, since these latter contradicted the Gospels. Logically they should simply have refused the Compact. But they shrewdly dissembled the last consequences of their doctrines and interpreted the imperial document, signed by Sigismund at Iglau, as the Magna Charta of Hussitism.

Rokytzana lost no time. The very next day after the ratification of the Compact he gave the chalice to lay persons in a non-Utraquist church of Iglau. Bishop Philibert of Constance, whom the Council charged with the execution of the Compact, had a difficult task. For the moment Rokytzana was forced to leave Prague, because of Sigismund's wrath at his persistent refusal to return to Basle for collaboration in the dogmatic constitution on the Sacrament of the Altar. This constitution (December 23, 1437) states clearly and precisely traditional Catholic doctrine. It was sent to Prague, but the Utraquist theologians and preachers ignored it completely. Philibert began to allot churches to each rite. But, while trying to save what could be saved, the noble prelate, highly esteemed by both parties, died as a victim of the plague (1439). Prague gave him an honorable funeral. Rokytzana now resided chiefly in the territory of Königgrätz, a citadel of Hussitism. A Catholic king might have succeeded, in spite of the Compact, in restoring Bohemia to the Church. But two Catholic rulers died in rapid succession. In December, 1437, Emperor Sigismund died at Znaim. With him the Luxemburg line, which had ruled Bohemia almost a century, was extinguished. His son-in-law and heir, the Hapsburg Albrecht, died in 1439. The Bohemian claims of his posthumous son, Ladislaus, were supported by his uncle, the German king, Frederick III, but were not generally acknowledged.

During the interregnum the law of the strong hand prevailed. Among the barons, who now usurped all power, Ulrich Rosenberg was the leader of the Catholic party. No Bohemian baron could compete in wealth with the Rosenbergs, the "kings of South Bohemia." Ulrich held court in Krumau. Two things rendered fruitless his championship of the Catholic cause. First, his selfishness seems to have prevented the election of a king. Secondly, he met his master in the young and gifted baron, George Podebrad, who, about 1435, became leader of the Utraquists. In the short, stocky figure of George lived an extraordinary spirit, revealed in flashing eyes. Though far below Rosenberg in resources, he entered the conflict resolutely. An inveterate Utraquist, he had two principal aims: the approval of Rokytzana's election as archbishop of Prague, and the exclusive dominion of the chalice in all Bohemian lands.

In 1448 Pope Nicholas V sent Cardinal John Carvajal as legate to Bohemia. On May 1 the cardinal solemnly entered Prague. A gorgeous parade of 500 horsemen, among them Ulrich Rosenberg and his three sons, accompanied the legate into the city. Deceived by that splendid reception, the legate tried to persuade the people of Prague to renounce the Compact. This proposal provoked the Utraquist clergy to extremes. They aroused the populace, and the cardinal was threatened with death. His position became intolerable. On May 23 he fled, protected by Rosenberg, but pursued by the mob with curses and stones, while the butchers of Prague swung meat-axes against Rosenberg's men. Then sudden rumor said that the legate had carried off the Compact. Four hundred horsemen set out in pursuit. In his haste Carvajal had really taken with him the document, which Podebrad had given him for information. With difficulty he persuaded his pursuers to wait till he reached Beneschau. There he returned the document.

These events sharpened the dividing lines. While that party which inclined to Catholicism, guided by Master Pribram, vanished entirely, some great lords renounced the chalice and returned to the Church. Among them were men like Meinrad of Neuhaus, next to Rosenberg the richest baron of Bohemia. Others joined Rokytzana, among them Master John Borotin, who had been an opponent. Three months later (September 2) Podebrad seized the capital, thus becoming master of Bohemia. Rokytzana returned, after eleven years of absence, and was received with almost as much pomp as when the papal legate had been received in May. All opponents—the cathedral chapter, the Catholic clergy, the German university students—left Prague, which now became the political and ecclesiastical center of Utraquism. The senate of Prague solemnly announced the Compact as the basis of Bohemian Church discipline, and at the same time strictly forbade the distribution of Holy Communion under one species. This procedure showed Rokytzana's intention to lead the bulk of the people purposely into error about the real contents of the Compact. From the pulpit of Teyn he thundered against the Roman Church, referring to the Holy Father as "the beast of the Apocalypse." Secret negotiations began with the Greek schismatics. The Catholic nobility, which under Rosenberg formed a federation, succumbed (1450). Podebrad was the undisputed ruler of Bohemia, even if his own adherents, out of jealousy, still refused him the title of imperial vice-regent.

Thirty years of confusion (1420-50) thus found temporary solution. The chaos, political and ecclesiastical, of the last decades had yielded to some sort of order and discipline. The remaining Taborites led a harmless life. All other Hussites followed Rokytzana. A third of the population was still Catholic, but Utraquism was now the established Church. If Podebrad and Rokytzana remained at the helm, Catholicism would in time be eliminated. Only where the majority was entirely Catholic, as for instance in Pilsen, could things go on as before. In Prague and elsewhere the lay chalice was, in violation of the Compact, introduced by force.

The Utraquists differed from Catholics only by the lay chalice and Communion for infants. While the Taborite priests celebrated Mass in secular dress and exclusively in the Czech language, the Utraquists retained tonsure and liturgical vestments, and celebrated Mass according to the Roman rite, with the exception of Epistle and Gospel, which were read in Czech. Ancient ecclesiastical customs were still honored. The Corpus Christi procession was celebrated with great splendor. Capistran once ridiculed the Hussite reformers with these words: "First you taught forty-five heretical articles. Then you discarded these one after another until only four were left. Now you maintain only one of these four." The lay chalice remained the only distinctive sign of a system which had begun by discarding all Church history, and by insisting on the Bible as the sole rule of faith. Instead of leading an international rebellion against Rome, the Hussites were now content with being a kind of High Church, outwardly in contact with the world-wide Roman Catholic Church.

But these champions of a "still-born reformation" were inwardly far from being true Catholics. Their Eucharistic doctrine was erroneous, supported by appeal to the Bible alone. The Wyclif-Hussite heresy, said Capistran, was revived by Rokytzana. The Utraquists, like the Taborites, refused submission to the Church. Yet the Utraquists, supported by the Compact, boasted of being true sons of the Church. The ban had been taken from them; they were not heretics. Pope Nicholas V and Callistus III addressed Rokytzana as "most beloved son." But this peace, a fruit of schism, rested on intrinsic insincerity. Even without Capistran's interference it would have broken down.

Utraquist leaders did not feel safe, in spite of the powerful position of Podebrad and Rokytzana in Bohemia. Foreign relations had suffered by the maltreatment of Carvajal. The Council of Basle had come to an inglorious end, and Nicholas V was universally acknowledged. The great German Empire, to which Bohemia belonged politically, obeyed the pope. Toward the end of the year 1449 Rokytzana decided to go to Rome himself, but turned back after reaching Salzburg. Rome had selected as mediator the German cardinal, Nicholas of Cusa, who was backed by the Catholic princes of neighboring countries.

Such being the situation, Capistran's proposed visit was welcome news in Bohemia, especially to Podebrad. Urged to submit his difficulties to this holy and learned man, Podebrad replied emphatically: "That I would do, even if no one urged me. These theological matters I do not understand. I cannot trust myself, nor can I rely on our priests." His later behavior does not stand in contradiction with this declaration. He supposed that Capistran would acknowledge the Compact. Without this, he said, Bohemia could have no continuation of the peace obtained by so many hard struggles on the battlefield. In case of necessity he was willing to drop even the candidature of Rokytzana for the archbishopric of Prague. But as to the Compact, he would allow no change, even if he had to resort to war.

Capistran, on the contrary, was dead set against the Compact. Two points were clear in his mind. First, the Utraquists were heretics, and Rokytzana a heresiarch, despite the Compact and absolution from the ban. Secondly, the Compact had no legal value, being null and void from the very start. And he fully realized what he would meet with. Cardinal Carvajal personally warned him. But concealment of truth was not in Capistran's nature. As he was going to Bohemia, not as negotiator, but as missioner, he counted confidently on a wonder of grace, and his companions shared his confidence. “If God grants to our father two more years,” writes Fara, “you will hear that all heresies in Bohemia have been eradicated. If he lives two or three years longer, even a great part of Turkey will accept the Catholic faith. The fame of his miracles has already reached there.”

Capistran uses the same kind of language. He is not going to Bohemia merely to make a number of converts. With the help of the Most High he will eradicate Hussitism. Surrounding Catholic countries fostered similar expectations; especially in Poland, where people feared Hussite infiltration, Capistran's approach was greeted with great joy. King Casimir and Cardinal Sbignev Olesnicki of Cracow sent special messengers to greet him in Moravia. Olesnicki is inclined to attribute former failures to a secret plan of divine providence, “which denied others a fame reserved for you.” This cardinal was an exquisitely educated prince of the Church, a champion of humanism in Poland. These lofty hopes were not altogether unfounded. Soldiers and diplomats had failed, but Capistran was a missioner, a remarkably gifted one. Was his triumphal march of these last months to halt suddenly at the borders of Bohemia? No. He must reach Prague, the citadel of Utraquism. He would gain people and leaders by the spell of his personality.

He went first to Moravia. In Bohemia, Catholicity had its chief strongholds in the castles of the nobility, and Utraquism in the cities. In Moravia the conditions were reversed. The nobility upheld the chalice, but the two principal cities, Brünn and Olmütz, remained, as Capistran put it, “completely Christian and Catholic.” His fame and the curiosity of the masses would draw pilgrimages. One triumph marked the day of his arrival. Baron Benesch of Boskowitz, who had heard Capistran preach in Vienna, returned solemnly to the Church on August 1, in the presence of a great throng assembled at the ceremony. This example had good effect. In two weeks about seven hundred other conversions followed, not counting many hundreds who followed their masters or employers. Benesch alone had about two thousand subjects. Of this new convert, Capistran writes that he did not know a more fervent

Catholic in all that territory. Benesch, his family, his whole influence, were entirely at the disposal of his spiritual father. He aided in the examination of people who had been cured. On August 15, the last day of Capistran's stay in Brünn, fifteen deaf persons were cured. Benesch called that day "the day of the deaf." Such miracles ought to make the Hussites ashamed of their own deafness, says Varese.

The Moravian landowners in general did remain deaf. Capistran wrote to John of Tobitschau and Zimburg, a relative of Podebrad, asking him to allow his subjects to attend the sermons at Olmütz. The answer was a curt refusal.

After the feast of the Assumption, Capistran went through the rich fields of the Hanna, crossed the Wischau, and entered Olmütz, the most important city of Moravia. In the name of the absent bishop he was solemnly received by the dean of the cathedral, Bohusz of Zwole. Again he had to preach in the open, in front of the cathedral, or upon the Oberring, or on the bleaching-ground outside the walls. He had two interpreters, one German, the other Moravian. The Hussites' seizure and imprisonment of pilgrims from Hradisch was the first answer to Capistran's Hussite sermons. The Catholic barons and prelate had urged him to treat disputed questions with the utmost leniency, and he had promised to do his best. But it was all in vain. "In the pulpit the spirit of God came upon him, and he was changed into another man," says Varese.

The animosity was increased by false rumors, such as one reporting that Capistran declared that all who had ever received Communion under both species were without exception condemned. Hussite theologians set to work. In Olmütz he received a written challenge from the Kremsians. A letter came from a priest, Stephen of Leskowetz, the chief of a sect which maintained that the adoration of the Holy Eucharist and the veneration of the saints were both idolatrous. In that letter Capistran is called; "the famous and crafty sophist, the verbose Italian, Brother John who preaches errors in Olmütz." Other epithets are added: "scurf of Behemoth," "tail of Antichrist," "Mohammed-like agitator." The letter ends with a challenge, demanding immediate answer.

With this letter came one from the governor himself, enclosing a letter from John Borotin, who represented the moderate Utraquists. The old master is much more polite than the violent Kremsians. He does not intend to disturb the missioner in his blessed work. But he does wish to let him know what is being said about him. He asks also for information, to defend him in case of necessity. Although, to his great sorrow, he hears that Capistran declares that all are condemned who participate in the chalice, he is willing to excuse these aberrations. Capistran, he thinks, is evidently a melancholic, and not quite right in his head. This queer diagnosis he bases on Aristotle, who said that "statesmen and heroes generally are melancholy." In corroboration he points to Capistran's practice of screaming, and of urging his hearers to scream. Borotin also demands an immediate answer.

CHAPTER XXV

Podebrad and Rokytzana

CAPISTRAN did give answer, not to personal invectives, but to the misstatements that would otherwise frustrate all his efforts. He gave answer in his great treatise against the Hussites, a treatise famous for his emphatic phrase. Dixi enim et dico ("I have said and I repeat"). The first part of this treatise he made public the day after he received Borotin's letter. It is addressed to the governor, with a copy for Borotin, and another for the Kremsians. He gave the three documents to the Bishop of Olmütz to be forwarded, but three years passed before the letters reached their destination. Was this delay owing to carelessness? Was it meant to quench controversy from the start? In any case the letters were not sent. When Capistran returned from Poland to Olmütz in 1454, he investigated, and the missing letters were found among the papers of the Bishop, who had died in the meantime. "May God forgive him. He kept my letters for three years in prison." Thus Capistran wrote to the Kremsians.

Although these letters remained hidden, the literary campaign continued. Catholics' literary efforts against the Hussites had been previously wanting, and theologians were lacking. Literary and scientific life was at a low level, as Hussitism had ruined the beautiful spirituality of Carolingian days. But on one doctrine, that of the Last Supper, Hussites were eloquent, and even the simplest could argue learnedly on this article and quote exactly the usual Scripture texts. Enea Silvio comments on the barbaric manners of the Hussites at Tabor. The cultured Italian felt as if he were among cannibals, yet he notes their love of knowledge, saying: "You find common citizens speaking Latin." Capistran's coming meant a new intellectual war, but he complained of great difficulties in getting his letters, treatises rather, copied and circulated.

His principal work against the Utraquists, called the Hussite treatise, seems never to have been finished. After refuting the charge that he condemned all who receive Communion under both species, he says he is merely enunciating a general principle, that to be a Catholic you must accept all that the Holy Roman Catholic Church believes, teaches, and practices. Whoever differs with Mother Church is a heretic and falls under the ban. This fundamental thesis is developed systematically. Many nights he must have spent poring over the great volumes that accompanied him everywhere. Utraquist theology was, indeed, poor and narrow. A few scriptural passages, a few citations from ancient Christian texts, and the Compact—that was all. But their endless repetitions made step-by-step refutation impossible. Capistran's voluminous treatise was answered with one four times as long.

The most frequently cited scriptural passage was from the sixth chapter of St. John, where Jesus says: "Amen, amen I say unto you: Except you eat the flesh of the Son of man, and drink His blood, you shall not have life in you" (John 6:54). The Utraquists drew a parallel between these words and the words of Jesus to Nicodemus: "Unless a man be born again of water and the Holy Ghost, he cannot enter the kingdom of God" (John 3:15). The absolute necessity of baptism, they argue, shows the absolute necessity of Communion under both species. Some Catholics replied by quoting certain patristic texts which seem to interpret this eating and drinking of the body and blood of Christ as a metaphorical expression of perfect union with Christ through faith.[1] This is not the common Catholic view. But Capistran joins the anti-Hussites. With fiery zeal he denies that these words of our Savior are to be taken as pointing literally to the Holy Eucharist. With a great display of erudition he interprets them as metaphorical.

But texts of Scripture were, in this matter, of secondary importance. The chalice had long since become a national

---

[1] Quoted for this view are Cusa, Enea Silvio, and Henry Tocke. The Council of Trent says: "Sed neque ex sermone illo apud Joannem sexto recte colligitur, utriusque speciei communionem a Domino praeceptum esse, utcunque juxta varias Patrum et Doctorum interpretationes intelligatur." Sess. XXI, chap. 1; cf. Denzinger, Enchiridion, 930 (ed. 14[a] et 15[a]).

movement, and confidence in the guidance of the Church had been deeply shaken. Hussitism was a popular reform movement, ignorant of history, bent on restoring the purity and simplicity of apostolic times. Capistran, seeing that the very idea of the Church was at stake, does not lose time over secondary questions. The development of the liturgy in the Western Church is a result of the powers which Christ gave to His Church, a certain freedom in proclaiming and formulating revealed truth and in regulating the liturgy. He quotes our Lord: "I have yet many things to say to you: but you cannot bear them now. But when He, the Spirit of truth, is come, He will teach you all truth" (John 15:12 f.). Referring to similar cases in the Old Testament, he goes so far as to assert that, even if Christ had commanded Communion under both species, the Church could not be denied the right to limit distribution of Communion to one species, when it found this method required by changed conditions. He admits that, in the primitive Church, Communion was given to the faithful under both species, but he denies any doctrinal obligation of this practice.

In the days before Constantine there had been greater freedom in liturgical matters. Afterward more specific regulations for the whole Church became necessary. That the Church gradually reserved participation in the chalice exclusively to the priest, was a reservation based on weighty reasons. Capistran enumerates twenty such reasons, which can be reduced to two: first, the danger of profanation; second, the danger of error in thinking that the whole Christ could not be received under one species. This last error was, in fact, the foundation of the Hussite system. Capistran, while voicing all tradition, quotes with preference St. Thomas Aquinas, particularly the latter's sequence Lauda Sion, which develops with dogmatic keenness and wonderful eloquence all details of the Eucharistic doctrine.

Here Capistran is at his best. How impressive and majestic is Catholic unity in faith, persisting through the centuries, when contrasted with the wretched confusion now pervading little Bohemia! The Utraquists insisted on Communion for sucklings. Other sects denied the presence of Christ in the sacrament of the altar and thereby rejected the Eucharist altogether. Anyone in the state of grace, they said, could receive Christ's body and blood in every food. The populace went still further, calling the sacred Host "idol" and "butterfly." But all alike based their claim on the Bible.

Why did Christ institute the Eucharist under two species? This question Capistran treats with particular care. He insists on the sublime, mystical meaning to which the separated species give expression. But since not all Christians are obliged to understand these lofty ideas, neither have all an obligation to receive Communion under both species.

In view of Utraquist exaggerations, Capistran is reserved on the question of frequent Communion. Since in those days frequent Communion was not generally considered a sign of greater piety, to urge the practice might, under the force of the chalice movement, be easily suspected as heretical.[2] Capistran was content with inculcating the obligatory annual Communion, but he did insist on worthy treatment for this great mystery. Utraquist irreverence was notorious. Capistran complains that Holy Communion is given to all kinds of vile and worthless people, even to those who have just come from taverns or even worse places. He turns one of their chief arguments against them. Paul's admonitions to the Corinthians sharply condemn the misconduct of the Utraquists.

But higher than all theological reasons stood the Compact, "the solemn confirmation of the lay chalice by the Church assembled in the Holy Ghost at Basle." Rokytzana, replies Capistran, violates the Compact more than anyone else does. Capistran, however, might have succeeded by making the facts known everywhere. If the Utraquists could be brought to observe the Compact as granted by the Council, they would be entirely on Catholic ground. If they did not, they would deprive themselves of their only support. But Capistran judged differently. He rejected the Compact altogether, refusing it any claim of legality and declaring that it had been confirmed neither by the Council nor by the pope.

Capistran quotes a rumor which said that Philibert had been

---

[2] A priest in Augsburg, who had educated his parish to receive daily, was in consequence denounced to the Inquisition.

commanded by the Council and the Pope to revoke the arbitrary concessions, especially the lay chalice; that he refused to obey and then, out of fear or shame, had not dared to return either to Basle or to Constance; and thus he had died in Prague. "Did his soul obtain eternal salvation?" Thus Capistran concludes.

Confusion and rumor prevented true knowledge of the facts. But Capistran would have been better advised not to attack the legality of the Compact. The Pope's decision could not, in any case, be delayed. The real question was whether the concessions made by the Council were a suitable means of restoring union. In denying that they had so far proved suitable, Capistran was quite correct, and later history confirmed his view. But he needlessly made his task heavier by his unsparing condemnation of the Compact. Capistran himself would not have thought so. He had no regard for diplomacy and in general little regard for his Bohemian opponents, looking on them as a grieved father looks on unmanageable children. He gives his temperament free rein. Kindness and severity, threats and tenderness, stand side by side in his Hussite letters. He has opprobrious names for Hus, whom his opponents had half-deified. He even quotes the popular satire of "the fat goose broiled in Constance." Like other outsiders, he failed to understand the complex national atmosphere in the Bohemia of those days. Appearances were taken for realities. His foes' tenacity remained a riddle for him, and their childish stubbornness exasperated him more and more. Yet his Hussite letters are not merely controversial. Only prejudice can miss the sincere keynote of his love and sorrow for his "friends," as he calls the Hussites again and again.

Capistran's condemnation of the Compact nullified the Hussite mission. Podebrad had been not unfavorably inclined. Now he was through with Capistran. Thus Prague became inaccessible. In the first days of September a messenger handed him a letter from Podebrad. Capistran replied, saying he could hardly believe that the message reflected Podebrad's true sentiments, and regretting that such a distinguished statesman was so deplorably misinformed about the Compact. He still hoped he might come to Prague to talk the matter over in detail. "Would that our Lord Jesus Christ gave me the grace to treat this topic in your presence, in the presence of the Pope, of cardinals and prelates, of the doctors of the University." The difficulty of his task is evident in a letter to the city of Bamberg. The slowness of results compels him to decline at present their kind invitation.

He has still no doubt about ultimate success. He writes to his confreres in St. Theobald: "We are well. God helps us more than we deserve. Since we left Vienna our companions have recorded more than 150 miracles. Last Sunday above 100,000 people were present at the sermon. Citizens act as guards, because we live here amid heretics. About 3,600 have returned to the Church, among them many nobles. I am satisfied. In Bohemia there is abundance of gossip. Yet we hope to bring everything to a happy end." In a similar hopeful vein he writes to Cardinal Olesnicki in Poland that he wishes to go to Poland, if only to pay his respects to a prelate so highly esteemed. He would, of course, prefer to convert the Bohemians first, if possible. These barons are not concerned about the faith and the Gospel truth as they hypocritically pretend. In greed and lust of power, they wish to be free like the brutes. But I still have good hopes. Daily sermons and daily wonders of God have already converted many. We are now going to Lord Rosenberg. In his castles we can preach in safety."

In the beginning of September, Capistran returned to Brünn and remained there another two weeks. There he received a second letter from Master Borotin, who was much offended at the apparent disregard of his first letter. The tone of his letter is marked by Utraquist vagueness. "We always obey Jesus Christ. We obey also the apostolic lord, though we reserve first place for Christ and His truth. But the apostolic lord rejects us and hinders our salvation." Toward the end he becomes very personal. "It would be better for you to remain in a hermitage or a monastery instead of going around to seduce people. How many you have already turned away from Communion under both species!" He quotes St. Jerome's word to the monk Rufus: "If you wish to be a real monk, why do you go about in cities? Cities are dwelling places for the masses, but not for hermits." This time Borotin received a prompt reply. "You accuse me of not having written to you. My dear John, I answered your first letter the very next day. If you did not receive my reply, the fault is not mine. I left my answer to you and your Kremsian colleagues back in Olmütz."

His tone then grows sharp. "Please tell me, since you praise the Council so emphatically, whether the laity in Basle receive Communion now under both species. Do Catholics in Germany? Or in Hungary, or in Scotland, or in Sweden? In Poland, Prussia, Burgundy, Brabant, Tours, Aquitania, Spain, Portugal, Navarre, Catalonia, Italy, Sardinia, Sicily, Dalmatia, Bosnia, Slavonia? Or in the kingdom of Cyprus, or in the Orient? My dear John, if only you would cooperate with me, another John, the Catholic truth would soon prevail. How I would long to see your face here in Moravia, to speak to you, to embrace you in the love of Christ! Your talk about seducing people does not disturb me in the least. My life and doctrine are sufficiently known in Italy, France, Germany, Spain, and other countries. I have spoken, not in nooks, not in hidden corners, but in public places, in universities. In your first letter you called me, without having even seen me, a melancholic, though I am indeed sanguine and choleric. Neither Aristotle nor Plato could pass judgment on a man they never saw. This time you call me a monk. But I am not a monk, I am a friar, of the Order of St. Francis. The Catholic Church has commanded me to preach, and to combat heretics anywhere in the whole world."

On the same day came a letter from Rokytzana, a polite and cautious letter. He says he is an unflinching opponent of all enemies of the discipline of the Church, and points to his struggles for the lay chalice at the Council of Basle. He welcomes the proposal of a disputation between the two of them. Let Capistran select one of the three places: Trübau in Moravia, Pellnitz, or Deutch-Brod, and send immediate answer. He would guarantee personal security. Capistran answered the same day. "You are very polite. No one else has written me in this tone." The offer of the disputation he accepted, though with apprehension. In a confidential letter to Cardinal Cusa he admits that much might be said in favor of Communion under both species. Rokytzana had asked that some authorized representatives be sent to him, to arrange the details, time, place, and witnesses, of the proposed disputation. But Rokytzana, too, must make sacrifices. "I have come a long distance, from Rome to Olmütz," says Capistran. The place must be acceptable to both parties, be secure for all participants. He sent copies of this letter to Podebrad, asking him to use his influence in this important matter. He also sent copies of the two letters to Ulrich Rosenberg and to Frederick III, asking the King to show it also to the professors of the University of Vienna.

But two or three days later he was obliged to leave Brünn. The number of conversions seriously alarmed the Hussites. Brünn and Olmütz received threatening letters, and feared that war against them was imminent. Capistran, to keep peace from being disturbed, went to Znaim in southern Bohemia. Rokytzana, upon receiving Capistran's letter from Brünn on September 25, started at once for Moravia in order, as he asserted later, to discuss with him the details for the disputation. Capistran had suspected from the beginning that the disputation plan had not been originally proposed by Rokytzana, but had been forced on him. As far as eloquence was concerned, Rokytzana had no fear, but his conscience was not clear. He had never observed the Compact. And Capistran was not the man to overlook this sore point.

Further, Rokytzana knew that the constitution of the Council (December 23, 1437) had never been made known to the Hussites, but was kept absolutely secret until Capistran published it. "I know," Capistran said, "that this document, provided with a leaden seal, was brought to Prague. You know best whether you still have it, or whether you have torn it or burned it. But even if the parchment is destroyed, the facts it contained remain in eternity." Rokytzana found himself in the same painful situation as he had been when Emperor Sigismund commanded him to go to Basle. But this time the demand of his own factionists was urging him to a discussion, and thus he made up his mind to finish this annoying task in the quickest and easiest way possible. But why did he insist on having the disputation in a small, remote place? The reason is clear enough. He was afraid of the public, and wanted his audience to be as small as possible.

The assembly at Neustadt in Moravia chose the castle of Lord Henry of Lipa, near Kromau in Moravia, as the place for the disputation. All would be admitted who understood the matter. Rokytzana would expound the doctrine of the chalice, according to the divine law, the practice of Christ, of the apostles, and of the ancient Church. Since Capistran on his way to Znaim had to pass through Kromau, the selection of this place signified a concession. Those barons honestly wished to bring the two men together. But the proposition with which they came from Neustadt represented exactly the contrary of what Capistran had demanded. They offered him, not proposals, but positive decisions, which he must accept or decline. Rokytzana acted as if he had nothing to do with these decisions. Later on he asserted that he had not been present at the assembly. His short inconsequential letter said nothing of a disputation. He referred Capistran for all details to the messengers. But these messengers did not find Capistran in Brünn. Since it was rumored that he was already on his way to Rosenberg, they left their letters to be dispatched to Krumau. Capistran at Znaim waited in vain for a reply.

How much he was preoccupied by the imminent disputation is shown by his letter to the Vienna University (September 24). He begs the University to send him their best men. "Vienna would have suited me best as a place for the disputation. But wherever it is held, we hope to overcome the Bohemians with the help of God. Next to God, I put my trust in you. If you assist me, I do not need any other help." With his success in Moravia he is well satisfied: "More than 4,000, among them many barons, noblemen, and priests, have abjured their errors. All Bohemia is aroused. The Hussite lords fear the conversion of the whole nation and have therefore prompted Rokytzana to this disputation." Joyous confidence is reflected also in his letter to King Casimir of Poland. Poland and Lithuania longed for his coming, to unite the Russians and the Ruthenians. The strong expressions in Casimir's letter about the Hussites and their infamous actions were water on Capistran's mill. He sent copies of that letter in every direction. His letter promises the King that he will come, but for the present he is bound to Bohemia. A great public disputation is near at hand. "I hope it will become for many the way to salvation. I do not doubt our victory."

After two weeks' delay, he left Znaim. Five or six days he spent in Eggenburg. From there he sent five requests to the Pope. Two of them concerned the Hussite mission: first, the authorization to absolve from all Church penalties reserved to the Holy See; secondly, a papal declaration that the Compact was invalid. His messengers carried also a long letter to the citizens of Aquila. He commends to them his confreres, who wish to hold their chapter with the Observants at San Giuliano rather than in the city with the Conventuals. Then he scolds them for neglecting to build a worthy memorial church over the remains of St. Bernardine. The churches and chapels dedicated to St. Bernardine since he left Rome, he says, can hardly be counted. And Aquila has his body. But where? In a little chapel, where it is exposed to profanation. They ought to frame him in gold and build a beautiful temple over him. He did not know that Aquila was already fulfilling this his dearest wish. Pope Nicholas V had granted the erection both of a memorial church and of an Observant convent.

From Eggenburg he went to the Cistercian monastery of Zwettl, where Abbot John George of Amberg gave him a friendly reception. Here he received a letter from Ulrich Rosenberg. He answers exultingly: "Tomorrow we advance to Weitra." There he would await Rosenberg's escort. But when he arrived in Weitra he had to wait two days for the arrival of Rosenberg's people. He occupied the time with preaching. On October 17 he arrived at Krumau castle, the home of the Rosenberg family.

CHAPTER XXVI

In Bayreuth and Eger

CAPISTRAN'S joy at finding himself at last on Bohemian ground was dampened by a threatening letter from Prague. Podebrad had forbidden Rosenberg to take Capistran as guest into his castle. Here also he finally received the messengers of Rokytzana. He answered energetically: "It is not your business, but mine, to select place and judges. I am apostolic commissioner and general inquisitor for the whole earth, whom you have to obey as if I were Pope, if you still wish to be a Christian. And you propose a village for this disputation, which requires learned and experienced men. You have boasted of your sharp and noble mind, of your merits at the Council of Basle. And now would you let your light shine before cart-drivers and shepherds? I thought you would select a time-honored city where scholars abound. And you choose Kromau, where, Lord Henry and his noble family excepted, only uneducated people live. I will not accept this place under any circumstances. I propose for your choice Naples, Siena, Perugia, Florence, Bologna, Ferrara, Padua, Pavia, Turin, Paris, Toulouse, Dôle, Oxford, Cambridge, Cologne, Erfurt. But if these cities are too far away, then I select Cracow or Vienna. If you are at all in earnest, then accept at least Eger. And I choose as judge, Pope Nicholas V, whose office it is to explain the divine law and the Holy Scriptures; for these Scriptures are dumb and cannot talk. Besides him I choose all cardinals, patriarchs, archbishops, and metropolitans of the Church of God. If you prefer kings and princes, then I propose: the kings and princes of France, of England, of Hungary, Bohemia, Spain, Aragon, Portugal, Navarre, Poland, Hesse, Cyprus; the dukes of Burgundy, Savoy, Milan, and Bavaria, all of whom, together with others, receive Communion under one species."

Eger would have been the most appropriate place for a

religious disputation, since Rokytzana declined cities outside Bohemia. King Frederick had summoned a diet to meet at Eger (December 4), at which the papal legate, Nicholas of Cusa, would confer with the barons of Bohemia and Moravia on the definite settlement of these ecclesiastical questions. "I will gladly go there," writes Capistran to Rokytzana, "if you accept the proposal." But he must have an armed escort. He could no longer trust Podebrad. "What would he not do with me if he caught me?"

Rosenberg did not submit to Podebrad's order of expulsion. Krumau was like a peaceful island surrounded by the Hussite ocean. The Minorites here and the poor Clares had repeatedly offered refuge to fugitive religious. For four weeks the Rosenbergs now enjoyed the presence of their guest. Capistran issued (October 28) the customary document of affliliation for Ulrich, and his children Henry, John, Jodok, Agnes, Bertha, and Ludmila. Jodok later on became bishop of Breslau. Bertha, the sorely tried wife of a count of Lichtenstein, lives on today in local legend as the White Woman. In the presence of Capistran, Ulrich solemnly resigned in favor of Henry, his eldest son, reserving for himself a mere subsistence. In a letter to Nicholas V, Capistran gives full vent to his admiration for Ulrich Rosenberg. His fame is great. But the reality is still greater. Ulrich has for thirty-six years stood unbroken against the Hussite storm. His estates are ruined. He has testified his fidelity to the Church even unto blood.

One other man Capistran praises highly. If the house of Rosenberg has remained a stronghold of the faith, this perseverance is owing in great measure to the influence of Dr. Wenzel of Krumau, doctor of canon law, and canon of the cathedral chapter of Prague, who has for many years been Ulrich's private secretary. Dr. Wenzel is the greatest personality among the Bohemian clergy. He is an indefatigable worker, full of energy, very eloquent, and of blameless life. If Capistran from this time on uses more severe language against Rokytzana, we may find the reason in the information he received from Wenzel. Rokytzana, who sent his reply from Prague (November 12), has changed his tone. All polite phrasing is absent. "Blasphemer," "religious without religion," and similar epithets abound. Capistran's miraculous cures are like the tricks of Egyptian conjurers. Rokytzana says he himself is slandered like St. Paul, when he is considered a heretic. Outside Bohemia he will not go. Capistran is afraid of George Podebrad, who has never broken his word. "But there, where you want to drag me, are thousands of my enemies." Furthermore, crimes are to be judged where they have been committed. "Since your crime of leading people to abjure the chalice was committed in Bohemia and Moravia, the matter must be settled right here." His reasons for rejecting Eger betray embarrassment. "Is not Eger a country town just like Kromau? Is there perhaps a university in Eger? Can you get more barons there than in Kromau?"

He falls into the usual contradiction when he speaks of the teaching office of the Church. The Pope cannot be judge in matters already decided by the words of Scripture. St. Paul's teaching was: "Let a man prove himself, and so let him eat of that bread and drink of the chalice." Holy Scripture far surpasses the authority of all bishops. Yet again he speaks respectfully of the Apostolic See and the Council of Basle. The latter, he insists, had approved his doctrine of the chalice, and Pope Eugene confirmed the Compact. This impudence is not intelligible unless we remember that Rokytzana wrote thus only because he intended this letter for his adherents in Bohemia rather than for his opponents. To Capistran's insistence on the indisputable fact that the entire Church outside of Bohemia received Communion under one species only, Rokytzana replies with a subterfuge cherished by the heretics of all ages, namely, that the truth is not always to be found on the side of the majority. Christ had stood alone with His little community. Elias too. "Many are called, but few are chosen." Oriental nations have, in spite of Communion under both species, been reunited with the Church. But the Hussites differed from the Roman Church in doctrine, not merely in rite. This Rokytzana conceals.

Rokytzana is not an honest opponent. He misrepresents facts in asserting that the barons in Neustadt fixed time and place for the disputation according to Capistran's wishes. Equally dishonest is his charge that Capistran fled from Moravia to escape the disputation, since, in truth, to get to Prague, the residence of Podebrad and Rokytzana, was Capistran's steady aim. Only when the gates of Prague were closed against him did he propose Eger. Rokytzana's rejection of Eger proves that Capistran was right in saying that Rokytzana from the very start had never really wished for a disputation. After this letter Rokytzana wraps himself in complete silence. His one great aim is to keep Capistran away from Prague.

Capistran had left Krumau before he received Rokytzana's letter. As the shortest way to Eger, via Pilsen, was not safe, he chose the road through Bavaria. In Passau a large crowd, even at the risk of life, climbed to the roof of the church to see him and to hear him preach: "Blessed devotion of the Germans," remarks Varese. On November 22 he passed through Vilshofen, and the next day arrived in Ratisbon. December 2 he was a guest in the Cistercian abbey of Waldsassen, where the mayor of Eger came to welcome him. Probably on the following day he reached Eger. Here disappointment awaited him. The disputation, planned for the next day, had been canceled. Cardinal Cusa had declared that he would go to Eger only if the Bohemians would first acknowledge him as papal legate, and would promise to submit to his decisions. When this demand was promptly refused by the Bohemian negotiators, Cardinal Cusa left further deliberations with the Hussites to the neighboring German princes. Among these princes two Hohenzollern margraves, Albrecht Achilles of Ansbach and John of Bayreuth, were foremost. They got a number of princes to meet in Bayreuth.

Capistran now learned, to his great disappointment, what concessions would have been offered to the Utraquists at the diet of Eger. Cardinal Cusa would have given the Bohemian delegates 4,000 ducats to cover traveling expenses. The Pope would appoint an archbishop for Prague, who with papal permission would grant to the Bohemians the lay chalice in the form conceded by the Compact. Sequestered church property would be allowed to remain in the possession of the present holders for their lifetime. Albrecht asserted that he had gained the Cardinal's consent to these concessions. Capistran could hardly believe this. He writes to the

Pope: "To my mind such concessions are a shame, not an honor, to the Holy Church of God, and to Your Holiness." He wrote at once to Cusa to find out the truth.

The assembly at Bayreuth decided to invite the Bohemian delegates anew to a discussion with Cardinal Cusa in Eger, on the fourth Sunday of Lent (March 19). Capistran informs the Pope of the warlike atmosphere in Bayreuth. "I find them all ready to serve you, with their possessions, with their people, even with their lives. People say that, since the rise of Hussitism, no such enthusiasm has been seen here." Capistran may have taken the remarks made at that meeting too seriously. Much was lacking for a new Hussite war. Very influential people blamed Capistran for too much sharpness.

Shortly before Christmas the papal messenger, Bartholomew of Siena, surprised him in Eger with a letter, dated October 28, from Pope Nicholas V. Bartholomew had left Rome before Capistran's messengers from Eggenburg arrived there. The motu proprio of the Pope contains a few words of appreciation for Capistran's activity in Moravia and Bohemia, and also a few privileges usually granted to itinerant missioners. Chief among them was the faculty of absolving, but only in the internal forum of conscience, those who had received Communion under both species, or had separated from the Church in other ways.

Capistran read the unexpected limitation of his former faculties with dismay. In his letter of thanks to the Pope, he candidly gives expression to his feelings. Even as a young religious he had received from Pope Martin V, as lately even from Pope Nicholas himself, the power to proceed against all heretics by public trial, and to invoke the assistance of the secular arm. In Bohemia he needs these faculties more urgently than in Italy. "Most Holy Father, the vineyard I labor in is yours. It is your field that I plow. Yours are the souls, entrusted to your care by Him who made them. Trust your useless servant. I would rather die than allow any dishonor to the Apostolic See. I do not ask for money, for honors, for titles. All I ask is authorization for the defense of Catholic truth."

Petitions to Rome must have occasioned this papal letter. A

letter from Frederick III, from Wiener-Neustadt, received about the same time, flatly refuses Capistran's request to assign a place for the disputation with Rokytzana. All efforts of his predecessors, Sigismund and Albrecht, all efforts of the Council of Basle, had been in vain. Further, since the matter concerned religion, the King says he must first consult the Pope. In conclusion, he referred Capistran to Cardinal Cusa, the legate, who, on St. Martin's Day, was to meet the Bohemians in Leitmeritz. The hint thus conveyed, that Capistran should not interfere in the legate's business, was quite out of place, since the two missions were independent of each other. Only after Utraquist submission to the Church could Cusa, as he himself said, enter Bohemian territory. To gain this previous submission was the task of Capistran, whose strenuous methods were the real reason for hesitation.

We must think of Enea Silvio as standing behind Frederick III. Silvio's view was that the Utraquists should be brought to union by concessions. He could not sympathize with Capistran's energetic attack on the Compact. This attack, he feared, would merely introduce new entanglements. Silvio must have inspired Frederick III's warning letter, and also the papal motu proprio of October 28. Capistran must limit his activity to exclusively pastoral work, to preaching and hearing confessions.

Yet the papal document became a useful weapon against Rokytzana, who had insinuated doubts whether the Apostolic See, famous for its century-old wisdom, had really sent this troublesome friar to Bohemia. Now the papal letter, almost in Capistran's own language, states that those who receive Communion under both species are on a level with those who resist Church union. This statement almost condemns the Compact. Capistran sent copies of the papal document in every direction to disprove the orthodoxy of the Bohemians. A letter of the Polish king, Casimir IV, served the same purpose. Casimir again invited Capistran to come and reunite the Ruthenians, and to leave the stubborn Bohemians to their own conceits. Capistran sent a copy of this letter also to Rokytzana, that he might see what the Catholic world beyond Bohemia thought of him.

In confident tone Capistran writes from Eger to his friends in Znaim. These friends, complaining of his long silence, had informed him of their worries. The Hussites were singing satirical rhymes, and the city was in fear of violent acts. Olmütz, Brünn, and Znaim were urged to accept the chalice. But Capistran had learned already from Benesch of Boskowitz that the suggestion was universally rejected. Further, John Hunyadi, the administrator of Hungary, had declared himself ready to march into Moravia as soon as Capistran would give command. Capistran consoled his friends with word that he had already commended them to Hunyadi's protection.

Christmas, 1451, Capistran was still in Eger, awaiting the return of his messengers from Rome, and also Cusa's decision about the meeting to be held on March 19. On Christmas Eve he began his reply to Rokytzana's letter of November 12. The answer grew into a long treatise. No assertion of his opponent is passed over in silence. In contrast to the Hussite treatise, this Eger production is sharply polemic. Capistran gives full rein to pugnacity. Objective statements, seasoned with biting irony, glide rapidly into pleadings, entreaties, and threats, clothed in the powerful language of Scripture. The harshest accusations jostle with affectionate invitations. "Oh, how I should like to win you and all your adherents for Christ, with all possible arguments, those of kindness and those of strictness!" The chief lines of the discussion are again two: The drinking of Christ's blood, and the Compact. Under the spell of a fixed idea Rokytzana clings tenaciously to the words: "Unless you drink My blood," and "let a man prove himself, and then drink of this chalice." Capistran replies: "Do you not see that you are cutting off your nose with your own knife? How shall babies prove themselves? Yet they receive Communion under both species." And the Compact. Why, Rokytzana himself is the enemy and destroyer. He cites Rokytzana's written reply to a pastor who has asked advice on giving Communion to infants: "Cling to Hussite custom. Be not frightened. You have not yet resisted unto blood."

Capistran replies: "Were it only true! How much innocent blood have your accomplices already shed! They have spared neither bishops nor abbots, neither priors nor provosts, neither pastors nor priests, neither clerics nor laymen. Some they have wounded, some they have killed. Others they have plundered, and thrown into prison. And how many of your own duped adherents have died a miserable death! Your own blood, quite true, has not yet been shed. But beware lest in the approaching judgment your blood, too, be spilled and licked up by the dogs. I do not wish this, I do not prophesy it. But ask God it may not come. And if blood must be shed, then may your blood, like that of the repentant Achab, be spilled for your eternal salvation. If your blood must be licked up by dogs, let it not be like the blood of the wicked and obdurate Jezabel. Oh, be converted to the true Catholic faith, be obedient to our most Holy Father, Pope Nicholas V, be reconciled to the Holy Roman Church. Come, then, my dear friend, return. Turn, O Sulamitess. Turn back that we may see you. Return to your Lord and God."

Again he writes: "All I seek is the restoration of the unity and harmony between nations by restoring them to their holy mother the Church. For this am I an exile in these Bohemian lands formerly so flourishing. Bohemia was a duchy, and Prague a bishopric. Afterward Prague was elevated. The duchy became a kingdom, the bishopric an archbishopric, with a flourishing university. I wish to restore what you are destroying. I do not desire to ruin you, but to win you. Gaze at your once glorious city. See how low it has fallen under John of Rokytzana. O my dearest John! Better are the wounds struck by a lover than the kisses given by an enemy. Rage not. Give up your ambition for Prague. You will never obtain that archbishopric. You are a heretic. You forced your way in, and did not enter through the gate. Me you call a monk. But you are neither monk nor canon. Many assert that you are not even a priest. Were you a genuine priest you would love me as your friend. You would not revile me: you would not call me "antichrist" or "Mohammed" or "blasphemer" or "sorcerer." Augustine was right when he wrote to Faustus: "Madmen refuse to be bound, sleepyheads refuse to wake. But true love will find the madman, and will awake the sleepyhead. Both will feel offended, both rage. Their rage is on account of their sickness. When they are cured, they rejoice."

To awake his correspondent, Capistran does not shrink from

the harshest expressions. "Senseless beast," he calls Rokytzana. "Those very men whom you quote, holy and learned men, men like Augustine, Jerome, Gregory, Basil, Bernard, all these and many others were monks. Why do you besmirch the name 'monk' with your filthy mouth, you prey of worms, you food of the fire, you heap of rottenness, you man of sin, you son of perdition, you slave of hell. Forgive me. You called me to the combat. Be ready, then, for the shining lance. I will not kill you. But unhorse you I will, you invincible knight, you unconquerable heretic. And now you are down, come to me, the grand inquisitor, the representative of the Pope. Come to abjure. Humble your soul. Recognize your errors. Become a teacher of the truth. Come and ask for absolution. Be reconciled with your noble mother. Cease to be the brood of vipers, who devour their mother's entrails. I shall receive you. Come at once. Come today."

Capistran finished this letter January 7, 1452. The making of copies encountered many difficulties. Copies of his own and Rokytzana's letters he wished to send to Pope Nicholas V, but could not. "Nearly a hundred pages. And I have no copyists." His correspondence is immense: invitations, petitions, recommendations. His word counts much at royal courts. Ulrich Rosenberg asks for three letters in favor of family affairs, one to the Pope, one to Charles VII of France, one to Philip of Burgundy. Philip had a special veneration for Capistran.

Rokytzana left Capistran's letter unanswered. But the city of Eger received orders from Prague to expel the monk. They were more afraid of him, he writes to the Pope, than of thirty thousand besieging soldiers. The Hussite nobles sang satires, held a court-martial, and burned him in effigy. Prague repeated a popular saying: They would rather admit a hundred thousand devils than Capistran. Rokytzana, mistrusting this movement, had an order passed forbidding anyone to say anything about Capistran, good or bad.

Since the efforts to hold the debate in Eger were unsuccessful, Capistran went to preach in Saxony, in order to make a new attempt to reach Prague from Brüx.

CHAPTER XXVII

In Brüx and Ratisbon

DURING February and March, Capistran preached in the more important towns of southern Saxony, Ölsnitz, Zwickau, Chemnitz, Freiberg, Meissen, the residence of the elector Frederick; and from there back by way of Freiberg and Layda to Brüx in Bohemia. This circle of towns retained the memory of Capistran's visits until the eve of the Reformation. One week he spent in Freiberg, another in Meissen. At Meissen the conflux of people exhausted the bread supply, and Dresden had to furnish every second day three truckloads. His sermon on the vice of gambling was followed by a "bonfire of vanities."

At Dresden, which should have been next, great preparations were made, including a thorough cleaning of the market place, a task undertaken only on extraordinary occasions. Usually the people let their pigs, goats, and geese run free in the streets and public places. No wonder that every rain turned the streets, only partly paved, into a quagmire, into which ladies would not venture without wooden shoes, and with their trains carried after them by menials. On this occasion men and women worked three days to reduce the market place to decency. But all this labor was in vain. "The devout father" did not come. Prompted to resume the Hussite mission in Brüx, he interrupted his tour through Saxony. The elector provided him with a body guard. The Franciscan friary of St. Lawrence had been destroyed by the Hussites in 1421, but a second friary, inside the walls, was now flourishing under the protection of Saxony. Capistran called the elector a champion of the faith; the Bohemians called him an enemy of the country.

Capistran's Saxon tour was felt in Prague as a new challenge. What was gained by keeping him out of Prague, if all neighboring countries received him? What hurt them most was the papal document of October 28, in which the Utraquists appear almost as heretics. On Ash Wednesday (February 23), while Capistran was still preaching in Saxony, Podebrad staged a counter-demonstration in favor of the Compact. The Minorite monk, John of Capistrano, is their enemy. In the name of the devil, this monk, supported by a bull of the present Pope, proclaims that all who receive Communion under both species are heretics. The present Pope, Nicholas V, has refused the demands of the legates sent to his coronation. Pope Eugene IV is mentioned with respect, as having approved the Compact. But Nicholas V wishes to destroy what his predecessor and the Council had built up. "If the Roman Church uses violence, we must defend our rights. Our disgrace may, like a spark, turn into a mighty flame. We do not wish it. But if we are forced to it, we are excused before the whole world."

For this demonstration Capistran regarded Rokytzana as solely responsible. In this he seems to have been mistaken. Podebrad, the administrator of the kingdom, a very independent character, disliked Rokytzana's obstinate and domineering manner, and the two men were not intimate. Podebrad's interest in the Compact was primarily political. It was the guaranty of a dearly bought peace, and must not be touched. In dogmatic questions he did not agree with Rokytzana's views. Enea Silvio and Capistran were correct in believing that Podebrad could easily be gained for the Church, were it not for Rokytzana. The situation filled Capistran with indignation and bitterness. That such a worthless man should rule the whole Bohemian nation! Putting aside all regard for Rokytzana's person, he would show the Bohemians whom they were following.

The feast of St. George, April 23, the day set for the Diet of Prague, was approaching. Capistran composed a memorandum, the third of his Hussite treatises. The barons do not know the true Rokytzana. "When once the wretched and unclean life of this man is known, you will see how he lies against his head. The poisonous serpent can but spit poison. Against his shameless attacks I have only the shield of the invincible Catholic truth. No one can endure such a man, who dishonors his people, who puts his nation to shame, simply that he may continue his own corrupt life."

Rokytzana, he repeats, is a heresiarch. He insults Nicholas V, he insults the cardinals and prelates of the Church, he calls Catholic princes and kings heretics. "No reasonable man can blame me for calling him a heretic. When I tried to rouse him from deadly slumber, he called me a sacrilegious man, a seducer, a fortune-teller, an antichrist, though in truth I am commissioned by the Apostolic See to weed out his heretical views, and then to restore to him all offices and titles which he has lost, and to admit him again to the community of the Church, if he puts off his wolf's nature and truly does penance. But the heart of Pharaoh is hardened, and some openly assert that he is not even a priest. Without being ordained himself, he would have the temerity to 'ordain' others unless he had been prevented. My noble lords, who can resist despising such a man, who, himself blind, despises the most famous teachers of Christendom? Grown up in vices, he would dictate to Christianity. He has urged that the Christian houses of worship be pulled down, that pictures of the saints be destroyed, the holy vessels be carried away. Thus he brings worthy sacrifices to God! Is not he himself an antichrist? Against papal prohibition, he usurps the dignity of an archbishop. He lets the body and blood of Christ be trodden under foot. You may see the blood of Christ dripping from men's beards like broth. You may see little children spit it out like dirt. You may see all receive it like common food.

"O you illustrious barons, you famous lords, of the glorious kingdom of Bohemia! Why tolerate in your midst such corruption and disgrace? Did your ancestors die as rebels against the Roman Church? No. The contrary is true. They loved and honored the Church more than other peoples on earth. In the splendor of divine service this noble realm was not excelled by any other country. Where are now the numberless churches they built and endowed? Where the legions of religious who lived on pious donations? Where is the ancient piety, the union of faith? Many among you deny the presence of Christ in the consecrated Host. How many thousands of Bohemians are not properly baptized, if baptized at all? How many for want of bishops are not confirmed? Peasants go to Communion without confession, just as they might go to dinner.

Rokytzana lords over all this like a second God. I say nothing of those who are forced to receive Communion under two species; for that is plainly against the Compact. The city of Saaz heard in a public sermon that Christ is not to be adored in Communion. Wicked men gad about pretending to be priests, even daring to say Mass. Where, illustrious lords, is now your famous university, once an ornament not only of Prague, not only of this kingdom, but of the whole Christian world? From it flowed forth, like the rolling Danube, a stream of light upon all nations.

"What does Rokytzana reply? Will he dare assert that Hus, Wyclif, Jacobellus, were more concerned for the welfare of this kingdom than your fathers and ancestors, who through so many centuries never infringed the rights and customs of the Roman Church, but rather guarded them more faithfully than others, as the apple of their eye? And where is your archbishop? Who has brought on you all these evils? Rokytzana and his teachers brought this leprosy into the country. Rokytzana still defends their damnable doctrines. Though I have pity on the misled multitude, I wonder how so many noble barons can be deceived, who would be able to govern not only Bohemia but hundreds of such kingdoms. They surely do not need the counsel of that corrupt man. I adjure you, my lords, remember your ancestors, who were the best sons of the holy Roman Catholic Church. Remember also your own last hour, in which Rokytzana's idle words will not help you.

"I would prefer by far to speak to you than to write. My words would impress you, wretch though I am. Well then, I beg you, do the work yourselves. Bring that deluded creature back to the Church. You, without assistance, will have freed this glorious Kingdom of Bohemia from the slavery of Satan. Against Rokytzana's calumnies listen to the voices of Italy, Flanders, France, Burgundy, and Germany, where for thirty-six years I have preached without interruption. Listen to those countries where I am known by reputation: England, Spain, Portugal, Catalonia, Dalmatia, Hungary, and Poland. And yet you, Rokytzana, you most wretched of men, you call me a vagabond, a seducer, an antichrist. My noble barons, does Rokytzana see more clearly than the whole Catholic world, than the universities of Rome, Naples, Siena, Perugia, Florence, Ferrara, Bologna, Padua, Pavia, where I have preached the word of God for so many years, and where my doctrine has not been condemned, but praised? And you dare call me a seducer, you senseless beast?

"Are these examples too far away? Then take one from your next neighbor. A stranger, unacquainted with German, I was received by the University of Vienna with the highest honors. Their famous doctors and masters listened to my teaching for fifty days, and praised it highly. Multitudes flocked to hear me. In Olmütz a hundred thousand persons came to one of my Sunday sermons. Nowhere in our day was a religious received with such honors as I was, in Austria, in Olmütz, Brünn, Znaim, by the lords of Rosenberg, in Passau, Ratisbon, and Eger. And you, mouthpiece of slander, call me a sixty-six-year-old tramp, a seducer and antichrist. Will Rokytzana say I am boasting? But I am not praising myself; I glorify my Creator, who chooses the lowly to confound the strong. His divine majesty has made me known to foreign peoples, so that Rokytzana and his adherents may see that Brother John Capistran is not a tramp, not a seducer, not an antichrist, but the legal ambassador of the Apostolic See. What I wish is the salvation of Bohemia. God is my witness. I wish to bring peace and rest to this kingdom. If I desired honors, I would go to Poland or to Hungary or to Germany or to Italy, whose princes invite me with urgent petitions. Let Rokytzana's serpent tongue cease hissing against me. For his soul am I enduring these labors. He is now unmasked. Beware of his poison. Tolerate him no longer. He is a stain on your honor. I will pray without ceasing for all of you, for each of you individually, even for my Rokytzana. I say 'my Rokytzana,' in the hope that he will return to Mother Church."

This effort of Capistran ended in bitter disappointment. He entrusted the letter to Nicholas of Lobkowitz, a nobleman who had extensive possessions in the neighborhood of Brüx and was generally considered a courageous representative of the Catholic cause. Nicholas promised to present the letter to the diet and to demand that it be read there. But events ran contrary to Capistran's aim. Frederick III had advised the Bohemians to acknowledge Podebrad as his representative. Hence (April 27) Podebrad was elected unanimously as administrator. Absent lords, among them the Rosenbergs, had to yield by August 15, or be treated as public disturbers. Next came the ecclesiastical question. The Catholic representatives did indeed refuse certain requests of the Utraquist clergy, and succeeded in reintroducing many Catholic customs, such as the blessing of water and of ashes. But they accepted the Compact, and even took Rokytzana under their protection. All that was now needed was papal approval, and this they hoped to obtain through the legate, Cardinal Cusa. Cusa, urged by Albrecht Achilles of Ansbach, invited the Bohemian delegates to meet in Ratisbon (June 4). Margrave Albrecht and Duke Louis guaranteed safe conduct. A delegate of Albrecht brought this offer to the Diet of Prague. The offer was accepted, and delegates were appointed. Under these circumstances Nicholas of Lobkowitz thought it useless to present Capistran's vehement accusations against Rokytzana.

Capistran was naturally pained when he remained unheard at the diet. But what pained him still more was the agreement signed by the Catholics and the Utraquists. "Not by the Holy Ghost, but by the devil, was this attained." Thus he wrote to Ulrich Rosenberg. It was a justification of Utraquist errors, an express approval of heretics. He writes in detail to the Catholic barons and commends their zeal against Utraquist abuses, and says he will send their letter to the Pope. But they should have refused to debate the Compact. That belongs to the Pope, to the Church. Duty would have urged them rather to assist him, the inquisitor, in the fulfillment of his office. He fears for the good name of Nicholas Rosenberg, now that he has promised to protect Rokytzana and his adherents. Difficulties are no excuse; faith is absolutely first among all interests. For his country, son may rise against father, father against son. How much more when faith is in danger. Avarice, he writes to Cusa, is the deeper reason for this agreement. Church property shared by Catholic barons would now remain undisputed in their possession.

In some way the lords of Prague finally received that letter from Brüx. But the Catholic barons should not be blamed for not expecting good results from reading it in the diet. The facts were known in Bohemia. Rokytzana's doubtful ordination and his usurpation of episcopal rights had been condemned by other opponents. Capistran's picture of the past glories of Bohemia might well have done good. But the Hussites blamed the Catholics for the unspeakable misery which had come over their country. As long as the Utraquist barons clung to their political and national aims, for which Rokytzana fought with full energy, all talking against the man was in vain. On the other hand, the effect of Capistran's writings on the Catholic world must not be undervalued. In this sense Capistran had really unmasked Rokytzana. That the Bohemians feared Capistran's influence is proved by the Ash Wednesday note of protest, signed first by Podebrad himself. Capistran is not vainglorious when he repeatedly throws his international reputation into the scale. The Bohemians feared his European powers of propaganda.

In the second edition of his Brüxian treatise, he pillories a recent vile trick of Rokytzana. While Rokytzana was preaching, there entered a Utraquist priest, hired for the purpose, and accused him of heresy. Rokytzana refuted him successfully, whereupon the defeated opponent solemnly withdrew his accusation. Capistran informed Cusa, and told the barons that if they let this infamous trick pass unpunished, he would report the affair to the Pope, the prelates, to all the kings and princes of Christendom. Was this comedy offered to the people as a substitute for the expected debate? Or is it a sign of Rokytzana's increasing nervousness? He must certainly have known that the Catholic movement was making rapid progress. Thirteen hundred Utraquists came from afar to Brüx, renounced before Capistran the use of the chalice. But none came from Prague as all roads were closed. "Had the people been free to come to us, we would have made the greatest catch in the history of Hussitism. By the grace of God we have not lost our time. God be praised for everything. I continue in God's word, though the Bohemians do not want to hear, and have shut their ears."

He was still striving to reach Prague. From Brüx he sent one letter after another, to the administrator, to influential barons, to men like Sternberg and Smiricky. He even approached Jakoubek of Wresowitz, an old Hussite incendiary, since this man was considered a confidant of Podebrad. He asked also the help of neighboring German princes, Louis and Otto of Bavaria, Albrecht and John of Brandenburg. To save appearances, his opponents offered him another opportunity to debate with Rokytzana, not in Prague, but in a remote friary in a small village, "where sheep and oxen abound," said Capistran. Smiricky wrote that he would accompany Capistran, if Capistran were ready to have his tonsure enlarged. Whether Smiricky doubted his own ability or, as Capistran thought, merely spoke words of mockery, this much was clear, that Rokytzana refused any debate under reasonable and acceptable conditions. Capistran's refusal to go to the village proposed was interpreted, of course, to Rokytzana's advantage. He now talked more frequently of the monk from Capistrano, who positively refused to debate with him in Bohemia, and wanted to drag him to foreign cities, whereas he himself wanted to dispute only in the presence of Bohemians, so they could decide whether he was right or wrong.

Rokytzana left writing to his friends. Podebrad himself wrote to Capistran, as did also the magistrate of Prague. Both productions were weak. But both held firmly to Rokytzana, who, they say, leads a clean life. The false prophet is Capistran himself. But his crazy ideas will never lead them away from evangelical truth.

John of Nedelist, a physician, now entered the lists. He had written anonymously while Capistran was still in Eger. He had said that Capistran's behavior in the pulpit was altogether improper, especially his shrieking, his exclamations, his gesticulations. At that time Capistran answered shortly and sharply: "Whosoever you may be, you talk like a heretic. Mind your own business, heretic, afraid to let yourself be known." Nedelist now wrote in his own name. As answer he received a small treatise, though Nedelist was unimportant. Some thought the name was a mere mask for Rokytzana or Borotin. Capistran did not share this opinion. But Nedelist may, if he wishes, give the reply also to the other two Johns. The language is strong, as it had been against Rokytzana. A layman dares instruct the theologian and inquisitor! "I could instruct you, as the proverb says, even in my sleep." He excuses his rough, blunt pen. "I am not guided by hatred, but rather by love. Like St. Gregory I get angry with sinners but I do not despise them. I seek your salvation, which you make light of."

This letter is an abridgement of all he had told the Hussites. He defends his elocution with Quintilian's doctrine. Pathos is becoming in a Christian orator. Like the Danube at high water, the preacher must carry his audience with him. "Had your preachers not been dumb dogs, unable to bark, the devil would never have had such a triumph in Bohemia. And you, devoid of all knowledge, sacred and secular, dare to criticize my exclamations, though Scripture is full of them! The true preacher must not fall asleep while preaching, as was the case with your preachers. He must teach, touch, and move. Against vices he must hurl thunder and lightning. Consequently he must raise cry and clamor. Hence I will continue to raise my voice and to gesticulate. On my fingers I will count, before a hundred thousand people, your ugly misdeeds. You cannot silence me. Two kinds of people hate me: Jews and heretics. Against these I have always been severe, but with justice and fairness. They never intimidated me. Neither can you."

Prague was still closed. Two months had passed in Brüx. After trying for ten months to meet the Utraquist leaders, he began to doubt whether he would be invited even to the imperial diet in Ratisbon. Catholics were not entirely satisfied with his methods. On May 9, after five months' absence, his messengers returned from Rome, where they had seen Frederick III crowned emperor. The three papal bulls they brought partially granted two of his requests. First, full faculties for the confessional; secondly, the power to affiliate new houses with the Italian family of the Order. But what of his chief requests, the faculty, namely, of inquisitory procedure against the Hussites, and of an express declaration that the Compact was invalid? These were passed over in silence. But the documents do praise Capistran's efforts against the abominable sect of the Hussites which, condemned by the Council of Constance, is still spreading its poison like a cancer farther and farther. The Observant foundations are called ramparts against Hussitism. This new public condemnation of Utraquism was quickly utilized by Capistran. He sent a copy of the bull to Nicholas of Lobkowitz, to encourage that baron. Another copy was sent to Ulrich Rosenberg, with a request to make it known to the other barons. "I wish there were copies of it in every corner of Bohemia."

The restrictions, however, show Rome's intention of keeping the road clear for Cardinal Cusa. Capistran is to limit his activity to strictly missionary work: preaching, and absolving in the realm of conscience only. Possibly Cusa himself appealed to Rome. He certainly did not share in every respect the views of Capistran on the Hussite question. He was angry that Rokytzana and the Bohemians had been branded as heretics. Capistran was much pained. His long letter to Cusa is pervaded by restrained indignation. "Contradiction of view compels me to accuse of heresy, either Rokytzana on one side, or the Pope and Catholic rulers on the other. Read Rokytzana's letters carefully, and then you may judge whether my inspiration came from God or from the devil. If we excuse heretics, we condemn ourselves. In matters of faith I have never learned to straddle. I believe in the One, Holy, Catholic, Apostolic Church. I for one cannot find that Church with Rokytzana. Do I not fight for you? Is it not for you that I expose myself to such dangers? Unbelief is included in this disobedience to the Apostolic See. Thus it stands in your own letters. In four bulls, addressed to me, the Pope calls the Bohemians heretics. And now these heretics accuse me before you, and senselessly demand that I call them Catholics!"

This letter shows Capistran's fear that the legate, not sufficiently informed, might make at Ratisbon the concessions planned by the princes in Bayreuth. These princes, without deeper ecclesiastical concern, wanted at any price a final regulation of the Bohemian affair. Capistran's frankness can be excused by the seriousness of his apprehensions. "If one rebellious nation can force the Church to concessions, what may not all other nations demand? Beware, my lord, lest to win Prague you lose the rest of Christendom. The law says that heretics, far from being rewarded, should be subjected to punishment, should be deprived of property, and that a plenary indulgence be granted to all those who take the field against them. Shall these flatterers, with honeyed words, induce you to grant them Communion under both species and let them retain Church property? You cut into your own flesh with such yielding. In Rome I heard you say that the cardinal's hat did not mean that others should bow their knees before you, but that you were to perform a great work for the Church. Pardon my boldness, but such concessions to heretics seem to me to be, not a great work for God, but something far less."

Capistran may have thought this frankness would exclude him at Ratisbon. But, without sensitiveness, the Cardinal decided to call Capistran to audience. If Capistran cares at all for the honor of God and the obedience toward the Church, he will be present, on Sunday after Vitus and Modestus (June 18), at the diet in Ratisbon. Capistran made immediate preparations. Further, he urged Rokytzana to come to Ratisbon. The admonition was useless. As Ulrich Rosenberg said, Rokytzana could not be gotten out of his hole at any price.

Capistran was still at Brüx when his term as vicar-general of the cismontane Observants expired. Assembling all the brethren who could be reached, he spoke with deep emotion about the gifts of the Holy Ghost. Extending his arms, he turned to all parts of the world, crying: "You are my witnesses that I receive all the faithful in every part of the world into our community. I grant them all, as far as it in me lies, a share in all our good works."

In far away Aquila an immense concourse of Observants (Pentecost, 1452) elected Mark of Bologna as Capistran's successor. But instead of being released, Capistran was declared vicar for Austria, Styria, Hungary, and Bohemia. Five foundations already existed, three in Vienna, one in Klosterneuburg near Vienna, one in Brünn (Moravia). This last foundation was owing to the coadjutor bishop, William of Olmütz, who contributed the first sum. A papal bull (March 6, 1452) raised these new foundations to the rank of a vicariate. Capistran predicted that "his little dogs," in spite of all resistance, would reach Prague. This word was fulfilled a few years after his death, but while Podebrad and Rokytzana were still alive.

A seven days' journey brought Capistran to Ratisbon, probably by way of Saxony. He arrived there on the 15th or 16th of June.

While waiting for the opening of the imperial diet, Capistran preached. The whole market place had to be covered with straw on account of the mud. As Corpus Christi had just been celebrated, he preached first on the sacrament of the altar, incidentally referring to the heresy in Bohemia. Then he treated the subject of recreation. Some games are morally right. Games without investment of money are justified. Chess, for instance, promotes ingenuity. Ball-playing develops the body. Archery serves the defense of liberty. But games of chance where money is staked are sinful, sinful even for those who merely assist by bringing in light or by watching the game or by preparing the dice. He enumerates fifty sins which result from unbridled gambling. Italian examples abound. A student in Siena, the night before his promotion, gambled away his property and then hanged himself. King Martin of Sicily (1386-1409) won a vassal's whole property, and then bought him a rope. A cleric in Ratisbon who reviled these sermons as exaggerations was, says Fara, overtaken by divine judgment. The usual mighty bonfire destroyed a mass of gambling apparatus. Gambling in German lands had perhaps less ruinous consequences than it had in Italy. Capistran himself insists on differences in time, place, and custom. He is severe on dancing. Ceremonial dances, as, for instance, at the reception of a king, he lets pass. But he condemns without reserve dancing with persons of the other sex. His own experience is his witness. Up to his thirtieth year he had danced very much. He says that dancing tempts all the senses of the body. "Better, young man, take coals of fire into your hands than the hand of a girl. Better for you, young lady, to dance on fiery coals than on the slippery and dangerous dancing floor."

Two princes, four bishops, many nobles and prelates, came to the diet. Ulrich Rosenberg sent Dr. Wenzel as his representative. The Bohemian delegates were escorted by two hundred horsemen; and, at their request, a second retinue met them at Cham. This pomp contrasted strongly with their instructions. When and where would the legate meet the estates of the realm? This was the sole question they were authorized to treat. They urged the legate to visit Prague immediately. "Their words were sweeter than honey," says a member of the diet. Toward Capistran, too, these gentlemen were extremely polite. He must accompany the cardinal under all circumstances. Sternberg, a clever but unprincipled and selfish man, tried to insinuate himself into Capistran's favor, but in vain. When confronted with the contradiction between their captivating words and the letters from Prague, they pretended ignorance. Capistran was not deceived. Dr. Wenzel writes to Rosenberg: "The Bohemian ambassadors, especially Sternberg, have been hauled over the coals by Friar John." Nor did the ambassadors succeed with Cusa. Rome was not disposed to surrender a papal legate a second time to the mob of Prague. Cusa had orders not to pass the Bohemian borders until the Utraquists had signed their submission to the Church. Since the Bohemian deputation would not guarantee even a safe-conduct, their invitation could not be taken seriously. Cusa's views had begun to change. Dr. Wenzel writes: "The legate also is very strict with them, even if he mixed some honey with his bitter words. The cardinal knows their method well." The only important result of the diet at Ratisbon was that the legate recognized the real condition in Bohemia.

Since the ambassadors declared that they had no authorization to sign a document of submission to the Roman Church, Duke Louis of Bavaria and Margrave Albrecht Achilles tried to mediate. For St. Gall's Day (October 16) a new diet was planned, this time at Eger. There the Bohemians would submit to Rome. Then the apostolic legate would go to Bohemia and announce to them the delayed jubilee indulgence, and consecrate bishops and ordain priests. The Bohemian ambassadors pledged themselves to promote the Eger diet. About St. Bartholomew's Day (August 24) they would answer. "The Bohemians leave today," writes Dr. Wenzel on June 26, about three o'clock in the morning. "They are not at all satisfied. They were treated vigorously by the legate and by Capistran and got slaps they will remember. Your Highness will rejoice to hear how splendidly they were dispatched."

Catholic opinion was much divided. Wenzel writes: "Some

think they will return to obedience. But I fear they promised with a faithless heart." Another member of the diet said no reliance could be placed on their word. Cardinal Cusa still had hopes, and prepared a most splendid celebration at Eger, to surround the Bohemian homage with corresponding solemnity. He sent two chaplains with the Bohemian delegation to visit Bohemia and Moravia, and to learn by personal observation the true disposition of the country. For this purpose they carried with them a circular of the Cardinal. This letter shows that Ratisbon had led the legate much closer to Capistran. His language now resembles Capistran's. The Hussites, he writes, "are so blind, that they do not see the light; so bestial, that they do not honor their own mother." He had been deceived, the legate says. Formerly he had ignored Capistran's views. He now expressly defends Capistran against the accusation, ceaselessly spread by his opponents, that he had condemned without distinction all those who, on the basis of the Compact, had received Communion under both species. "Neither Capistran, a man of holy zeal and much knowledge, nor anybody else has ever asserted such a thing." On the Compact, too, he agrees in essentials with Capistran, though he insists, not on the lack of canonical justification, but rather on the Utraquist failure to fulfill the conditions laid down by the Compact. Furthermore, he does not, in general, think much of such contracts. "Children should cling to their mother without stipulations and contracts. She is a kind mother. What is harmful to her children you cannot wring from her by any contract. What is wholesome she gives them without contract."

The diet at Ratisbon had discussed also the situation in Austria, whence nobles had arrived with bad news. Dissensions over Ladislaus threatened to end in open rebellion. While Frederick was on his way to Rome, disaffected nobles had formed a federation, which included John Hunyadi and Ulrich Rosenberg. Rosenberg saw in that federation a support against Podebrad. Ladislaus, as king of Bohemia, would be a Catholic ruler, and they themselves would enjoy his special favor. The Austrian delegates asked the princes assembled in Ratisbon to make a last effort at mediation. There was danger that the Emperor would make common cause with the Bohemians, and that the Hungarians would seek the assistance of the Turks. The delegates also adjured Capistran to mediate, and he therefore promptly wrote to the Emperor, urging him to yield. To the Elector of Saxony, a relative of the Emperor, he sent a courier. In a special memorandum he added numerous reasons, juridical and historical, to convince the Elector.

Capistran had left Brüx most reluctantly. Why did he not return after the diet in Ratisbon? His Bohemian mission closed with his departure from Brüx in June, 1452. Perhaps Cardinal Cusa, however much in sympathy with Capistran's view, thought that prudence now required Capistran's absence from Bohemian territory. As far as the Cardinal needed a representative to keep in touch with the Bohemians, his chaplain, John Dursmit, took Capistran's place.

Capistran spent the following months in the neighboring German provinces. Nuremberg came first. The magistrate wrote that the entire city was pleading with uplifted arms for his coming.

CHAPTER XXVIII

Nuremberg, Erfurt, and Jena

ON July 2, 1452, Capistran arrived at Amberg, the principal city of the Upper Palatinate. Here he received the third invitation from Nuremberg. Calamity now made that city clamor for his appearance. For two full years Nuremberg had been trying to make peace with its princely neighbor, the Hohenzollern margrave, Albrecht of Ansbach. To understand this situation, we must recall the long struggle that distracted the German Empire toward the end of the Middle Ages: the struggle between princes and free cities. The economic activities of the cities were penetrating in most embarrassing fashion into the dominions of the princes. To dominate these cities was naturally the aim of sovereigns. The citizens, on the other hand, saw in their freedom the guaranty of wealth, comfort, and protection. By hiring nobles to enter their service they were extending their influence indirectly even into princedoms. Nuremberg's granting of feudal rights to neighboring nobles had moved Albrecht (July 2, 1449) to send a herald, dressed in black and white, into the city with a declaration of war. Thirty cities held with Nuremberg. Albrecht had on his side twenty-two princes, many counts, and a great number of barons. Over seven thousand feud-letters arrived in Nuremberg, among them one from Podebrad, who sided with Albrecht, because Bohemia's enemy, the elector of Saxony, was on the side of Nuremberg. Thus the rich and mighty Nuremberg, called by contemporaries "the center of Europe," and Margrave Albrecht, the most distinguished among the German princes of those days, came to a clash.

Albrecht was enterprising, tenacious, and versatile; an alert diplomat, a knight without fear or reproach. Scars from uncounted feuds covered his body. Albrecht Achilles he was called by admiring countrymen, while foreigners called him "the German fox."

Personally he was an affable, jovial man, who liked to mingle with the people. At the Diet of Ratisbon he joined the riflemen in target-shooting, and enjoyed their hospitality. Nuremberg had between 20,000 and 30,000 inhabitants, and the citizens lived comfortably in roomy houses, which in wartime harbored many refugees. At the beginning of the feud the 10,000 farmers in Nuremberg territory were ordered into the city.

Now followed twelve months of killing, plundering, and burning, without one real battle. Countless hamlets and villages went up in flames. In March, 1450, the Nuremberg forces won a victory near Pillenreuth; in June came an armistice in consequence of mutual exhaustion. Many peace discussions followed without result. Repeatedly Frederick III summoned the parties to his court. When, in June, 1451, the diplomats from Nuremberg heard Capistran preach, and sent reports home, they were promptly ordered by the magistrate to beg the holy man's intervention and to invite him to Nuremberg. For the moment Capistran sent them the usual diploma of aggregation. When he arrived in Eger, the magistrate again invited him. One of these letters, in genuine humanist manner, paints exuberantly the city's yearnings for him. Albrecht Achilles also desired Capistran's mediation. A member of the diet at Ratisbon asserted that the margrave intended to let himself be guided entirely by the venerable father. Cardinal Cusa, too, urged Capistran to do all he could in the cause of peace. As peacemaking was one of the most prominent activities of the Franciscan itinerants, Capistran cheerfully accepted this mission of charity.

From Amberg he went to Eichstätt. On his way he visited Otto, count of the Palatinate. Then, on July 17, halfway between Nuremberg and Hilpoltstein, he met the Nuremberg delegates, Dr. Gregory Heimburg and Nicholas Muffel. Dr. Heimburg was Germany's most prominent lawyer. Imposing in appearance, stately in figure, with intelligent features, bold eyes, and a high forehead, he was the picture of dignity. But in character this highly gifted man was selfish and false. He was a rude, blustering demagogue, who abused even the princes of the Church. How far this representative of Nuremberg was responsible for the failure of Capistran's peace efforts is hard to say. Capistran was unpleasantly impressed by this first discussion in Hilpoltstein. Margrave Albrecht's presentation of the case was essentially different from that of Nuremberg. Quite different was the information sent by Cardinal Cusa. Capistran no longer knew what to think.

Pompously escorted, Capistran entered Nuremberg the same evening. A Nuremberg physician, Hartmann Schedel, gives us a pen-picture: "A small man, sixty-five years old, with meager and emaciated body, reduced to skin, veins, and bone." In Nuremberg, Capistran saw, probably for the first time north of the Alps, an Observant cloister not founded by himself. This Nuremberg convent belonged to the province of Strassburg. The Nuremberg magistrate had accused the Conventuals of leading a disorderly life, and the city would no longer tolerate such conditions. Eugene IV (1446) ordered a reform of the friary, and Bishop Antonius of Bamberg, by papal orders, gave the cloisters to the Observants. When, after the death of Eugene IV rumor said that the new Pope intended to restore the Conventuals, the magistrates promptly appealed to Nicholas V, reporting that the Conventuals had been incorrigible, but that the Observants were mirrors of Christian life, whose prayers had saved the city. If the Conventuals returned, people would leave the city.

Capistran quieted this fear. He went further. He placed the convent of the Poor Clares under the Observance, a step long since prepared by the abbess, Clara Gundelfingerin. On July 24 St. Clare received great company. Accompanied by the provincial, the guardian, and several brothers, some city councilors and others, Capistran made a visit to the convent. The sisters gathered in the refectory. In an address which the provincial translated into German, Capistran exhorted them to return to their first mother, St. Clare. After this he applied to each one individually the relics of St. Bernardine, and dedicated the rooms of the convent. The next day the community placed itself in due form under the guidance of the Observance.

Nuremberg offered the same picture as Vienna did the year

before. From July 18 until August 13 Capistran preached daily. In front of Our Lady's Church they had erected a pulpit, near the platform from which once a year the sacred ensigns of the Empire were shown to the people. Divisions were railed off in the market place: men, women, the Jews, the sick, the latter on one occasion numbering 1,800 people. Distinguished people, including Charles of Baden, had arcades near the pulpit. The twenty-seven sermons in Nuremberg treat three subjects, beginning with a series of sermons on the Creed, which is the foundation and groundplan of God's kingdom on earth. Every citizen of that kingdom must know these articles.

The second sermon insists that the Jews, too, have to come. The next day they are present. "I will prove to you the articles of our faith with the authority of your own law, the Old Testament." The next day: "I will continue this subject, hoping it will benefit our friends, the Jews." He addresses them: "Our most dear Jews." This address was not ironical. He says with St. Hilary: "If I do not love the Jews I am not a good Christian. Was not Christ a Jew? And the Blessed Virgin Mary? Were not the apostles Jews? To obtain graces for the Jews, of whose race Christ willed to be born, do I preach these sermons." Though all Jew-baiting is absent, he does, on occasion, condemn Jewish profanation of pawned liturgical vessels. He says that the Jews once made an attempt on his life.

In general his treatment is objective and scientific. The Messianic announcements of their prophets have been fulfilled in and through Christ. All these sermons show burning zeal to remove the veil from the eyes of a deluded people. He anticipates objections. "The Jews said in their hearts: 'That girl of Jairus was not dead; He did not raise her to life.' And of the youth of Naim they said: 'He was not dead. He was in a swoon.' But the raising of Lazarus your ancestors could not deny." He quotes long text from Isaias: "Read the 52nd and the 53rd chapters. Had he been an evangelist he could not have spoken more clearly. Oh, how beautifully have your prophets foretold the mysteries of your Messias!" Christian auditors he warns against the Jewish view that one can find salvation in any faith. "If everyone can be saved by his own religion, then there must be as many religions as there are men. Go your own way. But do not say longer: In the name of the Lord, or, I believe in God." In this endeavor of the Jews to infect their Christian hosts with religious indifferentism he sees the danger of Judaism. To counteract this danger only two ways are open: Either the Jews embrace Christian truth; or, if they remain stubborn, the laws about them have to be strictly enforced.

On Saturday, July 22, he preached on Mary Magdalen, his favorite saint, on whose feast he himself had been converted. "Examine yourselves as she did. What did you do in your fifth year, your sixth, your seventh? Prove conversion by deeds. Magdalen dried the feet of the Lord with her hair. If you have gambled with dice or cards, you must hand those things over to me." St. Lawrence Day, August 10, saw the "bonfire of vanities." Reports speak of 3,000 checkerboards, of 40,000 dice sets, besides a load of padded hats, pointed shoes, and the like. An immense fire, a gruesome cloud of blue smoke, says a chronicle. The Jews were forced by Christians to throw gaming tables into the fire. Colored wagons and sleighs were also burned, to atone for nightly joyrides, in which women participated. This violation of female decorum brought harsh words. "These are no noble women; they are hussies. May God punish men who tolerate such things. They are not nobles." On Friday, July 28, he began to preach against usury. These addresses were courses in moral theology, presented with concrete and penetrating rhetoric. In Germany he seems to have preached even more frequently and sharply than in Italy against taking interest. Transcripts are preserved not only in Nuremberg, but also in Halle, Leipzig, and Breslau. The Germans, he says with indignation, had almost entirely reconciled themselves with this method of lending at interest. In Leipzig he expresses his astonishment that certain cities had legalized the taking of interest. "These cities certainly do not belong to the *civitas Dei*."

He pursues his theme even on feast days. On August 1, feast of St. Peter's Chains, he begins by saying that the pope is above the council. But he soon turns again to his theme. His transitions are curious. "The death of the apostle pleased the Jews. They are pleased likewise with business. They gather treasures, yet not for heaven but for earth." On Portiuncula Day (August 2) he relates the origin of that feast, but turns promptly to his lecture on usury. But on August 4 he does dedicate a whole sermon to St. Dominic, praising his labors for the Church, and the merits of the mendicant orders in promoting knowledge.

The treatise on usury concluded, he began to speak about peace, the great problem of Nuremberg. "If thou also hadst known the things that are to thy peace" (Luke 20:42) is his text. He is concerned only with honoring God, not at all with favoring either city or prince. He speaks about peace in heaven, peace among men, peace in nature. Sin has disturbed the God-given order. A fourfold war is the result: between God and men, between the inner and the outer man, between man and angels, finally between men and men. Peace means man's return to a well-regulated order of life, within himself, with his neighbor, with God. Each of these points has four divisions. He paints the horrors of war, the ruined fields beyond the walls being his witness: material loss, personal loss, spiritual loss, loss for eternity. He tells how a civil war had decimated his own relationship: "Twelve of my relatives were killed in two days, the ancestral houses of my father and mother were burned down." Ruin of wealth: "During wartime only fools dare to go out to the fields, which thus run to weeds. The vineyards are ruined, the house destroyed, churches and hospitals neglected. The common welfare declines. Citizens have no rest. Nuremberg has three hundred watchtowers, each requiring eight or ten men. People are abed. Suddenly they are alarmed: 'The enemy is coming!' There is disturbance as if the foe were already inside the walls. And thus people have no rest."

He passes to higher motives, praising the heroism which consists in bearing, enduring, forgiving, and yielding. Look at the animals. The lion will not kill a fly. It plays with its young ones without harming them. Ravens live peacefully with ravens, and doves with doves. Magnanimity of heart guarantees peace among men. With mildness one can tame even wild animals. "Let me tell you what happened to me twice. Seven dogs rushed upon me. I cried 'Jesus,' and they ran away." He adds advice. "Let the ravening dog have a piece of bread, and you hurry away. It is better the dog eat your bread than your calves." Peace flows from charity. He tells simply how he himself forgave the murderers of his relatives. His activity as peacemaker in Italy showed him the divine judgments which fall on the enemies of peace. Nature shows the equivalent of noble self-denial. How bitter are green nuts! But when women gather them and keep them in water, they become delicacies.

These five peace sermons are masterpieces. Although the chronicles are usually brief in reporting his sermons, a Nuremberg chronicler reports in full the three narratives which Capistran inserted into his last peace sermon, on the feast of St. Lawrence. Side by side with his sermons went parleys on peace. This task was very disagreeable since each of the parties supposed that his opponent was wrong. Capistran demanded clear information on the cause of the war. But the Nuremberg magistrates could not be induced to compose the desired memorandum. Both parties refused at first to discuss the affair in Capistran's presence, with the excuse that all efforts of that kind at former meetings had been in vain. Finally they consented. Capistran assigned August 2 as the date for the parley. But the margrave refused to go to Nuremberg. He proposed the cloister of Pillenreuth, about halfway between Nuremberg and Schwabach. The delegates from Nuremberg were led by Dr. Heimburg; the margrave delegation, by the abbot of Heilbronn. The parties discussed their affairs with Capistran, but in separate rooms. The margrave party related to him very explicitly the whole story of the war. "He stayed rather long with them," remarks the Nuremberg protocol. Continuation was set for the following day.

Capistran went back to the city. He would not omit his sermons even in these days. On the second day Heimburg spoke in Capistran's presence. The margrave requested Capistran to come with him to Schwabach, where he would make known his final conditions. The prince promised to follow him rather than anybody else. But Albrecht's principal demand, payment of compensation for damages, was promptly refused by the Nuremberg delegates. They would not arbitrate with the prince at all until he had restored all that he had taken from them. Capistran forwarded the counterdemand of the council, and advised them to drop the demand of compensation. But the council would not consent.

Capistran felt that the aldermen were not fully candid. He asked them to tell him sincerely their full demands, if not publicly, then secretly. He would keep silence. Their refusal would be a sign of distrust in him, and he could do nothing but commend the whole matter to God. The council assured him solemnly of their full trust in him; but his reverence should remember that they had to act as governors in the way prescribed by their duty toward the city. Capistran felt his role as arbitrator was at an end, especially since the margrave continually shifted in his views. In this sense he wrote to the margrave, who thanked him in a letter from Schwabach. The aldermen told Capistran he had now learned to know that prince, and would learn to know him still better. They, too, thanked him and commended the city to him also for the future.

The sermon on August 12 was in honor of St. Clare. Capistran attacked Rokytzana's assertion that religious life is an invention of the devil. On the evening of August 13 he rode away toward Forchheim. At the gate he blessed the aldermen, who were sad that he had to leave them without establishing peace, and feared they might have lost his benevolence. They sent after him some casks of their best wines. Nuremberg finally had to accept the conditions which Capistran had advised, and pay the indemnities demanded by Albrecht. He in turn gave back the castles he had conquered. But Nuremberg remained a free city, a power which neighboring princes had to respect. During the Turkish war, in the year 1456, Nuremberg, to Capistran's delight, sent a large troop of soldiers to Hungary. There, near the Turkish border, and shortly before his death, Capistran blessed for the last time his faithful Nurembergers.

After preaching in Forchheim on the eve of the Assumption, Capistran came to Bamberg where he remained five days, preaching on the Blessed Virgin, with sharp attacks on the Hussites. His friend and benefactor, Bishop Anthony of Rotenhann, was an old warrior, who had himself fought against the Hussites. The feast of St. Louis of France (August 19), the saintly Franciscan of royal blood, led him to praise the religious life. To illustrate the hardships of the apostolic itinerant, he speaks of forty-four interpreters who served him since he entered German territory.

Turning north from Bamberg, the party entered Saxony, Jena being their destination. Duke William III, a brother of the Elector of Saxony, had invited Capistran. Thuringia lay in ruins, like Franconia. About three hundred villages had been burned by the Hussites. Then had come civil war. William III, dissatisfied with his share of the inheritance, waged a six-year war (1445-51) against his brother Frederick. Gera and many other towns went up in flames. Then the Schwarzenberg feud covered the land with ruins. Besides, the plague was raging. Via Koburg, Capistran reached Arnstadt, the residence of Henry of Schwarzenberg, who had made the jubilee pilgrimage to Rome (1450-51). Arnstadt escorted the Franciscans with all honors, and at their arrival offered them its best wine. Capistran was lodged in the Observant cloister, where a provincial chapter was being held, of which he was made honorary president.

In Thuringia the Reform had grown rapidly. The Conventuals had indeed protested that the Observants were not entitled to an independent vicar, and the Observants yielded for the moment. But the Duke wrote to Pope Nicholas, using strong language and accusing the Conventuals of preventing the progress of the Reform. Unless the Pope intervenes the Observants will die out. Capistran's arrival now encouraged the intimidated Observants. The provincial chapter of Arnstadt elected as vicar Henning Sele, who guided the Saxon Observants for the next fifteen years, at the end of which they had sixteen friaries.

Leaving Arnstadt, he came to Erfurt (August 27), which was ruled by the archbishop of Mainz. Numerous churches, convents, chapels, and hospitals gave the city the name of "Little Rome." The mayor of that time, Hartung Cammermeister, chronicles the devout father's visit, telling with loving detail how the horses of the brethren were led to the stables and fed. The mission met with a deeply religious mood. People gathered in the spacious market place in the early hours of the morning. The clergy sang in Latin Ave praeclara and Veni sancte Spiritus, continued by the people in German versions, until the venerable father arrived in solemn procession from the monastery. The outdoor pulpit was a covered tribune erected under a flying buttress of the cathedral.

During his four weeks in Erfurt he paid a visit to Jena (September 6), which finally established two more cloisters for the Observants, one in Weimar, the other in Langensalza.

His Erfurt sermons, dwelling on wisdom, are addressed to fathers of families and directors of communities. Wisdom is based on self-control. Without control of himself and of his household, how can a man preside over a community or guide a diocese or rule a kingdom? Rulers must have prudence, justice, and kindness. Despotism has no duration. A palm tree begins to bear in its hundredth year, a cucumber in its first year. Charles IV of Luxemburg is the example of a ruler devoted to peace; his son Wenceslaus, of a ruler whose weakness leads to anarchy. His own King Ladislaus of Naples, once idolized, now serves as a warning against despotism. Mercy must go hand in hand with justice. Capital sentences must be carried out quickly and without torture. Civil communities belong to the mystical body of Christ and can be preserved only by harmony, justice, and self-control. Taxes are a duty of conscience. The country must be preserved and developed.

He failed to influence the University of Erfurt. Whereas the universities of Vienna and Leipzig and Cracow brought him numerous novices, Erfurt failed him entirely. Why? Certainly not because of any liberal or irreligious spirit, though one of the sharpest critics of Capistran's miraculous cures came from the University of Erfurt. But as a recruiting place for Observants, Erfurt was not suited. It had famous cloisters of its own, in intimate contact with life in the University. The Erfurt Augustinian Hermits gave the theological faculty some of its best professors. The same holds good of the Carthusians. Both of these monastic institutions had carried out a strict reform. The Franciscan Conventuals there also took a lively interest in the theological faculty. Erfurt, therefore, was not a suitable field for Observant propaganda.

His Erfurt sermons repeatedly touch on Hussite affairs. Two

events seem to him providential. During the Hus celebration of that year the Hussite church in Prague was destroyed by fire, wherein many writings of Wyclif and of Jacobell perished. And besides that, the magistrates of Nuremberg could report that Podebrad's party had been seriously defeated by the Taborites. "Since Christians are asleep, God allows the heretics to war among themselves." The meeting planned for Eger collapsed; the Bohemians were not ready for absolute submission to the Pope. The Utraquist leaders were negotiating with the Greek Church. Cardinal Cusa, indeed, admonished the Bohemians to change their evil ways, but he failed as Capistran had failed. His circular provoked the Hussites to a libelous tract.

For the last sermon in Erfurt, Cammermeister says the audience numbered 100,000, though Capistran puts the number at 60,000. The "bonfire of vanities" included the long tresses of many women.

CHAPTER XXIX

Halle, Magdeburg, and Leipzig

UNABLE to go to Bohemia, Capistran went to Magdeburg, invited there by the archbishop, Frederick of Bichlingen, a noble, upright character, affable and benevolent, but relentless in the reform of his diocese. A layman at the time of his election, he adapted himself quickly to the duties of his new office. He took instructions in theology from one of his canons, declined a coadjutor, and personally fulfilled all the duties of a shepherd. To reform cloisters, he called on John Busch of Halle. Cardinal Cusa, who had presided over a synod in Magdeburg, declared he had not found in all Germany a shepherd equal to Frederick.

On his way to Magdeburg, Capistran paused in Halle, where he was met by Archbishop Frederick, in whose presence he preached. John Busch, a confidant of the Archbishop, though filled with the same fervor for reform as Capistran was, did not like Capistran's southern vivacity. "He preaches from two to three hours with hands and feet." Preaching on St. Clare as a model, Capistran contrasts her with modern young women who demand daily two pounds of bread and a proportionate measure of wine or beer, not counting other viands. If swamps can be kept free of frogs and snakes, then can these gluttons be free from temptations of the flesh. Of his last sermon at Halle—on the Creed, the Decalogue, and the Our Father—the chronicler remarks that "it was very long," and that the preacher "shouted terribly" when speaking of usury.

On October 7 he entered the cathedral of Magdeburg. His Magdeburg sermons treated the Ten Commandments, especially the third commandment. The bonfire of vanities included even tools for starching clothes. For the clergy Capistran held special conferences in the cathedral.

In Magdeburg, Capistran had to give much attention to a

controversy which for fifty years had been agitating the surrounding territory. In Wilsnack, a town in Brandenburg, in the diocese of Havelberg, the church was destroyed by fire in 1383. In the ruins the pastor is said to have found three consecrated hosts, uninjured, but showing spots of blood. Crowds of pilgrims began to come, and Wilsnack soon outstripped all rivals. Rivals these may be called, because ever since the twelfth century stories of miraculous hosts had circulated far and wide. Credulity and imposture played their part. The fame of Wilsnack at length provoked decided opposition. The Archbishop of Prague sent a commission to Wilsnack. When this commission reported unfavorably, he held a synod (1405) which forbade pilgrimages from Prague to Wilsnack. John Hus, one of the members of that commission, published a tract against the miracle of Wilsnack. But Wilsnack found its chief opponent in the provost of Magdeburg, Henry Tocke. Careful investigations had convinced him that fraud was at the bottom. Wilsnack hosts did not have the appearance either of bread or of blood.

Tocke gained new hope for success when Frederick became archbishop, since Wilsnack was in the diocese of Havelberg, and hence in the province of Magdeburg. The new Archbishop called Wilsnack the sorest spot in his province, and was determined to make order. The Wilsnack debate flamed anew. The Council of Basle excepted, no other topic so engaged people's minds. The chief opponent was Tocke; the chief defender, the Franciscan provincial, Matthias Döring. The metropolitan had to be prudent since against him were his suffragan, Bishop Conrad of Havelberg, and the ruler of the country, Elector Frederick II of Brandenburg, and also popular enthusiasm for Wilsnack. From the Netherlands, Bohemia, Hungary, Poland, and even Scandinavia, pilgrims came by thousands. Repeated conferences between the representatives of both parties proved fruitless. The Franciscan Conventual, John Kannemann, authorized by the sovereign, went to Rome in 1446 to obtain indulgences and privileges for Wilsnack. These were granted by Eugene IV and confirmed by Nicholas V.

Archbishop Frederick did not yield. The Elector now

withdrew, but Bishop Conrad of Havelberg persisted. For the provincial synod of Magdeburg (1451), Tocke and his supporter, Provost Eberhard Woltmann, had collected voluminous material. Cardinal Cusa, president of the synod, favored the opponents of Wilsnack. In a circular to all metropolitans of Germany, dated July 5, 1451, he dealt with the general question of bleeding hosts, and forbade their veneration by the faithful. In a sermon he admonished the people to adore the sacrament of the altar in their own parish church rather than to continue running to Wilsnack. Stubborn resistance at length led the legate to excommunicate the Bishop of Havelberg and to put the city of Wilsnack under interdict. Bishop Conrad retaliated by excommunicating his own metropolitan. Open hostilities followed. Havelberg knights plundered Magdeburg, and Magdeburg knights retaliated.

While affairs stood thus, a group of Hungarian pilgrims passed through Magdeburg on their way to Wilsnack. They showed a letter of recommendation from John Capistran. Following the custom of those days, Capistran had really given a letter of greeting to the miraculous blood of Wilsnack. Archbishop Frederick was deeply hurt. He at once sent Provost Woltmann to Capistran with a copy of that letter and with the circular of Cardinal Cusa. Woltmann found him in Zwickau. Capistran was startled at this news. But he did what duty prescribed. He had the circular of the papal delegate read to the people from the pulpit, with an interpreter to explain. So now when Capistran arrived in Halle, October 1, 1452, Provost Woltmann awaited him, and on the journey from there to Magdeburg spoke to him incessantly about the Wilsnack affair. Capistran's counsel, it seems, led the Archbishop to refer the whole matter to Rome. An accusation against his disobedient suffragan in Havelberg, which he had already sent to Rome, had remained unanswered. Capistran wrote to the Pope about this affair, and also to a cardinal, and to another high official.

He himself, he says, cannot decide on which side the truth lies. He urgently advises that a trustworthy official be sent to examine everything on the spot, but this advice was not followed. Decision came that what was left of the Wilsnack hosts was not to be exposed for adoration unless a newly consecrated host was simultaneously exposed. Rome allowed pilgrimages to continue and removed the interdict. In fact, pilgrimages continued, and reached their climax in the next two decades, and did not cease until 1552, when the Lutheran pastor of Wilsnack burned the hosts.

The historical origin of the pilgrimage did not interest Capistran nearly so much as did the theological background of the whole controversy. In our Lord's Resurrection, was all the blood shed during His Passion reunited with His glorified body? On this question, then much ventilated, Dominicans were opposed to Franciscans. The latter defended the view that parts of the precious blood could have remained on earth; hence they were inclined to defend the genuineness of the Wilsnack miracle. From this arose the further question: How far could the relics of Christ's blood become an object of adoration? On this question Capistran became involved in a very lively discussion with Woltmann, who fell into dogmatically indefensible positions. And as he also criticized the popes disrespectfully, the correspondence soon assumed an unpleasant character. Capistran censured Woltmann's irreverence. Woltmann charged Capistran with a lack of Franciscan humility. Fortunately Capistran was soon removed from the stage of this disagreeable controversy.

News of the course of events in Austria urged Capistran to return promptly to the borders of Bohemia. Dissatisfaction with Emperor Frederick's attitude toward his ward Ladislaus had finally led to open rebellion. On August 27, 1452, the insurgents besieged the Emperor in Wiener-Neustadt. Henry Rosenberg had joined forces with the insurgents. On September 1, Frederick surrendered his ward, stipulating that the young prince should live privately near Vienna until his majority. Count Ulrich of Cilli, guardian of Ladislaus, flouted these arrangements and led the prince triumphantly to Vienna. On St. Martin's Day (November 11), Ladislaus was to be proclaimed king of Bohemia. Capistran wrote to Ulrich Rosenberg, who had sent him the news: "I find no words to express my joy. I am convinced that Ladislaus has been given to us by God, that he may redeem his people, now sitting in the shadow of death." He wrote in similar terms to the Emperor, who probably did not relish the letter.

But Capistran still feared that the young Ladislaus might be induced to gain the Bohemians through dangerous concessions. Rosenberg had indicated some doubts in that direction. Capistran rejects the idea with indignation. If Ladislaus promises the Bohemians not to molest them in matters of faith, their return to the Church will be hopeless, and they will even bring many Catholics over to their side. Rosenberg must throw his whole influence in Vienna against such concessions. "If you give them a finger, they will take your whole hand. If you give them one word, they will multiply it by a thousand. Remember the Compact." In matters of faith direct them to the pope. Let Ladislaus not promise them anything at all, not even his mediation. Thus he could, if they persevered in their obduracy, restore ecclesiastical union even at the point of the sword. Let him, like his famous ancestors, protect the Church. "I speak openly," says Capistran, "like a faithful servant to his master. If you promise them what they demand, you will besmirch your name, and will most grievously offend God. You will leave the Bohemian kingdom built upon sand. Consider this well and act accordingly. Beware. In seeking earthly glory you may lose heavenly and eternal glory. Do not, in order to rule the bodies of men, deliver their souls to eternal damnation."

He promptly interrupted his work at Magdeburg, where he had been only eight days, and by way of Zerbst and Wittenberg came to Leipzig (October 20). Here he received more news, but very bad news.

On September 1, the day on which Frederick opened the doors of Wiener-Neustadt to the insurgents, Tabor in Bohemia surrendered to Podebrad. The latter then moved rapidly toward the south against his only remaining opponent, the Rosenbergs. Henry Rosenberg with all his forces was away in Austria. Ulrich surrendered (September 17) and acknowledged Podebrad as administrator of the realm, with one reservation: that neither he himself nor his confederates nor his subjects should ever be forced to do anything contrary to his obedience toward the Church or toward King Ladislaus. At this news, crushing in its effect on the Church, not only in Bohemia, but in all surrounding countries, even Capistran lost his composure. His letter to Ulrich Rosenberg was written in tears.

"O cursed covenant, incredible deed, satanic counsel! A noble baron submits to a base man, to a heretic. The Catholic stronghold now shelters heretics. A father of noble sons feared where there was no fear. Why did you not wait for these sons, instead of yielding to those whom you once abhorred, of whom you yourself said that their leader was not worthy to be your servant? O noble Lord, what shame have you brought upon yourself! What joy have you given your enemies! Your ancient glory, attained by the trials and combats of forty years, your merit before God, has all been destroyed and buried in a moment of vain fear. Your son Henry was already approaching. Victory was near." He urges Rosenberg to cancel that treaty. "It does not bind you, even if you had signed it with 10,000 seals. You are not allowed to keep it. On the contrary, since you have been enlightened, you have the duty to revoke it. All Germany is talking about you. The fame of the house of Rosenberg has been destroyed."

He becomes even more severe. How bitter for Rosenberg, now an old man, who had seen all his ambitious plans frustrated, to be told by the spiritual friend of his house that he was now good for nothing. "All hope rests now on your noble sons, on Henry especially, who by delivering King Ladislaus has made a great name for himself. You must give up that federation with heretics and entrust yourself entirely into the hands of your sons." Capistran enumerates ten reasons for withdrawal, some of them very humiliating for the old warrior. Let him say he did not know how to read. Let him say he had entrusted the government to his sons. "Let a few heretics abuse you, lest all Christendom do so. Become once more what you were: the Catholic champion, the invincible shield, the guardian of everything good, the avenger of evil."

Capistran feels that he himself has been dishonored. "I have proclaimed your praise everywhere, in the pulpit, by the pen." In his plans and calculations the house of Rosenberg had been the cornerstone. Now that Podebrad has become an obdurate heretic, every strengthening of his power is a threat to Catholic possession of Bohemia. Hence opposition to Podebrad is a duty of conscience.

Did Capistran in his glowing desire for Bohemia's conversion misconstrue the political possibilities? Ulrich Rosenberg, always a cool head, had simply drawn conclusions which, under the conditions, he considered inevitable. Capistran indeed judged differently. "Ladislaus, supported by the Catholic party of the kingdom, could have ended Podebrad's dominion and given a death-blow to Hussitism in Bohemia. Victory had been so near. You already had your king. You could easily have eradicated all heresies."

But Rosenberg could insist that at that time he was unable to resist Podebrad successfully. The principal question was this: How would the Austrian and Hungarian estates treat the Bohemian problems of Church and king? Again, the counselors of Ladislaus did not in any way share the views of Capistran. Vienna was inclined to allow the Bohemians a free hand in religious matters if they would but accept Ladislaus as king. That was just what Capistran had feared. He now proposed to hasten to Vienna. But Henry Rosenberg expressed his misgivings. The Emperor had invited Podebrad, who would not come if Capistran was to be there. Capistran yielded, but carried on the campaign by messenger and letter. He sent Father Peter with bundles of letters to Austria. These were addressed, not only to the Emperor, to his brother Duke Albrecht, and to Ladislaus, but also to a long list of influential men of Bohemia, Austria, and Hungary.

He stayed a full month in Leipzig (October 20 to November 20), preaching continually in church and market place. His main theme was the religious state, which has thirteen privileges and nine advantages, whereas life in the world has twenty dangers. Five days were devoted to usury. His interpreter was unable to translate the technical terms into German. But university circles were deeply interested. The armor of God is compared to contemporary warfare, under thirteen headings. The last three may illustrate. With the ballista we must shoot seven fiery arrows of love against the enemy.

With the bombarda we hurl seven glowing stones, and with the machina thirty. These thirty are thirty scriptural woes, to be hurled against thirty scandals in secular life. The theme of his sermon (November 4), preached in the assembly hall of the University, was the sublimity of the priesthood, the purity it demands, and the punishment of unworthy priests.

The Leipzig sermons were open propaganda for vocations to the religious life. Following St. Thomas, he induces others to choose life in a religious order. This life is the way to the fatherland, and it would be a sin to keep anyone from it. "I have not seen this sin here in Leipzig. But I have noticed elsewhere that doctors and masters discourage youths from entering the cloister. Scotus says such people are bound, as reparation, either to enter a monastery themselves or to induce somebody else to do so. Pay what you owe." Students should not postpone entrance in order to get the master's degree. Children may enter even against the will of their parents. He tells of judgments inflicted by God on parents who prevented their children from joining an order. He tells secular priests and married people how to proceed if they wish to choose the religious life, and complains that no sermons are preached on this topic.

He reviews the chief religious orders of the Church. Basil, Augustine, and Benedict are compared to the three youths in the Babylonian furnace. The mysterious fourth figure, who comes to aid these youths, represents Francis of Assisi. The furnace is the world; greed, pride, and lust furnish the fuel. Perfect renunciation of property is the source of Franciscan strength, growth, and agility. He describes in exact numbers the rapid growth of the Observance. Even persons of royal houses have taken the habit of St. Francis. The sum total is now 100,000 members, as he had seen in the registers of the Roman Curia. These 100,000 beggars are richer than people in the world. "I have now a thousand times more than I gave up. The whole world is mine. Wherever I come, I find churches, cloisters, sacristies, ready for me. And if they are not yet there, people are preparing to build them.

"Poverty, of course, pinches at times. It may mean a whole day in streaming rain, without a morsel of bread and without shelter for the approaching night. But in the cities we are amply provided for. The sick are better cared for in the Observance than if they were sons of barons, even if sacristies have to be plundered. Traveling brothers have their feet washed and kissed. This perfect poverty brings a high degree of spiritual freedom. Whose head is more bothered, that of the illustrious king of the Romans, or that of Brother Capistrano? The king's, of course. Ambassadors from all sides. Affairs without end. I occupy myself with one thing, knowledge of the divine truth. You are anxious about your forests, meadows, fields, your money, garments, and jewelry, for your family, sons, and wife. John of Capistrano does not bother about any of these things. He has but one wish: to spend his life in the praise of almighty God. From this freedom flow great works, especially great advances in theological science."

These sermons brought fruit. Candidates came from the University. After the sermon on October 28 he invested two, one from Salzburg and one from Meissen. On All Saints Day he clothed seven, two of them as lay brothers. Four came on November 4, eight on November 5. Seventy in all came during the month. A witness writes: "No wonder that this man, a model of holy life, with an immaculate reputation, can prompt so many excellent men to enter his Order." Some candidates, about half the number, were sent to the convents in Nuremberg and Vienna. The others he intended to take with him to Breslau, where a new Observant friary was planned. Those young people whom he had selected for Nuremberg and Vienna he entrusted to Christopher Varese. A letter to the guardian at Nuremberg betrays some apprehensions. The convent, lately reformed, seems to have retained certain Conventual customs. With unusual strictness he repeats several demands which he had already made orally.

Capistran's sermons on flight from the world are based on his own conversion, since he knows the dangers of the world by personal experience. He wishes, like St. Paul, that all would follow his example. But why devote a whole cycle of sermons to that topic, when only a few listeners would be called to the religious life? The reason lay in the times. Thorough instruction in the evangelical ideal was necessary in an age of widespread decline in monastic discipline. Even the candle which St. Francis lighted had burned low. Capistran's zeal in restoring the genuine Franciscan spirit aided the whole Church. His ideal of Christian perfection, illustrated in the great representatives of religious life, St. Francis, St. Clare, St. Dominic, and especially St. Bernardine, was a positive contribution to the reform of ecclesiastical life.

Those who think him guilty of exaggerating the evangelical counsels, and mendicant poverty in particular, should weigh the following words: "I consider it a little matter to go barefoot, to sleep in the habit, to live secluded, and even to shed my blood. But I consider it something great to control myself lest I fall into the snares of the devil. That is the greatest care and endeavor of the religious. Scourging oneself, fasting, and similar practices would not be sufficient." And with all his emphasis on the evangelical counsels, he defends also the other states of Christian life. Thence comes his fervent propaganda of the Third Order, and his love for St. Elizabeth of Thuringia. His sermons on the duties of the married state were liked. The neglect of children's education is the principal cause of the evils of the time. Charmingly he paints the mother, bringing forth in pain, losing sleep, bathing and dressing the children, giving milk. Impressively he speaks of the sanctity of the married state, and of the merit of conjugal intercourse as the fulfillment of the divine command to increase and multiply. A threefold woe he calls down upon mothers who, with some wicked potion, nip life in the bud. Merchants, physicians, judges, princes, are told with all frankness the duties of their state. Merchants especially have a dangerous calling. Rulers must cooperate with citizens, like the head with the members. Discord has weakened German rulers. "Beware of all quarrels lest you be dismembered."

In university cities he naturally addresses himself to students. He speaks of their difficulties and their prospects. Study well; then you can become a master, receive your 1,200 ducats, eat what you want, and appear before the prince. But shun ambitious place-hunting. Search your pocketbook before you spend. Perhaps you may die before you become master or doctor. Aim at wisdom, not merely at knowledge. Science should lead to wisdom. Science deals with earthly values, wisdom with everlasting values. Grammar, rhetoric, logic, music, arithmetic, geometry, and astronomy march like servants at the side of theology. Knowledge, unless animated by humility, becomes a fatal tumor. His stock example is the master in Paris who died in his flowering years, and three days after his death appeared, wrapped in a white mantle completely ornamented with syllogisms. Asked how he fared, he answered: "Don't you see what is under the mantle?" With that he opened the mantle, showing his whole figure swathed in fire. Why thus, he was asked, since he had died weeping. The answer came: "Those tears were not tears of contrition, they were tears of disappointment that I had to die so soon. I had counted on living long, having a good time, and enjoying my fame." But he has also encouraging examples. Two contemporary popes, Innocent VII and Nicholas V, had been born poor, and yet had risen to the highest dignity in Christendom.

In dealing with the well-known disorders in the secular and the religious clergy, Capistran was a model. Preachers who thundered against the clergy were always welcome to the audience. But such preachers helped to undermine the confidence of the people in the guidance of the Church, without removing the cause of the evil which they criticized. The better representatives of the Franciscan school counteracted this abuse. Capistran's sermons for the clergy were held in church, the laity not being admitted. In his public addresses he dwelt on the dignity and exaltation of the Catholic priesthood. His listeners in Breslau, after waiting in vain for the usual invectives against bad priests, began to murmur. In a sermon that followed, Capistran said: "You wish me to reproach priests publicly, as I have publicly praised them. That I will not do. The priests are your fathers; you are their sons. The priest of Christ is the head of the people of Christ."

In general, Capistran did not dwell on the wickedness of the times. He had fears for the future, and his ideals were high. But he did not look on the general condition of the Church with the deeply pessimistic views so common in the ascetic literature of the late Middle Ages. His whole missionary spirit was one of optimism, which sprang in part from his cheerful temperament, but more largely from his personal experience. His own life taught him the inexhaustible power of the Church in sanctifying souls. The irresistible progress of the reform was a still deeper source of this apostolic optimism.

In the meantime the diet in Prague decided it would accept Ladislaus as king, provided he would fulfill three conditions: the right of the Bohemians to elect their king; the validity of the Compact; the promotion of Rokytzana to the episcopal see of Prague. Ulrich Rosenberg, who was present at the diet, wrote Capistran in general terms, saying he dared not report details. Capistran answered ironically that the details hinted at were in everybody's mouth. He again urges Ulrich to restore his own honor at the forthcoming diet in Vienna.

Ladislaus himself, raised in a strictly Catholic manner, would personally have been inclined to refuse concessions to the Bohemians in ecclesiastical matters. Not so his council. They were convinced that, to save the crown, Ladislaus would have to defend the Compact and Rokytzana. In matters of faith he must let the Bohemians do as they please. Podebrad did not go to the meeting in Vienna at all. The question of Ladislaus as king of Bohemia remained unsettled.

CHAPTER XXX

The Jews and Breslau

ACCOMPANIED by about thirty novices, Capistran (November 20) left Leipzig. After pausing at three towns in response to invitations, he arrived on Christmas Day in Dresden. All preparations had been made. The market place had its pulpit and benches. The Barefoot Friars housed his retinue, and also his library, which, in a special wagon, followed the venerable father everywhere. Councilors served the guests. Capistran invested several young men, and left Dresden on December 27, escorted on city vehicles to Kamenz.

Here Capistran entered the territory of the "six cities." These six cities, just north of Bohemia, had suffered much from Hussite invasions. The town of Lauban had been ravaged twenty-five times, and the population was in extreme poverty. Hence they feared the consequences of Capistran's visit. Podebrad had sent threatening letters in advance to all places where Capistran was expected to preach. Bautzen, a fortified city, bluntly defied him, but the defenseless towns yielded. "If I find," wrote Capistran, "that these cities do not wish me to announce the full truth of Christ, I will go on to Breslau." But some of the "six cities" he did visit. Görlitz had written to him in Dresden and had presented him with two woolen cloaks. On Wednesday, January 10, he reached Görlitz and spent fourteen days in that devoted city. The market place saw, instead of public dancing, a public bonfire of vanities. At Lauban, which he reached on January 26, he preached from the balcony of the King's house. Toward the end of January he left the territory of the "six cities." For the Observance he had found no suitable place. The Conventuals lived after his visit as before.

Traveling eastward, Capistran's company came to Liegnitz, where Breslau's invitation reached him, relieving him of worry. Obstacles hindered his efforts for a foundation in Breslau, which felt that it was well supplied already with cloisters and that the city was too small and too poor to support more mendicant orders. The bishop, Peter Nowak, had written in this sense, and Capistran felt depressed. The deputies consoled him with the assurance that the city awaited his coming with "devotion, fervor, and ardent desire." The Bishop, too, had sent him a letter of welcome. The deputies sent word to Breslau to prepare for at least forty persons. They have seen, they add, how lame persons were suddenly cured.

On Shrove Tuesday all Breslau gathered on the meadows outside St. Nicholas' Gate. A group of women hurried a long stretch ahead on the road toward Liegnitz. At four o'clock he arrived. Clergy, council, and people escorted him into the city. At the cathedral he was awaited by the chapter. The *Te Deum* and the peal of bells ended the solemn reception. The next day, Ash Wednesday, he began the Lenten series. By way of introduction he compared himself to the queen of Saba, enraptured and surprised at the reception by Solomon. Further he employs the words of St. Paul (I Thess. 1:2 f.): "We give thanks to God always for you all ... being mindful of the work of your faith and labor and charity, and of the enduring of the hope of our Lord Jesus Christ." Breslau deserved his particular predilection. It had proved its Catholic fidelity splendidly during the Hussite troubles. Austria, Hungary, Poland, and western Germany had to be on their guard against Hussite infiltration. But Breslau, and indeed all Silesia, never wavered. Capistran was delighted with its fullness of practical Catholic life. In all Christendom, he writes to Cardinal Cusa, he had never seen such splendor in divine service.

His Lenten series had three cycles, the first devoted to the laws on fasting, the second to the Last Judgment, the third to the sacrament of penance. These instructions on confession, with all their scholastic exactness, are still models of concreteness. We select a few examples. First, love of one's enemies. "You find your enemy on a bridge, in danger of falling into the water. Instead of saving him, you let him fall in and drown. You are condemned. Even if you had built churches, practiced fasting, prayer, and alms; even if the fellow had murdered your father and mother, robbed you of your possessions, unless you save him you deliver yourself to the devil." Secondly, the examination of conscience. "In church, while running from one picture to another, did you forget to make the usual reverence before the Blessed Sacrament? At the consecration, did you bend both knees, not only one? Or who made that other knee, the devil? Does a sick man who eats break the fast? No, even if he eats a whole cow." But, in Bernardine's style, he laughs at people who worry about fasting. "The day before, they say: 'Tomorrow is a fast day, let us have an extra good meal today.' Next day they say: 'Today is fast day, let's have a big dinner.' And the day after they say: 'Yesterday was fast day, let us eat early today.' "

Some details are excessively strict. Examination of conscience should be continued over several days. An extremely subtle jurist, he finds reasons for excommunication even in pranks, as when a washwoman, for instance, pours water out of the window on a passing priest; or when a bold boy snatches at the bridle of a priest's horse. Priests should not rinse their mouth before Mass, lest they break the Eucharistic fast. But we must not exaggerate these details. Capistran emphasizes energetically the intention, the disposition of the will, a man's habitual thoughts, the conscience. "Suppose there were no God. Imagine that no man could be condemned. Suppose your soul perishes like your body. Suppose further that no one could discover your deed. Conscience alone warns and condemns you. Give more attention to the interior voice of your conscience than to all reproaches of men." The reason for fasting lies in man's double nature, sensual and spiritual. The keynote of his sermons on confession is the mercy of God and the expiating power of penance. With all his insistence on most exact confessions, he says again and again that perfect contrition effects reconciliation with God, and even before confession. He loves Mary Magdalen. "I profit more by the atoning penance of the fallen Magdalen than by the unimpeachable virginity of her sister Mary." How warm his tone when he urges discouraged sinners to dwell on God's goodness, which surpasses all expectations. To confessors he says: "It is better to dismiss a penitent with one Hail Mary than to impose a heavy penance and drive him to despair. It is better to give an account for too great leniency than for too great strictness. If you can rescue the sinner from the devil, you may leave the rest to purgatory."

We may be surprised to find that he does not insist on frequent reception of Holy Communion. With his usual exactness, he explains the Communion practice of the Church, saying that priests, and even lay people, may go to Communion as often as they wish. But he quotes St. Augustine: "Daily Communion I neither praise nor censure." To refrain from frequent Communion on account of a feeling of unworthiness he regards as laudable. But we of today must not forget that our modern practice of frequent Communion was then rare, even in the cloister, and that the Utraquists were guilty of an opposite extreme.

Passion Sunday (March 18) witnessed two great events. The first was the bonfire of vanities. On the Saltring, where now stands the memorial of General Blücher, the mighty pyre was erected. Holding a skull in his hand, Capistran painted the twelve pains of the hour of death. Lifting the skull on high, he cried: "Here is your mirror. Look in, and see what you have done. Where is that nose which inhaled such pleasing odors? Where is that hair which once delighted you? Where is that tongue that slandered? Worms have devoured all." The second great event on that Sunday was the solemn transfer of the site for a new cloister of the Observance. After the sermon a great procession moved out toward the city walls, to a district covered with gardens and houses, where the new cloister of St. Bernardine was to be erected. Bishop Peter, the city council, and the chief captain of the country, Conrad Eisenreich, transferred the property in due form to Capistran. Among the guests for the day was Duke John of Brieg. The community was lodged for the present in the houses of the donated district. The numerous novices brought from Leipzig needed urgently a definite foundation, where they could begin an orderly monastic life. In a temporary structure, built in a week's time, choir services began.

Other noteworthy sermons of this period were one on the twelve prerogatives of the Mother of God, preached on the feast of the Annunciation, and one on the name of Jesus, preached on Palm Sunday. In other sermons, too, he insisted on devotion to the name of Jesus, lamenting that even in Breslau this devotion had shortly before been forbidden.

These Breslau sermons touched the Hussite heresy only occasionally. Yet even this sufficed to have Capistran again denounced in Prague. Master Paul, the son of a Jewish family, had been brought up by a Bohemian in Utraquism. As a student in Vienna he had renounced Hussitism. After studying art and medicine in Italy, he was ordained in Ratisbon and then returned to Prague, where he was engaged as a teacher. Unstable in character, he left Prague, going first to Cracow and then to Breslau. His Prague benefices kept him in touch with the heads of Utraquism. He now reported that Capistran was preaching against the Bohemians and Rokytzana and he advised the sending of some Utraquists, whose names he mentions, from Prague to Breslau as observers. He would have quarters ready for them. But these letters were intercepted by the Breslau magistrates, and Paul went to jail. When this news reached Prague, George Podebrad demanded that Paul be immediately released and sent to Prague, since he was fully justified in thus proceeding against a disturber of the Compact. Breslau, he added, had done great wrong in receiving the monk Capistran so solemnly, and in permitting him to condemn agreements sanctioned by the Council of Basle, and to call the Bohemians heretics. If Breslau is disposed to uphold the Compact, let her no longer tolerate that monk, "our enemy," in her midst. How the Council answered this quasi-ultimatum we do not know. But in any case the event had no influence on Capistran's departure.

After Easter he intended to go to Poland. But, in fact, he remained four months more in Breslau. One reason lay in his own sickness. During Holy Week he became seriously ill. When Podebrad's letter came, Capistran was near death. The unusually severe winter, the hardships of the journey, and the unbroken strain of the past few years had again sapped his strength. On Good Friday his interpreter, Father Frederick, took the pulpit.

Good Friday preaching was at that time an ordeal. Custom prescribed addresses lasting for hours. People expected an ornamented and detailed narrative of the Passion. In some places the sermon began at midnight. The seven canonical hours suggested a sermon in seven sections, with intervals for rest. Thus the sermon occupied six, seven, and even nine hours. Geiler of Kaisersberg had condemned this practice most energetically. At first he had himself preached five or six hours. Evil experiences made him limit himself to two sermons of an hour each, one in the morning and one in the afternoon.

Capistran's Good Friday sermon, of which more manuscript copies exist than of any other, presents a happy contrast to other Passion sermons of his time, which were filled with legends about Pilate, Herod, the good thief, and so on. Capistran's sermon is indeed very, very long, but follows the Gospel closely. The ten roads traversed by our Lord furnish the ten divisions. Each division begins with the words: "Tell us, O Mary, what did Jesus do on this road?" Each of Mary's answers is subdivided into six points. These sixty points would have filled long hours. But Father Frederick managed to shorten the sermon considerably. He did so, he said, in order not to diminish the devotion of the people.

On Easter Sunday, Capistran was sufficiently recovered to attend the sermon of Father Frederick. He thanked the Bishop, the captain, the mayor, and the aldermen, who had repeatedly visited him. He thanked all for their prayers. He had been sure his end was come. Prayers saved his life. "I was already at the gates of paradise; you have kept me back. I do not refuse to die, but neither do I refuse to work. Let God dispose of me as He wills."

In the impression that he was over his illness he was mistaken. He suffered seriously during the whole month of April. Only now and then could he deliver a sermon, one in the open (April 22), outside St. Vincent's Gate, one (April 27) in the cathedral, behind closed doors, a conference for the clergy. On Monday, April 30, he left Breslau and went with the bishop to Neisse. The solemn farewell celebration in Breslau was not intended for a transient absence. But unexpected events brought him back to Breslau three weeks later.

Scarcely had Capistran left the city when rumors began to circulate that, during the recent Holy Week, the Jews of Breslau had committed sacrileges against the Blessed Sacrament. The militia entered the Jewish quarters of Breslau, and led the population with their possessions to the royal castle. The judicial examination resulted in the following declarations. The leader of the Jewish community in Breslau had instigated a young Jew to bring the "God of the Christians." A Polish peasant from Langwiese near Öes, a few miles from Breslau, was bribed for the deed.

On Wednesday before Holy Thursday (March 28) he stole the ciborium from the village church in Langwiese. Frightened in an open field by a sudden thunderstorm, he threw the ciborium away, having first taken out ten or eleven particles. These particles he gave to the wife of a soldier to bring to the Jews in Breslau. There in the synagogue, in the presence of some twenty persons, these Hosts were lashed with whips and stabbed with knives. From the mistreated Hosts blood streamed forth on the bystanders. The bloodstained switches were thrown into a brook. A month later the crime became known. The church robber was brought before court and confessed. King Ladislaus sent two representatives to deal with the case, but before they arrived one of the chief prisoners, Meyer, committed suicide in prison. About the middle of May Capistran returned from Neisse to Breslau. The Bishop, whose guest Capistran was in Neisse, had not been informed of the procedure, and wrote (June 2) to express his astonishment at this neglect. He admonishes the aldermen to proceed very cautiously, as he heard they had arrested even innocent persons. Since business prevented him from coming in person, he requested Capistran (June 14) to make the necessary investigations, and to insist that the trial be soon brought to a close, to avoid scandal. In that sense he wrote also to King Ladislaus.

The court examinations brought new revelations. The wife of a citizen of Breslau, a baptized Jewess, accused her own father, in his presence, of horrible crimes, committed sixteen years before. In a cellar at Löwenberg he tried to burn consecrated Hosts, which he had bought from a woman. Three times he threw them into the fire, and each time they leaped out again. An old Jewess, seeing this miracle, had gone to her knees, and confessed her faith in the God of the Christians. She was murdered on the spot, and her body was burned in that cellar. A Host placed on a small table and cut into four parts with a knife, had bled so profusely that neither knife nor table could be washed clean and both were therefore thrown into the Bober.

The plaintiff further accused another Jew, Jonas by name, of having in the same cellar committed ritual murder on a three-year-old Christian boy, whom he had bought from a peasant. The defendants denied everything. A commission sent from Breslau to Löwenberg found at the assigned place traces of that fire, as also the bones of a woman and a child. The remains were brought to Breslau and handed over to Capistran. Nicholas Fara says himself he had seen Capistran holding the relics of the boy in his hands. Other Jewish communities in Silesia became entangled in this process. Some of the Hosts robbed at Langwiese were sent to Schweidnitz, and were there similarly desecrated in the synagogue. A rabbi then brought some of these Hosts into his house, and cut three of them with a knife. Blood spurted up a span high. One of these Hosts the rabbi sent to the Jews in Posen. In consequence, during the second half of June, 318 Silesian Jews were imprisoned, and their possessions sequestered.

In the report of the trial on June 22, Capistran's name does not appear. In that of July 9, he is mentioned as one of the presiding officers. On July 7 the royal deputy, Reichol, writes to Vienna that the first death sentences had been executed, two of them by fire. Sigismund Rosicz, a contemporary canon, confirms this report. Hence the widespread belief that forty-one Jews were burned on the fourth of July can no longer be sustained. Executions were on different days during July and August, and in various towns. A report from Schweidnitz, says that seventeen Jews were burned to death there on August 13. In Liegnitz a great number perished when the prison burned at the beginning of July. All other Jews, about three hundred in number, were exiled from Silesia. Their entire property was turned over to the King. Children under the age of seven were taken-away from their parents, were baptized, and placed in Christian households.

In the Saltring of Breslau an iron cross of expiation stood for centuries on the spot where the Jews underwent death by fire. In our times that cross made way for a memorial to Blücher. But the memory of those gruesome events is alive today. What is to be said of the part which Capistran played in this terrible drama? His first biographers found therein one of Capistran's glories. The Catholic observer today sees therein an object of regret. Jewish historians mention Capistran's name with horror. Where does the truth lie?

We must begin with the question of guilt. Did the Silesian Jews, in fact, commit the crimes which they were accused of? If so, Capistran's position is unassailable. Ritual murder, sacrilegious crimes, would even today be severely punished. The sentences of 1453 were entirely in harmony with contemporary European ideas of justice. Hence even the most severe critics of Capistran's juridical activity must suppose innocence in those he condemned. At the outset we must admit that medieval accounts of Jews as guilty of murdering children and of desecrating Hosts must be carefully sifted. Some of these accounts, based on prejudice, are pure inventions. Stories of Hosts that bleed and leap into the air recur with a suspicious frequency, often in rapid succession in neighboring territories.

Belief in a bleeding Host was often merely a convenient tool for initiating a persecution of the Jews, as when, for instance, deeply indebted Christians found no other way to get rid of their Jewish creditors. A bleeding Host was easier to obtain than the corpse of a Christian child. On the other hand, Jewish historians go decidedly too far when they brand all such accusations as mere fables or psychological impossibilities. Unimpeachable evidence shows that cases of robbery and desecration of consecrated Hosts did occur in the Middle Ages, and still occur in our own days. Admitting that Jews as a class were not guilty, what reason can be given for denying that individual Jews never gave vent to their hatred of Christ by committing such crimes? But Christians were guilty of grievous injustice when, instead of punishing individuals who were guilty, they punished also the innocent majority. They were guilty also of credulity in easily accepting charges against Jews.

The credulity was partly an unintended consequence of the anti-Jewish laws. Under the influence of this stigma, public opinion was inclined to take for granted that Jews were likely to do any kind of wickedness. These wild outbreaks of wrath against Jews find their deplorable counterpart in the frenzy against witches. Even sincere judges were perhaps often misled by this delusion. In judicial procedure, the emphasis lay, not in discovering the real facts, but in getting those accused to declare themselves guilty. Reicholf, one of the royal commissioners, writes of the Breslau proceedings: "We have never seen a more obdurate and callous people. These Jews endure torture unto death or commit suicide rather than admit guilt." Bishop Nowak warned against precipitation and condemned the arrest of the innocent. But was the accusation against the Silesian Jews nothing more than a criminal plot, set in motion to get rid of pressing creditors? Who can answer that question today? The detailed account of the robberies, the precise reports on places and times, the definite description of all persons concerned, even of accused Christians, all this must incline us to believe in the trustworthiness of the charges. But, on the other hand, some of these testimonies were obtained under torture, and hence their reliability remains doubtful.

We are not surprised that novelists are the class most busy in lifting the veil from this mystery. The historian must, for the present at least, limit himself to this observation: If this whole procedure was owing to a plot, its extraordinary ingenuity and precaution become historically remarkable. With all allowances for the imperfect juridical procedure of those days, and for the prejudices of judges, how shall we account for the remarkable fact that even those who condemned the expulsion of the Jews as unchristian, still do not manifest the least doubt about the truth of the accusations. Take, for instance, Peter Eschenloer, who came to Breslau in 1455, and in 1470 wrote of the affair in the sense just quoted. Nearly twenty years had passed when he wrote, fifteen of which he had spent on the spot. Must we admit a plot so deep that none of the real facts ever came to the knowledge of the public? And if we admit such a plot, then we must also say that the judges were victims of invincible error. Calumny and prejudice would be responsible. If we suppose this state of things, one question remains. How far did Capistran's activity in Breslau affect, at least indirectly, the course of events leading to this catastrophe?

Just before the Jewish persecution started, Capistran had preached a Lenten series in Breslau. Did those sermons arouse the populace to animosity against the Jews? A chorus of critics say, Yes. But these critics have not read those sermons, they have not even read the extensive excerpts that now lie printed before us. Once, and only once, do we find in those forty sermons a reference to the Jews. In his thirty-second sermon Capistran advises the people not to refrain from work on Saturdays, not even out of veneration for the Mother of God. His reason? That the Jews may not interpret this rest as a participation in their Sabbath celebration. In Vienna and Nuremberg, Capistran gave much attention to the Jews. Breslau seems to have had only an insignificant Jewish population, which did not require much notice. The popular conception of Capistran thundering for forty days against the Jews, is the purest fiction. In Breslau as elsewhere, he may have insisted on the observance of the laws laid down for the Jews, especially on the prohibition of usury. At the utmost, then, we may admit the possibility that the presence of the preacher, known as a sharp opponent of unlawful Jewish practices, may have encouraged wicked elements to go ahead with their evil plans.

The popular tradition needs other corrections. Capistran had nothing to do with the arrest of the Jews, nor was the supreme direction of the trial in his hands. During the first two weeks after the arrest he was not in Breslau at all, but was the guest of the Bishop at Neisse. The sources give us with certainty only one fact, namely, that Capistran together with other clerics attended the sessions of the court. That he acted thus in obedience to the express wish of the prudent and moderate Bishop, who insisted that the trial be ended before the departure of his guest, puts the affair in an entirely different light.

But did not Capistran personally instruct the torturers in the use of their instruments? If so, we have the finishing touch in painting the man who gloated in executing Jews. But the very fact is historically questionable. Further, even if we suppose the fact, did those instructions tend to increase the sufferings of the unhappy prisoners? Most certainly not. Capistran's whole career cries out in protest.[1] That punishment must never be allowed to go beyond strict legal limits, had been his attitude as judge in the Neapolitan courts. Hence the historian is constrained to think that these Breslau instructions, if given at all, aimed at shielding the victims from illegal excesses. Oral tradition in Italy, as we saw above, says that torture led to successive untruths rather than to the truth. But we cannot expect that a judge could at once upset a practice so deeply rooted in law and custom.

Further we admit, in view of Capistran's reputation as jurist and inquisitor, and in view of the general veneration which he enjoyed, that his attitude may have had great influence on the final sentence. But would that sentence have been essentially different if Capistran had not been present at all? Sacrileges were punished by death. That was the general European practice, which meted out the death penalty even for much lesser crimes. Even the banishment of all Jews corresponded in such cases with the general view of the public. Jews were merely tolerated. The state believed itself justified, whenever public welfare required, in banishing Jews and confiscating their property. In the Breslau incident the number of Jewish communities involved made of this general law a precaution against future danger. Finally, we should note in this Breslau affair the absence of all outbursts of popular feeling, which elsewhere so often led to lynch-justice against the Jews.

This trial at Breslau is referred to over and over again, to paint Capistran in the blackest colors. Yet the historical facts are in this case more inaccessible than in any other episode of his life. The final verdict must rest on sources distinct and dependable.

Capistran's general attitude toward the Jews stands out clearly in his sermons. The Franciscan itinerants of those days live still in the popular mind as examples of Jew-haters. Some of them did transgress the proper limits, and had to accept correction from

[1] Cf. supra, p. 12.

superiors, both spiritual and secular. Capistran especially is pictured as a fanatical denouncer of sin and vice, and a preacher of hatred against heretics, Jews, and Turks. What are the facts? He did, indeed, deliver special sermons for the Jews, especially in cities with large Jewish communities. Further, he insisted on the custom of holding special sermons for the Jews, who were obliged by law to attend. But the usual imagination, that on such occasions he aroused popular sentiment against the Jews, is not true.

Occasional remarks occur that could be interpreted in that sense. Thus he once asserted that the Jews believed themselves entitled to kill all Christians, but that on account of their small number they did not dare to say this publicly. But when he occupies himself directly with the Jews, he aims at their conversion. Sorrow and disappointment over the obstinacy of this race often find expression. Yet he never treats them contemptuously or disdainfully, but takes them seriously. He calls them "our friends." We find no trace of racial hatred. The Jewish question is for him a religious one. When a Jew believes in Christ and is baptized, there is no difference between the Christian and the Jew. He even goes so far as to assure them from the pulpit that, if they will but hear the word of God, he will love them as he loves his nearest relatives. He is always aware that faith cannot be compelled: the Jews must never be forced, but are to be kindly encouraged. However, the laws of the Christian past must be observed. The Jews, if they will not believe, must be kept separated from Christians. Hence he always opposes privileges that would weaken or abrogate those protective measures of Christian society, and he urges that spiritual rulers insist on the strict observance of the laws concerning Jews and on the abrogation of contrary privileges. In this effort he did not stand alone. Many other reformers condemned the arbitrariness and laxity manifested in this matter. The Council of Basle earnestly reminded the public of this element in canonical justice. Cardinal Cusa decreed strict enforcement of these laws.

Capistran's efforts to keep the Jews behind these barriers were rooted, first of all, in his temperament. Others, not Jews alone, felt the energetic activity of this strong man, and his own confreres had similar experiences. Even before the papal throne he spoke frankly. Danger for the faith in a free contact between Jews and Christians was one idea that underlay this legislation. Capistran points out this danger occasionally, and is even stricter than St. Thomas Aquinas. But his animosity against Jews, if we wish to call it by that name, had its deepest roots in his predominating religious idea. He is entirely possessed by the thought of the Christian empire of God here on earth. Christ is King, and Christ's Church is the kingdom of God. The Jews are the descendants of those who killed this King. They have inherited hatred against Christ from their ancestors, and they give it full vent wherever they can do so with impunity. Therefore we are justified in suspecting them. They are now simply our enemies and are known as such. They have crucified our Lord Jesus Christ.

That the members of this race were domiciled in Christian lands and were tolerated as fellow citizens, was hard to bear. But that Jews should rule the children of God's kingdom, contradicted Capistran's high sense of Christian dignity. Christians must not, in any shape or form, become dependent on Jews. Are Christians permitted to buy from Jews those parts of butchered animals which the Jews for ritual reasons discarded as unclean? The lawyer who put this question was inclined to say, Yes. Capistran decidedly said, No. "Christians would thus appear inferior in the eyes of Jews. The Jews consider unclean anything touched by Christians. They will not buy or eat animals butchered by Christians. Why should Christians take and use what is set aside by the wicked hands of unbelieving and perfidious Jews? Let the Jews buy and eat what they like. That is their own business.

But let them have no occasion to think contemptuously of our immaculate faith and to consider themselves better than us."

He urges Christians not to buy wine from Jews. "Our dignity forbids us to consume the dirt that falls from their hands and feet when they tread the grapes. In many cities matters are so regulated that the Jews buy grapes for their own use. Their unholy feet must never soil that wine which our priests use in the Holy Sacrifice. From their own meat let the Jews make offerings according to their custom. Or, if they will, let them feed that meat to the dogs who catch the quails and pheasants for their delicious banquets." He admonishes his questioner to keep his conscience clear, and not to allow our Lord Jesus Christ to be grieved by association between His perfidious enemies and His faithful people.

To prevent commercial and social contacts by strict enforcement of the laws concerning Jews, and to abrogate all privileges that stood against this plan, was the fundamental idea of Capistran's policy. How far did he succeed? That he deeply injured Jewish interests in many lands is the assertion of Jewish historians. Detailed proof of that assertion is lacking. In Italy he did succeed in having edicts issued to abrogate Jewish privileges. But their execution met with obstacles that soon made them ineffective. Beyond the Alps his efforts in this direction met with the same results. Two pronounced friends of the Jews, Emperor Frederick III and King Casimir IV of Poland, would not yield on this point, despite their great esteem for him. Many measures that were adopted are, without good reason, traced to his influence. Indirectly, of course, he may have sharpened the public conscience. Jewish communities were everywhere afraid of him. In certain places they offered him gifts, which he refused with a smile. But to stigmatize him as one obsessed by hatred of Jews is to ignore entirely contemporary Jewish legislation. The question of Jewish privileges cannot be regarded as a war of medieval intolerance against the approaching dawn of noble humanitarianism. Far different things were in question. Not humane emotions, but interests merely selfish, dictated those privileges to the Jews. As a rule Jews paid dearly for these liberties. Even Frederick III treated his Jewish agents harshly when money was in question.

CHAPTER XXXI

Capistran's Character and Work

EVEN Capistran was not immune to deception. Human weakness often puts whole generations under fixed ideas, from which even the best and noblest characters cannot free themselves. Like witchcraft, anti-Semitism was an obsession, which, instead of punishing individual crimes, made the whole race accountable, and easily believed accusations maliciously invented. We cannot prove that Capistran was immune from the credulity of his age. But credulity is not identical with malice. To get a true picture of Capistran, we must rely, not on partial and dubious reports of his animus against Jews and heretics, but on the reliable records left by men who knew him and, while venerating him, still disagreed with him.

Prominent contemporaries who had personal contact with Capistran paint pictures quite at variance with the harsh and sinister portrait familiar to our times. Enea Silvio, for instance, one of Capistran's great admirers, was assuredly no adherent of morose ascetism. The jovial Hohenzollern prince, Albrecht Achilles of Brandenburg, was delighted with Capistran and chose him as his intimate counselor. An unknown contemporary in Germany prefers the company of Capistran to all the pleasures of the world. His first biographers never tire of praising his kindness of heart, his tender compassion. He was easily moved to tears, especially in prayer. This gift of tears he himself appreciated highly. He would break into tears in the midst of a sermon. In a circle of confreres, when he happened to mention something that had formerly touched him, tears would promptly roll down his cheeks. And all miseries, spiritual and bodily, called forth not only compassionate feelings, but also compassionate deeds. Care for the sick occupied most of the time not given to preaching. Once or twice a day he visited the long line of invalids brought on stretchers from all directions. Suppressing all feelings of abhorrence, he touched their loathsome wounds, washed their sore eyes, put his finger into the ears of the deaf. Special commiseration he showed to those sentenced to death. Once he asked for the bodies of five criminals to give them decent burial. On another occasion he collected the scattered remains of such a criminal. Passing a gallows, he saw hanging thereon the body of a criminal, who had been executed several days before. The intolerable stench made Capistran instinctively hurry his steps, holding his nose closed. At once, feeling he had done a great wrong to an unfortunate fellow man, he took upon himself a horrible penance. He climbed the ladder to the gibbet, embraced the corpse, and let his head rest for some moments on that putrifying mass.

Appeals to his sympathy must have been frequent. His correspondence abounds with intercession for unhappy people, sometimes for total strangers. Even for criminals he demands Christian charity, in tones that sound as if he were pleading for his own relatives. As example, we mention two letters, one in which he implores mercy from the Prince Bishop of Trent for a youth condemned to death, one to Philip of Burgundy for the city of Ghent, which was awaiting harsh punishment. Anybody who has read merely these two letters can never more doubt that Capistran was a man of universal compassion, and will recognize the error in the often repeated phrase, "the saint with the heart of stone." In view of the customs of that age, Capistran's whole activity as inquisitor and preacher bears no marks of unnecessary harshness. Like other great churchmen of his day, he also cautions earnestly against excessively rigorous use of ecclesiastical punishment. Strict in the pulpit, he was lenient in the confessional. Even in doctrine he condemned exaggerations. In Church law he favored liberal interpretation, for example, in the law of annual Communion. Some theologians taught that the faithful were bound, under pain of mortal sin, to receive Communion on Easter Sunday. Others said any time in Holy Week would suffice. Capistran recommended receiving the sacrament at Easter. But strict obligation, he said, was satisfied by receiving at any suitable time during the year. In this he was much milder than the present law.

The crucial test of his charity lies in his attitude toward his confreres. His office of superior began almost with his profession, and he was practically independent during his whole religious life. His time was perpetually claimed by the world. Men of such renown easily lose contact with their confreres. But on this point he was never censured, not even by his opponents, whether Conventuals or Observants. All of them realized that his brethren lived in his heart; that he sacrificed time, energy, and unusual talents for his religious family, and that this family clung to him with love and enthusiasm. They appreciated especially his tender consideration in regulating occasional disorders and faults. His words often contain paternal admonition, which he considered an excellent means to preserve the spirit of his communities. But when he had to correct hidden faults, then not even his most confidential advisers knew of it. Such matters were settled under four eyes. Even odious and stubborn characters he treated with respect. Lastly, from the day of his conversion he exercised in heroic fashion the difficult law of loving one's enemies. We must believe him when he says: "For the salvation of Rokytzana's soul I would be willing to die. I love him. Our Lord's commandment binds me."

We are not insinuating that Capistran's character had no shadows. But we do say that repulsive traits of roughness and heartlessness were put into his picture by the views and sentiments of a far later time. His own contemporaries, even his sharpest critics, knew nothing of Capistran in that light. That in dealing with heretics and Jews he transgressed established bounds and thereby failed against Christian charity, is a thought practically unknown to contemporaries. He was at times censured as impractical, but never as uncharitable or inhuman. Even Döring, one of his severest critics, finds nothing to blame in Capistran's behavior toward the Jews in Breslau.

Other questions will bear investigation, as, for instance, ambition and irascibility. But here, too, we must avoid exaggeration. Preaching in the open air and celebrating Mass on a high platform, often attributed to vanity and pomposity, were simply the national customs of Italy. But a point that is open to animadversion is his manner of preaching. He talks much of himself, of his experiences, of his former faults, but also of his success, and especially of his miraculous cures, and he announced even greater wonders for the future. He threatens skeptics and scoffers with divine judgments. While we note that he ascribed all these miracles to the intercession of St. Bernardine, we must admit that temperament and imagination at times led him astray. He exaggerates the number of his listeners beyond all probability. His desires and hopes become certain expectations. He accepts too easily legends and miraculous reports. But our standards must still be suited to our saints. Christian perfection does not exclude but rather includes personal characteristics. And Capistran was markedly individual. Nicholas V, jesting on Capistran's name, called him *Capo strano* ("Queerhead"). One of his own confreres, displeased by what he considered Capistran's vainglory in the pulpit, even refused to give him absolution. Later this confrere admitted he had done wrong and begged Capistran's pardon. And Enea Silvio, who in a particular case said that Capistran was prompted by an inordinate desire for honor, defended him in general against this suspicion most energetically. Silvio proved his point by Capistran's undisturbed cheerfulness, since people who thirst for honor are frequently sad on account of the many disappointments they experience.

To conclude from noisy celebrations in big cities to a lack of interior life would be using commonplace men to measure the saints. Energetic external activity is, in the saints, a fruit of their yearning desire for contemplative rest and solitude. Of this mysterious union of opposites in one soul, the holy Curé of Ars is a modern example. Superficially viewed, Capistran does not show that he felt his exterior work as a personal sacrifice. But his confidential companions relate how, after a solemn reception, he went quickly to his cell, and there he wept bitterly from interior confusion. When he could manage to do so, he chose the hours of the night for arriving and departing, thus to escape the cheering crowds.

The deep remorse that took possession of him on the day of

his conversion never left him and remained the dominant attitude of his mind. Frequent weeping in solitude was the chief source of a painful inflammation in his eyes. This penitential disposition underlay his preaching. Setting aside all reserve, he would make public confession in the pulpit, thus emulating the penitent Magdalen, his favorite saint. He wished the most despised spot in the world as a grave for his rebellious body. These words were not empty sounds. They were in the end fulfilled in a very remarkable way.

We are not surprised that such an energetic temperamental nature, always ready for action and battle, did not escape reproaches of irascibility and impetuosity. Contradictions he found intolerable, say his critics. "Prouder than the devil, craftier than Satan," is his own self-description. But he adds that he has done his best to master these tendencies. Of craftiness hardly a trace can be discovered. Even those who are not particularly enthusiastic about him acknowledge his utter sincerity and straightforwardness. Absolute frankness, in face of friend and foe, is an excelling trait of his character. Less success he may have had in controlling the emotions of anger, a weakness found in other saints for their humiliation. But we must not lose sight of personal ill humor in his critics themselves. Nicholas Fara, who defends Capistran against the accusations of sinful irascibility, admits vehement passionateness, but adds that those who are not passionate are not apt for practicing heroic virtue, which consists in control of passion. "John, just and merciful, was angry against sin in the manner of the prophets and the apostles." "Even when you are angry, the eye of love must not go blind," was Capistran's own saying. Of any serious indulgence in this his greatest weakness he never became guilty. Strict in judging himself, he could still say of his whole religious life: "I think I have watched myself well."

The reason for Capistran's return (May, 1453) from Neisse to Breslau probably lies, not at all in the Jewish affair, but in the interests of his Order. During the following weeks the second chapter of the newly created Austro-Bohemian vicariate met at Breslau under his direction.

The young vicariate had grown rapidly. By the spring of 1453, two hundred novices had entered, mostly from the universities of Vienna and Leipzig, later on from Cracow, and finally from Breslau itself. The year 1452 had seen new foundations in Amberg, Langensalza, and Weimar. Amberg was assigned to the vicariate of Strassburg, Langensalza and Weimar to the Saxon observance. But the two new foundations of 1453, Olmütz and Breslau, were assigned to the new vicariate. New growth was expected in the province of Silesia. The four Silesian Franciscan convents–Beuthen, Kosel, Leobschütz, and Oberglogau–having carried out a partial reform, now wished to be associated with the Observants and sent their vicar, Nicholas of Glatz, as their representative to the Breslau chapter. Besides, Pope Nicholas V had given Capistran (May 4, 1453) unlimited power to make new foundations. This authorization brought new difficulties. Gabriel of Verona, who had been elected vicar in the previous year, had proved excessively zealous. He thought the Germans needed unrelenting strictness, but the brethren found his prescriptions too harsh. The chapter in Breslau chose in his place Christopher of Varese.

The Observance was gaining new ground beyond the Alps. But meanwhile it seemed to be losing out in its Italian motherland, where since 1446 it had been a practically independent Order, bound only outwardly to the Conventuals by having the same general. Transfer of Observants to the Conventuals was strictly prohibited, but Conventuals could join the Observants at will. Soon after Capistran's departure for the north, the Conventuals moved to regain the old status of mutual transfer. This would let Observants join a lax convent with a more commodious program of life. The strict discipline of the Observants would no longer be possible. Difficult characters could force superiors to satisfy their whims.

These anticipations came to pass. The entanglements of the following years started with the greatest of the Observant preachers, Robert of Lecce. Not yet thirty years old, this remarkably gifted man enjoyed undisputed renown, even in the papal court. He was compared to St. Paul. Robert exemplifies the dangers of reaching too quickly the climax of fame. To secure greater freedom of activity for these popular preachers, the pope withdrew them at times, by a special privilege, from obedience to lower superiors. Only men established in virtue can profit by such privileges. Robert did not stand the test. Success went to his head. He had answered an order of Capistran with the remark: "I owe obedience to the vicar-general only as far as it suits me." Capistran had expressed his apprehension: "This young man will have a bad end." But things had gone fairly well until the general chapter in Aquila at Pentecost, 1452. Robert evidently counted on receiving some office of honor. When the chapter disregarded him, he was highly offended and curtly refused the request of the chapter to preach the Lenten sermons in Aquila the following year. From now on he turned to the Conventuals. The general, Angelus Christophori, no great friend of the Observance, treated Robert as a Conventual and sent him (1453) as preacher to Rome. Here he was an enemy to the Observants, accusing them of false pretenses in obtaining the papal decree of Eugene IV. Consequently, he argued, their privileges of 1446 were null and void. He added a list of twenty-four Observant preachers, who, he said, supported his views. Finally, he claimed that most of the provincial vicars of the Observance held the same ideas. His fame gained him support in the papal court, and the situation for the Observants became critical. The cardinal protector of the whole Franciscan Order, Capranica, upheld Robert. The general and most of the provincials supported him zealously. The provincial of Milan, James Bussolini of Mozzanica, excelled as opponent of the Observants.

Pope Nicholas V, deeply concerned, summoned the vicar-general of the cismontanes, Marcus of Bologna, to Rome for a report. Mark advised calling in the vicars and other representatives of the Observance. This was done. From Italy, France, and Spain delegates hurried to Rome. The Austro-Bohemian vicariate was represented by their first vicar, Gabriel of Verona. Although they unanimously gave their support to the bull of Eugene IV, Robert still continued his agitation, even dragging the matter into the pulpit. In an outdoor sermon, at Campo Fiori, before an immense throng of listeners, he gave twelve reasons to show that the whole Observant family was in the state of mortal sin, that of disobedience to their lawful superiors. The Pope, acting with great circumspection, submitted the contested bull to a council of thirty-five doctors drawn from the chief universities of Italy. Their views were then examined by a commission of cardinals. Both commissions pronounced unanimously: first, that the bull of Eugene IV was fully legal; secondly, that the present condition of the Observance was in no way in contradiction with the Rule of St. Francis.

The Pope now called numerous representatives of both parties and announced the result of the investigation. Everything should be left in its present condition, with two exceptions. First, Observants who find their life too hard, may pass to the Conventuals. Second, the Observants are not allowed to take over any cloister from the Conventuals. But the Conventuals were not satisfied. Mozzanica attempted to prove to the Pope that the bull of Eugene IV contradicted the Rule. But the Pope cut him short. "Your Order is immense. Let this new branch have its own guides. Your provincials have enough cares. Your task is well done, if you govern well those brethren who are entrusted to your care."

But the Observants, too, were dissatisfied. The bull of Eugene IV indeed remained intact. But the free transfer of Observants to the Conventuals aroused a feeling that the Pope had, after all, sided with the Conventuals. Not only in Rome but also in smaller places the dispute became the topic of the day. The public divided into parties, for and against the Observants: some blamed Robert's lust for power; others regarded him as a victim of envious confreres. A good illustration of the situation has been preserved for us in a letter written to Capistran by a member of the noble branch of the Colonna family, a great friend of the Observance. Hurry home, says the letter. "I am willing to suppose you can turn Germany, Russia, the whole north, to God. I am ready to accept reports and that you are working miracles, and even raising the dead. But your poor family here, exposed to the storm, will suffer shipwreck. What incalculable loss for all Christendom! Dearest Father, you are their only hope, you who can prevail with God and men, you who can bend the neck of the proud and silence the tongue of babblers. Come home to your flock. You have done enough up there. The tree on which your deeds are the fruit is in danger of being uprooted. Come. All good people long for you." Capistran responded by writing letters to the Pope, to the cardinals, to the general, threatening the latter with divine judgments.

The sequel heightened his fame as a prophet. Angelus died in Perugia, his native city, a few weeks after his re-election as general. From all sides the Observants, marching day and night, says Mark of Bologna, hurried to the funeral in Perugia. The Conventuals gratefully acknowledged this act of reverence. The Pope chose the provincial of Milan, James Bussolini of Mozzanica, to fill out the term of office. "Till now he has roared against us like a lion, now he promises everything good," writes Mark to Capistran. Mozzanica wrote personally to Capistran announcing his own appointment and praising Capistran's work, his sanctity, and his special gifts. He asks for prayers and offers his services. Capistran, even beyond the Alps, was a power to be reckoned with. Even Robert of Lecce, the habitual companion of Mozzanica, sent greetings to Capistran, asking the prayers of one whom he was denouncing in Rome as a falsifier of papal bulls. The Italian Observants, who did not trust him, called him "the sneaking fox." His intimate friendship with Mozzanica made them suspicious.

The Observants were, nevertheless, in a confident mood. Toward the close of the year 1453 Mark of Bologna reported a victory gained by Capistran. But he was mistaken when he added: "Our bulls have not been changed by one iota."

These controversies penetrated also into the German provinces. Matthias Döring, the most prominent advocate of German Conventualism, submitted to the University of Erfurt a legal opinion, dated October 16, 1451, on the use of money. Döring appealed to papal privileges. He was answered by a German Observant, perhaps John of Brandenburg, then vicar of the Saxon Observants, who invoked the Rule of St. Francis and Capistran's authority.

Up to this time the Conventuals found little reason to complain of Capistran, who had respected their establishments.

Weimar and Langensalza were founded at the expense of the sovereign. Leipzig, earnest in reform, still remained in the Conventual province. In Saxony, Breslau alone had two cloisters, one Conventual, one Observant. Döring accepted this arrangement (July 15, 1453). The new cloister would not harm the Conventuals of St. James if the latter will but live right. Let both cloisters work in harmony. But he complains to the Breslau council of certain priests who dissuade the faithful from giving money to the Conventuals, declaring this practice deserving of excommunication. If the brethren in St. Bernardine, says Döring, do not accept alms in money, this is praiseworthy. The other custom, however, based on papal privilege, is not reprehensible. But Döring goes too far when he adds that Capistran and his brethren "are well satisfied with me and my brethren." Capistran did, indeed, shun collision with the Conventuals. But in Germany, as in Italy, he emphasized the contrast between Observance and Conventualism. As illustration we may cite his instruction to the guardian of Nuremberg: "Just as in the interior life, so also in the exterior, you are to differ from the Conventuals."

The letter just quoted deals chiefly with the training of novices. The emphasis is on the interior life, especially on a daily hour of meditative prayer. Subjects of meditation are: The Passion of Christ, our own miseries, sins committed in the past, the hour of death, the pains of hell, the promised glory of heaven. In reciting the daily Rosary let them pause at those mysteries which offer the soul special attraction. They shall confess twice a week, revealing also their evil imaginations as a remedy against relapse. The same letter blames two practices, preserved in Nuremberg from their Conventual days. First, too much singing. "The novices shall learn to sing, but also to weep and to pray. But too much singing distracts the mind and reduces time for work, bodily and spiritual, so that none of you can deliver a good sermon, and thus souls suffer harm. Limit your singing to Mass and Vespers."

The second practice is that of inviting seculars to their table, a practice that must be altogether discontinued. "If the guests complain, tell them I have commanded it. Do not claim old custom.

It is contrary to the religious spirit, and is the custom of Conventuals and of people in the world. And do not say: 'We will lose the donations that guests bring to us.' Better be satisfied with bread and onions than sit together with people of the world enjoying royal dishes. Let seculars be served in the room reserved for outsiders. Religious excepted, do not admit people to the refectory, except perhaps prelates who would be offended if they were excluded. My brethren, shun intercourse with seculars and seek solitude. Believe me, the more you flee from people of the world the more they will appreciate you and love you. So spoke our holy Father St. Francis. But when they see you familiarly they no longer note any difference between you and others. But when they do not see you often, they will take you for angels. Many will come to join you, and the family will prosper."

The same letter shows that scourging was prescribed for Monday, Wednesday, and Friday. But Capistran condemns categorically the practice of scourging one another. This custom is wicked, improper, and very dangerous. Let them eradicate it, or send his novices back. Incidentally we learn that the signal for Matins was given at one or two o'clock in the morning.

Deep differences existed between Conventuals and Observants. Capistran sums them up in three catchwords: Pueri, petulantia, pecunia. These three P's must be reformed, he said to Eugene IV. By pueri (boys) he meant the acceptance of candidates who were still too young. By petulantia he meant easygoing, lukewarm, careless superiors. By pecunia he meant relaxation in poverty, especially in the use of cash money. A similar word of his, enumerating three things that wreck the Order, mentions pride in superiors, stubbornness in lay brothers, and dissension and sensuality in priests.

To understand his severity we must remember conditions. Reform involved battle against the laxity prevalent in Conventualism. Extreme youth in candidates was the enemy of chastity. Even the canonical age limit of fourteen years did not satisfy him. He demanded for his Order as a minimum the completion of seventeen years of age. The Observance differed from

Conventualism chiefly in three ways. First, by the strictest practice of Franciscan poverty, excluding real estate, money, and every kind of regular revenue. Secondly, by the greater measure of penitential exercises. Thirdly, by a much greater emphasis on the interior life, on love for prayer, solitude, and meditation. Meditation had indeed been zealously practiced before Capistran. But he made it a daily obligation. A year after his death the general chapter urges superiors to withdraw the brethren from superfluous occupations, and to train them in the practice of the interior life. Christopher of Varese, Capistran's most intimate companion, says that lack of meditation would destroy the Observance.

Capistran's long stay in Breslau was probably caused by his weakened condition. And when his strength did return, a decision about where to go next was difficult. Italy was calling him back. Hungary and Poland desired him as visitor. Sbignev of Cracow wrote that he was waiting for Capistran's arrival. The grand master of the Teutonic Knights had invited him to Elbing in Prussia. He himself still thought of the Utraquists in Bohemia and Moravia. Ladislaus had sent him an invitation to come to Vienna by way of Olmütz. The royal messenger, Reicholf, writes to Vienna on July 9: "I bring you joyful news. The devout father will soon come to Vienna." He adds that Vienna should give him as grand a reception as Breslau had done. The coronation of Ladislaus as Bohemian king meant new hopes for Capistran. He welcomed the King's invitation. But a new development kept him from Vienna and led him to Poland. The betrothal of the Polish king, Casimir IV, with Elizabeth, the sister of Ladislaus, was to be celebrated in Breslau. Apparently both kings wished Capistran to honor this festival. Further, King Casimir wished that his delegates to Breslau would then bring Capistran with them to visit Poland, to officiate at Casimir's nuptials with Elizabeth. The King's wishes were fulfilled. On August 10, Breslau witnessed the gorgeous entrance of the representatives of both kings. At the betrothal itself (August 20) Capistran delivered the oration. A *Te Deum* in church closed the day. Two days later the Polish delegates left Breslau, taking Capistran with them.

CHAPTER XXXII

In Poland

CAPISTRAN'S party was met (August 28), two miles outside of Cracow, by a great crowd of people. The solemn reception took place just before the city walls. King Casimir, his royal mother Sophia, and Cardinal Sbignev Olesnicki, had come to greet their guest. Capistran was domiciled with George Schwarz in the great square of Cracow. For the Divine Office all the brethren met in Capistran's quarters. The Franciscans at Cracow either had no room for so many guests or perhaps refused to harbor them. These Conventuals had been stubborn supporters of the Basle schism to the very end.

At once Capistran began to preach, in the open as usual. The great preacher was welcomed and appreciated. Discipline in all ranks had weakened. Among the reformers two were distinguished: the vicar-general, John Elgot, and Nicholas Tempelfeld of Breslau, who for a number of years had been a preacher in Cracow. King Casimir IV was considered careless and easygoing. Harmony was lacking between him and Cardinal Olesnicki. Sbignev, outwardly imposing, intellectually gifted, animated by an energetic desire for activity, had found the right field for his work when he was made bishop of Cracow in 1423. As bishop of the capital, he was considered the first minister of the state. He had become involved in a question of rank with the Archbishop of Gnesen, who was the primate of Poland. But Olesnicki did not lose himself in politics. The duties of a shepherd of souls remained foremost. At his own expense he built churches and supported poor students. Hussitism found in him its sharpest opponent. As chancellor of the Cracow University he suppressed all movements in favor of the heresy. Cracow, like Vienna, remained faithful to the Church. The Cracow professors pledged themselves by oath never to accept Hussitism.

On the other hand, the University had favored the Council of Basle. Even Sbignev's cardinalate was originally a gift of the antipope, Felix V. When (1447) Sbignev submitted to Nicholas V, the latter also made him cardinal (1449). Among the humanists Olesnicki stood in high esteem. As a pioneer of the new ideas in education, he zealously promoted the historical studies of his friend, John Dlugosz, one of the most prominent historians of that age. With Enea Silvio he kept up a very friendly correspondence and would gladly have had him as his guest.

The Cardinal now kept Capistran for almost nine months in his episcopal residence. In previous correspondence, Olesnicki had planned first of all to employ Capistran in regaining the schismatic Ruthenians. But, in fact, we have no record either that Capistran ever left Cracow during those nine months, or that any move was made in the Ruthenian affair. Olesnicki surely did not drop the idea, but Capistran probably refused to go farther to the East. His gaze was still directed to the West. Leaving a problem half-finished was not his way. And just now the coronation of a Hapsburg as king of the Bohemians offered good hopes for Capistran's Hussite mission. Moreover, Cracow, a university city, was a favorable center from which to extend the Observance in Poland, especially in those portions where the German language was used. Cracow, in fact, remained preponderatingly German until 1550. Deterred from going to Prague because of its Hussitism, students began to attend the universities of Leipzig and Cracow.

An Observant foundation in Cracow had long been planned by the King and the Cardinal. Capistran soon invested five young men. A tract of land was given by the Count of Sandomir, a brother of the King, who said he was happy to have found such a heir.

The duties of his office forced Olesnicki to travel, and his intention to return promptly to Cracow was frustrated. The old man fell seriously ill and was bedridden for many weeks outside his diocese. Rumor even said he had died, but that his death was kept secret. The sick prelate, worried because the King also was absent, wrote to Capistran not to grow weary of Cracow, where he could do so much good and where his daily preaching had already removed a number of evil conditions.

On October 28, 1453, in the cathedral of St. Vitus in Prague, Ladislaus was solemnly crowned by the Bishop of Olmütz, in the presence of all the secular and religious dignitaries of the kingdom. The interregnum was past. Capistran felt he could now make a new attempt to go to Prague, especially since the young King had invited him, twice in one year, to come to his court. He wrote to the King, saying he had no greater wish on earth than to come to Prague and he adjures the King to give him a reliable escort. He protests energetically against the insinuation that he is an enemy of the Bohemians. "God is my witness that I do not desire my own salvation more fervently than I do theirs. I love the Bohemians so much that I could not wish for anything more delightful than to conclude my earthly pilgrimage among them." He yields even on the question of the Compact, provided the Pope approves. What the Holy Father approves, Capistran will defend. Similar letters he wrote to Podebrad and other influential dignitaries. His faithful friend, Benesch of Boskowitz, the vice-chamberlain of Moravia, received a whole bundle of letters from Cracow, to be forwarded by special couriers to Prague.

But Capistran's hope turned out to be a chimera. The cathedral chapter, headed by Wenzel of Krumau, did indeed return to Prague from its exile in Pilsen. But the two principal demands of the Utraquist party remained firm. Ladislaus bought his coronation with a promise, not only to respect the Compact but also to make Rokytzana bishop of Prague. And Prague knew well that Capistran would do his very best to have Rome reject the Compact. They knew, too, that he would influence the citizens in that spirit. His letter to Ladislaus showed that clearly. The Bohemians, he says, should at least listen to him. Perfect reunion of the Utraquists with Rome was his goal. But Podebrad used his power to keep Capistran away. Ladislaus, personally Catholic-minded but unable to challenge Podebrad, who was the real master of Bohemia, made him his viceroy and lord chief steward. The royal chancery now informed Capistran (December 13) that for various reasons permission could not be granted. He should patiently await further information.

Podebrad's personal answer was still plainer. He would have preferred to leave Capistran's letter unanswered, but Boskowitz had ordered his messenger not to return without an answer. Now, since Ladislaus himself had written to Capistran, Podebrad yielded. His short brusque letter (December 22) repeats the accustomed Utraquist accusations. Capistran, an enemy of the Bohemians, slanders them everywhere and starts discords where people have finally found peace. "Your absence is more pleasing to us than your presence would be. You will not get an escort. We are not disposed to bow to your will."

At Cracow, where Capistran, while awaiting the answer from Prague, continued to preach daily, an old figure re-emerged on the scene. This was Master Paul, the wandering Jew of Prague. Capistran had him arrested. Sbignev declared himself perfectly satisfied with this procedure, though he later relented. From prison Paul wrote doleful letters to Capistran, imploring mercy, promising to go with him to Prague and help him against Rokytzana.

In January, 1454, the messenger of Benesch of Boskowitz arrived with the desired letter. In a personal message Benesch announces that, after a visit in Prague to see the King, he intends to come to Cracow to see Capistran.

Capistran still persevered. He wrote a very long letter to Podebrad. Since he knew that Podebrad, an illiterate man, would not bother with that long message, he added a resume of the strongest passages. The long letter was meant for the public. Podebrad's last letter again asserted that Capistran had formerly been offered a reliable escort to Prague and had refused it. Capistran now reveals the whole story. Not Prague, but country villages, "with lots of oxen and sheep," had been offered to him as places for disputation. From Brüx he had asked for an escort, but received no answer. Since then they have persecuted him from city to city.

In one impression Capistran was mistaken. He still thought that Podebrad was controlled by Rokytzana. Therefore his efforts to eliminate Rokytzana's influence on Podebrad. "If I were sure, my dear George, that the letter which came to me over your name represents your real sentiments, I would treat you as the insolent writer of that letter deserves. But since I cannot presume such rudeness in a nobleman, I will answer more mildly than wise men think I should. How can a man so qualified in secular affairs let himself be controlled by heretics who abuse his ignorance of reading and writing to cover him with disgrace and shame? Can you not see that they force me to expose you before kings, princes, prelates, and universities, and before the whole Christian world? Will the Christian world not look on you as a rude and uneducated heretic if I am compelled to answer their questions regarding that lying and abusive letter which you have written? No one anywhere can heap more shame on you than I can, I, little brother John of Capistrano, who am listened to by thousands. Kings, princes, prelates, people, all love and honor me, not by reason of my virtues, but by reason of their humility and their veneration for the Apostolic See. I could easily give you a name which water would never wash off, which time would not erase. Do you really enjoy being ridiculed? Is that the glory you aim at, to be proclaimed before the Christian world as protector of heretics, rebel against the Church, son and pupil of that poisonous heresiarch called Rokytzana?

"What wrong have I done to you that you persecute me wherever I go? My only wrong has been my zeal for the honor of God and the salvation of souls. You know well enough that I preach nothing but the doctrine of the universal Church. I do no wrong when I call those men heretics who have really stained themselves with heresy. I was sent to love Catholics, to honor them, to strengthen them in Christian faith, but also to fight against the heretics, to cry out and to thunder against vice and sin. I will not be a dumb dog. My dear George, I do not hate Rokytzana or his friends, as you imagine. But I do hate their misdeeds, their heresies, their false ideas. If they cannot endure being called heretics, let them become Catholics. Let them abjure and humbly ask for absolution, if they want to escape the eternal fire. Your Rokytzana, my dear George, is he not, according to Christ's word, a thief, a robber, who did not come through the door into the sheepfold? What devil placed over you this shepherd, who exercises the priesthood without being a priest? who preaches, celebrates Mass, and absolves without having received the power to do so?"

Podebrad had asserted that Capistran would come to Prague to start discord. "Let answer be given," says Capistran, "by all the nations among whom I have worked these many years: the Italians, the Bavarians, the Franconians, the Thuringians. I am an Italian. But I was received by the Germans as a German, by the Poles as a Pole, by the Catholics of Bohemia as a Bohemian. In Vienna, Nuremberg, Brünn, Olmütz, Oppeln, Amberg; in Hungary, in Langensalza, in Cracow, and in Breslau, I was given good cloisters, which I have populated with religious, drawn from the universities of Vienna, Leipzig, and Cracow. Two years ago I came from Italy with twelve companions. Now I have four hundred confreres to combat Rokytzana's errors."

He ends by saying that for this time he has endeavored to be still indulgent. But if Podebrad does not declare that Rokytzana was responsible, then he will change his style. "But a good tone between you and me would be better."

The shorter letter is even sharper. Podebrad is represented as the principal originator of the schism in Prague. "You are he who stained Prague with innocent blood. You desecrated consecrated places. You tore to pieces the seamless garment of Jesus Christ. Beware! More powerful than you was Lucifer, whose son you plainly prove yourself. Stronger were the giants and mighty potentates of olden days: Artaxerxes; Sennacherib, killed by his own sons; Pharaoh, drowned in the sea; Caesar, the invincible, who fell with twenty-four wounds; Nero the cruel, cruelly killed; Domitian, Maximian, Diocletian, and many others. None of them escaped the judgment of God. Do you, my dear George, really believe that you alone will escape the divine wrath?"

Capistran's manner of procedure was not favored by his friends in Moravia. When the messenger came with this letter to Moravia, the Observants indeed, by Capistran's order, multiplied it for public circulation. But the citizens of Brünn, on learning its contents, shook their heads. They delayed the courier until Benesch of Boskowitz returned. Then they held council, to which they also called the suffragan bishop, William of Olmütz. Since copies of the letter were already in circulation, they decided to let the original be delivered to Podebrad. No record exists of Podebrad's answer.

Capistran still hoped in the King, who wrote to him to return before long to Breslau and there await arrangements. Meanwhile the approaching marriage of Casimir with Elizabeth of Austria kept Capistran in Cracow. On February 2, Austrian noblemen brought Elizabeth to Teschen, where she was received by a Polish embassy. Casimir had sent 2,000 horsemen to meet his spouse, and her own escort numbered 900. Deep snow covered the country. The cavalcade needed a week to reach the capital. Court and nobility put on their greatest splendor. The Observants of St. Bernardine, eighty in number, drew much attention. Their poor penitential appearance contrasted strangely with the knights in precious armor, riding on richly caparisoned steeds. People shed tears, says a chronicler. Knights and courtiers whispered to one another: "The Lord God belongs to those men there; they can obtain from Him anything they wish." And as they rode by they recommended themselves, with bows and courtesies, to the prayers of the men of God. The splendid scene suffered much from bad weather, as it rained heavily all day.

Who was to perform the marriage ceremony for the royal pair? The Archbishop of Gnesen as primate of the realm? Or the diocesan Bishop of Cracow? The decision reached was to submit the matter for future occasions to the Pope, but for the present case to let Capistran perform the ceremony. Capistran, the canonist, declared that the right belonged exclusively to the bishop of the diocese, from whom alone he would accept delegation. As he spoke he bent his knee, and received Cardinal Sbignev's authorization. A new difficulty arose. Capistran could speak neither German nor Polish. So, after all, the Cardinal performed the wedding ceremony, while the primate offered the coronation Mass and anointed the royal couple. Evening was near when pontifical High Mass began. The primate, says the chronicler, "sang like a torrent." Capistran's prayers for the royal couple bore splendid fruits. This matrimony, blessed by a saint, brought forth a saint. Prince Casimir, born 1458, lived a life of piety and innocence, died at the age of twenty-five, and was canonized by Pope Leo X.

The wedding feast lasted eight days. When the guests returned home, Capistran would have preferred to go with them. But urged by the court, especially by the King's mother, he reluctantly consented to remain till Easter. The King himself was probably less urgent. His relations with Capistran were not too smooth. The Jewish question led to serious differences. In contrast to his father Casimir III, who had consistently upheld canon law, Casimir IV was very liberal. Without asking the advice of the Cardinal of Cracow or of the barons, probably under the influence of the Count Palatine of the Empire, he granted the Jews all the liberties of his realm, liberties which they enjoyed nowhere else in those days. Capistran earnestly admonished the King not to forget his duties as a Christian ruler. Let him not exalt the enemies of the Cross of Christ by granting them liberty to oppress Christians. Let him revoke these thoughtless privileges. But the Count Palatine frustrated all these efforts.

Another source of difference lay in the King's warlike preparations against Prussia, then governed by Teutonic Knights. Attempts to reform the decaying order had been frustrated by the knights themselves, who were given to luxurious life. The very efficient grand master, Henry of Plauen, had succeeded, after the disaster of Tannenberg (1410), in saving the state. He now planned to give the state a broader foundation, by granting the nobility and the cities a share in the administration and the rights of representation. The knights, embittered by these measures, deposed him, but thereby prepared their own ruin. Unbearable taxation led to the formation of a Prussian union against the Order. On February 6, 1454, the union gave notice to the grand master that they would no longer obey him, and offered dominion over the territory to King Casimir. Poland was divided in opinion. Cardinal Sbignev and Capistran were opposed to the offer. Capistran based his view on the religious character of the Order. He suggested submitting the quarrel to the Pope's decision. The Polish King should act as mediator in reconciling the opposing parties.

Such is the historical truth in this matter. But in Germany rumor said that Capistran had instigated the Poles against the Teutonic Knights. His presence in Cracow and his unusually long stay in Poland may have lent color to the false suspicion. Further, he had declined an invitation to visit the lands of the Order, pleading his obligation to return to Bohemia. When in reality he then went instead to Poland, this step could easily be misconstrued at the residence of the grand master.

When King Casimir invited Cardinal Sbignev to a diet in Lanziz, to discuss the Prussian affair, the Cardinal declined. His relations with the King were already strained. In a memorial he protests, not only against the King's illegal favors to the Jews, but also against other encroachments on ecclesiastical jurisdiction. He even threatens excommunication, saying: "No one stands so high as to be immune in matters of faith." He reminds him of King Boleslaus, the murderer of St. Stanislaus. He himself will also, in case of necessity, resist injustice, even to the shedding of blood. To Lanziz he cannot come. Age and bodily infirmity forbid. Moreover, what he thinks of the Prussian problem, is already known to the King. In general he is disgusted with these diets, where there is more damning than planning. Also for Capistran's sake, who is preparing to depart, he must remain in Cracow.

Shortly before Easter, Ladislaus, the new king of Bohemia, again wrote to Capistran, asking him to return to Breslau. On May 14, after nine months in Poland, Capistran left Cracow, escorted at the Cardinal's expense.

CHAPTER XXXIII

Later History of Utraquism

BY way of Beuthen, Gross-Strehlitz, and Oppeln, Capistran reached Breslau again on May 29. The city's third reception was as solemn and enthusiastic as if he were coming for the first time. But the prospect of a long stay in Breslau did not please Capistran himself. In spite of his predilection for that city, he awaited only the King's permission to go to Prague by way of Olmütz. "At Olmütz my work would bring far better results than here in Breslau, where I have already preached the word of God so many months."

Meanwhile the annual chapter of the Obervants met in Breslau under his presidency. At this third chapter of the new vicariate ten convents were represented: Vienna, Kloster-Neuburg, Brünn, Olmütz, Breslau, Cracow, Oppeln, Beuthen, Kosel, and Leobschütz. Christopher Varese, who was ailing in consequence of a fall from a horse, resigned his office of vicar, and Gabriel of Verona was again entrusted with the post.

Capistran's urge to get away from Breslau was probably prompted by other reasons. The oath of allegiance to King Ladislaus had divided the citizens into passionate parties. Superficially the question was one of formality, since Breslau and all Silesia looked on Ladislaus as their rightful king. But deeper things were involved. These border states of the Bohemian crown: what were their real rights? The Czechoslovak nobility had, under Podebrad's leadership, passed a resolution at the Bohemian diet, which annulled the right of succession to the throne for the King's children, and reserved to the Bohemian estates the right to elect a new king. Only as a king-elect was Ladislaus allowed to come to Prague and be crowned there. The Vienna government had yielded to this demand. But the other countries under the crown of Wenceslaus had not been consulted at all when this revolutionary measure was passed. They now decided they would swear allegiance to Ladislaus as heir of the crown. Moravia had acted thus even before Ladislaus was crowned. The same procedure was being planned by Oberlausitz and Niederlausitz, by Silesia, by Breslau, and by Schweidnitz-Jauer.

Prague wished to prevent this procedure. When the ambassadors of Oberlausitz came to Prague to take the oath, they were handed the Bohemian formula, which they had to sign. Now Breslau was summoned to Prague. The city decided not to go; for in the past, it had not sworn allegiance to a new king until the king visited Breslau the first time. Simultaneously, when the king came to Breslau, princes also came to swear fealty, thus clearly emphasizing the rank of Breslau as the second capital of the Bohemian realm. If Breslau now went to Prague, the Silesian princes would have to do likewise. This step they regarded as destructive of their national rights.

A still deeper reason for reluctance lay in the disgust harbored by the Silesians, originally German colonists, for the heretics in Prague. Heretical triumph, they felt, was unbearable. Magistrates and citizens, clergy and laymen, were all of one mind. But how should they treat that command to come to Prague? Here opinions were divided. The civil powers advised, as the lesser evil, to yield for the present time. Thus too the Bishop and the higher clergy. But the great mass of the citizens, led by the lower clergy, insisted passionately on their constitutional rights, and urged an absolute refusal to go. Under the leadership of Nicholas Tempelfeld, they succeeded in gaining the councilors, and at first even the Bishop and the prelates. The dominion of heretical Prague over the neighboring provinces was a danger for the Church. Thus the preachers justified their interference in the question. When the magistrates, in spite of opposition, did send a delegation to Prague, they were forced by public opinion to send a second delegation on the heels of the first, to cancel all authorization to take the oath of fealty, and to declare that only at Breslau would Breslau honor its hereditary king. Podebrad was prudent. He did not drive things to extremes, especially since the other Silesians were still reluctant. The agreement reached was this: Breslau would not have to come to Prague, but a delegation from the King would come to Breslau, and there accept homage in the King's name. But when the Prague deputation came to Breslau, in early May, Dr. Tempelfeld found means to frustrate even this concession. The delegates had to return with a message which said the King must come himself. The citizens were determined even to employ force.

Thus matters stood when Capistran returned to Breslau. His judgment was that the city was right in principle, and wrote in this sense to the King. "If the Bohemians insist that you guarantee their ancient privileges, why should you not do the same for the people of Breslau? Are the Bohemians perhaps more faithful to you than the people of Breslau, who have never refused you obedience? When the Bohemians insist on Breslau doing homage in Prague, are they not aiming to bring Breslau also under the yoke of the heretics when you are dead?"

Agreeing thus with Breslau on the question of principle, Capistran would not decide what the city ought to do in case the King would persist in his command. His letter to King Ladislaus shows great reserve, though he does urge the wish of all the citizens of Breslau that the King should soon come to their city to receive their oath of loyalty. This question was not a question of faith, and Capistran remained neutral, even when things came to a crisis. In the King's name the city received a harsh reprimand, and Prague prepared to use force. But Breslau remained steadfast and strengthened its fortifications. Bishop Peter Nowak went personally to Prague as intermediary. Podebrad treated him with such distinction that the people of Prague grew angry. They said that now Capistran himself might just as well be admitted.

The presence of a Catholic king was no great advantage to the Catholic cause in Bohemia. Ladislaus had indeed restored the Carthusians, and also the pastor of St. Benedict's Church. But, as Wenzel of Krumau writes to Capistran, the King himself was surprised that the Utraquist preachers had not yet cried alarm. Wenzel adds that the restoration of other churches is expected and that the King is preparing the downfall of Rokytzana. But for the present, he adds, prospects for all these things are very poor.

Rokytzana is oppressing the Catholics just as before, is teaching false doctrines to the clergy, especially on the authority of the Pope, and, to crown all, pretends that all his acts have been authorized by the King. He thus brings the innocent King into bad repute. Further details, he concludes, Capistran will learn orally from Jodok Rosenberg, since it is too dangerous to write everything. He himself can hardly accompany the King on his journey to Breslau. His church might fall a prey to ravening wolves.

Meanwhile Capistran had received the King's consent to go to Olmütz and Vienna. On July 18, two months after his arrival from Cracow, he preached his farewell sermon. This was possibly the occasion of his famous prediction that Breslau would have, first, a Bohemian captain, then a Bohemian bishop, and third a Bohemian king; that under them the city would be more oppressed than ever before; but that if the city preserved peace and harmony it would overcome all these evils. All these things came to pass. Henry Rosenberg became viceroy of Moravia; his brother Jodok became bishop of Breslau, and George Podebrad became king of Bohemia. Breslau complained of Capistran's unexpected departure, since his presence was greatly needed. Although one deputation followed another, he was determined to go. He consoled the delegates with the prospect of a return. But they would have to ask for him earnestly, and give him serious reasons for returning.

Serious reasons did in fact soon appear. Shortly after his departure, Bishop Peter returned from Prague with strict orders from the King to urge the people to obedience. But all his urging was in vain. The magistrates and the citizens declared unanimously they would abide by their resolution, even to death if necessary. Then Bishop and cathedral chapter went to the council and explained the dangers of opposition. The council yielded, but not so the citizens. They would rather die, they cried, than become faithless to their resolution. Popular indignation ran high, against council, Bishop, and clergy. The priests were accused of misleading the people, since they themselves did not keep the obligations they had so often preached. Bishop and magistrates gave them three days for reflection. The magistrates wrote to Capistran that they saw no way out of the turmoil except his return to Breslau. Father Christopher of Meissen, guardian of St. Bernardine, sent two detailed reports to Capistran in Moravia. The people's party too, guided by Tempelfeld, asked by letter for his advice. All these letters show that he had succeeded in keeping himself above the parties in this crisis.

Just after Capistran's departure from Breslau a new order arrived there from Prague, signed by the Bohemian chancellor, Procopius of Rabenstein, saying Capistran was to stay in Breslau instead of going to Olmütz. The reason given was sad enough. Moravia was summoning troops, and Capistran's presence there might deter the Utraquists from enlisting. In the interests of peace he should stay away from Moravia for the present. Here was evidence, black on white, that the Bohemian government would not support his missionary efforts, and that the King could not bring him to Prague.

In Olmütz, Capistran received a startling letter from Enea Silvio. It said, first, that Capistran must abandon all hope of reaching Prague. "Those who advise you otherwise deceive you." But, secondly, a more important task now awaited the great preacher. Constantinople had fallen into the hands of the Turks.[1] The threatening Turkish cloud overhung Europe. Capistran should go at once to Frankfort-on-Main and urge the German congress to energetic war against the archenemy of Christendom. Silvio himself would most probably come as imperial ambassador. They could then discuss details.

Enea Silvio, who four years before had brought Capistran to Austria, now sends him against the Crescent. Capistran accepted this commission as coming from the Emperor, though acceptance meant sacrifice. His work in Olmütz was reaching thousands of people, and many were coming to abjure the chalice. His old adversaries, the Kremsians, were again on the scene, accusing him of not having answered their former treatise of two years before. Only now did Capistran learn that his answer to them had never been sent. It was found among the papers of Bishop John of Olmütz,

---

[1] May 29, 1453.

who had died in the meantime. This former answer he now sent to the Kremsians, and with it an explicit reply to their new treatise. Here the matter ended. He was preparing to go to the imperial diet at Frankfort, intending on the way to visit several princes, to interest them in the new crusade. Besides, incorrigible optimist that he was, he hoped that this new commission would still open for him the gates of Prague. He wrote to Podebrad, asking for an escort thither. His tone is this time much milder. But religion is still uppermost. Let Podebrad, who has labored for fame, now care for his immortal soul. The Hussite correspondence, from beginning to end, shows Capistran as a zealous shepherd of souls.

Capistran, who did not think his Hussite mission was ended, looked on the crusade as a transient interruption of his work in Bohemia. But since his work in Bohemia was in fact ended, let us weigh its results. Enea Silvio declared flatly that Capistran's Hussite mission was a total failure. Bohemia, he says, remained what it was before. The number of converts, twelve thousand, was small in proportion to the great mass of heretics. And most of these converts had hardly been conscious heretics. They had been separated from union with the Church chiefly in the rite of Communion. Few of them shared the erroneous doctrines of their leaders. The real danger lay, not in the fact that so many thousands shared the chalice, but in the fact that, under cover of ecclesiastical concessions, the whole kingdom was on the way to estrangement from the Church. A century later many countries in Europe permanently lost contact with the Church without being aware of what was really happening. Bohemia was already, under Rokytzana's tenacious leadership, headed for the same fate.

But a distinction must be noted. The heretics of the fifteenth century had against them the solid unity of the whole Catholic West. Hence they had felt obliged to remain, at least outwardly, in union with the pope, the head of the universal Church. Hence also their incessant efforts to obtain the solemn acknowledgment of the Compact and, if possible, the elevation of Rokytzana to the archiepiscopal see of Prague. Convinced interior acknowledgment of the pope, and of the supreme authority of the Church of Rome in matters of faith and doctrine, was not to be found in the leaders of Utraquism. George Podebrad declared, in a later Bohemian diet, that the Roman Church was for him not synonymous with the Christian Church.

From all this it follows that Capistran's views on the Bohemian Church question were essentially correct. The leaders of the movement must be regained or else repudiated. He was at first convinced he could regain them. Results partly justified his daring expectations. In those districts of Moravia and western Bohemia where he could preach undisturbed, the Utraquist sect vanished entirely. If he could make the Utraquists, including their leaders, Catholic again in all fundamental questions, then all the other barriers, based on ecclesiastical exceptions, would vanish of themselves. In the perfect accomplishment of this program he was, alas, forcibly prevented by the dictators in Prague. Hence he saw only one other way, and that was to obtain a solemn rejection of the Compact by the Apostolic See. The leaders of the sect would thereby be forced to declare their position openly. The state of untruthfulness and hypocrisy, which the Bohemian separate Church had inherited from her hollow peace with Basle, would come to an end.

But these ideas of Capistran were not shared by leading ecclesiastical circles. The two most influential counselors of the papal curia in this question were Cardinal Cusa and Enea Silvio. Both favored papal approval of the Compact, as did likewise the neighboring Catholic rulers, Emperor Frederick III and King Ladislaus Posthumous. Capistran stood alone. This isolation was tragic. But it shows too, perhaps more than any other event of his career, the depth of his genius for leadership. But did the tragedy mean complete failure? He opened the eyes of the Catholic world. Herein lay his chief merit.

Incomplete sources prevent us from seeing how far the course of events in Bohemia itself were influenced by his activity. But the further course of events completely justified Capistran's views. Enea Silvio himself, when he became Pope Pius II, solemnly condemned the Compact and thereby declared open war against the unmasked

Bohemian heresy. Capistran did not live to see this result, but he had prepared the way. Even his failure to meet the leaders of Utraquism face to face turned out to be an advantage. The literary efforts, to which he turned instead, made the whole Catholic world his board of arbitrators. His Hussite correspondence had an immense circulation, and everywhere efforts were made to obtain a complete collection of his controversial writings. Catholic eyes were open everywhere to the danger symbolized by Rokytzana. Even Bohemia was benefited, since Catholicity grew strong in and around Bohemia. The Observant convents of Vienna, Brünn, Olmütz, Breslau, Leipzig, Weimar, Langensalza, Nuremberg, and Amberg surrounded the heretical territory like a crown of watchtowers. Two of the three episcopal sees of the kingdom were occupied by members of those families that had been the chief pillars of his Hussite mission. Jodok Rosenberg, Ulrich Rosenberg's son, became bishop of Breslau (1456). Prothasius, son of Benesch of Boskowitz, became bishop of Olmütz. The see of Prague remained deserted. But the administrator of the Catholic consistory in Prague, Dr. Wenzel of Krumau, Capistran's true and able friend, gained increasing influence after the coronation of King Ladislaus.

Why was final settlement of the Bohemian question still delayed so many years? Because the fact that the throne was occupied by a Catholic Hapsburg seemed to offer guaranty for a satisfactory solution. The outside Catholic world seems to have thought so, although Ladislaus, bound by his coronation promise, protected the Utraquists, and Rokytzana's deportment showed no change. Podebrad, moderate and prudent, always aiming at a reconciliation of both parties, did his best to establish permanent peace with the Church. The transactions with Rome were now taken up again, under Callistus III, an aged, obliging, and indulgent man, who in 1455 followed Nicholas V in the chair of Peter. But Callistus was wholly preoccupied with the Turkish war, and Capistran was preaching the crusade in far-off Hungary.

In 1456 the Bohemians prepared a solemn embassy to Rome. The promotion of Enea Silvio to the cardinalate seems to have created new hopes. Rumor said that the new cardinal was the attorney of Utraquism at the papal curia; that he felt bound to save the Compact and to promote Rokytzana to the archiepiscopal see of Prague, or even to the cardinalate. Capistran wrote from Budapest to Enea Silvio in Rome. Was it possible that he could betray the Catholic faith in this fashion? Afterward Capistran learned, from the cardinal legate, John Carvajal, that approval of the Compact was really under consideration in Rome. Cardinal Silvio had advised Pope Callistus to take this step. In deepest sorrow Capistran wrote instantly to the Pope, admonishing and warning. "The Hussites have already profited much by abusing the Compact. What will they not do if the Compact finds approval? I fear Hussitism will flame up anew in other countries, in Bohemia, Moravia, Hungary, Transylvania, along the Moldau, and still farther. These countries are already infected by this damnable heresy. I have found elsewhere traitors against God and men, but nowhere have I found rebels against the Church as infamous as the Hussites. Let the Pope use the utmost circumspection. While here in Hungary we are trying to save Christendom, the Church over there behind us may be entirely destroyed."

The sudden death of King Ladislaus (November, 1457) put an end to the idea of an embassy to Rome. The Utraquist majority put Podebrad on the throne (March 2, 1458). But he was uneasy, fearing resistance. Catholic provinces depending on Bohemia were dissatisfied, as was also the house of Hapsburg, and other neighboring states. Podebrad, to secure his throne, sought papal acknowledgment. As a first move he planned to accept the crown from the hand of a Catholic bishop. But the see of Prague was still vacant. Prothasius of Olmütz had not yet been inducted into office. The bishop of Breslau, Jodok Rosenberg, refused to perform the coronation. In this predicament help came from the new king of Hungary, Matthias Corvinus, Podebrad's future son-in-law, who sent two Hungarian bishops to the coronation. These bishops insisted indeed that the King take the Catholic oath of coronation, but allowed him to do so secretly, and to postpone its execution temporarily.

Podebrad now vowed obedience and loyalty to the Roman

Catholic Church. He swore to protect the Church with all his might, to keep his subjects free from all error and schism, and to lead them back again to Catholic unity in cult and rites. Thereby he solemnly abjured the Compact. Then followed (May 7, 1458) his solemn coronation in the cathedral of Prague. Now also the Catholics of the kingdom swore allegiance to him, with the sole exception of Breslau. There Dr. Tempelfeld started passionate and energetic resistance against this King of the heretics. Capistran was now dead, but his influence is clearly felt in Tempelfeld's tracts, especially in his condemnation of the Compact. Imitating Capistran explicitly, Tempelfeld claims that Podebrad was a real heretic, and therefore could not be acknowledged as king.

The event proved Tempelfeld right. The proverb which Capistran occasionally quoted, namely, that one could never trust a Bohemian, was in this instance most strikingly exemplified. Who could have suspected that Podebrad, at this very time, had also taken oaths, equally secret and solemn, to protect the Utraquists and to be faithful to the Compact?

Enea Silvio, who had now ascended the papal throne, let himself at first be deceived by Podebrad. By letters and legates he obtained the acknowledgment of Podebrad as king, and brought even Breslau to submission. The Pope made Wenzel of Krumau the exclusive administrator of the archbishopric of Prague. But Rokytzana had no intention whatever of resigning his leadership of an independent Utraquist consistory, though, according to the oath of coronation, Utraquism had no longer any legal foundation. Catholics at least thought so. But, to their great surprise, they now heard the King say that he knew his duties toward both parties and was going to fulfill them. On the other hand he showed open favors to Catholics, since he still hoped to be crowned as German king. He even established the Franciscan Observants in Prague, thereby fulfilling a prophecy made by Capistran. But Rokytzana soon managed to undo this step. In 1460 the Catholics lost their best support. Dr. Wenzel of Krumau paid for his zeal by dying of poison.

The peace with Rome was hollow and soon went to pieces. The very presence of Gabriel of Verona, guardian of the cloister in

Prague, irritated the Utraquists. On Holy Thursday, 1461, Bishop Jodok of Breslau preached in the cathedral against the chalice. Rokytzana in turn thundered against the King himself. To quiet the storm Podebrad declared publicly that he would protect the Compact. The final breach with Rome was now but a question of time. In 1462 the Bohemian delegation finally went to Rome. But instead of leading the nation to unity with the Church, as had been promised in the coronation oath, the ambassadors demanded the approval of the Compact. In a public consistory, attended by four thousand people, Pius II presented the reasons that spoke against the granting of the chalice to the laity. Then the final decision was read: "The Compact which the Council of Basle granted to Utraquist Bohemia is hereby revoked and annulled."

In the Diet of Prague (August 12, 1462), Podebrad replied that he would give crown and life for the Compact. His further measures against Catholics and the Pope brought on him, in 1466, the major excommunication. The result was a new civil and religious war. The king of Hungary, Matthias Corvinus, who had become the Catholic leader, conquered Moravia in 1468, but could not subdue Bohemia. Mutual exhaustion led to a truce in 1470. King Podebrad, who was ailing and desired peace, withdrew more and more from Rokytzana. On February 22, 1471, the latter died in despair, according to a contemporary report, which says that on his deathbed he acknowledged that he had never been a priest. Podebrad, delivered from his evil genius, promised to make peace with the Church. Just when a papal legate to Bohemia was appointed, Podebrad also died, exactly one month after Rokytzana (March 22, 1471).

Utraquism, deprived of great leaders, now dwindled in importance. Podebrad's successor, Ladislaus, guaranteed equal rights to both parties. Externally, in ceremonial, Utraquism approached Catholicism more and more. In the sixteenth century Lutheranism led one party of Utraquists to return to the Church. But the genuine Hussites welcomed the German reformers as friends and comrades. Luther said that Hussite treatises revealed him to himself as a thorough Hussite. The heresy of the fifteenth century prepared the great apostasy of the sixteenth century. Did

Capistran foresee this fateful development? We have reason to think so when we reflect on the unbending will and mighty energy shown by this old man against the Utraquists. From Budapest, in his last months, he wrote to Pope Callistus III: "The Hussite danger is the greatest to which the Church had been exposed since the days of the apostles."

Capistran's Hussite mission, when all is said, was not a failure. Though to Capistran himself it was indeed a keen disappointment, he had not wasted his time. His religious foundations bore lasting fruit. But proper judgment here depends on our view of the general importance to be assigned to the itinerant preachers of the late Middle Ages.

Momentary successes were often extraordinary, never attained by the pulpit of later centuries. Capistran sums up the matter in a Vienna sermon. Italy, he says, had been a chaos, political and religious. But when preaching again came into honor, first in Bernardine, and afterward in me, poor sinner, Italy was renewed and resembled a great cloister. However, a generation later, a confrere of Capistran, Blessed Bernardine of Aquila, while praising the classical age of the great preachers, casts a glance at his own times which leads him to break out into bitter laments. People, high and low, are worse than before. "Many have joined religious orders. Some people in the world have changed their way of living. Religious in general, under the influence of Bernardine's life and miracles, have become more strict. But with the great mass of people everything turns to the worse. God alone knows what may still come."

Itinerant preaching, then, did not influence public life with sufficient permanence.[2] The preachers themselves complain often enough of serious failures. "The preacher sows the seed, but, alas, how little he reaps," cries Capistran from the pulpit in Nuremberg. "This must be attributed, not to the sermon, but to the people." And we may add that it must be attributed to the very nature of itinerant preaching. Extraordinary care of souls is not a panacea. Many other

[2] Pastor remarks that too little attention has as yet been bestowed on the action of these preachers of penance (I, 33).

factors must cooperate. First of all, the ordinary care of souls must stand on a high level. Excitement, enormous concourses of people, the soul-stirring appeals and emotional cries for mercy, are evanescent, and not subject to frequent repetition. This is why the preachers themselves did not like to stay for a longer time in the same place. Emotional conversions have to be fostered and strengthened by daily self-sacrificing work in detail. And this requisite was in great measure missing, especially when the local clergy, secular or religious, were not favorably disposed to the preachers and their methods. A second factor was the helping hand of the secular power. Where this power entered in, as in Perugia, better conditions were lasting.

But we must not omit another reflection. Deficient in permanency of positive upbuilding, itinerant preaching may still claim the merit of having saved Italy from the invasion of Protestantism. Capistran declared in Vienna: "Had the office of preaching not been rekindled, Catholic faith might have entirely collapsed, or at least have retained but few adherents."

So much for itinerant preaching in Italy. Capistran's mission to the north was an isolated incident. Hence we cannot expect fully the same results. Investigation would have to cover each particular scene of his activity. But, in fact, our only sources are the casual reports of tradition. His canonization, begun ten years later, offered opportunity for testimony about him. And these petitions do speak with fervor and enthusiasm of the successful activity of the holy man, but generally they do not give us concrete details. The Bishop of Meissen and the city of Görlitz stress the fact that he brought a great number of hardened sinners back to penance. Halle reports that his influence put an end to usury in that city, and that the Jews, who would not yield on this point, had to leave the city. Their report adds that many of their people had joined religious orders. "We are convinced that he could not have obtained such results by mere human means: he was guided by the inward teacher, the Spirit of God." Nuremberg praises the moral renovation of their own city and of many other German cities. Leipzig points to the seventy members of their university who had joined his Order. Many among these were masters, many were esteemed for nobility or wealth or other advantages.

We have also still earlier reports. Shortly after Capistran's departure from Leipzig, the Conventuals of the city, both Dominicans and Franciscans, informed the magistrates of their resolution to join the Reform with all their hearts. Peter Eschenloer, the historian of Breslau, says that Capistran turned the citizens into religious. Legislation likewise shows Capistran's influence. His great patron, William of Thuringia, issued (October 27, 1452) regulations to end the abuses censured by Capistran at Jena. The chief headings are: Sunday observance, gambling, drinking, concubinage, laziness, and usury. The penalties are imprisonment and banishment. Criminals are granted a three days' delay for reception of the sacraments, with opportunity for confession at the place of execution. Similar regulations were made at Ratisbon.

The city council of Leipzig (December 20, 1452) forbade also the wearing of pointed shoes. This edict seems to be the first in a long line of regulations, in Saxony and elsewhere, against intolerable extravagances in dress, indulged in particularly by men. Another decree (1454) checks the extravagance prevailing at family feasts, and forbids games for money. Even as late as 1463 the influence of Capistran's sermons can clearly be traced in the dress regulations at Leipzig. In opposition to usury also Leipzig remained the docile pupil of Capistran. The University there multiplied copies of his tract De cupiditate, which contains the essentials of his doctrine. Usury was henceforth the favorite theme of the jurists. The perennial interest, shown by numerous manuscripts, which the University of Leipzig manifested in this and cognate questions originated most likely in the impetus given by Capistran.

A book written about fifty years later offers valuable testimony. A Leipzig jurist, Dr. Christopher Kuppener (1511), wrote in Latin and German a profound treatise on usury. Kuppener says he was led to this work, not for merely academic reasons, but chiefly to aid confessors and business men. If we recall that Leipzig was then well on the way to become a world market, this remark of Kuppener is significant. These business men, he adds, prefer the salvation of their souls to temporal and earthly gain.

These facts must be considered in reducing to proper balance the generalized complaints we hear of Capistran's lack of success. Thus, soon after Capistran's death, we hear a chronicler complain: "How often and how loud did he cry while he lived! How energetically he urged us to be faithful to God! But the holy man could not reach what he aimed at." And Albert Krantz, dean of the Hamburg cathedral, himself a Catholic reformer, who died in the first year of the German Reformation, closes his history of Saxony with these words on Capistran: "He was an extraordinary man; but what he effected did not endure. Only too soon did the old wretched conditions return, in the cities and in the country." Still we would be wrong if we compared his influence to a straw-fire, since we find his memory alive even in places where he passed but a few days. The city of Kamenz, where he spent only four days, says that his memory there will never be forgotten. Such reports are numerous.

In summing up the merits of Capistran's forty years of apostolic activity, we must assign first place to his work as leader of the Observance. His work in this field was lasting on both sides of the Alps. And the Observant movement, we must remember, was carried on in the name of the papacy and in favor of the whole Church. Capistran went to central Europe, not only as a public missioner, but also as a pioneer of a fresh and powerful reform movement in the whole Church, with the Observance furnishing the vanguard. We may even say, looking at the situation in Italy, that Capistran sacrificed the Observance to his love for the Church as a whole. His long absence jeopardized the independence of the Observants in Italy. The Conventuals profited by the absence of their strongest opponent to renew their battle against Observant independence. His brethren kept calling for him, their only hope. He had to choose, and never in his life was choice so difficult. Hungary kept demanding his assistance against the Turks. Calls from Italy were ever more insistent and alarming. Deeper insight into the Italian crisis will help us to surmise how great was Capistran's personal sacrifice when he chose to dedicate the rest of his life to the task of defending the Cross against the Crescent.

CHAPTER XXXIV

At the Diet of Frankfort

MAY 29, 1453, the day on which Constantinople fell to the Turks, was a fateful day in the history of the West. The Turks had indeed, a century before, entered Europe, and had subdued the greater part of the Balkan peninsula. But as long as Constantinople, the strongest fortress of the world, remained unconquered, Turkish dominion in Europe was not secure. Now the fall of the Greek Empire sealed for centuries the destiny of southeastern Europe. Christendom realized that the loss of Constantinople was not merely the loss of another fortified city. When on July 8 Robert of Lecce, in a sermon at Rome, announced this catastrophe to the people, they broke out in loud wailing.

When Capistran, in Cracow, learned the terrible news, he at once announced his intention to preach a crusade against the Turks. At the wedding feast of the Polish King (February 10, 1454) he urged the King and the guests to take the cross. But prospects for a crusade were not promising. Pope Nicholas V did indeed contemplate comprehensive measures. His bull against the Turks (September 30, 1453) endeavored to rekindle enthusiasm in the West. Christian powers are admonished to keep peace, and the obdurate are threatened with the ban. This was aimed chiefly at the Italian states, which were lacerating one another like dogs. Milan was at war with Venice, Genoa with Naples. With great difficulty the feuds were ended, and for a few years Italy enjoyed profound peace. But the forces thus released did not advance the crusade movement. Since in the first months after the fall of Constantinople no further undertakings by the Turks were reported, the first scare soon evaporated. Italy wished to enjoy her long-desired rest, and was loath to rearm. "Italy is taking her vacation," so writes John Dlugosz to Capistran in Breslau. And Cardinal Sbignev writes repeatedly to Capistran that for the present he sees no hope that the Christian states will fight against the Crescent. Venice and Genoa have even concluded peace with the Turks. Hungary wants peace, not war.

Capistran's own efforts showed the correctness of the Cardinal's view. From Breslau he sent the papal bull to King Ladislaus in Prague for publication. But the Bohemian government had something more important in hand. They were preparing for war against Saxony. The King's councilors delayed the publication of the bull. Capistran urged them not to sacrifice matters of faith to secular aims. But the old enthusiasm for the crusades was dead. Emperor Frederick III did issue an invitation for a great assembly, to meet on St. George's Day (April 23, 1454) at Ratisbon. But the Emperor himself did not go personally. Of non-German princes only Duke Philip of Burgundy appeared. The Pope and Savoy sent representatives. Of the numerous German princes, only Albrecht of Brandenburg and Louis of Bavaria appeared. Ladislaus of Bohemia-Hungary did not even send a delegate.

Cardinal Cusa and Enea Silvio, the representatives of the Emperor, worked in vain. The Germans busied themselves with their grievances against the Emperor. They pretended that the impending war of Poland against Prussia prevented any crusade against the Turks. Cardinal Cusa promptly wrote to Capistran, who he supposed was still in Poland, to prevent bloodshed between Poland and Prussia. If the Prussian difficulties could be settled, Poland might be counted on for the crusade, for that country was a powerful kingdom under a young and enterprising ruler. Cardinal Sbignev outlined a far-reaching plan. Poland could easily bring up an army of 200,000 men, but efforts should be made first of all to employ the Tartars, the archenemies of the Turks. After the infidel dogs have torn each other to pieces, the Polish King, with fresh and vigorous troops, would fall on the weary Turks and annihilate them. To make this plan feasible, the Pope should arrange peace between Poland and Prussia and should assist the King financially, to gain the Tartars for an attack on the Turks. Sbignev imagined the peace with Prussia as entirely favorable to Poland. Patriotic enthusiasm had drowned all scruples against the annexation of Prussia.

The only result of the Diet of Ratisbon was the calling of a second diet, to meet on St. Michael's Day (September 29) at Nuremberg, if the Emperor came personally, otherwise at Frankfort-on-Main. Enea Silvio, as we have seen, invited Capistran to the diet. Capistran looked upon this invitation as expressing the Pope's will. But the decision to leave Olmütz, where a new movement of conversions was setting in, was indeed a hard one.

As he could not pass through Prague, he went through Austria to Bavaria. Arrived at Munich, he wrote to King Ladislaus, admonishing him to send delegates to Frankfort, saying that the success of the diet depends chiefly on the mood of the Hungarians, who are the first to be threatened by the Turks. Capistran cannot comprehend how Ladislaus is now contemplating a war with Saxony. Does the King not know his own precarious situation? The good will of his neighbor nations is indispensable. His immediate advisers, since they do not keep faith with God, will still less keep faith with the King. They wish to involve the young monarch with their own enemies, either to drive him out of the kingdom or to get him so thoroughly into their own power that he will be their subject rather than their ruler. Already they hold all the fortified places, all the cities, even the Catholic cities, which formerly they could not get even by force of arms. Let the King set out to visit his hereditary lands, especially Hungary, before it is too late. Otherwise, instead of winning Bohemia, he may lose everything, not only Bohemia but also Austria, Moravia, and Hungary.

Capistran's journey, rapid though it was, suffered interruptions. The imperial city of Augsburg held him six days. Arriving on September 18, he was conducted to the cathedral of St. Ulrich. Here, as he knelt before the tabernacle, the diocesan clergy, the Benedictines, and the friars sang a number of hymns. Then Capistran embraced them and gave them the kiss of peace. Two of the city fathers with a group of soldiers were his constant escort, that people might not crush him to death. He preached in the open, before the bishop's palace, where his platform was decorated with silk hangings and relics of saints. In the afternoon he visited the sick. Among the three or four hundred who daily awaited him, those who had firm confidence, says Frank, the Benedictine chronicler, were by God's grace cured. He adds that thousands could witness that Capistran cured many of them.

Capistran's average audience at Augsburg was about 20,000, a number, says Capistran, which rivaled that of his audience in Breslau. In this Augsburg crowd history calls attention to a boy, then ten years old, who later on painted from memory a famous picture of the preacher. His name was Thomas Burgkmair, father of the still more famous Hans Burgkmair. The preacher is represented standing composedly in the pulpit, his long fingers grasping the rail of the platform. Energetically closed lips betray the man of action. His steady gaze rests upon the surging multitude, as if watching the results of his words which the interpreter is translating into German. Sunday, September 22, saw an immense bonfire of vanities. The next morning, after saying Mass in the open, he blessed the people once more, and rode away, leaving great weeping and lamenting behind him. Hurrying on, he barely paused at Dillingen and Nördlingen, and in the last days of September reached Frankfort. He was very weary, but began at once a month of preaching. On weekdays he preached in St. Bartholomew's, on Sundays on the Roman mount, where the people were accustomed to do homage to a new emperor. To avoid disorder the gates of the city were closed. Invalids came in such enormous numbers that the perplexed authorities consulted Capistran about their accommodation.

Capistran was now expected to re-enact the part of St. Bernard of Clairvaux, who just three hundred years before, in the neighboring city of Spires, had fired the reluctant Germans on to the crusade. But the days of St. Bernard had passed. The Diet of Frankfort was indeed better attended than that of Ratisbon. Four German princes had arrived: the elector of Mainz, the elector of Trier, Albrecht of Brandenburg, and the margrave of Baden. The Emperor was represented by Enea Silvio and the Bishop of Gurk, the Pope by a bishop, John Castiglione of Padua.

That Philip of Burgundy did not come, was a great

disappointment to Capistran, who placed his chief hope on this man. He was the son of John of Burgundy, who in the battle of Nicopolis (1396) fell into Turkish captivity. Philip from that time on dreamed of reconquering the Holy Sepulcher and never forgot that Burgundy was the birthplace of the crusades. Two years before he had sent delegations to invite Poland and Aragon to join him in regaining the Holy Land. Capistran strengthened this holy enthusiasm in the soul of the Burgundian. When Philip was at war with the rebellious city of Ghent, and was just prepared for its entire destruction, Capistran had intervened, probably by request of the threatened city. Philip, writes Capistran, must keep his sword strong and sharp for the war against the infidels. The prince who will free the sepulcher of Christ must remember what souls redeemed by Christ's glorious blood will suffer by war. "I will suffer with them. You have conquered others; now conquer yourself. Think of Christ's mercy. He died for His enemies. There is no greater honor than that of forgiving."

Capistran's hopes were strengthened by Philip's personal presence at the Diet of Ratisbon in the previous year. How sorely he missed him now in Frankfort! He wrote again to the Burgundian. The crusade will depend on him. He has been chosen by divine providence to save Christendom. From the diet itself he expects nothing.

In this last view Capistran was right. The public meetings heard much talking about the crusade, but the real planning was in secret, and was directed against the Emperor. Capistran thundered from the pulpit, but in vain. In vain did he assure them that he and all his confreres would go with them against the Turks. The diet replied with complaints against the Pope, complaints that were then common, and echoed even by Enea Silvio. Capistran defended the Pope and read publicly the bull against the Turks. This step, so he reported to the Pope, made a deep impression. But he himself in this same report complains of the negligence now prevailing in Rome. For example, the sending of a mere bishop as papal legate had made a bad impression. Rome did not seem to care much about the whole matter. He himself could have attained far different results if he had received from Rome a definite commission. Even of the crusade bull he possessed a mere copy. He had not received an original document with an official seal. Reports are common that the treasure of St. Peter is being squandered on costly buildings. To that accusation he has difficulty in finding an answer. That Pope Nicholas V was by this time incapacitated, broken in body and spirit, and that therefore even important affairs at the Curia were at a standstill, was a situation not known in far-off countries.

Capistran felt that the Turkish situation was dangerous. The Cardinal of Cracow wrote that the Turks had broken into Serbia with 40,000 men and were preparing to attack Belgrade, and then to advance along the Danube. That Italy was threatened had already been reported to Rome by Cardinal Isidore, who escaped from Constantinople. Hungary alone seemed to be the only hope for the moment. But the Hungarian ambassadors told Capistran that, unless the German Empire assisted them energetically, they would have to sign a pact of peace with the Turks. They would need at least 70,000 foot soldiers. The 12,000 cavalry and 30,000 infantry which the diet had granted them were insufficient. Further, the details had been postponed to the next diet, which was to be held on Candlemas Day (February 2, 1455) at the Emperor's court in Wiener-Neustadt. Any effective help from Germany could not be expected before August. This prospect filled Capistran with grief. "Many talk as if this diet had done great things. I think that very little, next to nothing, has been done." Thus he wrote to the Pope. "If Hungary makes peace with the sultan, woe to thee, Italy, woe to thee, Rome!" Let the Pope do his utmost to have German troops in Hungary by May at the latest.

Before the diet ended, Capistran arranged to go from Frankfort directly to Hungary. He writes to the Pope: "Tomorrow I leave here, and go to the Emperor. From there I go directly to Hungary, to prevent hasty agreement with the Turks." From this resolution nothing deterred him. Henry VI of England invited him to come from Frankfort to England. Capistran replied that he could not come now. Henry, the last of the house of Lancaster, was pining away, and evidently expected to be cured by the wonder-worker.

Capistran reminded him of the blessings of the Cross, telling him that his sickness is a gift of God. "Should I mourn over a sentence which God has decreed?" He closes with an urgent plea that the King mobilize his whole power against the Turks. He alone would suffice to beat them. This sounds like a compliment. England was exhausted from long war with France, and stood now at the outbreak of a civil war, which would last thirty years. Pope Nicholas V tried in vain to preserve peace in the island kingdom.

Capistran also refused all urgings to return to Italy and felt he would never see Italy again. He wrote to ask for two confreres from his homeland in the Abruzzi. These two were Ambrose of Aquila and John of Tagliacozzo. He hoped these two might close his eyes to this world, and bring his books and documents back to Capistrano. The two came to him in Frankfort and with them the lay brother, Philip of Massa, to report on conditions in Italy.

We must now say a word about these conditions. Mozzanica, the new general of the Conventuals, answered Capistran's congratulations with an obliging letter, ending with a request to urge the Observants to harmony, obedience, and brotherly love. But Mozzanica's real intentions were revealed when he refused to confirm the new vicar-general of the ultramontane Observants, John Quiesdeber. The general pretended he must first confer with the Pope. But Quiesdeber, on the basis of the regulations provided by Pope Eugene IV, considered himself confirmed. Still he applied promptly to Capistran for assistance, since he feared the new general wanted to take away from them, step for step, all the advantages Capistran had obtained for the Observants. This appeal from France shows that Capistran is the shield of the Observance everywhere. From Rome, at the same time, he received a touching proof of veneration. The Roman Observant province, at its Pentecost chapter, addressed him officially as the "source of our renovation." The letter was written by the aged Father James of Rieti. They do not ask him to return. They will go with him to battle. They place their province at his disposal: all the brothers, all their convents, their life, their strength. Humbly and uncomplainingly they will obey him and go wherever he sends.

Regarding the liberty of choosing between Conventuals and Observants, Pope Nicholas tried to console the vicar-general, Mark of Bologna. "If they do not wish to behave, let them go." But the question was whether even well-disposed brothers would be able to resist the allurements for any length of time. With surprising frequency Conventuals now visited Observant convents. Even Mozzanica did so. As an inducement to join the Conventuals, uneducated lay persons were promoted to orders. Young fathers were promoted to high positions as preachers. Even brothers guilty of misdemeanors could count on a good reception, and even an office in the Order. The foremost adversary of the Observance was still Robert of Lecce, now at the height of fame in the papal curia. At the fall of Constantinople he had, in grandiloquent terms, placed himself and his companions at the Pope's disposal. The Pope let the vicar-general plainly understand that Robert stood high in favor, and thus the superiors had simply to be silent.

Cardinal Capranica, the protector of the Order, was no longer a support. Observants were shown the door and told not to come again. Even Capistran had fallen into disfavor. "Fables," said the Cardinal, on hearing the reports about miraculous cures. We understand, of course, that these endless quarrels grated on the nerves of the cardinals. But where did the fault lie? Pope Eugene IV had clearly regulated relations between the two branches of the Order. Why had the question been reopened?

Nevertheless the cismontane vicar-general, Mark of Bologna, was optimistic. But Capistran thought otherwise and reproached the vicar-general on his rosy views. Why does the vicar-general so seldom approach the Curia? And to Cardinal Latino Orsini, a sincere friend and patron of the Observance, Capistran writes that the Conventuals are seeking to extirpate the very name of the Observance. He encloses a report to the Pope, in which he complains that, after repeated messages, he had not been deemed worthy of answer. "God be praised for all this. I know that I do not seek my own honor. I seek God's honor and the salvation of souls, that are entrusted to Your Holiness. Those who seek their own honor find easier hearing." He reminds the Pope of two of his predecessors of the same name, Nicholas III and Nicholas IV, whose benevolence and favors to the Order the fifth Nicholas should not diminish but rather increase.

His letter to the cardinal protector, Capranica, is a masterpiece. He confesses first his long silence, the chief reason being the pain he has felt, and still feels, at the severe treatment accorded to his confreres. Then he defends his religious family in the strongest terms. The Observance is a work of the Holy Ghost. Why is the Cardinal an opponent rather than protector of these 20,000 zealous brethren? He will remain devoted to the prince of the Church in life and in death. But that the Cardinal ridicules miraculous cures, this he can hardly believe. In times past he and the Cardinal have had frequent intimate conversations on life, death, and eternity. Now the reality is at hand. We must meet the Turks. Let us then no longer worry these poor servants of Christ, who wish only to keep their vows. Let them be protected in their holy rights.

Referring to Capranica's taunt that he had not dared to enter Prague he concludes: "My Roman masters, when the Grand Turk visits you, he will have new hats and mantles for you. Alleluia, alleluia! I am hurrying on to Hungary, to martyrdom. I invite you all to come and give me an example. I will follow you at least from afar. You blame me for not going to Prague. If you still think I ought to tempt God, though escorts were refused me almost a hundred times, then I will still go there. I offer you eternal thanks for everything."

These letters were, objectively, in some degree unjust. Of many facts Capistran was ignorant. First of all, he did not know the difficulty of approaching the Pope. Sad incidents had made the sickly Pope so gloomy that even cardinals could not easily obtain audience. The vicar-general was urged on all sides to undertake no further steps concerning the bulls of Eugene IV. Capistran's reports did not reach the Pope at all, and no cardinal spoke a word to the Pope about what Capistran had written. Thus the vicar now wrote to Capistran, adding that the recommendations sent by princes and prelates had no effect whatever. Perhaps the situation would change if letters came from the Emperor and from kings.

Mark is hurt by Capistran's mistrust, which he blames on Brother Philip of Massa, who had seriously angered the Pope by saying to a bishop that the Observants, if forced to subjection under the Conventuals, would appeal to the Council of Constance. Only with difficulty had the Pope been quieted. Philip remained under stigma. But Capistran, misled by the brother's zeal, had let him receive holy orders. The Italian brethren had been shocked. They now consider fortunate the fact that the sick Pope knew nothing of Capistran's letters from Frankfort. "Woe to him," said the brethren, "if the Pope hears that he has let himself be counseled by Brother Philip." The vicar-general clung to his view that the Conventuals had failed, and that the bulls of Eugene IV were still in force. Those who were going over to the other branch were people who deserved to be dismissed, not only from the Observance, but from the Order altogether. When these consoling explanations came, Capistran was far away from Frankfort.

Deep sorrow for his confreres led Capistran, on his way back to Austria, to recommend them to prominent and influential protectors, who during the following months sent to Rome earnest representations in favor of the Observance. These petitions show that the success of the Franciscan reform is essential to the public welfare. Emperor Frederick III sent three letters. Enea Silvio sent a personal appeal to Cardinal Capranica. Having expressed his veneration for St. Bernardine, he continues: "I simply must assist this holy family. Sinner though I am, I love these men of clean and chaste life. Just as in battle the fainthearted find support in the brave, so too in the ship of Peter. The wise and determined are the salvation of the cowardly and neglectful." And now his humanist pen sketches a splendid picture of the Observants. They are the beaming light upon the mountain. They carry on the work of the Gospel. He does not like to see Observants pass over to the Conventuals. "The road which leads to perdition must be closed. Open the door which leads to life. The Conventuals are still numerous, but their convents are decaying while those of the Observants increase and flourish. Princes listen to them. Bishops and prelates are favorable. They do not infringe parochial rights.

They are not burdens to the secular priests, but supporters, while the Conventuals solicit contributions or quarrel about burial rights. Hence the people like the Observants better than the Conventuals. On the difference in their mode of life I prefer to remain silent. The Pope will do well to favor this strong army of 20,000 men. Brother John is a man of God. To the people of these German states he is a prophet. He would but need to crook a finger if he wished to unloose a storm. But you need not fear. He will not become faithless." Capistran's dedication to the common cause of Christendom should have been an example for princes and rulers. He refused even his old friend, the former Bishop of Gurk, John Schallermann who begged him to give at least one month to his oppressed brethren in Italy. At the close of the diet he set out at once for Hungary. But the fears of the ambassadors that his visit would again be delayed were not altogether unfounded. Half a year elapsed before he finally crossed the borders of Hungary.

CHAPTER XXXV

Nuremberg and Wiener-Neustadt

ALL SAINTS DAY finds him in Aschaffenburg. Then Würzburg kept him a few days, and from there he went to Nuremberg, to call this valiant imperial city to battle against the Turks. Here he found many students from Leipzig among the novices. Here, too, he passed through a period of uncertainty whether he should continue his journey or not. From Breslau came news that the dispute on the oath of homage had ended: the court at Prague had yielded; Podebrad would come with the King. Here was a dilemma. In Breslau he could at long last meet "his George" and the King, and at the Bohemian court he could work as effectively against the Turks as he could in Hungary. On the other hand, Hungary was greatly in need of his encouraging words. The nation, if forsaken, would settle matters in its own way. Not knowing what to do, as usual in such dilemmas he tried to force a decision by prayer. After the common night prayer he asked his confreres to say three more Our Fathers with outstretched arms. During that night he had a dream which he interpreted as meaning he was soon to die in Hungary without attaining the crown of martyrdom. During Mass the next morning he heard a loud call: "On to Hungary!" The cry was repeated later while he was preaching in the open. That settled the matter.

From Nuremberg he hurried on to Ratisbon, and there on Bavarian soil he learned for the first time what silly reports were afloat. Rumor said that he had been arrested by the Elector of Mainz on charges of instigating the Poles against Prussia. Only papal intervention had set him free. To quiet the people he condemned this gossip from the pulpit. The Elector had treated him with the greatest generosity and liberality. Then, with twenty-eight companions and several horses, he embarked on the Danube. But in Passau he had to pause for a week. Late in December, after a toilsome and dangerous voyage, he reached Vienna, having suffered much from the cold.

Should he go on at once to the court of the Emperor in Wiener-Neustadt? Enea Silvio urged him to remain for the present in Vienna. The royal family, especially the Empress, would, of course, give him honorable reception at any time. But to make himself useful at Wiener-Neustadt he would have to wait till the princes arrived for the diet, then he would have to do a great work. The edifice erected in Frankfort was tumbling. Three beasts were endangering all Christendom: effeminate life, ambition, and greed. The princes are selfish, proud, and indifferent; none will obey the other, none will undertake any hardship. They will let public welfare go to ruin rather than leave their castles in bad weather. To save mankind they would not abstain a single day from their accustomed pleasures. Look at the Venetian pact with the Turks. Silvio writes: "All Christendom could be bought for a price; everybody obeys Turkish money. Unless we change our lives we shall perish. Capistran has for thirty years been fighting these three monsters successfully, in Italy, in France, in Germany. If he succeeds now in Neustadt we need not fear the Turks."

Of the almost three months Capistran waited in Vienna, we have few records and no extracts of sermons. The book of miracles records only two cures. Capistran's appearance was no longer a sensation. The curiosity of the people was satisfied. This same phenomenon was noted also in Munich, Augsburg, Eichstätt, and Frankfort. But his activity was by no means unfruitful in Vienna. He developed the Austro-Bohemian vicariate of the Observance. To the ten convents already existing he now added Warsaw in Poland and Maria Enzersdorf in Lower Austria. Further settlements were planned. Emperor Frederick III intended to give the cloister at Judenburg in Styria to the Observants, and Jamnitz in Moravia was another prospect. In Lower Austria, Capistran received an offer of three places at once: one between Krems and Stein, one at Langenlois, and one at St. Pölten. The people and the secular princes asked for Observant convents, while the clergy, secular and religious, objected. The opposition was chiefly economic, on the ground that existing cloisters and churches might suffer harm. Capistran usually retreated in such cases. Thus he advised the brothers at Maria Enzersdorf to leave that place again when he learned that the pastor of Mödling was opposed. But the founder, the powerful Ulrich of Cilli, promised to remove all difficulties. At St. Pölten protest came from the prior of the Augustinians and from the Bishop of Passau. Capistran dropped the plan and admonished his benefactors at St. Pölten to do likewise.

Nor were internal difficulties lacking. Capistran's heart was delighted by the brothers in Vienna, whom he calls angels. But in the Polish and the Silesian convents some were dissatisfied, saying that certain practices of piety and penance customary in the Observance were arbitrary, not demanded by the Rule. To those dangerous propagandists Capistran wrote two energetic circulars. These prayers and acts of mortification had always been in practice. Let them look at St. Francis and his first brethren. "Where are today the penitential shirts which those men wore upon their bare bodies, emaciated by fasting? Where are those frequent fasts on bread and water? Where the uninterrupted prayer? Where the frequent night watches? Where the scourgings? Which of you kisses the wounds of lepers? Who finds it his greatest pleasure to be despised? Who crosses land and sea to share the martyrdom of our Lord? I cannot go on when I think of all this. Why can we not go back to their manner of living? If our frailty does not permit, let us at least keep near their footsteps. With this intention did our Italian fathers add that little amount of watching, fasting, scourging, and other self-denials. What graces of God have thus been drawn down on us!" Lastly, he traces this spirit of dissatisfaction to Brother Peter of Ödenburg, his own earlier companion, a baptized Jew and former Conventual, whom he had left in Cracow. This fatherly admonition was well received in Cracow. The guardian wrote back in May: "We are in good health, thanks be to God, and live in brotherly harmony and continual prayer."

The Conventual mode of living was, nevertheless, a perpetual temptation for less zealous brothers. And some less qualified candidates had found admission. Four years had seen the birth and growth of a new province of more than 500 members, the strongest cloisters being those of Vienna, Breslau, and Cracow. But these numbers soon diminished. After Capistran's departure Cracow, for example, in May, 1455, had twenty priests, fourteen lay brothers, and forty clerics, but only four novices.

Capistran never lost sight of the progress of the Observance in Italy. The memorial church of St. Bernardine in Aquila remained his chief concern. By 1454 the project was at a standstill. The Conventuals wanted simply a side chapel, annexed to their own church of St. Francis. Finally the government of Aquila also dropped the plan of building a new church. This report reached Capistran in Cracow. He wrote to the magistrates of Aquila that they had pierced his heart. Contrary to his custom, he wrote in Italian, in the plain blunt style of the Abruzzi, a heart-to-heart talk which the rulers of the proud city of Aquila would not endure from anyone except "poor old John of Capistrano." He sees himself exposed before the whole world. Deceived by their repeated promises, he had spoken everywhere about the grand edifice which Aquila was erecting. In the short time of three years he had founded fourteen new cloisters, eight of them dedicated to St. Bernardine. "And now the illustrious government of Aquila will build him a mere chapel." Verona had built a Bernardine convent, one of the finest in Italy. Padua, with two Franciscan cloisters, had built a third one to honor Bernardine. But Aquila says: Just a chapel. "Shame on them. The thing stinks throughout Italy. All countries surpass you, even such as Bernardine never visited. The whole world builds him convents and churches. But Aquila, which possesses his body, thinks him unworthy of a church. O damnable ingratitude! All the waters of the Danube and the Po will not wash away that stigma. Nay, judgment will fall on them. Bernardine made your city prosperous. Are you challenging God, to let your faces grow lean again?" As to finances let them not be afraid. The King of Naples had already given 5,000 ducats. "Your city will grow in fame. The chief ornaments of a city are beautiful churches and cloisters." Here again Capistran was prophetic. St. Bernardine's Church in Aquila became the boast of the Abruzzi.

In July, 1454, when James of the Marches came to Aquila and

read Capistran's letter to the people, they broke into loud weeping. On July 28 James blessed the cornerstone. The people's devotion and enthusiasm, he wrote to Capistran, would challenge the eloquence of Cicero and Homer. Criticism, however, still lamented the immense proportions of the new church.

But the Turkish war was now Capistran's dominant idea. Three years before he had urged the students of Vienna to the religious life. Now he aroused them against the external enemy. Hundreds took the cross from his hands and pledged themselves to go to Hungary. His letters and messengers went out in all directions, even into his native land, into the Abruzzi. The feudal lord of Celano, Count Leonello Acclozemora, enraptured by his reports, wished to fight at his side against the Turks. But he needed the consent of his lord, the King of Naples. Capistran wrote at once to King Alfonso, urging the God-given opportunity to gain an immortal name.

Reports from Hungary were serious. Hunyadi had indeed undertaken several successful incursions into the Ottoman borders, and had stormed and burned the strong fortress of Widdin on the Danube. But in a long report to the Emperor he insisted that Hungary was unable alone to continue the struggle. The Sultan was concentrating strong forces near Sofia, and cavalry was raiding southern Hungary. Serbia's help depended on further development of her strongholds, chiefly Belgrade.

In Neustadt things dragged on. Ambassadors spent their time at the watering places, awaiting the arrival of the Emperor. Thus wrote Enea Silvio, who added: "In Italy all is silence and neglect. We do not even have an answer to our letter from Frankfort." To Capistran's urgent question Enea again answered that Capistran would be heartily welcome at any time. But both the Emperor and the Elector of Trier felt that participants were still too few, and Capistran had better wait until Podebrad came. Toward the end of February, Podebrad did come to Vienna. Whether the two old opponents, Capistran and Podebrad, ever met personally, either in Vienna or in Neustadt, is an unanswered question. But Capistran now learned with deepest sorrow that the Bohemian lords were still set on promoting the elevation of Rokytzana to the see of Prague. This concession alone would fully reconcile the Utraquists with the Church.

At length, about the middle of March, the diet opened. It failed even more pitifully than the one at Frankfort. The German imperial estates were meagerly represented, and those present had little interest in the crusade. Order in Germany, they told the Hungarians, must come first. Again they demanded reforms from the Emperor. Podebrad, to Capistran's great satisfaction, offered to the crusade the whole power of Bohemia. But he added an ominous proviso: Bohemia must be guaranteed peace with her neighbors. This proviso was pointed against Saxony. In vain Enea Silvio, Vitez of Hungary, and Capistran urged the assembly to forget all else but the great common crisis of Christendom. Instead the delegates trifled. Much valuable time was lost in questions of precedence, before the members could even be seated. News of the death of Nicholas IV (March 24) came almost as a release from an unbearable situation. With an agreement to meet again the following year and to be ready for war by the feast of the Ascension, the contemptible congress dispersed.

This fiasco did not dampen Capistran's ardor for the crusade. While his friend, Enea Silvio, homesick for the sunny south, was counting the days he must still spend among the barbarians, Capistran longed for his journey toward suffering and death. But his journey to Hungary was somewhat roundabout. Emperor Frederick had offered him the almost depopulated cloister of the Conventuals at Judenburg in Styria. So Capistran went for a few days back to Vienna, leaving there at the end of April, with a feeling that he would never again see these confreres here on earth. He could not hide his emotion. After morning prayers he gave the great community of St. Theobald his last admonitions, urging discipline and warning against innovators. He spoke till daybreak. Then, dissolved in tears, he kissed each brother farewell.

PART VI
UNDER CALLISTUS III
(1455–58)

CHAPTER XXXVI

Capistran in Hungary

FROM Judenburg he wrote a long letter to the new Pope, the aged Spanish cardinal, Alfonso Borgia, now Callistus III. Borgia, long a friend and patron of Capistran, was an excellent canonist, but also a man of simple, pious character. In an audience granted to Father James of Rieti, he spoke most kindly of Capistran, saying he was a saint and martyr, who fought incessantly for the faith. Capistran, he said, like St. Vincent Ferrer, "has always desired to see me in this position." Borgia had always believed in St. Vincent's prediction, and had often referred to it in confidential conversation. Capistran, reminding the Pope of the exact day and place they had spoken of the matter, said he had been so impressed that he resolved not to write to the Cardinal again until he could address him as the anointed of the Lord. Hence the first sentence of his letter: "I lay my pen aside, and in veneration of Your Holiness, in the presence of three brothers, I kiss the ground."

The letter, of course, deals with the Turkish war. His tone is sincere, familiar, and confident. The Pope must open his treasures, spiritual and temporal. Grand buildings and churches are good, but the poor are still more precious. The gold and silver of St. Peter's, St. Paul's, and the Lateran, would better be sacrificed to the crusade than robbed by invading Turks. He urges three particular measures. First, since the Germans will do nothing until next summer, let the Pope, in love for the many Christians who will meanwhile fall into the hands of the Turks, spur on the King of Naples to join the crusade. Secondly, let the Pope reissue the crusade bull of his predecessor. Thirdly, let the Pope send everywhere as preachers of the Cross men who were absolutely unselfish, men who despised money.

Callistus was already doing what Capistran urged. His special mission, he said, entrusted to him by divine providence, was to be the protector and champion of Christendom against Islam. He published the crusade bull on May 15, 1455. To all Christian countries he sent legates and preachers to re-establish harmony among Christian rulers and bring them to a united front against the Crescent. The Pope at first intended to call Capistran back from the north. But at the last moment, advised by Capranica, he gave up the idea since, so he wrote to Capistran, he would have to send him back again where he already was.

The Italian Observants also labored to bring Capistran home, intending to elect him vicar-general at the general chapter in Bologna. Mark, the outgoing vicar-general, sent him peremptory orders to be present at the Bologna chapter. This order overlooked the fact that Capistran, as general inquisitor, was exempt from the superiors of the Order. Capistran answered in no uncertain terms, and poor Mark wilted. Capistran adds that he would be too late in any event. "I would need the wings of an eagle. Think of the long and difficult roads. Think of my immense baggage in books. Think of the sermons I would have to preach daily simply to get drivers and wagons." But he did send Gabriel of Verona and Nicholas Fara as representatives of the young Austro-Bohemian vicariate.

"Would Capistran accept the election? Would he come if he were elected?" These were the dominant questions on Pentecost Saturday, May 24, when the chapter got ready to vote. Gabriel of Verona said, Yes. Audiences at Capistran's sermons had diminished. Their devotion had been satisfied. The Hungarians had seen him already in Vienna, and would not be so enthusiastic about him as the Germans. But Gabriel was emphatically contradicted by Nicholas Fara. Capistran, he said, would not come home again except by express command of the Pope himself. Capistran had personally written to Mark in the same sense. Rome reported that the Pope would not consider Capistran's return. So the chapter gave up this hope, and chose for vicar-general Father Baptist Tagliacarne of Levanto, who had been a companion of Capistran. The chapter reconfirmed Capistran in his privileges and sent him two brothers. The rise of a flourishing Observant vicariate north of the Alps was joyfully welcomed by the chapter. But the good fathers still expressed doubts whether northern barbarians would remain true to the spirit of the Observance.

On the other hand Nicholas Fara, in his report to Capistran, complained of a certain narrow-mindedness in the Italians. The provincial vicar of the Abruzzi, who had been the most obstinate in working for Capistran's re-election, was guided by one narrow desire, to have the great preacher in Aquila and thus ensure the erection of St. Bernardine's Church in that city. Thus they sacrificed great problems to small ones. Still Fara's reports are in general very consoling. The election was marked by perfect unanimity. The electors were willing to obey even a lay brother. Efficient young preachers were coming forth, among them a certain Father Michael, who in power of speech seemed to excel even Robert of Lecce. The brethren were praying he might not follow in Robert's footsteps. History shows these hopes were fulfilled. Michael of Carcano became not merely the greatest preacher of Italy in the second half of the fifteenth century, but also a great light among the Observants, who count him among their blessed. The new vicar-general animated the brethren with joy and trust. He was a simple, apostolic man, who kindled enthusiasm. The new Pope was kindly disposed; even Capranica was now friendly. Callistus III had asked the Observants for six preachers. These they had granted, Capistran being the first. The self-sacrificing appeal of the aged Pope made the deepest impression upon the brothers. Fired by the eloquence of Mark of Bologna, the brethren rose up in a body, crossed their arms on their breasts, and declared with tears their readiness to go to death with the Pope.

The chapter was mistaken in thinking that Pope Callistus III stood on their side against the Conventuals. When Tagliacarne came to Rome he found that a new storm against the Observance was approaching. The minister general, Mozzanica, far from confirming the election of Tagliacarne, was determined rather to use this opportunity to annul with one stroke the independence of the Observants. Callistus III, though he appreciated men like Capistran and James of the Marches, had never rid himself entirely of certain prejudices against the reform movement. As cardinal legate in Catalonia he had to deal with the sect founded by Berbegall, a Spanish zealot, who resembled the Fraticelli. On this attitude of the Pope, Mozzanica built his hopes and aimed at obtaining a formal repeal of Eugene IV's bull of separation. Efforts would be made to prove that the bull of 1446 was surreptitiously obtained. But if the bull were acknowledged as genuine, then the Observants would no longer be children of St. Francis and would have to adopt another name.

The monstrous assertion that Capistran had brought that bull through the papal chancery without the knowledge of the Pope, was treated seriously at the papal court. Even Callistus made the remark that Eugene IV had never seen that bull. Capranica, who was protector of the Order at that time, also declared that he had never heard of the bull.[1] The basis of these doubts is unknown. But if the doubts were justified, then certainly nobody could doubt the reasonableness of investigation. But Mozzanica's way of acting does not show him in a good light. The man whom he accused as a forger was far away. He continually told the Observants that they were, one and all, beginning with Capistran, in the state of mortal sin and would all go to hell if they did not make perfect reparation before death. Capistran, he said, had started something worse than a hundred murders. Tagliacarne, not at all intimidated by the roaring lion, defended Capistran's honor. On one occasion, in the presence of Cardinal Capranica, after Mozzanica had repeated his accusations, Tagliacarne uttered a solemn protest, called the Cardinal himself to witness, and threatened to send a full report to Capistran. As Mozzanica would not yield, Tagliacarne carried out his threat.

But, as accusations increased, all the Observants came under suspicion. Their preachers, it was asserted, were giving scandal and were offending prelates. Even their orthodoxy was questioned. Especially their preachers in Germany, a land always under suspicion in Italy, were accused of heresy. The aged Pope,

---

[1] Bernardine of Aquila traces this remark to Capranica's multiplicity of duties, and consequent forgetfulness of details.

preoccupied with the Turkish troubles, was much influenced by these representations. His remarks showed that the cause of the Observance was in serious danger. Even of Capistran he spoke slightingly at times. That he did not immediately proceed to unify the Order was because of the efforts of Father James of the Marches, in whom he had much confidence, and whom alone he admitted to audience on this matter. But the confreres of Father James were not all assured that he would be successful. He was a holy religious, a zealous apostle, an excellent preacher. But he was not an organizer like Capistran. At the last election of a vicar-general he had received but one or two votes. His brethren now feared that, in holy simplicity, he would make too great concessions.

The Observants did indeed gain a small initial success when Callistus III decided that the bull of Eugene IV should, for the time being, remain in force. But the Pope went on to order a general meeting in Assisi for November 1. There the provincials of the Conventuals and the vicars of the Observants were to submit their ideas on the unification of both branches. Mozzanica told Father James that the meeting had been dated so early in order to prevent Capistran from being present. Thus affairs were now just where they had been twenty-five years before, when Martin V called both parties to a general chapter in Assisi. Now, however, the Observants were on the defensive, in spite of twenty-five years of development.

Once more the Observants urged Capistran to return. Tagliacarne sent couriers to him with most pleading petitions: "We implore you with bare heads and on bended knees. Come back to your orphaned brethren. They will die unless their one and only physician comes to their rescue."

These appeals for help reached Capistran at the borders of Transylvania. The decision was now still harder. But much as he loved his religious family, the general interest and welfare of the Church were predominant. Besides, he could not reach Assisi by November 1. So once more he took up his pen. It was nerve racking to see the fruits of a thirty-years' struggle for the existence of a reform suddenly endangered, and to begin the whole work anew.

His long letter deserves a place beside the letters of Bernard of

Clairvaux and Catherine of Siena. With the frankness and zeal of a saint he holds up to the Pope the duties of the papal office. It is his last appeal in favor of the Observance. He sketches its history, and lays bare the fundamental questions. Based on the councils of Constance and Basle, on the decrees of Nicholas V and Eugene IV, "we wish for nothing but to live forever in the observance of the Rule, even unto death and the shedding of blood. If we are forced to give up our claim to the decrees mentioned, then that force is against justice, against the holy councils, against the decrees of the Popes. To me this course appears unthinkable. What will Christian nations say when they hear that the poor servants of Christ, precisely because they wish to keep their vows, are subjected to persecution and suppression from those who should have protected them? Beware, Holy Father, you are putting a weapon into the hand of those princes and superiors, secular and clerical, who are seeking a pretext to withdraw from obedience to holy Church."

Capistran's letter to Capranica is short. Let the Cardinal, if he will, believe all rumors unfavorable to Capistran. Favorable rumors let him consider only in so far as Capistran is the instrument of Christ.

Many other appeals came to Rome in favor of the Observants. The petition sent by the Hungarian congress was very energetic. They do not understand how the Pope can favor the Conventuals as teachers of the Franciscan Rule. The Conventuals, at least in Hungary, do not observe that Rule themselves. The Hungarians will drive all Conventuals from their country rather than permit the Observants to be subjected to them.

These petitions were so numerous, said Capistran, that a donkey would have had to work hard to drag them along. But they were in vain. The Pope, wrote Tagliacarne, did not read them at all. He was fixed in his determination to attain unification of the Order at any price.

To the chapter in Assisi the Pope sent as legate, Blase Ghilinus, the Benedictine abbot of Sant' Ambrogio in Milan. The papal letter, which Abbot Blase read in the presence of both parties, sounded like a lecture for the Observants. Then he dealt with each party separately, his task being to receive their suggestions on the re-establishment of union. Only with difficulty could the Observants persuade him to take a meal with them at the Portiuncula. What he saw there moved him deeply. The extreme poverty of the brothers, their recollected bearing, and their deep spirit of piety brought tears to his eyes. Abbot Blase was an excellent prelate, highly educated, and, though young, widely experienced. His report made an impression on the Pope.

Long and disagreeable negotiations followed. The Conventuals demanded the abrogation of three Observant rights: first, that of special officials, vicars, or procurators; second, that of founding new settlements without the consent of the Conventual superiors; third, that of preaching in places where Conventuals already resided. The Observants, on the other hand, insisted simply on the basis established by the bull of Eugene IV. Their only concession was to grant the general superior a greater influence. Tagliacarne had brought from Assisi six brothers, but they had little influence as negotiators, since the Pope saw no one except Father James. Even the cardinal protector was excluded from the discussions. The Pope did indeed answer Capistran's memorandum from Hungary. But, while praising Capistran's work and granting the authorizations asked for, the Pope referred but slightly to the principal contents of Capistran's letter. Capistran felt that further efforts for the Observance would be useless. One of the six brothers describes their work with these words: "During the deliberations we sit at home in our cell, meditating with folded hands, like women after the death of their husbands."

Desperation led them again to Cardinal Capranica. Greatly pleased, the protector tried to save what could be saved. A compromise was reached. The unification bull (February 2, 1456), which had made the Pope, as he said, "sweat blood," did indeed revoke the bull of separation (1446), but still gave to the Observants a certain degree of independence. They were allowed to have their own vicars. On the other hand this independence was limited in several ways. First, in the election of the general of the whole Order, the Observants could vote, but could not be voted for. Secondly, their own general chapters cannot elect vicars-general. But regarding the right of changing from either branch to the other the bull again approaches the ideals of Eugene IV. More could not be obtained, writes Tagliacarne to Capistran. "You failed us in this hard task. Oh, father, may God forgive you! Never before has your family gone through such trials. We have passed through eight months of martyrdom."

Capistran could no longer busy himself with these questions. The cannons of Mohammed II were obliterating all other sorrows. Higher things were at stake than the privileges of the Observants. Yet these last months of his life were saddened by the uncertain fate of his family. This was the last test of his obedience to the vicar of Christ. His loyalty was equal to any trial, and his family proved worthy of its leader. "As duty demands, we have in all this humbly submitted to the apostolic regulations. We hope we have disposed the Curia and the Protector a little more in our favor." So wrote the vicar-general to Capistran. In reality things were not so bad as they seemed. What the Conventuals had obtained was but a momentary success. The final victory of the reform was but a matter of time.

Judenburg, one of Capistran's last foundations, brought him deep sorrows. When he accepted it he was not aware that Pope Nicholas V had forbidden the Observants to take over Conventual cloisters. He feared he might have incurred censures. But Callistus III, partly out of regard for the Emperor, who had shown great personal interest in the new foundations, subsequently confirmed the new settlement. After a few days in Graz, Capistran turned south again and reached the Hungarian borders, which he crossed about the middle of May. From Oberlimbach he sent his faithful interpreter, Father Frederick, as messenger to Italy. His own next destination was Raab, where in June a Hungarian diet was to deliberate on the Turkish war. On May 24 he passed by Papa, and on May 28 by the famous Benedictine abbey of Martinsberg, reaching Raab a few days later.

Here he found gathered a great number of Hungarian barons and prelates. Fear of the Sultan prevailed. New reports of his immense preparations compelled serious attention. Present at the diet was George Brankovits, the prince of Serbia, a man of eighty years who still preserved a majestic appearance. A ruler endowed with splendid talents, an experienced general, a versatile diplomat, Brankovits ranks as the last great prince of medieval Serbia. Extensive estates in Hungary and Croatia made him one of the richest princes of his time. A second source of his power lay in southern Serbia, where gold mines and silver mines brought him yearly 120,000 ducats. Now on June 1, Novobrdo, the chief mining center, fell into the hands of the Sultan. All the noblemen of the city were executed; 320 young men were made Janizaries; 700 women were handed over to the soldiers.

A courier brought news of this catastrophe to Brankovits in Raab. The barons met that same day. Hunyadi, proposing a comprehensive plan, promised an army of 7,000 men at his own cost. Brankovits promised an equal number. King Ladislaus would have to furnish 20,000 men. Both the Pope and the Duke of Burgundy were expected to do the same, while the King of Naples and the other Italian princes were each to furnish 10,000 men. If he could get pay for these 100,000 soldiers three months in advance, he would be able, said Hunyadi, to drive the Turks out of Europe, to recover Constantinople, and to carry the war into Asia, where the Christian army could be maintained at the expense of the Turks. Possibly even the Holy Land might be regained. He urged that the Pope be asked to send a cardinal legate, who, well supplied financially, would head the crusaders. For this position the Cardinal of Gran would be fitted. Lastly, the King of Naples must simultaneously attack the Turks by sea.

Capistran brought these splendid plans at once to the knowledge of the Pope. Hunyadi's program was by no means so fantastic as it may appear today. The great general knew Turkish conditions, and was always sober in his calculations. Would the Christian powers respond? That was the question. Poland, Germany, England, and France had not yet been included in Hunyadi's plan. How could help be expected from these distant powers if the lands immediately threatened did not grasp the seriousness of the situation? King Ladislaus would prefer to fight against his uncle, Emperor Frederick III, than against the Turks. The responsibility for this most inopportune feud in the house of Hapsburg rests on the counselors of the young King, and chiefly on Ulrich of Cilli, the head of the aspiring family of the counts of Sanok in southern Styria. Cilli disliked Hunyadi and feared him. Behind Hunyadi's back he had invaded Croatia and had since then called himself the Banus of Croatia. He was popularly accused of a secret agreement with the Turks. He associated with Hunyadi's personal enemies, as, for instance, with the Hungarian palatine Ladislaus Gara, and with the voivode of Transylvania, Nicholas of Ilok. He aroused the Saxons in Transylvania against Hunyadi. He filled his royal master with suspicion, alleging that Hunyadi was planning for the crown, even for the life of the King. Finally he lured Hunyadi to come to Vienna to be judged.

Cilli fell into his own trap. Hunyadi captured him and revealed all his plots to the public. The Hungarian nobles, enraged at Cilli's treachery, clung more faithfully than ever to Hunyadi. But the latter still had powerful opponents, among them George Brankovits, Cilli's father-in-law. This Serbian prince, loving his own cause, the quiet possession of his own land, more than the common cause of Christendom, was ready at any time for a favorable agreement with the Turks. Besides, as Capistran learned in Raab, Roman Catholics living in Serbia were oppressed by the government. Capistran's efforts in their behalf were repulsed by the Prince, who was a faithful adherent of the Greek schism. At the same time Brankovits boasted of a bull in which Pope Nicholas called him a faithful son of the Church. Capistran considered it his duty to inform the Pope. From Raab he sent an exact report, ending with the question whether under such circumstances it was any longer advisable to deal with that man.

During the following months Capistran strove to unravel this web of enmity and suspicion, and to bring the leading men of Austria and Hungary to harmonious cooperation. These men held him in high veneration and gladly did him favors, but they were not Italians, who, though hot-blooded, were more easily moved to better ways. These northerners were more persistent in their ill will.

During the first half of July, Capistran set out from Raab for Budapest. On the way he spent a few days with Cardinal Dionysius Szechi in Gran, who would willingly have kept him still longer. But important decisions were waiting in Budapest. Hunyadi resigned all his offices except that of general in southern Hungary. He allied himself with Cilli by allowing his younger son, Matthias, to become engaged to Elizabeth, the daughter of Cilli. Matthias was sent to Vienna, ostensibly as a student, really as a hostage. At the same time Ladislaus, Hunyadi's elder son, married a daughter of the Count Palatine, Ladislaus Gara. After publishing all these arrangements on August 1, Hunyadi returned to Transylvania, Capistran promising to follow him very soon.

Meanwhile Capistran preached in western Hungary. The fear that the Hungarians would be slower than the Germans in coming to hear him proved unfounded. People flocked to him from far and near, quite as if a great jubilee indulgence had been announced. In Stuhlweissenburg, for instance, he preached for at least a whole week to immense crowds.

In the meantime, too, the Hungarian estates continued to deliberate at Budapest. But no military preparations were made. A poor harvest made them hesitate. Besides, the southern Turkish invasion had brought in a pestilence which was now entering Transylvania and Hungary. And since Brankovits had succeeded in getting the Turks to leave Serbia, no attack was feared during the current year.

CHAPTER XXXVII

Capistran in Transylvania

HUNYADI'S invitation to preach in Transylvania led Capistran to hope for a rich harvest among the numerous schismatics who lived on the estates of the Catholic lords. By way of Szegedin, Capistran went to Csanad, where he remained a few days during the second half of September. That territory had been twice visited by Turkish cohorts, and the traces of their presence could be seen everywhere. Here Capistran received renewed calls for help from his afflicted confreres in Italy, but all he could do was to encourage them by letters. The exhausted old man must have suffered fearfully. In his letter to Callistus III he speaks of mystical tortures of soul. The news from Rome had stabbed his heart like a dagger. He speaks of these mysterious experiences also in a letter to Cardinal Capranica. In the pulpit at Csanad, during the pause filled by the interpreter who repeated his address, Capistran had had a terrifying vision. He saw great battles in the sky: sun, moon, and stars at war. The moon and the stars rushed on the sun and overcame it. Then he heard a voice: "Sun is subdued by the moon; God's judgments are a deep abyss." And again he heard a voice: "God's judgments are inscrutable; deep calls unto deep." Again he pondered, then heard the final sentence: "The higher must serve the lower; the end is near."

In Stuhlweissenburg three weeks earlier he had seen streams coming from the four ends of heaven. These streams plunged into the sea, then recoiled, seeming to drag the whole ocean with them. The western stream remained victorious in this struggle. These two visions Capistran reported to Cardinal Capranica, without making an attempt to explain them. Did this great champion of the Church see the future of that Church? Some weeks later (January, 1456) in Temesvar, he must have had still deeper revelations. During the afternoon rest Jerome of Udine was frightened by hearing Capistran weep convulsively. Repeatedly asked what had happened, the saint could answer only with sobbing and groaning. Udine called some other brothers. They gathered around him, helplessly listening, while he, bathed in tears, in a voice broken by sorrow called continually on the mercy of God, invoking in long line the mysteries and the instruments of Christ's Passion. To the questioning brothers he answered that he had seen in a single moment the unspeakable woe and misery that the world would have to go through.

Urgent invitations reached him en route. The citizens of Lippa said they would gladly come to him if he could not come to them, but that their city had a large number of Jews, schismatics, and infidels, who certainly would not go with them. The cathedral chapter of Arad sent two canons to him, who gave a vivid description of the evils which the Church there had to suffer from Turks and schismatics. Toward the end of October he arrived at Karansebes. In November he reached Hunyad, the ancestral seat of John Hunyadi, whose wife Elizabeth had urged the man of God to come quickly. Her future daughter-in-law, the daughter of Count Ulrich of Cilli, was at the brink of death. But even if she should die, he still should come, for it was in his power to revive her again. For Christmas he was invited to visit Matthew, Bishop of Weissenburg.

Three months were now devoted to the crusade and the schismatics. In Transylvania, as in Moldavia and Wallachia, the schismatics, people and clergy, lived in great ignorance. Capistran was energetically supported by two native Franciscans, Matthew and John. The common people could easily have been gained, but the resistance of the schismatic clergy frustrated all efforts, in spite of full cooperation by Bishop Matthew and John Hunyadi. The first step was to eliminate the influence of John Wladika, who called himself the bishop of the schismatics and stood in high repute among the people. Hunyadi arrested him, burned his house in Hunyad, and sent him prisoner to Capistran. Capistran thereupon subjected Wladika to a strict examination and found that he was exceedingly ignorant. He followed qA1neither the Latin nor the Greek rite. But he showed himself docile, admitting his ignorance and asking for instruction. Capistran sent him to Budapest, later baptized him there solemnly, and then sent him to Rome. After a period in Rome, Wladika became a legitimate bishop of the Greek Uniat Church, and returned to his native country. The progress of union was accelerated when Peter, the prince of Moldavia, acknowledged the Roman Church.

In January, Capistran was recalled to Budapest. He had just sent a circular to the Catholic barons of Transylvania, urging them to burn all schismatic chapels in their territories and to offer the schismatic clergy an ultimatum: either to accept the Roman Catholic Church or to leave their country. But the barons were not willing. In case of mass conversions these lords would have had to provide Catholic churches, schools, and clergy. Even Hunyadi hesitated. After some delay he gave the order, revoked it, though later on he put it into effect.

The command which made Capistran return to Budapest came from the new legate for Germany and Hungary, Cardinal John Carvajal, who was himself under orders from the Pope to get at once into touch with Capistran. The delegate's first impressions were very rosy. He found the young King fervent for the crusade. Like David, Ladislaus in his unsullied innocence would be victorious over the heathen. Cilli, too, showed entire good will. But Hunyadi was the real Maccabean of his time. The fact that Hunyadi and a papal legate were at the head of the crusade would bring together such immense forces that food would be wanting rather than warriors.

Capistran promptly got ready for the journey. Hunyadi, together with his wife and younger son Matthias, the future King Corvinus, accompanied him to Temesvar. The winter was again very severe. Capistran's hardships on this march through the Hungarian steppes would have been enough, so he writes to the legate, to crush a rock. He expresses doubts about the date fixed by the legate. Repeated Turkish raids made him fear an attack by the main army even before Easter. The banus of the Mačva, John Korogh, had informed him that an attack on Semendria and Belgrade was to be expected in March.

On February 6 King Ladislaus and the papal legate arrived in

Budapest. On February 14, the first Sunday of Lent, Capistran received from the legate the papal brief, which gave him all the authority of a crusade preacher. With the brief he received a special crucifix, blessed for him by the Pope. Capistran wept freely. "I will defend it with my blood, a hundred times a day if it must be." So he wrote to the Pope. The following weeks he remained in the capital preaching daily. Toward the end of March he wrote to the Pope: "A very great number of prelates and barons have taken the cross." Generally it was during the divine services that he received the vow to join the crusade. Those thus enrolled he dismissed to their homes, with orders to join the army as soon as he would call them. He was always surrounded by great throngs. Everybody wanted to take the cross from his hands. The legate was hardly noticed, though Capistran tried his best to direct the attention of the people to the papal envoy.

The diet was slow and reluctant. National conditions were too unsettled. Carvajal tried in vain to bring King Ladislaus and the Emperor to an agreement. Hunyadi, who had not wanted to come to the congress at all, when he did come brought with him a strong detachment of soldiers. Capistran, the common friend and counselor of all, of Emperor, King, Hunyadi, and Cilli, found the situation painful. Each expected the saint to side with him. Finally the estates granted the necessary funds. Each hundred of citizens had to furnish ten horsemen and two foot soldiers. But the general opinion was that nothing could be done before August when the new harvest would be ready. In the presence of the King these resolutions were made known to the apostolic legate.

Thus the diet ended. But on the following day came terrible news. Mohammed II was already leading a vast army against the southern border of Hungary. So the King at once summoned forces to occupy the strongholds and to secure the crossings over the Danube. Many barons took the cross. Hunyadi, though full reconciliation with the King was still lacking, was made commander-in-chief. Appeals for assistance were sent in all directions. King Ladislaus wrote to the Pope and to the Duke of Milan. Carvajal entreated the Pope to send the fleet immediately against Constantinople. The next day the legate wrote to the Pope again: "The danger is such that delay of one day, nay, even of a few hours, may lead to a catastrophe over which Christianity would weep forever."

But again these first fears passed away. Carvajal, in a letter (April 17) to the Duke of Milan, complains of the general lukewarmness. One waits for the other; each says he will do as much as others do. Some console themselves with trust in God, who has always protected the Christian faith. The worst example was given by the government itself. For the shameful inactivity of the King, Cilli is held responsible. He did not wish to help his rival to new laurels. Hunyadi would fight the Turks even if no one helped him. And the honor of a hero's death was just what Cilli wished him most sincerely.

The crusade preachers were full of fervor: the Dominican, Archbishop Kalteisen, in Germany; Carvajal in Austria, assisted by the Franciscan, Gabriel of Verona. To Poland, Capistran himself sent an appeal, and this settled rumors of his death, which had been circulating in Moravia and Bohemia. Benesch of Boskowitz had tried to send a special messenger to Hungary, but had found nobody willing to go. In Cracow people had been praying for the repose of his soul. Hence his appeal aroused unusual joy. "We preach the crusade with utmost zeal." Thus wrote the guardian in Cracow, Father Ladislaus, a native Hungarian. But he would have much preferred to read in Capistran's letter: "Take the cross and follow me."

In Hungary the three Johns were busy: John Carvajal the legate, John Hunyadi the commander-in-chief, and John Capistran the preacher. After the diet Hunyadi hurried to Belgrade, the key fortress of Hungary:

Capistran, leaving Budapest about the middle of April, went to preach the crusade in southern Hungary. Among his helpers were two of his countrymen, John of Tagliacozzo and Ambrose of Aquila. Capistran's tone on this tour was unusually solemn. Repeatedly he offered his own body to ward off all the dangers threatening Christendom. He felt his end was approaching and that he would never return. Again and again he invited Father Gabriel to pay him a last visit in Budapest. He had written his farewell letter to his relatives in Italy. It was at the same time his first letter to them since he left Italy to go north. He has not forgotten them, he says, and has often sent them greetings. "But I must write myself. My first letter may be my last as I am about to go with the Christian forces against the infidels. My longing is to close my life by martyrdom for Him who died for us on the Cross. My fear is that I am not worthy of such a grace." His last petition commends to them the little cloister in Capistrano. His relatives are blessed with earthly goods. "Next after spiritual goods, nothing in life is dearer to me than that cloister."

Ships were at his disposal on this journey. He crossed southern Hungary in all directions, answering urgent invitations. In reply to his request for news about the Turks, the Archbishop of Kalocza urged him to come for eight days. On May 15 the prelate renewed his invitation.

Meanwhile, in Budapest, the Cardinal was doing his utmost. He fully intended to march at the head of the army against the Turks, even if it should bring him the lot of the cardinal legate Cesarini in 1444. "In the first years of the Church, popes gave themselves to a martyr's death, I should like to do the same." Thus he wrote to Capistran. And he added: "Not in weapons do I put my trust. My suite is forbidden to wear arms. My hope rests in the prayer of the Church." The court party was still against Hunyadi, and when he asked the legate for a meeting, the King and his counselors were decidedly opposed. But Carvajal did not yield. He went to meet Hunyadi in Szegedin. The legate placed himself entirely at the disposal of the experienced field marshal. Carvajal himself wished to go from Szegedin directly to the south, in order to await in Peterwardein the approach of the crusade army. But Hunyadi insisted that the legate return to Budapest, since from there he could far better influence the Christian princes toward energetic assistance. Besides, a most unfavorable impression would arise if the legate came to the border with such weak forces as had so far assembled. Carvajal yielded. But he sent as his representative

Bishop Francis Oddi to Peterwardein, to keep the crusaders there together, and to send him frequent reports.

But now all hopes seemed doomed. Hunyadi objected to using untrained soldiers as crusaders. He counted naturally, in the first place, on an army of trained soldiers, not only from Hungary, but also from foreign lands, especially from Milan and Burgundy whose rulers had repeatedly promised assistance. To untrained forces Hunyadi gave only occupations of a subordinate nature. The legate did not agree with that idea at first. He expected Capistran to continue preaching in the border districts, so as to have, in the decisive moment, sufficient troops ready to move. If Capistran thought it best, the legate would join him at once. "Here I accomplish nothing anyhow." Thus he wrote on May 23.

The legate, when he wrote thus, did not consider the danger immediate. Even on June 2, just one month before the siege of Belgrade began, he wrote to Capistran to come and see the Emperor, and to urge him to more promptness. "I should like to have you in many places at once. I know how much you can accomplish at any time." Evidently the legate was still under the impression that the attacks of the Christian navy and the powerful preparations of Skanderbeg in Albania, news just then in circulation, would delay the march of the Turkish main army against Hungary. Similar consoling news of an impending attack by the Christian fleet came to Capistran from the Pope and from Cardinal Scarampi, the commander of the papal fleet. Yet a few days sufficed to falsify these hopes. Hunyadi sent word that the Turkish army was near the Hungarian border.

Carvajal sent a copy of this letter to Capistran (June 5), ordering him to lead all those who had taken the cross promptly to the border. "I do the same from here," he says, adding: "The King has gone out hunting and has not yet returned." This hunting trip was only a pretext. At Cilli's prompting the royal court had secretly fled to Vienna. This example had its effect. Hungarian law obliged the nobility to follow military summons only when the King's power was insufficient. Hence the prelates and the barons now considered themselves no longer bound to their vows as crusaders.

They fled from the capital, and retired to their castles and villages. Regarding only their personal security, they left the kingdom to its fate. The citadel of Budapest itself remained half a month without any garrison. Hunyadi's appeals met with no response. He waited in Szegedin, but waited in vain, for reinforcements. Only one baron joined him, the one who was nearest the danger, Michael Korogh of Mačva.

As the Sultan marched rapidly toward Belgrade, Hunyadi left Szegedin on June 12 and hurried to the border. He informed the legate that he would take up his position near the town of Keve on the Danube, opposite the mouth of the Morava. There he would prevent the Turkish fleet from entering the Danube. If the Turks, he said, can blockade Belgrade also from the riverside, then the city will be almost entirely lost, since it can no longer be provided either with provisions or with reinforcements. The legate should therefore send to Keve all those who had taken the cross. But they would have to be there before the Turkish ships reached the Danube. He himself would be in position there on the feast of St. John the Baptist.

On June 22 Hunyadi summoned the Saxon communities of Transylvania. The Sultan was only four days south of the Danube. Let them now get ready and meet him in Keve, even if they had not respected the King's summons. But all in vain. He remained alone. Brankovits too, the Serbian despot, did not make a move. His letter to Cardinal Carvajal (June 25) from Becskerek has plainly no other purpose than to lessen the unfavorable impression of his inactivity. His statement that Hunyadi was waiting with his whole army at the Danube and that the barons were now ready to join him was real mockery. Deceitfully he adds that the legate should tell him what he should do against the Turks. Brankovits knew only too well what the legate expected of him. So did all the barons of the Empire. Brankovits' real plan was to preserve a cautious neutrality, and thus assure for himself favorable peace terms from the Sultan.

Alarming letters came to Capistran, not only from Hunyadi, but also from Szilagyis, the commander of Belgrade. They asked him to stop preaching and to bring at once as many crusaders as he could get. The number of those who in Hungary alone had taken the cross would have formed a respectable army. Capistran had personally fastened the cross on the shoulders of 27,000 men. Many others had received it from the hand of the legate and from other missioners. In Hungary alone about 40,000 men had pledged themselves. Nor were the efforts of the crusade preachers in foreign lands, especially in Germany, without result. But until these armed and trained forces could reach the seat of war many weeks would pass. The Turks had arrived a full month sooner than expected. According to Carvajal's calculation, a real army could not be placed in the field before the middle of August. All that could be done for the moment was to recruit men near the scene of action.

Capistran did as he was told. He ceased preaching and sent messengers in all directions, to admonish prelates and barons to do their duty. But this appeal, like Hunyadi's, remained unanswered. An extremely depressed mood came over him. Only a few hundred men, quite insufficiently armed, came at first. Then some more hundreds came slowly from more distant districts. But no time could be lost in bringing the first reinforcements to Belgrade. Five boats, obtained in a hurry, were loaded with provisions and a part of the forces. The rest of the crusaders were to march along the shore. With only a few thousand men, he began his march to Belgrade. During the past year he had dreamed of a splendid army of crusaders, led by kings and princes. And now, a pitiful handful against a mighty army.

In those days Pope Callistus III called all Christendom to fervent prayer. Rome was disturbed, not merely by the immense infidel army at Belgrade, but also by the appearance of a comet, by an earthquake, and by a terrible pestilence. But while everybody fled from Rome, the Pope remained at his post. He did so, as he told an ambassador, because the Sultan did not pause, even when thousands in his army fell victims to the plague. The feast of the Apostles brought forth the famous bull against the Turks. The Pope urges Christians to prayer, fasting, and penance. He adjures them "to return to the Lord that He may again turn to us." On the first Sunday of each month rogation processions are to be held everywhere. Votive Masses "*Contra paganos*" are ordered. Sermons are to be preached. Daily in all churches bells are to be rung between None and Vespers. When the bell is heard, three Our Fathers and Hail Marys shall be recited. This bell became popularly known as the "Turk-bell."

Perhaps we may see one of the first fruits of this universal prayer in a vision granted to Capistran shortly before his army set out. During the Memento for the Dead he saw an arrow fall from heaven upon the altar. On the arrow were written in golden letters these words: "Fear not, John. Go down quickly. In the power of My name and of the holy Cross thou wilt conquer the Turks." He spoke of this vision, not only to his confreres, but to the people from the pulpit. His recent despondency was swept away. Joy and zeal marked his last preparations. Sailing down the Danube, his little army caught sight of Belgrade in the early morning of July 2, the feast of the Visitation. Few though they were, they were greeted by the city with loud cries of welcome. Perhaps no other city had ever waited for him with such longings as Belgrade, now threatened by the shadows of death. To the sound of music, Capistran and his band were escorted into the fortress.

CHAPTER XXXVIII

The Battle on the Danube

HUNYADI'S orders were that Capistran, leaving part of his troops, should sail on down the Danube to Keve. To this the commander of Belgrade objected. It was too late. Capistran would simply fall into the hands of the Turks. Besides, he would be needed in Belgrade more than in Keve. But Capistran did not yield. He celebrated Mass at once, then preached. After dinner he set forth with three boats toward Keve, forty-four miles down the Danube. Soon afterward Szilagis heard that the Turkish ships had already passed Keve. Hunyadi had been unable to do anything against them. So the commander of Belgrade dispatched a messenger. But Capistran sailed on. At whatever risk he would bring help to Hunyadi. The weather was beautiful: the sun shone in a cloudless sky; the winds were silent; the flowing river was smooth as glass. Perfect visibility would let them see the Turkish ships in time to land, and they would then proceed on the left bank of the river. Then suddenly a heavy thunderstorm broke upon them. But far from harming them, it saved them. Darkness and high waves forced them to land. When the storm passed, they saw the Turkish ships near at hand. During the night Capistran made his way back to Belgrade by land.

The rest of the crusaders arrived the next day, July 3. To Capistran's great satisfaction they had some cannon with them. That same day he sent a report to the Bishop of Assisi at Peterwardein. "The Turkish fleet has already occupied the Danube, and controls below Belgrade all passes into Hungary. Today we expect the siege to begin. Never before have the Turks put such a large force into action. Christendom is in extreme danger. Hunyadi fights daily against the Turks. But what can he do without assistance?" Let the Bishop inform the legate, and let the legate do his utmost to move kings and princes to come as quickly as possible.

The time for sleep and laziness is gone. It is time to get up. The unbelievable has happened. If kings, princes, barons, and prelates do not wish to be visited by the Turks, let them come here. If they wish to keep their own possessions, let them send their soldiers here, to the place of resistance. Here is the place to fight, before the Turks become masters on land, as they are already on water." He himself cannot now write to the legate. He is too deep in pain, sorrow, and fatigue. Will the Bishop please write for him?

These last words do not contradict Tagliacozzo, who says that, since the vision in Peterwardein, no one had noticed in Capistran a trace of sadness. Capistran did not indeed let others notice his interior struggle, but kept his people in good spirits. Yet these were the most terrible days of his life. His soul was sad unto death. This inward sadness appears in the letter just quoted, as it does in his letter to the Pope on the very day when Belgrade was finally delivered.

The same day, July 3, when the first Turkish troops appeared before the walls, Capistran's eagerness flamed up at first sight of the infidels. He suggested immediate attack. "Who will follow me?" But no one responded. This word was a mere temperamental outburst. His actions were prudent and far-seeing. In a few hours the city would be entirely blockaded, cut off from all contact with the world outside. But contact simply had to be maintained. Capistran decided to leave the city before the river was closed. Sunday, July 4, he said Mass in the fortress. Then he exhorted the garrison to perseverance until rescue should arrive. He ordered some of the priests to stay in the city. They were not, he said, to participate personally in battle, not even by handing weapons to the soldiers. Their business was to support the defense by prayer, to perform their priestly duties, and do works of charity. For the lay brothers he left no particular instructions. Let them act as God inspired. He himself with four brothers left the city. He would soon be back, he told the inhabitants, with such an army that Christians and Turks would be equally surprised.

The commander ordered two ships for his protection, since some Turkish vessels were seen near at hand. But the crews on these two ships were displeased when Capistran, soon after sailing, ordered his boat to land: he heard a neighboring village had been abandoned. Since in such cases helpless people were often left behind, he ordered a thorough search. They found just one, a girl, the child of a schismatic. He baptized the child and confided it to a family in Slankamen, not far from Peterwardein, which he now made his headquarters. From here he went personally to the Archbishop of Bacs. But even this prelate, Capistran's personal friend, refused to provide any military assistance. His expressed reason was that Hungary as a whole was staying away. But he was known to be a personal adversary of Hunyadi. Hunyadi himself, amid daily skirmishes with Turkish outposts, had made his way up the left bank of the Danube, and now stood just across from Belgrade, where he awaited reinforcements.

The river blockade by the Turks proceeded slowly. Their fleet waited until the land forces were settled in their camps, and had placed their siege guns in position. July 7 saw the center of the army settling outside the city. Unbroken masses of white tents soon covered the wide plain and the slopes of the hills south of the city. The Turkish army, says an eyewitness, looked like a wide expanse of freshly fallen snow. Out of the white mass of tents emerged many a pompous pavilion, decorated with multicolored banners. High above all others rose the Sultan's gorgeous tent, with its green banner of the Prophet. In general this Turkish expedition displayed the magnificence of a triumphal parade. What did little Belgrade mean in the path of the conqueror of Constantinople?

Belgrade watched in wonder as the baggage trains arrived. Endless lines of wagons—wooden, brass, iron—carrying artillery and ammunition. Then camels, buffaloes, and oxen without number. Finally, an astonishing multitude of dogs, destined, so ran the rumor, to tear Christians to pieces. The right wing, with the Sultan and his European contingents, stretched down toward the Danube. The left wing, under a pasha with the Asiatic troops, reached out to the right bank of the Save, which flows into the Danube at Belgrade. What chiefly frightened the Christians was the amount of artillery, which, according to Hunyadi, was four times as large as the Turks had ever before brought together. Two hundred cannons faced the city, among them twenty with mouths large enough for a man to sit down in. Then seven catapults that could throw stones too big for a man to encompass with his arms. Tagliacozzo says that the Turks might have shattered, not merely the walls of Belgrade, but even the highest mountains. And to think that the Sultan's best artillerymen were Christians! Marshaled in three long lines, the guns controlled every part of the city. Walls and ditches, to protect the gunners, changed these batteries into little forts.

On the size of the Turkish army, estimates differed very much even then. The unusually great number of women in the Turkish army was variously explained.[1]

With the encirclement by land completed, the fleet proceeded to blockade the riverside. In the Danube, above Belgrade, was a large island called Semlin, beyond which the main fleet took its station. The entire flotilla consisted of about 200 ships, among them 64 galleys. The admiral's ship, beautifully decorated with banners, often came forth to the sound of music and sailed along near the city. Tagliacozzo reports with satisfaction how the great vessel was destroyed by a Turkish cannon ball fired over the city. Belgrade sailors plundered the beautiful vessel and killed the shipwrecked crew. In this cruel war neither side respected law or right. The Turks in their turn massacred captive Christians in view of the city.

In the Turkish camp opinions were divided. The grand vizier, Karadja Pasha, advised against attempting to take the city by storm. Its high hills slope down till they reach the Danube which defends it on the north and the Save which defends it on the west. These natural advantages were reinforced by lines of fortification that were the admiration of competent contemporary critics. A Burgundian knight, Bertrandon, who visited Belgrade on his way from the Holy Land, praises the double line of walls surmounted by good towers. The city had five strong forts, well supplied with artillery. Three of these forts were up on the hills, the other two on the right bank of the Danube. Beneath these lower forts, in the

---

[1] To tempt the crusaders. To make the Turkish army seem larger. To further the Sultan's plan of colonizing in conquered territory. These reasons have been given.

river, was a harbor, protected by chains. This description corresponds in essentials with that given by Tagliacozzo, who adds details. The upper forts were defended by unusually strong walls and a deep moat. Approach was by a single drawbridge. The smallest of the forts stood on the highest point of the city and was crowned by a watchtower, called *Noli timere*. In this tower was a sort of loud-speaker, which occasionally hurled invectives across to the Turkish camp. Here also were the royal apartments, the windows of which looked down on the whole city. In this fort were now lodged the Franciscans of Capistran's retinue, and were stored the books and relics he had brought along. By a hidden passage those inside the fort could reach the Danube. Between the two encircling outer walls was a moat of unusual width.

This description shows why Karadja Pasha, the ablest of the Turkish field marshals, was decidedly against the idea of storming the fortress. He reminded the young Sultan of the defeat of his father, who in 1440 had besieged Belgrade for six months in vain. The plan he suggested was to leave the city under blockade, and meanwhile subdue the whole province between the rivers Save and Drave, thus cutting off Belgrade from the regions back of it. Happily for the Christians the Sultan rejected this plan. With contemptible words for his own father, the Sultan declared that he would subdue the city within two weeks. Within two months he wished to celebrate the Ramadan in Budapest. Thus the bombardment began.

While the artillery thundered against the city, the Turkish troops worked their way through a network of trenches toward the wall. At night the bombardment became fiercer. The defenders feared chiefly the colossal stone balls. Tagliacozzo regards as a miracle the fact that only one person, a woman, was killed by these missiles. These stone balls indicated their coming by a mighty sound. Then a bell in the citadel gave a signal, and everybody rushed for cover. When one of these stones broke through the roof of a church where Tagliacozzo was saying Mass, the congregation ran out. From then on he celebrated in the open.

The good Franciscan speaks candidly. Desire for martyrdom had yielded to anguish.

The friars visited the defenders upon the walls. But, obedient to Capistran's command, they did not even lift up a stone, although other members of the clergy did not heed this admonition. Tagliacozzo once watched a chaplain, who with three shots sent seven Turks to the next world. We ourselves, he adds, unused to such gruesome business, were overcome by horror. We prayed and wept. We repented of our sins and confessed them. Most of the time we spent in silence, awaiting from one hour to another the sabers of the Turks. Plague soon attacked the crowded city. Tagliacozzo and several of his brethren fell ill. Provisions grew scarce. And the hungry people saw the Turks, in the waving fields beyond the Danube, gather in rich supplies of grain. Sometimes the commander came to visit the trembling brethren. "Courage," he would say; "Hunyadi and Capistran will soon bring us help."

Hunyadi had in the meantime set up a fortified camp, probably on the Titel plateau, near the junction of Danube and Theiss, north of Belgrade. He now met Capistran in Slankamen. Discussion showed views widely apart. Until now Hunyadi had manifested the greatest interest in defending Belgrade. But when he saw the immensity of Turkish preparation, he found the obstacle insurmountable. He was indeed accustomed to win victories with inferior forces: at Varna, for instance, with 16,000 men against 100,000. But those 16,000 were trained soldiers. Now his own army was far smaller, and part of it was isolated in Belgrade.

Throngs of men from all ranks were daily assembling, especially in Slankamen, where the leaders were now conferring. But what kind of soldiers would these newcomers be? "Poor naked folks," a chronicler calls them. It was a motley assembly, poorly armed, without training. Hunyadi told Capistran bluntly that he could not do a thing with these people. His heart bled to think that Hungary would be overrun by the Turks, but under the conditions he could do nothing to rescue Belgrade. With these views of Hunyadi the cardinal legate was in accord. He had asked both Hunyadi and Capistran not to risk fighting with these volunteers alone. Catastrophe would be the inevitable result. Hunyadi was to wait until the feast of the Assumption, by which time the legate hoped to come himself with a well equipped army.

But could Belgrade hold out a full month? No. The hourly thunder of the Turkish artillery, heard far beyond Hunyadi's camp, gave the answer. The sending of supplies to the fortress was now impossible. The Turks had arrived far earlier than was generally expected. The legate's advice came too late to meet the situation. An army in the open field can retreat, but a besieged fortress cannot. One of two courses lay open to Hunyadi: he could attempt to break through the lines of the enemy on the Danube, enter Belgrade, and thus reestablish contact with supplies in the rear; or, this plan failing, he must propose a parley with the Sultan, in order to save Christian lives. The idea of a treaty with the Sultan was popular in Hungary at the time. Carvajal sent word to Venice that the Hungarians intended to settle with the Turks peacefully, and that Hunyadi might assent. What the Turks wanted, he said, was a free road to Italy. Such a disgraceful proposal was certainly not in Hunyadi's mind. But he may have contemplated some agreement in order to prevent the worst. He had made such agreements in the past. One plausible report says he had such a move in mind when he called Capistran away from Belgrade. He would thus not only save Capistran from death, but also secure for the city more favorable peace terms, since the presence of the famous preacher would have irritated the infidels to the utmost.

Capistran rejected absolutely the idea of an agreement. Victory lay in God's hands. On this he insisted, vehemently and repeatedly. The debate was long. Finally Hunyadi yielded. Veneration for his saintly friend moved him, as did also his own reputation. Even without Hunyadi's cooperation, Capistran would go to Belgrade. Could the noble general leave these untrained and inexperienced crowds to themselves? Could he abandon this saintly priest, so highly venerated all over Christendom?

Hunyadi's command brought together 200 vessels, most of them small boats. With these he would sail down the Danube. What a contrast to the legate's plan, which contemplated the papal fleet sailing up the Danube, while the great boats from Budapest, each holding 500 men, would sail down to attack the Turkish fleet simultaneously! Among the 200 vessels now at hand, only one was large enough to carry a few cannons, as protection for the small boats which carried the soldiers.

Hunyadi set July 14 as the date for the attack. Spies who made their way during the night into Belgrade brought orders to the local commander to have the sailors in Belgrade ready to attack the Turks in the rear. The army at the moment of sailing numbered about 18,000. The Hungarian lords were still absent, though Capistran had threatened them with the ban. The only galley of the Christian fleet was manned by Hunyadi's own troops.

At nightfall on July 14, Capistran pronounced over the army a general absolution. Then he again impressed on them the practice in which he had been drilling them for weeks, namely, to be ready, when the signal should be given, to shout their war-cry in unison, and with the utmost strength of voice. That war cry was the one word "Jesus," thrice repeated.

Under a moonless night, they floated down the Danube, halting near the island of Semlin. Three thousand men remained in the boats. All others left the ships, with Hunyadi and Capistran. Some marched down the right bank, which here rises vertically from 50 to 70 feet above the river. These men were headed by the banner of the cross, carried by a nobleman named Peter. Behind this banner came Capistran. The others marched down the left bank.

The attack began at eight o'clock on the morning of July 15. A Latin antiphon was intoned as a signal. The Christians, moving down stream, made the best of their favorable position. They loaded boats with heavy sand, and released them into the swift current. These boats crashed into the Turkish ships, causing serious confusion. Amid wild battle cries on each side, the boats clashed along the whole line, and the battle raged from one bank to the other. The sailors of Belgrade had been waiting. They now came out with forty boats full of well-armed troops and fell on the Turks from the rear. High on the right shore, visible to friend and foe, stood Capistran, waving the banner of the cross. His voice rang out carrying the name of Jesus, now up to heaven, now out across the stream, or then pronouncing a denunciation of the enemies of the

Christian name.

This double attack, front and rear, completely confused the Turkish sailors. They fought on for five hours, then yielded. Three of their galleys had been sunk and as many captured. They had lost 2,500 men. Their defeat would have been still greater had not the Christians met with a serious mishap. From lack of caution among the gunners, fire broke out in the one good ship the Christians had. When the fire was quenched, the ship was found disabled and had to be retired. The other ships then gave up the pursuit, and the surviving Turks escaped down the river.

The adventure had ended in perfect success. Seriously damaged, the Turkish fleet took up a new position, somewhat below Belgrade, across from the Turkish camp. Christian ships now controlled the crossings over the Save and the Danube. Belgrade sailors patrolled the fortress. The other ships, swelled by new arrivals to the number of 300, were anchored at Semlin, above Belgrade, near the camp of the crusaders. The crusaders were naturally jubilant. But one incident showed a deeper feeling. Without Capistran's knowledge, they gathered all the booty of the battle, made an immense heap, and set it on fire. Why? Because they feared that the nobles, who had refused to come for battle, would still claim the spoils. But they did save two gorgeous garments, and brought them to Capistran as a present. He in turn sent them to the cardinal legate as a souvenir of victory.

CHAPTER XXXIX

The Day of Deliverance

HUNYADI and Capistran entered Belgrade the next day, July 16. The crusaders, those excepted who were needed in the fortress, put up their camp on the west bank of the Save near Semlin. While from towers and spires victorious banners were still waving, a group of Hunyadi's troops, bold with victory, went out to meet a contingent of Turks who approached the walls in challenge. That skirmish cost the Turks a number of dead and wounded, but the Hungarians lost their leader. Capistran, who had watched the fight from the wall, was later accused of being the cause of that useless encounter. But Tagliacozzo says that Capistran had merely asked the leader whether he had been to confession and Communion.

Capistran did not stay in Belgrade. He was needed in the camp near Semlin, where, in truth, he alone had supreme command. Each new troop, as it arrived, asked for Capistran, knelt for his blessing, and from him accepted their station. Without him neither Hunyadi nor Szilagyi could control these people. A week would elapse before the final battle on July 22. Only occasionally during that week did Capistran return to the fortress, either to bring relief forces or to get the sick and wounded, whom he sent to various villages upstream. In the camp itself he had to oversee all details, even the appointment of guards and sentinels. For this seventy-year-old man, frail and worn, the week was one of superhuman exertion. Accompanied by two trumpeters, he could be seen moving ceaselessly through the camp, now on foot, now on horseback. Tagliacozzo heard Capistran, on a later occasion, tell Hunyadi that in seventeen days he had slept altogether only seven hours. The fine horse that Hunyadi gave him broke down after some days. Three days passed at times before he found leisure for a meal. To solicitous warnings he answered with the words of Christ: "I have meat to eat which you know not."

Provisions for the army were plentiful. "It rained food," says Tagliacozzo. But the fare was monotonous, simply bread and weak wine. And the water was bad. When Capistran did find time to eat, he sat down amid his people, ate his hard biscuit like the rest, and sipped of the wine, now souring in July heat. His exterior he neglected entirely. He never changed clothing. His body was covered with a crust of dirt, which crept into his very mouth. He lost all sense of taste, and had to scratch the crust from his tongue and palate with a knife to prevent putrefaction.

Crusaders continued to arrive slowly from Hungary, Germany, Poland, Bohemia, and Bosnia. Estimates, probably too high, speak of sixty thousand men engaged in defending Belgrade. Twelve thousand of these were in the city for the decisive battle. The rest were in the camp near Semlin. The description which Tagliacozzo has left us of the excellent spirit of discipline that governed these masses sounds exaggerated. But we must remember that this army consisted, not of professional soldiers, but of men religiously devoted to Capistran, ready and eager to follow him even into captivity and death. Belgrade was but the climax of the universal enthusiasm surrounding Capistran wherever he went. These crowds in Semlin represented the multitudes that had swarmed around him as missioner.

The camp was governed by a spirit almost ascetic. Its discipline was that of a religious revival. The coming battle was simply an act of religion. Capistran said Mass and preached daily in the open, in full view of the Turkish camp on the opposite bank of the Save. The other priests too, chaplains who had arrived with their contingents, celebrated daily, and the members of religious orders sang their office, just as if they were at home in their cloisters. Multitudes came to receive the sacraments. The usual aberrations of military life were absent. "We have a holy captain. We must avoid all sin." Thus these simple men spoke to one another. Popular punishment was severe. One soldier had stolen a trifle. They cut off his right ear. Another sold bread above the fixed price. His whole supply was thrown into the Danube. He himself would have followed had he not been saved by two Franciscans who chanced to pass by. But even thus he did not escape a sound thrashing.

Capistran issued repeated warnings against pillage. "If we begin to think of plunder, the Turks will defeat us." All goods found by chance were burned to prevent quarrels. What welded this motley mass into an army was reverence for the holy man who filled them with longing for heroic death. At a sign, like novices, they went to carry water or get wood. Crowds went on their knees as he passed by. Higher than any king stood this foreign friar, who did not even know their language and had to address them through an interpreter. But mostly they read his mind by his gestures, as when he lifted his hands or spread his arms in the form of the Cross or waved the banner or began the march. What he willed, was done.

That Hunyadi introduced some military training may be taken for granted. The army consisted of beggars and peasants, clerics and scholars, monks and lay brothers, tertiaries and hermits, that is, of people who knew hardly anything of war. Weapons and equipment were wanting. The few horses at hand were used for the transport of provisions. Lances were not to be seen at all. Some wore shirts of mail, picked up at random, which made "one or the other look like David in Saul's armor," says Tagliacozzo. Swords, clubs, slings, and shepherds' staves were the chief weapons. Some few brought crossbows, rifles, or iron rods with barbed hooks. The prior of an eremitical cloister, who came with seven brothers, wore a shirt of mail under his habit, had a sword at his side, and was protected by a helmet and shield. Praying or singing aloud, like pilgrims, these crowds entered into the camp. They were armed better in spirit than in body.

Capistran's mode of training for battle was to inspire these crowds with unwavering confidence in the power of the holy name of Jesus. Heralds proclaimed in camp that victory lay in this name. All who would fight in this name were welcome. He announced a general religious peace, probably for the first time in his life. "Heretics, schismatics, even Jews, are our friends in fighting the Turks." He forbade the molestation of dissenters. And he treated these personally with special kindness. He imposed this one condition: They must join in the battle cry; "Jesus, Jesus, Jesus." Repeatedly he made the whole army repeat that cry, which rolled like thunder across the Save. He expected certain victory. He had his interpreter shout across the Save to the Turkish guards these words: "Tell your Grand Dog, that, if he does not cease from his heinous plan, the hand of the Lord will soon strike him." Instead of "Grand Turk," Capistran always called the Sultan "Grand Dog." His whole camp had to do the same. The Turks in turn tried to intimidate the crusaders. Tricks were employed which now seem childish. On both sides of the river mighty bonfires were kindled, around which rose deafening noises, made with shouting, ringing of bells, and anything and everything to make a clamor. The Christian army was in good spirits. A report from Belgrade says: "These devout and strong men thirst for the blood of the Turks, as the hart pants for water."

Hunyadi's chief care was to repair the fortifications, now seriously damaged. "Belgrade deserves no longer the name of stronghold. It lies open on all sides." Thus he wrote to the King. Even the extremely strong fortifications of the upper city had been seriously impaired. The chief tower showed a broad deep gap. Hunyadi doubted whether the city could be restored sufficiently to be defended. What he repaired by day was destroyed by the nightly cannonade.

The defeat on the Danube did not at all deter the Sultan from his plan. Rather he rushed preparations for the decisive battle. Time was beginning to work against him. Food in the Turkish camp was getting scarce. Because he had marched too rapidly, his supplies had fallen behind. He had planned on taking the fortress at the first attack, since by August he meant to be in Budapest. Besides, reports of hostile invasions into his Asiatic provinces now began to arrive. He had the first messengers put to the sword, and swore that anyone else who brought such news would be treated the same way.

Signs of the final storm increased. On all sides endless columns of Turks could be seen carrying materials of all kinds, wood, stones, sand, trees, to fill up the broad trenches in front of the fortress. All Italy would have to work a long time to heap up such mountains, says Tagliacozzo. On July 20 two deserters brought to Hunyadi positive word that an attack was planned for the following day. Hunyadi and Szilagyi, who the preceding day had repeatedly expressed their opinion that the city was lost, now stopped the work of repairing the fortifications. At a council held in the Christian camp, Hunyadi declared the situation hopeless. He had repeatedly beaten an overwhelming Turkish army by skillfully taking advantage of circumstances. Now he sees no possibility of further resistance. The walls are shattered, the barons had not come, the crusaders had no training. In a few hours the city would be a prey of the Turks. The legate had recently repeated his warning not to risk a battle, as it would lead to a catastrophe. The only thing left is to abandon the city. The Danube is still in the hands of the Christians. Garrison and citizens can still be saved.

Hunyadi's motive in suggesting retreat was praiseworthy. He wished to avoid a worse evil. But Capistran remained immovable. Against all doubts of the general, he opposed unshakable confidence in God. "We will hold the fortress and put our enemies to shame." He did not remain alone in his views. A young Bavarian, John Roth, private secretary of King Ladislaus, later bishop of Breslau, energetically urged perseverance in the defense. He prefers heroic death to a doubtful retreat. Hunyadi was now in a dilemma. He had no real authority over the crusaders. Capistran was determined to resist the Turks alone. To retire with his garrison and leave Capistran and his crusaders to their fate was something unthinkable. Once more Hunyadi yielded to Capistran's "stubbornness." In this light we must judge his further behavior. Hunyadi was still convinced that his chief obligation was to prepare the retreat of the garrison crusaders and the population to the northern shore of the Danube at the beginning of the catastrophe which he felt was unavoidable. All his measures point in this direction. Part of his men he left under Szilagyi to defend the citadel. He himself boarded a ship and sailed back and forth on the Save and on the Danube, to watch all further developments. That

Hunyadi was thinking also of his own safety cannot be denied, but such prudence is not blameworthy. If Belgrade fell, the experienced commander would be still more needed by the threatened kingdom.

The morning of July 21 saw the last preparations for the decisive battle. The Turkish cannonade ceased. Feverish activity developed in their camp, in spite of a terrible loss they suffered that same day in the death of Karadja Pasha, who was crushed by a stone ball. The Sultan declared he would now in person lead the attack, and was with difficulty dissuaded from this plan. Capistran selected 4,000 crusaders and led them into the city, where a depressive mood prevailed. Women and girls, especially those of rank, sought refuge in the camp of the crusaders. The sick, the wounded, and the crippled were quickly removed from the city. With glowing words Capistran spurred his people on. Leaving five of his brethren in the citadel, he himself returned to the camp to prepare the reserves.

The attack began in the cool hours of the evening. The battle music and the battle prayer of the Turks sounded like the roar of wild bulls. The crusaders began their own songs, shouting the name of Jesus. Beneath their floating banners they took their positions upon the walls and in the breaches. When Hunyadi heard the well-known war trumpet, he sent word to Capistran to assemble all those still in camp on the shore across from the fortress, and to have all boats in readiness. Retreat across the Danube was still in his mind. Capistran had scarcely taken his position on the shore when the attack began. Praying aloud, he watched the cruel spectacle on the other side. Under a hail of arrows which rained down upon the defenders the Turkish storm troops worked their way forward to the trenches. In spite of serious losses they succeeded in making some pathways across. Covered by the ruins of partly destroyed walls, they climbed by posts driven into the ground up to the walls. The crusaders fought with desperate courage. Women assisted. They brought up stones and arrows. They carried away the wounded, using hands and teeth to draw out the arrows.

Notwithstanding all heroism, Hunyadi's fear seemed justified. In the first hours of the night strong divisions of the enemy pushed through the breaches into the interior of the city. In hand to hand struggle they were driven back. Toward midnight the assault reached its climax. The Turks attacked along the whole line. Here and there a Turkish flag was seen fluttering on the wall. One Turkish division pushed its way through the city up to the drawbridge which led to the citadel on the height. Szilagyi thought the battle was lost, and ordered the garrison to escape by the inside tunnel to the Danube. People in the city followed this example, some jumping from the windows, others wading through the water up to their necks to reach the boats.

But the battle was not over. It still raged at the drawbridge, though the crusaders were now alone. Capistran had heard from Hunyadi that the city was already lost. But his trust in God remained unshaken. He brought fresh reserves into the citadel. Then occurred the incident which caused so much difficulty during the process of his canonization. A huge Janizary had climbed the wall. A robust Hungarian grasped him. The Hungarian, pushing the Turk to the edge of the wall, cried out to Capistran, asking whether his soul would be saved if he threw himself down with the Turk? Capistran said, Yes. Another twist, and both men with arms locked about each other, were hurled down into the depths.[2]

While the struggle still raged at the drawbridge, and more and more Turks pressed into the city, the defenders of the wall resorted to a measure which had once before (1440) saved the city. A mass of brushwood, saturated with powder, sulphur, pitch, and other inflammables, was in readiness. As if by command the whole mass was set on fire and sent headlong down upon the storming Turks. This long wall of fire was terrible in its effects. The storming troops yielded, broke, and fled. The Turks in the city, seeing the flames lighting up behind their back, hurried to gain the open field. It was almost morning. The worst was over. The tide had turned.

---

[2] An incident shows how deeply in this life-and-death defense against the Turks even Christian minds had grown wild and savage. Two young Turkish noblemen were captured. Capistran tried in vain to convert them. Hunyadi condemned them to death. Proposal was made to give them first a few days for reflection. Hunyadi answered scoffingly; "Baptize them, yes. But behead them first!" And Tagliacozzo defends and praises Hunyadi's deed!

As St. Magdalen's Day slowly dawned, the defenders saw from the wall a horrible scene. In the trench below lay thousands of Janizaries. The long line of burnt bodies, says Tagliacozzo, looked like an endless trough of salted meat. Noises were dying down. The walls grew quiet. The storm had passed. The city was saved. Szilagyi brought back the garrison, the fugitive citizens returned, and Hunyadi came into the city, but did not stay long. He was still wary, expecting a new attack. Hurriedly he gave the necessary instructions, insisting in particular on restraint. No sorties from the city against the Turks. Sailors were forbidden, under death, to bring crusaders across the Save against the Turkish camp. This done, Hunyadi returned to his ship to await further developments.

Events showed that Hunyadi's apprehensions were unfounded. Mohammed II felt he had failed and was preparing to retreat. Decisive for his resolution to end the siege may have been the serious losses of Janizaries. He ordered the Danube flotilla to be set on fire to prevent the ships from falling into the hands of the Christians, though the latter did succeed in looting the burning ships.

By noon the conditions foreseen by Hunyadi began to develop. They were caused by an insignificant incident. A small group of crusaders sneaked out of the city, climbed a hill, and began shooting into a division of Turkish guards, who took to their heels. The scene was witnessed from the walls. Enthusiasm mounted. A thousand men rushed out of the city, meeting no resistance. Capistran was on the watch and beheld their recklessness. He wanted by all means to have Hunyadi's orders respected and may himself have suspected an ambush. He called his men back, but his voice faded away unheard.

On what now happened the reports are deficient. Capistran's own account to the Pope says that, when he saw that his people could not be called back, he himself hurried out to save them from falling into a trap. Tagliacozzo adds a few details. To save the hundreds of storming crusaders, Capistran got into a boat and crossed the Save into the camp in order to bring out all the reserves, as a restraint against the comparatively small groups coming out of the city. But when he commanded transit for his troops over the Save, the sailors of Belgrade refused, since they respected Hunyadi's orders not to transfer crusaders. Then Capistran recrossed the river, accompanied only by Tagliacozzo and Ambrosius, the standard-bearer, and two men to row the boat. At four o'clock in the afternoon he reached the other shore.

The Turkish lines were still quiet. As Capistran approached the city, he was seen from the walls, and new crowds streamed out of the city. In the following events Tagliacozzo sees an evident miracle. But we must reckon with the supposition that the Turks, busied with preparations for retreat, had left only a few men for observation in the space between the city and their camp, and that the siege guns in front of the camp were without trained gunners. Now, as the crusaders took position in long lines on the opposite shore of the Save and began to shout their mighty war song, and as at the same time new divisions kept streaming out of the city, the Turkish groups around the heavy artillery took to flight.

To the Christians this was a signal. They stormed the batteries, capturing the three long lines without any fighting at all. Capistran now threw aside all scruples. He saw in this incident the hand of the Lord. Hunyadi's prohibition had been superseded by circumstances. Measures must now be fitted for the conditions created by the spontaneous attack initiated by the crusaders. Tagliacozzo and Ambrosius tried to hold him back. He repulsed them energetically. "Forty years have I been waiting for this choice morsel. Let cowards turn back." They left him and went back into the city. Tagliacozzo says that, like Peter, he preferred to watch the course of events from afar. Capistran, glowing with the enthusiasm of battle, dragged himself, in spite of exhaustion and suffocating heat, to follow his soldiers.

Details again become confused. So much seems certain: the Turks brought out reserves from the camp, to drive the Christians back from the guns, and to forestall an attack upon the camp itself. One scene of this final struggle has become the emblem of this momentous battle. Surrounded by the turmoil, Capistran climbed a heap of earth between the guns. There he stood, visible to all, his standard-bearer at his side. Heedless of death that whistled round him, he stood waving his cross, shouting words of encouragement to his children, or singing words of prayer to heaven. Darkness ended the struggle. The Christians held the conquered guns. The Turks retired to a fortified position to prevent an invasion of their camp.

Capistran had indeed intended to storm the camp, and in one grand sweep utterly to destroy the enemy. But for this plan the few thousand crusaders participating in that afternoon's battle would not have been enough. Cooperation by the Hungarian garrison in the city and by the remaining reserves beyond the Save depended on Hunyadi. Hence Capistran hurried back into the city. Here he was met by Tagliacozzo and Ambrosius, who, now ashamed, were returning to their father. But Hunyadi was not in the city. He was still on his ship. Szilagyi condemned Capistran's plan as dangerous and hopeless. How could the Christian army, being without cavalry, pursue a fleeing enemy? Capistran yielded, and ordered the crusaders to return into the fortress.

CHAPTER XL

Illness and Death

THUS ended this day of glory. Incessantly Capistran repeated the joyful words: "This is the day which the Lord hath made." Late that same night he wrote a short message to the Pope. On the following day he drew up a more detailed report. But neither in these two accounts nor in the later one (August 17) does he dwell much on details. He is entirely possessed by the greatness of the events, in which he sees only an act of God to save Christendom. Hence he emphasizes, on the one hand the terrible danger that threatened the Christians, on the other hand the greatness of the victory, particularly since it was won without military leadership. His second report shows keen annoyance at the absence of the papal legate.

Hunyadi's role causes Capistran evident embarrassment. In his second and third reports he omits Hunyadi's name entirely. In his first letter, describing the greatness of the affliction, he simply says that even Hunyadi, the brave champion of the Christians, stood for the evacuation of Belgrade. Coming to the first victory gained during the night, he adds that Hunyadi had strictly forbidden the defenders to sally forth against the enemy. That Hunyadi was personally away from the battlefield during decisive engagements, Capistran passes over with tactful silence. Circumstances compelled him, he writes to the Pope, to become the leader of the crusaders, and, like a second Joshua, to lead the army of God.

History must confirm Capistran's claim. What his modesty kept hidden is made clear in Tagliacozzo's report. "Belgrade was saved by the merits, the indefatigable activity, and the prayers of Capistran." Looking at the situation as it stood in June and July, 1456, we must admit that, without Capistran, no serious attempt would have been made to save Belgrade at all, and that the fortress would have fallen irretrievably into the hands of the Turks. The crusaders were summoned and organized by him. He, and he alone, kept that motley crowd together, imbued them with his own fiery spirit, and formed of them a strong, tenacious, and persevering army.

In detail we find that Capistran saved Belgrade three times. First, when he gained Hunyadi's unwilling consent to break through the Turkish flotilla which controlled the river. Secondly, when he opposed the evacuation of the city. Thirdly, in the night before St. Magdalen's Day, when even the brave Szylagyi left the citadel, when the city was fleeing and Hunyadi acted as if the city had already fallen. Still we must not forget that the decisive stroke, namely, the wall of fire hurled down on the storming Turks, was owing to the desperate self-defense of the citizens fighting for their homes. On the other hand the importance of the afternoon battle on July 22 has been frequently overestimated. It did indeed serve to bring the personal heroism of Capistran fully into the light. But no new turn in the situation resulted from this successful raid. The Turks may well have looked upon it as a rear-guard skirmish.

Among the deliverers of Belgrade, Capistran stands foremost, though we must also give full credit to the other leaders, notably Carvajal and Hunyadi. The legate had manifested zeal and energy. But what share did he have in the happy results? Pope Callistus III, in a letter of thanks to the legate, speaks as follows: "Your counsels and efforts were the chief element in preparing the victory. Your fervor summoned the crusaders and the Hungarian estates." But we must recall that, like Hunyadi, the legate had put all his hopes in the well-armed reserve troops, for which he had certainly worked with untiring zeal. But these troops were still on the march when the decision fell at Belgrade. The great majority of those who saved the city had come at Capistran's call. The Hungarian diet contributed next to nothing. Tagliacozzo gives the legate credit for providing the city with weapons and food, and for sending his representative, the Bishop of Assisi, to Peterwardein. With the legate's failure to arrive in time for the battle, Capistran was much displeased.

Hunyadi's chief merit lay in the great act of self-denial

whereby, in spite of all his military experience, he bowed to the great faith of his holy friend, and stayed near him till all was over. What would have happened if he had insisted upon his declaration at Slankamen? The fortress was under his command. Would the citizens have still had courage to resist? Would they not have yielded to the Turks?

Hunyadi's cooperation was undoubtedly a factor in the final victory. The measures of a leader in critical conditions are judged by the course which things finally take. Let us suppose that Belgrade had fallen, as Hunyadi was sure it would. No one, least of all the crusaders, would then have blamed him for "swimming around in the river." Rather they would have praised his prudence in preparing for an unavoidable retreat. But after the engagement had, against his expectations, ended so wonderfully, his behavior appeared naturally in a less favorable light. To remove this unpleasant impression is the aim of the official report, composed in Hunyadi's chancery on July 23. This report does not mention Capistran and his crusaders at all. The uninitiated reader would conclude that the victory was Hunyadi's personal merit. The report is silent on points of importance, and colors the picture in favor of Hunyadi.

Capistran's charitable silence was not imitated by other correspondents, who unsparingly criticize Hunyadi's attitude. Animosity against him was prevalent among the crusaders. Already exasperated at the absence of the Hungarian militia and at Hunyadi's prohibition against pursuing the defeated enemy, they flared up on learning that Hunyadi "had sailed about on the Save." Their anger increased when the general was reported as saying he would not be sorry if all these insubordinate crusaders were slain. Thus we understand how open hostilities between the crusaders and Hunyadi's people began on the day after the battle. Spoils from the forsaken Turkish camp were the occasion. The crusaders sent a herald through the city to proclaim that yesterday's victory was gained, not by the Hungarian lords, but solely by the power of the holy name of Jesus and His Cross, through the merits and circumspection of Father John Capistran. The Hungarians, in turn, seemed ready to attack the crusaders. Hunyadi had not returned to the city. Even now, after the retreat of the Turks, he did not leave his observation boat. Capistran had gone to him for a confidential parley, when the unrest in the city was reported. Hunyadi refused to intervene. So Capistran went to the city to calm his people. They must now, he said, return home. Shortage of food was setting in. They had fulfilled their mission in a splendid manner. The Turks were no longer to be feared, at least not in the present year.

The regular troops now began to arrive, and their leaders began to draw up daring plans for continuing the war. The cardinal legate had left Budapest on July 22 with 4,500 men. He had no idea that the decision at Belgrade had been reached that very day. A week later he arrived in the rescued city. He found Capistran preaching hopes of being able by Christmas to celebrate Mass in the church of the Holy Sepulcher in Jerusalem. But three great battles, he added, were still to be fought. Hunyadi, too, was determined to recapture Constantinople and to drive the Turks out of Europe.

A few weeks sufficed to shatter all these glorious plans. Pestilence followed war. Unburied corpses saturated the sultry summer air with putrefaction. When Tagliacozzo, by order of the cardinal legate, rode out with a companion to measure the forsaken Turkish camp, the two friars, although they hurried, had repeated attacks of painful vomiting. Beasts of prey invaded the field of death, howling horribly, especially at night. Conditions in the city were not the best. The camp epidemic spread rapidly. Hunyadi was one of the first victims. He was moved to the healthier climate of Semlin. But his days were numbered. Capistran never left the dying hero. On August 11, scarcely three weeks after the victory, Hunyadi died.

Capistran, too, had caught the deadly disease. On August 6 it came, with high fever and violent diarrhea. At Carvajal's advice he likewise sought quarters in Semlin, although this village, burned by the Turks, had very poor accommodations. A ruined hut was his resting place, with a mat on the ground for a bed, a log for a pillow, and his own cloak as covering. Thus he lay, shaken by fever, in the company of mice, snakes, lizards, and gnats. The Cardinal supplied him generously with food, but the patient could not retain anything. Medicines were none, since the Hungarians, says Tagliacozzo, have a horror of them. Carvajal, too, now left Belgrade, and took Capistran with him to Slankamen, where the latter found welcome in the rectory. But he did not stay there long. He wanted to recuperate in the Observant cloister at Ilok, a few miles up the Drave. Of his twelve brethren he sent four who were sick to a place in the neighborhood. Three helped him to reach Ilok. Two took his library to Budapest; three remained with him. Among these was John Tagliacozzo, the only countryman now at his side in this strange land.

He was still hopeful, though sometimes he suffered from melancholy. Weeping, he once said to Tagliacozzo: "Close my eyes if I die here and take my books home. But stay with me to the end." Still he did not think that the end was near. His tough nature would, he thought, master even this serious attack. His thoughts were bent on continuing the war. He still hoped to die in camp or on a battlefield. His third report to Pope Callistus III, without even a word about his sickness, still dwells on the glorious victory of our Lord Jesus Christ and adds details of Turkish losses. He paints the future. Now was the happy moment to drive the Turks from Europe and to recover the Holy Land. He begs the Pope to send, at his own expense, twelve thousand horsemen from Italy. A six-month campaign on Turkish territory would pay the cost of the war for three more years.

These were daring plans. Means for their execution were almost non-existent. The crusaders from the west were almost totally neglected. One soldier writes from Vienna to Salzburg (August 26) that both Vienna and Budapest had many crusaders, but they had no leader to tell them what to do. Thus they were loitering about, disgusted, and without provisions. A messenger sent by Carvajal to Rome confirmed this report. The crusading army, by reason of much sickness, was without order, suffering from lack of food and shelter. John Capistran, himself sick with fever, did what he could. But in his present condition he could no longer care for the arriving crowds as he had done in Belgrade, though he still dragged himself about leaning on his stick.

Who is to be the general, to replace Hunyadi? Capistran singles out the voivode of Transylvania, Baron Nicholas of Ilok, a man of excellent qualities. To the great alarm of his confreres, Capistran rode out with the Cardinal legate for a personal visit to Baron Nicholas. Riding along he surprised his companions by letting his horse run lustily. Nicholas accepted the proffered leadership. But he promptly sent Capistran back to Ilok to be taken care of. This was indeed an act of kindness. But the Baron had his own special motives. If John Capistran were to die, his grave would lend the greatest splendor to the Baron's ancestral castle. With mingled piety and brutality, Nicholas gave secret orders to keep Capistran, alive or dead, in Ilok.

Capistran also wished, in case his sickness should end in death, to be buried in Ilok where there was an Observant cloister which he had founded shortly before the battle of Belgrade. This cloister was especially dear to him, not only because it was the last of his foundations, but also because, being very near the schismatics and the Turks, it symbolized his own particular inclinations. But he knew his confreres thought differently. He had heard that they intended to abandon the place as soon as he was gone. But if he were to die there and there be buried, his confreres would be bound to remain.

Ilok is a healthy and beautiful place, situated on the southern bank of the Drave, high on the slope of the Fruska Gora. It offers a magnificent view into the Hungarian plains across the river. Here, in the circle of his brethren, the patient at first grew visibly better. Sometimes he could say Mass daily. When not able to do so, he was brought to the church for Holy Communion. If unable to recite the breviary, he had others recite it in his cell. Once in a while he came to the general meal. But a week after his return, in the night after the feast of Our Lady's Nativity, he was granted certainty of his approaching death. He spoke of it openly and with undisguised joy. That he was not to achieve a long-desired martyrdom, filled him with regret; but an unbloody martyrdom, a mortal illness of seventy-eight days, was a welcome substitute. To continuous fever and incurable diarrhea were now added pains in all parts of his body, especially in the intestines. Old ailments, hemorrhoids, gall stones, and a broken thigh-bone, completed the picture of the man of sorrow. He had indeed good care. Father Jerome of Udine nursed him with self-sacrificing devotion. Lords and ladies sent him choice food and delicacies. These meant good times for the brethren, since the patient could eat very little. Still none of those close to him believed that he was near the end. His unchanged freshness and liveliness of spirit deceived them all. Dominion over his body, obtained by many years of asceticism, lasted to the end. Clearness and determination continued to mark his decisions. He severely punished a brother who had resisted a superior.

Messages of sympathy coming from all sides brought him many joys. To illustrate. A letter came from the provincial vicar of the Abruzzi. The writer, Blessed Bernardine of Aquila, gave him good news from his native land, detailing the edifying death of Brothel Philip of Aquila. Capistran read the letter again and again, kissed it repeatedly, had it read to the people in church, and ordered copies of it to be sent to his friends. He told Tagliacozzo that the dead brother had struggled all his life against sensuality, but had been victorious. King Ladislaus visited the sick father twice. At one of these visits Capistran is said to have warned Ulrich of Cilli to be on his guard. Many dear visits were made by crusaders. Thus when the Nurembergers, a troop of 800 men, sent a delegation to visit him (October 15), one of them wrote home from Futak: "Our spiritual father Capistran received us with great love." He greeted his old friends with the words of St. Paul: "We were dead; but now we live again." He promised to write in their name to the Pope, and to pray to God for Nuremberg.

After the middle of October his condition grew worse. His exhausted body evacuated nothing but blood. A painful cough robbed him of rest. Yet he continued his usual occupations. He dictated and signed letters. He received visitors. October 18, thinking his end near, he called John Tagliacozzo, whom he had appointed superior of the brothers who were to return to Italy. Solicitude for the young brother fills his heart. "What will become of you when I am dead?" Thus he spoke tenderly, his hands on the young friar's shoulders. Faithful perseverance, loving care for his confreres, and special attention to Capistran's books: these were his last admonitions. Then, ordering the whole community to assemble in his room, he knelt down before them, begged forgiveness of his faults, commended himself to their prayers, and admonished the guardian to bury his body as soon as possible, and to retain that cloister. Then he prepared a lifelong confession, his last confession, which with wonderful clearness of memory he made on the following day to Father Tagliacozzo. Then on his knees he awaited the Viaticum. The house bell rang. The doors were locked to keep out the pressing crowds. The thirty brothers accompanied the Most Holy Sacrament into the room of their dying father. After receiving, Capistran ordered the recitation of the prayers for the dying up to the passage, *Proficiscere*. Then he dismissed them. He would let them know when to return and finish the prayers.

He suffered five days more. His unbroken vivacity still deceived those around him. The vicar of the Hungarian Observants, just then in Ilok on visitation, as he took leave, promised to return soon. The patient replied: "If you leave me now, you will not see me again."

In his last hours he was still thinking of his books. Most of them he had already sent back to Budapest, whence Tagliacozzo was to bring them to Vienna, and from there a Vienna friend would take them to Venice. Only his Hussite treatises were to remain in Vienna. All his other works were to be brought to the cloister in Capistrano, where that same year an unusually large and beautiful library had been finished. He still had seven folios with him. These he himself packed personally, using for the purpose the cloth which had covered his preaching desk on mission trips. Tagliacozzo was to bring his last greetings to his former traveling companions, Gabriel of Verona and Christopher of Varese. His habit, he added, was not to be sent back to Italy. This habit he wished to be his shroud, and the only ornament of this shroud would be the cross which the Pope had sent him. In that habit, and by that cross, he had defeated the Turks.

His last hours of bitter suffering he spent in giving blessings. First, he blessed imperiled Christendom. Then all his confreres. Tagliacozzo, sitting beside him, pronounced the long list of the names of the provinces, of the cloisters, of the brethren. As each name was pronounced, Capistran gave an individual blessing. Nor did he forget his countrymen, the citizens of Aquila, the Poor Clares, the Tertiaries. The day before his death he dictated three points, to be insisted on in all cloisters: zeal in the service of God, brotherly love, and correction of faults.

Death came on October 23. Consumed with thirst, he begged for a certain sweet drink commended by the medical practice of the day. But even this last refreshment was not at hand. When noon had passed, he ordered the prayers for the dying. Still clear in mind, he corrected the reader's many mispronunciations. Toward evening, while the community was reciting Vespers, his agony began. The brothers in the room said the last prayers. His voice gone, he gazed pleadingly from one brother to the other. As the prayers ended he became more quiet. He lay silent, his hands folded, his gaze fixed on a point above. Then came the end. He gave a sudden sign to lift him up. As Brother Jerome put his arms round him, Capistran died. Eyes wide open, lips tightly closed, he sank back on his couch. Tagliacozzo and Jerome closed his eyes.

Capistran's death was peaceful. His burial was not. The steward of Baron Nicholas had been long in the room of the patient, waiting for the moment of death in order to claim the body. Reluctantly he granted the permission to wash the body according to custom. The body itself was a pitiful sight, a few bones wrapped in skin, says Tagliacozzo, though on the face lay an unearthly beauty. Hurriedly the corpse was brought into the choir and put on the bier. The excited people were already threatening to break down the doors. The community suffered much. Those who had been their best friends now became a real burden. People feared that the dead body would be carried away secretly. King Ladislaus had, in fact, expressed his intention of having Capistran buried in Vienna. Hence the brethren tolled the bells, and started the funeral services at once. But to satisfy the increasing crowds they had, against the express order of the deceased, to postpone the burial from day to day. Since the corpse did not show any signs of putrefaction, but remained soft and flexible, the celebration might have continued indefinitely, had not the legate sent orders for immediate burial.

The burial took place on Friday, October 29. Baron Nicholas, arriving after the funeral, was indeed glad that Capistran had found his last resting place in Ilok. But he scolded the brothers roundly for having buried the holy man in a common grave. Their appeal to the legate's order did not move him at all. Face to face with the legate, he said that, whereas in Italy usurers and other great sinners were buried in churches, here a great servant of God who had done so much good had been stuck into the ground. Here, on his own property, he is not going to tolerate such action. In fact, he had the body promptly exhumed, and put into a metal case, secured with four locks. Thus enclosed, Capistran's remains were kept in a side chapel in the Franciscan church, pending the erection of a worthy memorial tomb.

CHAPTER XLI

Survival of Capistran's Work

THE victory of Belgrade, which Capistran had paid for with his life, did not fulfill the hopes it had raised. It did not lead to the end of Turkish power in Europe. Even so, Belgrade must not be underestimated. Where would Mohammed's victorious march have ended if Belgrade had fallen? But why was the favorable chance for a Christian counterthrust not utilized? The aged pope, Callistus III, did indeed increase his activity. All through the summer of 1456 new troops of crusaders, well prepared, kept arriving in Hungary. King Ladislaus fully intended to carry on the campaign. But since the death of Hunyadi and of Capistran the soul of the whole enterprise was missing. Ulrich of Cilli, who never left the King's side, had but one aim: to get rid of the sons of Hunyadi and thus take his place in Hungary. The noble-souled Carvajal did his very best. But he was not a Hunyadi or a Capistran.

Scarcely half a month after Capistran's death the old enmity between Cilli and Hunyadi led to bloodshed. When, on November 8, Ladislaus arrived at Belgrade, he was solemnly escorted into the city. But as soon as he and Cilli had entered the fortress, the gates were barred behind them. Their armed retinue was forbidden to enter. The following day brought a dispute between Cilli and the Hungarian lords, and dispute led to violence. Ladislaus Hunyadi was wounded, and Cilli was struck dead. Only with great difficulty did Ladislaus succeed in restraining his troops from attacking the castle. Dissolution of the crusaders seemed unavoidable. King and legate permitted them to return home. Treated like enemies by the Hungarians, they made their way back, swearing they would never again enter that country.

These returning crusaders spread Capistran's name far and wide. Even Greek chroniclers tell of his share in the Turkish defeat.

No other deed of his long and active life made him as famous as did the release of Belgrade. A frail Franciscan figure waving the banner of the Cross has become Capistran's historical symbol.

On the other hand, strange to say, Belgrade was a taint on Capistran's memory. The responsibility for this false view lies on those who wrote the official battle reports. Public opinion on the merits of that victory was formed in the long run, not by the tales told by returning warriors, but by princes' and prelates' chanceries that copied the reports of the Hungarian leader, Hunyadi. No matter how Hunyadi was hated by the court party, no matter how the battle had been won, it was simply accepted that the fame of that victory had to be attached to the name of the Hungarian commander-in-chief. Hunyadi became known to the world in general as "the great hero of Belgrade." In an audience granted to the ambassador of Milan, Callistus III expatiated on the merits of Hunyadi, calling him the most famous man the world had seen for three centuries.

In this atmosphere, Capistran's reports were bound to make an odious impression. Why had he said absolutely nothing about Hunyadi's heroic deeds? Himself he had called "the Joshua of the crusaders." Was not this arrogance and boasting? The papal court came to believe that each leader, Hunyadi and Capistran, tried to gain full credit for the victory by suppressing the share of the other. Enea Silvio gave classical expression to this view. Although he shields Capistran generally against the accusation of ambition, he looks on the present case as an exception, and proceeds to moralize on the sweetness of fame, which nobody can resist entirely, since losing a kingdom is easier than refusing fame. This judgment of Enea Silvio has been repeated times without number. Attempts to defend Capistran were frequently made, but failed, chiefly because of inadequate knowledge of the real history of the Belgrade campaign. Enea Silvio's picture of the battle was in possession and had obtained official sanction. This picture shows Hunyadi, soldier and leader in one person, directing that battle in a decisive manner.

On the other hand the vindication of Capistran's honor was undertaken by his companion, John Tagliacozzo, who lived through these terrible days at Capistran's side. But his three descriptions, the third especially voluminous and detailed, did not then find their way to the public, and indeed remained hidden as regards significant details down to our own times. Putting before us the testimony of this eyewitness, and of all other accessible sources, our judgment today must run thus: Capistran's contemporaries were quite mistaken when they accused him of ambition and envy. We now know that his silence was meant, not to shame Hunyadi, but to shield him. And we also know that what he lets us see of his own merits is far below what truth would have allowed him to claim. Capistran's Belgrade reports contain no word unbecoming in a saint.

How did Capistran's great life-problems fare after his death? Callistus III died on August 6, 1458, on the feast of Christ's Transfiguration, a feast instituted by himself in permanent memory of the victory at Belgrade. The aged Pope, untiring champion of imperiled Christendom, had not succeeded in initiating a universal crusade. The country most concerned, Hungary, was handicapped by domestic struggles. To avenge the murder of Cilli, the Hungarians accused the son of Hunyadi, Ladislaus, of a conspiracy against the King, and he was beheaded on March 16, 1457. And in that same year fate overtook King Ladislaus himself. Influenced by Podebrad, he went to Prague to celebrate his marriage with Magdalen of France. There he suddenly took sick, dying three days later. Was he a victim of Podebrad? Or did he die of the plague? We do not know with certainty. But people remembered how Capistran warned Ladislaus to stay away from Prague. The chief Hapsburg line came to an end with Ladislaus. The Bohemians made Podebrad their king. The Hungarians chose Matthias Corvinus, Hunyadi's younger son. Shortly before his death, Callistus III admonished the new King of Hungary to devote his whole energy to the battle against the infidels. But new difficulties directed the attention of the ambitious Corvinus toward the West.

The new pope was Pius II, that Enea Silvio who had been Capistran's friend. And we can easily see in the most notable acts of this Piccolomini pope an approval of Capistran's life. Pius II, once a partisan of the Council of Basle, now gave that council its deathblow. In regard to the Bohemian Compact, though he had for a long time been an opponent of Capistran, he found himself, as pope, compelled to enforce the very measures on which Capistran had never ceased to insist. In organizing a crusade the new Pope also failed. But here likewise he walked nobly in the footsteps of Capistran. Although feeble in health and exhausted by fever and gout, the Pope resolved in all earnest to sail, with the whole college of cardinals, at the head of a Christian fleet against the Turks, hoping by this supreme effort to arouse the whole West to its duty. Deathly sick, he reached Ancona (July, 1464) and saw the Venetian ships arrive in the harbor. But on the eve of the Assumption he closed his eyes in death.

The crusade had been Capistran's chief goal. Next in importance was the Observance. Here also Pius II carried on the work of his dead friend. The French Observants had, under Callistus III, made the false step of appealing against the pope to a council. Then, at the appeal of their cismontane brethren, they canceled this step and came to the general chapter of the Conventuals of 1457. But in this chapter, and in another a year later. Observants were excluded from voting for a general of the whole order. In this second case Callistus III himself had withdrawn this right, giving them instead the privilege of freely electing their own general.

Callistus' death created an entirely new condition. Pius II appointed a commission, including Cardinal Cusa, to examine the two bulls, one by Eugene IV and one by Callistus III. This commission advised the Pope to promote in every possible way the flourishing reform movement. Pius II canceled the bull of his predecessor. Thus the Observants were once more under the regulation laid down by Eugene IV. Capistran had triumphed again.

The Observance continued to grow and flourish. The transalpine branch did not indeed now grow as rapidly as it had in Capistran's time, being hindered by political entanglements. Still its growth remained steady until the Reformation. Under Pius II it had 800 brethren in 25 cloisters. In 1467 this cisalpine branch was divided into three vicariates: the Austrian, the Bohemian (including

Silesia), and the Polish, each of which flourished. All three vicariates had a powerful protector in Matthias Corvinus of Hungary, who at times controlled also certain parts of Austria and Silesia. Even a son of Podebrad appears among the promoters of the Observance. Austria and Styria, about the year 1500, had a dozen cloisters. In 1477 the Bohemian vicariate had 20 cloisters. In 1500 it had 27, of which 12 were situated in Silesia. But that part of Silesia which belonged to Saxony remained permanently closed to the Observance. In other parts of Saxony the reform gained visibly, increasing from 16 cloisters in 1472 to 37 in 1517. The upper German province had by that time 28 Observant cloisters. In southern and western Germany the Reform came more and more under French influence. In Austria, Bohemia, Poland, and part of Saxony, Capistran's preference of the Italian Observance remained dominant. The manner of living, and especially the form of the apostolic activity, were naturally accommodated to existing northern conditions. In developing and improving the office of preaching, Father Frederick of Thorn and Father Gabriel of Verona gained great merits.

The question of studies soon became very important also in German territories. Here, too, the establishment of special houses of study met opposition. But, under Capistran's inspiration, promotion of study began to prevail. The Observants did not indeed follow the Conventuals, who sent their young men to the universities. But home-studies were everywhere introduced. The large cloister of St. Bernardine at Breslau, which Capistran seems to have built for the purpose, remained a house of study until its dissolution. Interest in studies was owing in no small measure to the fact that the first members of these new vicariates were predominantly students from the universities of Vienna, Leipzig, and Cracow. The old predilection of the Franciscans for good large libraries remained in force also among the Observants. Capistran, while in Germany, often sent good books to his confreres in Italy.

The Observance flourished also in Italy. The Abruzzi province, built up almost from the beginning by Capistran himself, had by the end of the century more than 300 members in 19 cloisters. Two of these cloisters had occupied his mind up to his death. The first was in his native city, Capistrano. Since he was never to see it himself, he wished it should preserve, if not his body, then at least his beloved books and manuscripts. The second was the majestic memorial church over the body of St. Bernardine in Aquila. From afar, simply by the weight of his word, he had succeeded in building this monumental edifice. Aquila, a small city, already well provided with churches and cloisters, did not seem to need a new church, especially one of such dimensions. But Capistran insisted on a temple worthy of the memory of the great apostle of Italy. Thereby he gave to his native Abruzzi not only its chief sanctuary, but also its chief monument of native art. The entire structure, from its majestic cupola down to the smallest effort of chisel or brush, is the work of native artists.

Sixteen years passed since Capistran's death before Bernardine's remains could be transferred from San Francesco, the Conventuals' church in Aquila, to his own new church.

Does this church really belong to Bernardine? It does; but it belongs also to Capistran, being the crown of his efforts to glorify his great confrere. Six years he had given to Bernardine's canonization. Then followed six years of missionary activity, during which Europe, from Sicily to Poland, founded chapels, churches, cloisters, even whole provinces, under the name of Bernardine. The majestic memorial church in Aquila is a monument, not only to the greatness of Bernardine, but also to the incomparable energy of Capistran.

We must go a step farther. Bernardine's church, built by Capistran, is likewise a symbol of the Franciscan reform. In 1400 the Observance was next to unknown. A century later, in 1500, it had 45 provinces, 1,250 cloisters, 30,800 members.

Here, then, a word seems in place on the story of the Observance during the Reformation. By 1500 the Observants were as numerous as the Conventuals. Their coexistence under one common superior had become impossible. Prelates and monarchs petitioned the Apostolic See for definite regulation. Leo X replied (May 29, 1517) with the bull that created the Order of Friars Minor.

This order included the two Observant families, one cisalpine, one transalpine, both under one general, to be chosen alternately from each family.

The separation begun after the Council of Constance was completed one hundred years later. In this result, necessary though regrettable, Capistran had a large share, though we must not forget that among all Observant leaders he himself had held most tenaciously to the idea of unity. If in the end he preferred reform to formal union, he did so because he preferred the general welfare of the Church to the interests of his Order. And to the whole Order itself the reform movement brought new power and enthusiasm, and has preserved for the foundation of St. Francis its peculiar character.

A few months after the bull of separation came that ecclesiastico-religious revolution, which tore away great parts of Europe from the Catholic Church. Capistran's forebodings began to be fulfilled. The sixteenth century showed how greatly the Order had been in need of reform. The Conventuals in many places played an inglorious role, and furnished numerous apostates, as did also those Poor Clares who were under their control. Peter Fontinus was the first priest to preach the Lutheran doctrine in the cloister of Breslau, and he was followed by many confreres. The community of St. Bernardine's in the same city gave an opposite example, suffering dissolution rather than renounce their faith. Seventy years before, a ruler of the house of Haunold had zealously aided Capistran in erecting the edifice of St. Bernardine's cloister. Now another Haunold drove the disciples of St. Bernardine out of the city.

We must not exaggerate. Some Conventual communities also bravely refused to apostatize. Some individual Conventuals, like the famous Thomas Murner of Strassburg, defended the true faith with word and pen. And the Observants also lost some of their members. But on the other hand no other religious association furnished as many distinguished champions of the Catholic faith in German lands as did the Franciscan Observants. Of their number about 500 shed their blood for the faith between 1520 and 1620. By the free will of its inmates, not one Observant cloister was given to the heretics. The same holds good of those Poor Clares who were under Observant guidance. Well known is the heroism of St. Clare's convent in Nuremberg, under the leadership of Charitas Pirkheimer. And the spirit of Capistran persisted also elsewhere, not merely among his own direct disciples. The Dominicans in Leipzig, whom Capistran had won for the reform, remained unflinchingly faithful until they were dissolved by force (1539). They strongly supported Eck in his battle against Luther. Not in vain did Luther call the Franciscan Observants his most dangerous opponents.

CHAPTER XLII

Canonization

THE Franciscans remained grateful to their great son, "the crown and glory of our Order," as he is called by the cismontane vicar-general in a circular of February 5, 1457, in which he informs the whole Franciscan family of Capistran's death. Efforts for canonization soon began. Pope Nicholas V, during Bernardine's process, had said to Capistran in jest: "And who will take care of your canonization?" The pleasantry might seem a presentiment of the unusual difficulties which this canonization process had to meet. Capistran had effected the canonization of Bernardine in six years. His own process lasted 234 years. Canonization delays are indeed nothing extraordinary. But in this case they are remarkable. Nicholas V had said, this time in all earnestness, that if he lived longer than Capistran he would himself canonize him. The cardinal protector, Capranica, considered the noblest figure in the college of cardinals, prevented only by death from ascending to St. Peter's Chair, asserted repeatedly that he knew no second man who as preacher and saint could compare with Capistran. Callistus III and Pius II favored the canonization. But difficulty followed difficulty.

The process had to begin in Hungary where Capistran had died and was buried. But here, in a time of political troubles, the promoters had to deal with the opposition of Cardinal Carvajal, who dwelt on three special faults in the character of Capistran: imprudence, ambition, and irascible temper. Through that foolhearted eruption on the Turks from Belgrade, Carvajal judges, Capistran had exposed the cause of Christendom to the greatest danger. The final victory he ascribes to lucky chance. Silence on the merits of Hunyadi proves Capistran's ambition. Besides, he scolded harshly in the pulpit, and treated those who contradicted him in a very unkind fashion. This threefold accusation, raised by a noble and highly merited prince of the Church, while it was not the chief cause of delay, was still felt two centuries later.

Such unfavorable contemporary judgments are not unusual. Certain weaknesses of character, which cling even to real saints, sometimes to the end of their pilgrimage, often prevent close associates from seeing the whole picture. During the nerve-racking excitements of the Turkish war the aged Capistran may have occasionally lost his temper. In view of the shameful inactivity of so many leaders who should have been in the war, Capistran may not always have paused to pick and choose his words. Such outbursts would weigh heavy on men like Carvajal, a man of quiet and restrained temperament. But in regard to rashness and ambition, the Cardinal was, in essential matters, mistaken. Nor can he be considered an impartial witness. He, the official representative of the Pope at the crusade, had been pushed into the background by Capistran. Capistran himself was much annoyed by this situation, but could not change it. Further, the legate, though not on the spot, stubbornly insisted that Belgrade should simply await his own arrival. Actual events outran his instructions.

Capistran's confreres also increased the ill humor of the prelate. By word and pen they glorified Capistran, and equivalently blamed Carvajal. They spoke the truth, but did not thereby do good service to their dead father. Carvajal's resistance may have been directed less at Capistran himself than at his enthusiastic panegyrists. James of the Marches, Capistran's successor in the crusading army, tried in vain to interest the legate in the favors obtained through Capistran's intercession. After a sermon in Budapest, in the presence of the court and legate, he introduced a girl who had been cured of blindness. Witnesses testified to the fact of the cure. The legate took no interest in the matter. But Pope Callistus did, appointing a commission to investigate. Then the Pope died. James returned to Italy in broken health, leaving Stephen Warsan, the Hungarian vicar, to support Capistran's cause.

Pius II advised the Observants to send one of Capistran's companions to collect testimonials. John Tagliacozzo was chosen. Furnished with influential letters of recommendation to emperor and princes, Tagliacozzo again crossed the Alps and reached Hungary. Returning to Italy, he presented to the Pope the petitions of King Matthias Corvinus and of Nicholas of Ilok for the introduction of the canonization process. A similar request was forwarded to Rome by Emperor Frederick III, after he had sent a Franciscan delegation to visit the cities and courts of Germany and Poland where Capistran had preached ten years before. These delegates returned with a rich harvest of testimonials, some general and stereotyped, but many enthusiastic in devotion and gratitude. Besides, in May, 1462, a Hungarian delegation arrived in Rome, to promote this cause in the name of King Matthias.

Prospects were at this time very favorable. Peter of Odenburg was collecting the favors granted in Ilok and elsewhere. Nicholas Fara and Christopher Varese were writing biographies, one in Austria, the other in Italy. Tagliacozzo now wrote circumstantial reports on the events in Belgrade and on the last illness and death of Capistran.

But the formal process did not begin, impeded perhaps by the influence of Carvajal, who returned to Rome in 1461, and lived there till his death in 1469. And a strange fate followed the numerous petitions from the north. The Franciscan who was bringing them to Rome died on the way, after entrusting his post to a nobleman from Assisi then on his way home. This man, arriving in Assisi, deposited the letters there for the present, as duty obliged him to return to Germany. Then he, too, died. His heirs, not knowing the nature of the documents, deposited them carefully in the family archives. Thus the petitions disappeared. They were found and sent to Rome 150 years later.

August 8, 1473, four years after Carvajal's death, Elizabeth, the widow of John Hunyadi, petitioned Sixtus IV, a Franciscan Conventual, to initiate the process. A Turkish raid on Hungary had revived the memory of Capistran. But scruples and objections were not yet silenced. An unnamed chronicler of the years from 1420 to 1464 paints Capistran's character in a very unfavorable light. The great preacher is ill-humored unless received in pompous parade. He likes choice foods and delicious wines, just as he does the applause of the multitudes. Messengers precede him to propagate his fame. Contradiction he cannot stand. He will not preach except in public places, amid display and pomp. His miraculous cures are illusions, many patients having to reclaim their crutches from the churches. Capistran is cowardly. He dared not enter Bohemia without letters of safe-conduct. In Belgrade he advised the crusaders to take to flight. Belgrade, we recall, served Carvajal to accuse Capistran of foolhardy rashness. Here it serves to brand him as a coward.

This anonymous literary attack was pervaded by a slanderous spirit. Its author was Matthias Döring, leader of the Saxon Conventuals. Since 1461, when he was removed from his office as provincial, he had lived in a remote cloister of Brandenburg, his native land. Bitterness dominates his pen. The Council of Basle, which he called the holy council, was his ideal. He judges famous contemporaries by their attitude to the conciliar movement. Capistran was by no means his only victim. Cardinal Cusa and Archbishop Frederick of Magdeburg are treated most contemptuously. Even the noble Cardinal Cesarini gets not a word of acknowledgment.

In 1478, five years after the petition of Hunyadi's widow, the general chapter of the cismontane Observants at Pavia seems to have attempted a vindication of Capistran's honor. Nicholas Fara, who participated in that chapter as provincial of the Abruzzi, wrote in Pavia a preface to his life of Capistran, wherein he deals sharply with the critics of the blessed father. Probably under the influence of this chapter an Italian biography of Capistran was published in Como, the first to appear in print, and for a long time the only one. We may recall here the fact that, among all Capistran's literary remains, his treatise on usury was the only one printed before 1500.

Fifty years had passed since Capistran's death. Of immediate witnesses few were now living. But the wish to see Capistran lifted to the honors of the altar was not yet dead. Laurentius, the lord of Ilok, sent a petition to Alexander VI, noting that the district of Ilok was again seriously threatened by the Turks. The second successor of Alexander VI, Leo X, who decreed the final separation of

Observants from Conventuals, conferred upon the great champion of the reform the first ecclesiastical honors. On December 31, 1514, he allowed the diocese of Sulmona, in which the town Capistrano is situated, to celebrate the feast of Blessed John. Leo X was determined to carry through the canonization as soon as possible. He ordered the Bishop of Fünfkirchen, and an abbot of the same diocese, ta make the necessary researches. Leo's death brought these efforts to a stop. The Church did not yet have a permanent Canonization Commission, and each pontificate had a new commission.

Under the second Medici pope, Clement VII (1523-34), the preparatory work for the process was again set in motion. Petitions came from the Polish king, Sigismund I. Cardinal Campeggio wrote from Hungary that the people were demanding the canonization of Capistran. The Turks were again in the field; Suleiman the Magnificent was ready for a decisive stroke. Louis II, king of Hungary, utilized for military preparations even the sums collected for Capistran's canonization and was never able to restore the loan. He died in the battle at Mohacs, and Ilok (Capistran's resting-place) fell into the hands of the infidels, who held it for the next 170 years. The Turks now took revenge. They extinguished the votive light which for seventy years had burned over Capistran's body in a side chapel of the Franciscan church of Ilok.

What did the Turks do to his grave? Trustworthy contemporary reports are contradictory. One says that the Franciscans succeeded in removing Capistran's body, and carried it to Nagyszöllös in northern Hungary, near the Transylvanian border, far from Ilok. That cloister was afterward destroyed by Calvinists, who are said to have thrown the silver shrine, together with the remains of Capistran and other precious things, into a deep well. A modification of this report says that the heretics threw Capistran's remains into the Danube, but that the river in a miraculous fashion washed them again to shore. Diggings in the well at Nagyszöllös, undertaken in the seventeenth century, remained without results.

A second report says that the pillaging Turks carried Capistran's body away and that they refused to give it up in spite of diplomatic pleas. Then, much later, a nobleman bought back the treasure and entrusted it to the care of the Basilian cloister at Bistrica in Wallachia. Requests for permission to open the shrine at Bistrica were stubbornly refused by these schismatic monks. At last, in our own days, during the German occupation of Wallachia in World War I, General Mackensen allowed a Hungarian commission to open the sarcophagus. The investigation showed, not the corpse of Capistran, but that of some Greek saint.

We must conclude that Capistran's body is lost. A popular prophecy said that his body would be found again when Hungary would be freed from the infidels. The contradictory reports just cited show that dependable information is lacking. The most probable supposition is that the Turks destroyed the grave and scattered to the winds the remains of the great crusade preacher. Such a report actually circulated in Vienna shortly after these events.

Interest in the canonization of Capistran now disappears for nearly a century. Hungary suffered under the catastrophe of 1526. A year later Rome itself was seized by an army of Lutheran mercenaries. Two years later Suleiman stood before the gates of Vienna. St. Theobald, the Observant cloister outside the city, went up in flames, one hundred friars falling under Turkish scimitars.

Yet these sad events, unfavorable to the canonization process, seemed to revive in the faithful the memory of the zealous champion against heretics and Turks. In the year 1519 a monk of Marienmay printed at Augsburg selections of sermons preached by Capistran, together with a short biography in which he says that he knows old people who had personally seen Capistran. The booklet has an engraving in wood, by the Augsburger Schaeufelin, representing Capistran in the pulpit, looking down on a bonfire of vanities. The humanist controversialist, John Cochläus, published for the first time some letters of Capistran. Christopher Manlius of Gorlitz, a Protestant, in his history of the Lausitz, recorded carefully all reports he could find on Capistran, who, he says, was generally called a saint in his day, and whose fame is still widespread in Germany. He appeals to a word of St. Augustine to justify the burning of vanities. About the middle of the century three biographies, one by Udine, one by Fara, and one by Varese, were printed in Vienna, which had now become what Belgrade had been in Capistran's time. And in 1564, two years before Suleiman's last Hungarian campaign, these three lives were republished in Vienna.

But the canonization process itself had to wait for Gregory XV (1621-23), who counted much on the saints in his war against heretics. He who honored in a special manner Blessed John of Capistrano, and planned his canonization, began by extending Capistran's feast day to the whole Franciscan Order, an act which was equivalent to formal beatification. Gregory died, but Urban VIII continued the work by appointing commissions, one in Rome, a second in Capistrano. After the two commissions had reported, the process rested again for another twenty-five years.

The final step in Capistran's glorification was initiated by Luke Wadding, whose annals made the official documents on Capistran's life accessible to the public. Searching in Assisi, Wadding found that package of petitions which had been lost in 1462, and sent them to Urban VIII, but nothing further happened. A new period of oblivion might have set in, had not Cardinal Carlo Medici intervened. Among the Medici, veneration for Capistran was a kind of family tradition, dating back to Capistran's lifetime. Hence the zeal we have noted in both Medici popes, Leo X and Clement VII, for the canonization of Capistran. This tradition grew stronger after 1579 when the barony of Capistrano came into the hands of the Medici. Carlo Medici, elevated to the cardinalate by Pius V, devoted himself with great fervor to the cause, though he was otherwise worldly-minded. He commissioned Bernardine Barberio, Roman agent of the Spanish King, to promote the process. When Bernardine died, his nephew took over the work. This nephew, John Barberio, was destined, after 200 years' delay, to do for Capistran what Capistran had done for Bernardine. Adroit and versatile, unlimited in veneration for his hero, Barberio pursued his task with admirable tenacity.

This last phase of the long process began with a session of the Congregation of Rites, on July 13, 1649, in the presence of Innocent

X. The promotor fidei urged as the first objection that all previous efforts had been fruitless. Wadding's annals had recalled the views of Cardinal Carvajal and of Enea Silvio. Investigation of all these objections took some years. Then Capistran's literary legacy had to be examined. Innocent X passed away, but his successor, Alexander VII (1655-67), urged the continuation of the process, and affirmed the purity of Capistran's doctrine. On April 5, 1660, the advocate of the consistory, Julius Caesar Fagnanus, delivered a splendid panegyric on Capistran, which ended with an appeal for early canonization. A decree of the Congregation of Rites (September 17, 1662) declared that nothing now spoke against Capistran's reputation for sanctity. Barberio wrote an enthusiastic biography. Finally Alexander VII, on September 25, 1663, confirmed a decree of the Congregation on Capistran's heroic virtues.

The first part of the process had found a happy conclusion. Now followed examination of miracles. All fifteenth-century reports were declared insufficient for canonization, although without any intention of deciding against their reality. The Congregation demanded miracles that could be certified by living witnesses. Another ten years' delay followed. But on July 14, 1675, Clement X, out of many cases presented by Barberio, selected as satisfactory two sudden healings obtained by invoking Capistran.

At last. The endless process had ended. The Congregation of Rites decided unanimously (December 20, 1678) that the canonization could now take place. Innocent XI approved this decision (June 13, 1679). And yet, ten more years went by before canonization really took place, though such leaders as Cosimo III of Florence, Charles II of Spain, and Emperor Leopold I, petitioned urgently for an early procedure. Innocent XI himself was a devotee of the new saint. If the Church, he once said, had any honor higher than canonization, that honor would go to Capistran. Why, then, the delay? One reason was the protracted illness of the Pope. But the chief reason was a financial one. The Pope was sending every ducat he could spare to the Emperor in Vienna, which was again besieged by the Turks. During this fearful crisis Capistran's image stood above the high altar of Ara Coeli in Rome, with a votive light burning before it day and night. And in Bavaria, in a Franciscan church near Schleisheim, people claimed to have seen a wooden statue of Capistran turn on its pedestal toward Hungary, where at that moment (October 4, 1683) crusaders were battling the Turks. Two hours later the statue was easily brought back to its original position.

The final glorification of Capistran coincided with the decisive victory of Christendom over the Turks. The dominion of the Crescent over Hungary had been broken when the Eternal City prepared for the solemn canonization of the victor at Belgrade. On October 16, 1690, Pope Alexander VIII placed among the number of saints three Johns: John of Capistrano, John of St. Facundo, and John of God. Two others were canonized on that same day: the Franciscan lay brother, Paschal Baylon, and Capistran's contemporary and friend, Lorenzo Giustiniani, bishop of Venice.

As a saint in heaven, Capistran continued his apostolic activity upon earth. Canonization festivities became everywhere days of religious renewal. In Vienna, Emperor and court went in procession to the stone pulpit of Capistran in St. Stephen's cemetery. Belgrade had been lost again the previous year. Now, a few weeks later, near Slankamen, just between Ilok and Belgrade, the imperial army destroyed a great army of Turks.

In that one year of 1690 more biographies of Capistran were published than in all the 234 years since his death. Among these was the largest of all Capistran books, the *Capistranus triumphans*, written by the Franciscan Amandus Hermann. It is a folio of almost a thousand pages.

Not satisfied with the canonization of his hero, Barberio made a request that Capistran should solemnly be declared by the Church as "The Apostle of Europe." But his pious proposal remained unanswered.

Two centuries and a half have passed since Capistran's canonization. A popular saint, like Francis of Assisi or Anthony of Padua, he has not become. His greatness is too much intertwined with history. As conqueror of the Turks, he entered into the memory of men. With the climax of the Turkish crisis came his canonization. His image above the stone pulpit, on the outside wall of St. Stephen's in Vienna, remains typical. His figure is surrounded by trophies of victory; his right hand holds the banner of the Cross; his foot rests upon the body of a defeated Turk. Above his head hovers an angel, holding the name of Jesus. With the end of the Turkish wars, and the subsiding of the Reformation controversy, the cult of the great champion against heretics and Turks experienced a noticeable diminution.

The fifth centenary of his birth, celebrated in 1885, reminded the world of this forgotten saint. Since that year his feast has been celebrated in the whole Church on March 28. A bronze statue of Capistran was unveiled (November 22, 1922) in front of the fortress of Ofen. The saint is represented as pressing forward at the head of his crusaders, trampling beneath him the bodies of Janizaries. He seems to fly on the wings of a storm. Every muscle, every fiber of his sinewy figure, every fold of his habit, is in motion. Every line pushes forward. This symbolizes what Capistran was in the past, but still more what he is in the present. And what the statue says to the eye is made clear to the mind by the great biography of the saint, written in Hungarian by Bölcskey. And as a final illustration of Capistran's imperishable attractiveness we may mention an association established in Brussels, which aims at the study of life-problems in the full Catholic spirit, and which calls itself by Capistran's name. Its three catchwords are Initiative, Organization, Activity. These three words express the traits most characteristic of this indefatigable champion of God.

If we strive to understand the peculiarities of our saint's activities and struggles, if we are mindful of the days in which he lived, if we allow for the limitations inherent in human nature, then we shall see in John of Capistrano, not a dead hero, but a living saint, a guide for our own days and for the sad days still to come.

FINIS

www.ingramcontent.com/pod-product-compliance
Lightning Source LLC
Chambersburg PA
CBHW010346170726
48284CB00011B/2806

* 9 7 8 1 9 5 3 7 4 6 4 2 9 *